MANY NATIONS UNDER MANY GODS

MANY NATIONS UNDER MANY GODS

PUBLIC LAND MANAGEMENT
AND AMERICAN INDIAN
SACRED SITES

TODD ALLIN MORMAN

UNIVERSITY OF OKLAHOMA PRESS : NORMAN

Library of Congress Cataloging-in-Publication Data

Names: Morman, Todd Allin, 1969–, author.
Title: Many nations under many gods : public land management and American Indian sacred sites / Todd Allin Morman.
Description: Norman, Oklahoma : University of Oklahoma Press, 2018. | Includes bibliographical references and index.
Identifiers: LCCN 2018016678 | ISBN 978-0-8061-6172-3 (hardcover) ISBN 978-0-8061-9421-9 (paper)
Subjects: LCSH: Public lands—United States—Management. | Indians of North America—Legal status, laws, etc. | Indians of North America—Religion. | Sacred space—Conservation and restoration—United States. | Cultural property—Protection—United States. | Land use—Government policy—United States.
Classification: LCC KF5605 .M67 2018 | DDC 343.73/0256—dc23
LC record available at https://lccn.loc.gov/2018016678

The paper in this book meets the guidelines for permanence and durability of the Committee on Production Guidelines for Book Longevity of the Council on Library Resources, Inc. ∞

Copyright © 2018 by the University of Oklahoma Press, Norman, Publishing Division of the University. Afterword copyright © 2024 by the University of Oklahoma Press. Paperback published 2024. Manufactured in the U.S.A.

All rights reserved. No part of this publication may be reproduced, stored in a retrieval system, or transmitted, in any form or by any means, electronic, mechanical, photocopying, recording, or otherwise—except as permitted under Section 107 or 108 of the United States Copyright Act—without the prior written permission of the University of Oklahoma Press. To request permission to reproduce selections from this book, write to Permissions, University of Oklahoma Press, 2800 Venture Drive, Norman OK 73069, or email rights.oupress@ou.edu.

CONTENTS

Preface | vii

Introduction | 3

1. Protection of American Indian Religious Freedom and
   Sacred Sites: A Recent Development in the United States | 10
2. The Arizona Snowbowl Resort and the Hopis | 48
3. Cave Rock and the Washoe Tribe of Nevada and California | 89
4. Badger-Two Medicine and the Blackfeet Nation | 115
5. Four Nations and Five Controversies in
   Indian Religious Freedom | 137
6. Improving Protection of Indian Sacred Sites
   and Reconceiving Indian Sovereignty | 173

Conclusions | 198

Afterword | 211

Notes | 215
Bibliography | 241
Index | 253

PREFACE

The first time I had the privilege to attend a meeting of the University of Montana's Native American Law Student Association, our faculty adviser, Professor Raymond Cross of the Three Affiliated Tribes of the Fort Berthold Reservation, asked each of us to talk about what Indian nation we were from and why we were interested in Indian law. A non-Indian, I borrowed a quip from Will Durst ("whiter than the Osmond Family Christmas . . . in Sweden") before recalling another pop culture reference—a scene from the 1991 television miniseries *Separate but Equal*—for a more serious answer to Professor Cross's second question.

The film poignantly portrays the struggles of the Legal Defense Fund of the NAACP to eliminate segregation of public schools throughout the United States and to overturn the legal doctrine of "separate but equal." That pernicious legal doctrine proclaimed that as long as facilities and conditions were equal, the forced segregation of the races by state mandate comported with the Fourteenth Amendment to the Constitution of the United States and its requirement that no person could be denied the equal protection of the laws based on race. The NAACP Legal Defense Fund was led by Thurgood Marshall, played by Sidney Poitier in the film. The film started with scenes of children walking some distance to their school, a crowded and run-down old building. The head of this school in Clarendon County, South Carolina, visited the superintendent of the county schools and asked for a single bus, so that children might not tire themselves out walking to school. He noted that the white schools had more than thirty buses for students. He was refused, but this began the federal lawsuit *Briggs v. Elliot*. Initially the case was to simply challenge the undisputed fact that the different facilities were in no way equal—the county spent $179 on each white child and only $43 for every black student—but Marshall and his team expanded the case by presenting expert psychological testimony that separate was inherently unequal; that it crippled the self-esteem of African American children while damaging the moral development and character of white students. The case ended at the trial level with a split decision. The district court issued an order for school funding to be equalized, but the challenge to the doctrine of "separate but equal" failed. Marshall's efforts would not be vindicated until three years later, before the Supreme Court in *Brown v. Board of Education*.

The specific scene I recounted for my fellow members of the Native American Law Student Association followed Marshall's loss at the district court. Upon entering a cab to leave, Marshall says to his fellow NAACP attorneys, "Sometimes I get very weary trying to save the white man's soul." I shared that I was drawn to Indian law because I wanted to do something to save my own soul.

Like many who pursue a more just and compassionate world, however we participate in that effort, I realized at an early age that there was a huge gap between what was said and what was done in the United States, and millions suffer and die in this gap. I also understood my position of privilege: I knew I had more opportunities than those lost in this gap. I understood that I lacked the freedom to live with these material benefits and opportunities without the suffering of those lost in the gap. This began a lifetime of studying the gaps in what was said and what was done and working to find ways to close those gaps. At university I began to study international human rights and volunteered for Amnesty International.

Along the way I learned that the indigenous peoples of the United States and the world have suffered and continue to suffer the greatest material deprivations because of the gap in what is said and what is done. This history of systemic horror was barely hinted at in my schooling, from elementary school through completion of my undergraduate degree. The history of the United States includes many of the worst crimes against humanity, and the system cripples everyone involved by ignoring, hiding, and sometimes just lying about that history.

While finishing this book I worked at Central State University, a historically black university in Wilberforce, Ohio, and I came to understand how the materially disadvantaged are spiritually and intellectually advantaged compared to others. While many of my students had a great deal to learn about history and other topics, their education was in certain ways more advanced than that of the average American of European descent. The students of Central State University understood their life experiences and, by being awash in mainstream U.S. culture, what the United States pretended to be. They heard what was said as I had, but they lived in that gap that was the difference between what was said and what was done. They understood aspects of that gap that I would never fully appreciate because I had an education that had obfuscated and sometimes lied about the existence of the gap.

This brings us to this book and why I wrote it. This simple direct answer as to why I did this research was that I asked Professor Cross, of the University of Montana School of Law, what case he thought could use a historical treatment. He suggested *Navajo Nation v. Forest Service*, and circumstances led me to focus on the importance of the San Francisco Peaks to practitioners of traditional Hopi religion from among the thirteen indigenous religions that hold the Peaks as sacred. I later expanded my research to other cases involving indigenous sacred sites and religious freedom, placing the cases in the context of the relevant histories of the Indian nations struggling to survive to this day. The longer answer is, in part, found above. The most important first step in ending the gap between what we say and what we do is to honestly understand what was and is still being done. By beginning to talk about how things really are, we reduce the gap and can move forward together to make a future that is healthier for everyone involved.

This book provides a brief national history of the Indian peoples involved in many of the case studies, as well as an all-too-brief explanation of religious and cultural perspectives that place importance on indigenous sacred sites. I have endeavored to be accurate and respectful in the presentations of these histories. I do not have the benefit of having lived as a member of any of the cultures and societies presented here, though my role as a staff attorney for Anishinabe Legal Services, working before the court of the Leech Lake Band of Ojibwe, provided me new opportunities to learn every day.

I hope I am as accurate as a historian presenting brief histories of several European nations and the culture relevant to contemporary legal issues might be. At times I have oversimplified and almost certainly left out many details that are of crucial importance to people who have lived these histories and in these cultures. While I am much more confident of my presentation of the law and the state of the law regarding the issues covered, I hope the related national and cultural histories will aid in explaining the significance of the legal history—a history that far too often ignores the reality of indigenous histories.

A book of this length cannot be produced without the support, hard work, and love of many people.

I want to thank Aya Camui Chen (陳姣燕) for her consistent support and love in driving me to finish this project. If not for her tenacity, I would still be editing the manuscript and looking for a publisher. I also offer heartfelt thanks to my friends Agnes Simon and Lynn Chien-Hui Chiu (邱千蕙) for their advice and experience. Together with my family—the Cromer, Chen (陳), and Weisberg-Krumlauf clans—these women provided me the support necessary to complete this project. A special thanks to my father-in-law, Teng-Kuo Chen (陳登國), and my mother-in law, Yu-Chan Hung (洪玉盞), and thanks for the amazing map produced by my brother-in-law Ting-Yu Chen (陳庭右).

In addition to thanking all the faculty and staff of the History Department of the University of Missouri, I want to express my sincere gratitude to all the professors on my dissertation committee for their willingness to guide me in research that is unusually interdisciplinary, drawing as it does on the fields of geography, indigenous religion, American history, and law. To Professors Catherine Rymph and Mark Carroll go my thanks for patiently teaching me the writing style of a historian as opposed to that of an appellate brief writer. I thank Professor John Bullion for his guidance over the years. I offer special thanks to Professor Mark Palmer for providing perspective on the project from outside the field of history and for his encouragement during my search for a publisher. A special thanks to Professor Denny Smith of the University of Nebraska for his guidance and advice on moving forward with my work.

I thank Professor Raymond Cross of the University of Montana School of Law for suggesting this field of inquiry and sharing his insights into the field of federal Indian law. Though I did not realize it at the time, Professor Cross had worked for years, in significant ways, to improve the very human relations this work examines in the Indian law conferences he conducted every spring for Forest Service administrators and officials of Indian nations. It is only now, more than a decade later, that I have begun to understand his position on *Lyng v. Northwest Indian Cemetery Protective Association*, and I thank him now for the insights his words then provided me in understanding the complexities of the law involved in the management of indigenous sacred sites on public lands. I want to thank John Tottenham for all his encouragement and advice over the decades. I owe any intellectual success I have achieved to his mentoring in my formative years.

My initial research would have been considerably more difficult without Zackeree S. Kelin, former managing attorney for DNA Legal Services of the Navajo Nation, and Howard Shanker, attorney for the Navajo Nation, who assisted me in obtaining a copy of the trial transcript for *Navajo Nation v. Forest Service*. And I would be remiss if I did not thank my coworkers at Anishinabe Legal Services for allowing me the time off necessary to finish this project.

Thanks also to all those who produced editorial feedback in all the stages of development of this project, including but not limited to Adam Weisberg, Charlie Cromer, Bruce Cromer, Scott Dyson, Denny Smith, Betsy Patch, and my anonymous reviewers. I want to thank my editor, Alessandra J. Tamulevich, and the University of Oklahoma Press for taking a chance with this book.

Finally I want to thank Barbara Lee Allin, an amazing woman whose tenacity and determination taught me much about how this world treats women and set me on the path of seeking the truth about the way things are and thinking about how things could be. I thank her for my life. I am saddened she could not be in the world of the living to see the completion of this book or to meet my wonderful wife.

Though many have provided insight and assistance, any errors in judgment, reasoning, interpretation, or fact in this book, and all conclusions, especially those the reader does not care for, are entirely those of the author.

MANY NATIONS UNDER MANY GODS

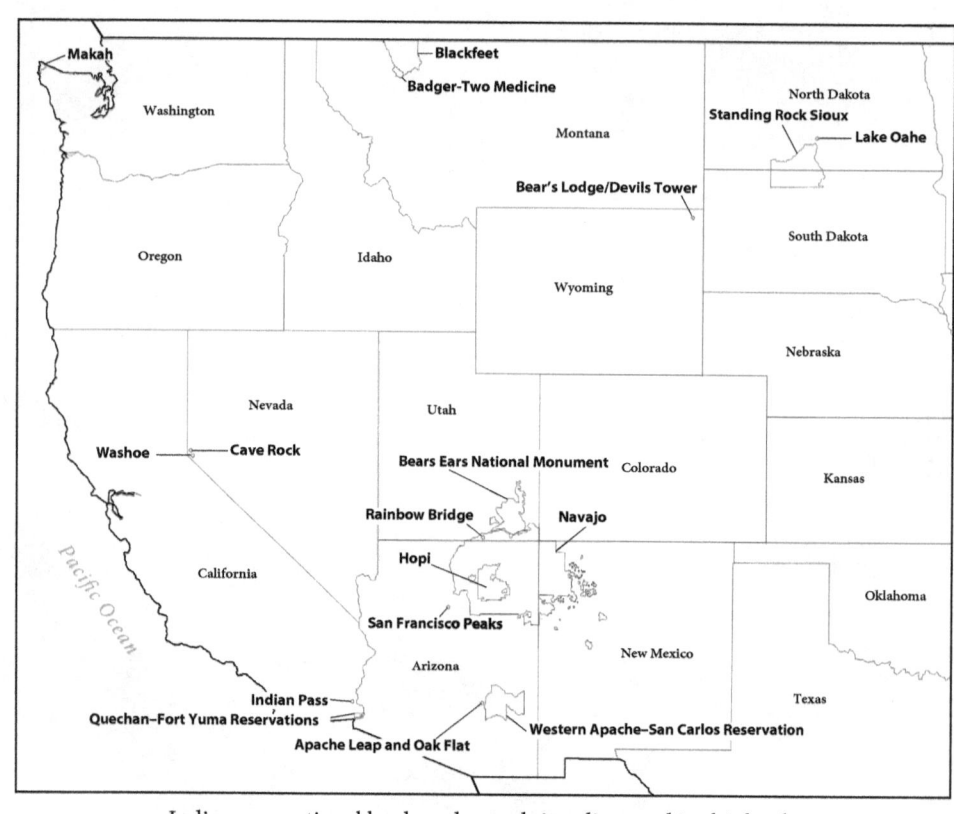

Indigenous national lands and sacred sites discussed in this book.
Cartography by Ting-Yu Chen.

INTRODUCTION

One August day in 2006, the founder of the Indigenous Law Institute, Steven Newcomb, had the opportunity to speak with Supreme Court justice Antonin Scalia at a reception following a presentation by the justice. Newcomb asked Justice Scalia for his opinion on the 1823 Supreme Court decision *Johnson v. M'Intosh*. *Johnson* is considered to be the foundational case of both property law and Indian law, and Newcomb thought Scalia would have an interesting perspective on the case, given his claims to being a constitutional originalist. Much to Newcomb's surprise, Scalia replied, "I've never heard of it. I've never read it."[1]

Johnson v. M'Intosh decided a land dispute in which two European Americans claimed the same parcel of land. Thomas Johnson had bought the land from the Piankeshaw Indians, while William McIntosh had purchased the same parcel from the federal government. Chief Justice John Marshall, who wrote the opinion for the court's majority, declared that under the Doctrine of Discovery, recognized in international law, the discovering Christian power, or its successor in interest, held the underlying title to lands that indigenous peoples had lived upon since time immemorial. The people discovered living on these lands merely retained the right to occupy them. The doctrine provided the discovering power or its successor in interest exclusive power to extinguish occupancy rights by sale or through just war. Marshall determined that McIntosh held the legitimate title, since his chain of ownership came from the federal government, the successor to the discovery rights of the British Empire and the only landowner the courts recognized.[2]

That evening in August 2006, Newcomb was quite astonished by Scalia's claim to have no knowledge of the case that offers the legal justification for U.S. sovereignty over lands in North America. Earlier that evening, Scalia had delivered an address entitled "Constitutional Originalism" at the University of San Diego. During the course of his talk, Scalia made reference to the 1833 book *Commentaries on the Constitution of the United States* by Justice Joseph Story. After Scalia claimed to have no knowledge of *Johnson*, Newcomb attempted to reengage Scalia by mentioning that the Supreme Court had just referred to the case in a decision Scalia had signed on to during the spring of the previous year. Rather than directly addressing this incongruity, Scalia instead compared the history of U.S. expansionism to that of the other settler states of Canada, New Zealand, and Australia. Scalia claimed that the courts of the United States came up with the principle for dealing with indigenous peoples through "a right of conquest." Newcomb asked if the justice could identify a single case in which the courts had made such a claim. When the justice could not, the conversation came to an end.[3]

Upon recalling the discussion with Scalia some years later, Newcomb noted how incredible it was for him to have no knowledge or recollection of such a foundational case as *Johnson*. The address Scalia delivered that August evening had directly referred to Story's *Commentaries*. The first section of *Commentaries* is entitled "Origin and Title to the Territory of the Colonies" and discusses the Doctrine of Discovery. Newcomb was quite disturbed that the nine members of the United States Supreme Court have nearly unchecked power in deciding the fates of millions of indigenous people yet remain nearly entirely ignorant of the history of relations with indigenous peoples and the law that governs those relations.[4]

In many ways Scalia's inability to notice Indians at the beginning of Story's book is the crux of life in the Americas today. The lands the United States claims sovereignty over, by the right of Christian discovery, are still home to more than five hundred Indian nations with their own distinct cultures, religions, languages, and histories. The heart of U.S. history is the history of taking land and suppressing Indian self-determination, for the United States would be impossible without this history. Yet somehow Indians and federal Indian law remain invisible to the intellectual and legal leaders of the governing class in the United States.

This book is an examination of part of the invisible history of several Indian nations and their later struggles to protect the integrity of sacred and cultural sites located on federal public lands. The focus of the book is the history of Indian peoples engaging in the legally mandated consultation process and the differing outcomes across several case studies. As Indian history has been rendered invisible to nearly all but those who have lived that history, each case study begins with an all-too-brief introduction to the history and religious perspectives of the Indian nations in question. While there are many commonalities between Indian cultures, there is more cultural diversity to be found among Indian peoples than among the peoples of Europe. To understand any particular Indian nation's participation in the legally mandated procedures that might protect its sacred and cultural sites, one must have some understanding of the history and culture that make those sites significant. Thus this history is included for two reasons: first, to provide the necessary context for explaining indigenous perspectives in the legal process; second, to help the reader understand that Indian nations and societies, like all societies, change over time and have their own unique cultural perspectives.

The current study brings several new avenues of investigation and conclusions to the study of the legal histories of Indian sacred sites, Indian religious freedom, and the place of these ongoing histories in the context of changes in Indian sovereignty. While other studies have examined aspects of these legal issues, those studies have been almost exclusively from a legal perspective.[5] This is the first book to examine the consultation process and the related administrative record and the first study to look at this administrative record for indigenous sacred sites as it relates to the changing and competing perspectives on sovereignty found in the courts, Congress, the executive branch, and Indian communities.

For more than a century, U.S. policies toward indigenous peoples were predicated on the assumption that Indian religions and cultures would disappear, making room for the invaders to take all of North America. Indian peoples refused to be eliminated. The U.S. government took Indian lands containing sacred sites, destroyed indigenous economies, caused famine, and tried to destroy the very fabric of Indian society by outlawing religions, forcibly removing children from their homes, destroying indigenous land management, and declaring that Indian nations lacked full national sovereignty because they were not Christian nations. While Indians stubbornly clung to their culture, religions, and societies, non-Indians managed to look past indigenous peoples, rendering them invisible in the most peculiar ways. Indian peoples found themselves involuntary minorities in their own homelands, with wealth and military power firmly in the hands of the Europeans who decided to stay. During the decades of plunder, the U.S. government incorporated many places of cultural significance to indigenous peoples, including sacred sites, into public lands administered by the federal government. Despite these enormous difficulties, indigenous peoples continued their fight to survive. Recalcitrant to this day, Indian peoples continue to survive as distinct cultures with their own religions, languages, and historical perspectives.

The failure of policies designed to eliminate Indian peoples from North America has led to the current reality in which the United States has to become a plurinational society whether it wants to admit it or not. Since the time of sustained contact between the hemispheres of the world, Christian nations have debated the status of indigenous peoples under international law. In 1831 Chief Justice Marshall, in *Cherokee Nation v. Georgia*, referred to this evolving body of international law, with reference to the precedent of *Johnson*, and claimed that indigenous nations had lost some part of their inherent sovereignty by being discovered by Christian Europeans. Thus Indian nations were not properly foreign nations. This body of international law has changed over time as people of European ancestry have learned more about those with whom they share the planet. The United Nations General Assembly adopted the Declaration on the Rights of Indigenous Peoples (UNDRIP) in 2007, for the first time recognizing the rights of indigenous peoples in such areas as self-determination, traditionally held lands, and the protection of and access to religious and cultural sites. U.S. president Barack Obama announced in 2010 that his nation would drop its official position as the last government in the world to oppose the declaration. (Initially, four nations—the United States, Canada, Australia, and New Zealand—voted against UNDRIP, but the others accepted it before the United States.)[6] World opinion has changed, even in the European nations, and eliminating Indian societies is no longer an acceptable option for the United States.

The Richard Nixon administration took tentative steps toward creating a society in which indigenous peoples could exercise meaningful cultural and political self-determination. President Nixon had the courage to renounce a policy implemented while he was vice president in the Eisenhower administration: termination. Termination policy was yet another attempt at the elimination of Indian nations as political and cultural communities within the United States. The Nixon administration undertook policies designed to improve respect for Indian societies and to bring about the practical implementation of greater Indian self-determination.

Another legacy of Nixon that few give that complex character credit for is the National Environmental Policy Act. This law from 1970 created the Environmental Protection Agency and the requirement that federal agencies promulgate environmental impact statements for proposed federal actions that significantly impact the natural environment. As many indigenous sacred sites are on federal lands and significantly impacted by federal actions, environmental impact statements, and the process by which one is created, would become significant in the lives of Indian sacred sites.[7]

The policy of government-to-government relations begun by Nixon continued beyond his administration with the passage of the Indian Religious Freedom Act of 1978. This law purported to reverse U.S. policy and make it the official position of the United States to protect and preserve Indian religions, guarantee the practitioners of indigenous religions access to sacred sites on public lands, and consult with Indian political and religious leaders when administrative decisions might impact Indian sacred sites.

Since 1978, the executive and legislative branches have continued to take steps toward creating a society based on mutual respect for cultural differences, while the Supreme Court and justices such as Scalia have engaged in a campaign to undermine Indian sovereignty and legal protections for religious diversity. Through a series of laws and executive orders in the late twentieth and early twenty-first century, the consultation process regarding sacred sites has been expanded and deepened, providing administrators with new legal options for protecting sacred sites. At the same time, the Supreme Court has removed all substantive constitutional protections for religious freedom, for Indians and non-Indians alike, and has restricted the self-determination of Indian governments again and again. The Supreme Court has acted against the emerging consensus of international opinion regarding indigenous rights and self-determination.

This book examines the history of the consultation process that has grown from the National Environmental Policy Act and the Indian Religious Freedom Act as it regards recent cases involving the administration of Indian sacred sites on public lands. The cases studied here do not have a uniform outcome. While the first case study, involving the San Francisco Peaks in the Coconino National Forest of Arizona, is infamous in its disregard for the opinions of many Indian peoples, overall the consultation process is not one in which indigenous interests universally lose. The strengths and weaknesses of the consultation process and attending legal protections (or lack thereof) will become apparent through the course of the case studies. The book concludes by examining the lessons of this recent legal history in the context of changing notions of indigenous sovereignty and by examining several proposed alterations in sovereign relations between Indians and non-Indians with regard to their efficacy in providing protections for Indian sacred and cultural sites outside the confines of current reservation borders.

Charting the rise of American Indian religious freedom as a historical question and as an important ideological challenge for contemporary society must begin with four major historical ideological approaches to the history of American Indians. The earliest is the frontier or conquest perspective, which viewed Indian societies as inevitably giving way to settler expansion. The second approach viewed humans as either racially or developmentally divided into hierarchies and saw indigenous and settler populations divided in one or both of these ways. The modernist approach examines social boundaries between settler and indigenous populations, conceiving of these boundaries as fixed but capable of being transcended. The fourth approach, which emerged beside the modernist approach in the post–World War II era, is the postmodern or postcolonial approach. It includes "[c]ontemporary writing in which texts and histories seek to deal with the tension between the liberating dissolution of boundaries and the constant reshaping of them as political memories of the colonial past."[8] This approach, while aware of and informed by postcolonial studies, takes a more universalist perspective that retains much of the modernist approach. This universalist perspective treats indigenous struggles for self-determination, sovereignty, and freedom as part of the human struggle for both individual and collective self-determination, sovereignty, and freedom, as is explained in more detail below.

Chapter 1 presents the theoretical background for this study and provides a brief history of Indian law in the United States up to 1978, as well as an introduction to First Amendment and relevant administrative law with regard to sacred sites and public lands management in the years leading up to the case studies of the present project. For those already familiar with the issues involved, this chapter is not strictly necessary, but general audiences should find this an excellent introduction to the law and history necessary to fully appreciate the case studies that follow.

The case studies of various Indian nations and their efforts to protect sacred sites on public lands begin with the second chapter. This chapter examines the history of the Hopi Nation and its ongoing interests in the management of the San Francisco Peaks in the face of an ever-growing ski resort in the midst of that sacred place. The third chapter examines the case of Cave Rock, the Washoe Indians, and efforts to protect that sacred site from the negative impacts of rock climbers. Chapter 4 examines the lengthy consultation process surrounding a new Forest Service travel management plan for Badger-Two Medicine, a place sacred to the Blackfeet people, adjacent to their reservation in Montana. Chapter 5 examines several related cases, none of which involve Forest Service administrative decisions but all involving actions relevant to the ongoing issues of public lands management and Indian religious freedom. Each case illuminates additional strengths and dangers inherent in the consultation process and covers the efforts of four Indian nations—the Makahs, the Quechans, the Western Apaches, and the Standing Rock Sioux—to protect their religious freedoms.

Chapter 6 examines the emerging legal context of continued struggles for protecting indigenous sacred sites and evaluates several proposals for altering indigenous sovereign relations with the U.S. government. The conclusion brings the disparate parts of these case studies together and examines the ongoing concerns of Indian peoples as related in a 2012 Forest Service internal evaluation of sacred site management.

The consultation process, flawed as it is, shows that understanding is possible, but non-Indians need to take up the challenge and educate their own communities about the invisible history of relations between indigenous peoples and European peoples. As Antonin Scalia and other alleged intellectual leaders of the non-Indian United States have repeatedly demonstrated, Indians are invisible and ignorance of their central place in U.S. history is staggering. Scalia, like so many political and intellectual leaders of the United States, was completely ignorant of the theoretical legal basis for U.S. claims to sovereignty over Indian land. The hope is that this book will play a small part in ending that invisibility and assist some in beginning to learn the multinational history of the central portion of North America. Then we might be able to work together to protect the many cultural and sacred sites of the many nations found in North America.

1 PROTECTION OF AMERICAN INDIAN RELIGIOUS FREEDOM AND SACRED SITES

A Recent Development in the United States

Indigenous struggles for freedom and self-determination cannot be forced to conform to the more familiar civil rights struggle within the existing legal framework. Some, with reference to the civil rights model of achieving freedom and self-determination, might mistakenly suggest that indigenous peoples are seeking special rights under the existing legal paradigm. The current approach starts from the position that aspirations for freedom, self-determination, and happiness are universal human pursuits. The complex historical details of this ongoing human struggle result in each people taking a unique path to achieve these universal aspirations. While there may be similarities in these historical trajectories to some extent, the conditions indigenous peoples face are so historically different that simply applying conventional legal notions of a civil rights struggle will necessarily fail to account for the systematic denial of the fundamental humanity of indigenous peoples for all of U.S. history. As will become clear as we examine some of these complex histories, in regard to religious freedom, sacred sites, and sovereignty, solutions to ongoing complexities must acknowledge that Indian peoples must determine how their societies relate to other peoples, rather than having formal relationships largely determined by outside forces and societies, as remains the case to this day.

The history of American Indians is generally broken into six broad periods directly linked to the changing Indian policies of non-Indian governments. The policies of each period impacted practical expressions of Indian national sovereignty and religious freedom. The current U.S. government and its predecessor governments altered policies as society changed and developed. Scholarship on these changing policies and on Indian history has changed over time as Western civilization has made progress in accepting cultural diversity. There are more than thirty thousand books on American Indians, and Indian scholarship has been largely the province of anthropologists. Non-Indians have produced more than 90 percent of the literature on American Indians.[1]

The major eras of policy and history of American Indians are (1) the international relations phase; (2) the domestic dependent nation phase; (3) allotment and assimilation; (4) the Indian Reorganization Act or "Indian New Deal"; (5) termination; and (6) sovereignty and government-to-government relations. While certain policy changes came with distinctive historical actions, such as the Indian Reorganization Act, the transition between other periods was more gradual. Similarly, the scholarship has a large amount of overlap from one era of historical approach to another. It should be noted that a great deal of history addresses the era before transatlantic contact became regularized, and while its study is a growing field, this period is generally not considered part of American Indian legal history. In a sense, it would perhaps be better to say there are six periods in which non-Indian governments have been trying to conceptualize indigenous people as existing within the Anglo-American legal system.

INTERNATIONAL RELATIONS

The initial interactions between European settlers and the indigenous population of North America were those governed by international relations and international law, from the perspective of the non-Indians. Beginning in the seventeenth century, various settler and European governments entered into trade treaties as well as military alliances with various Indian nations, within a context of international law. For example, the first British settlers at Plymouth survived the early years only because of their military alliance with the Wampanoag Nation. The Seven Years' War saw both the French and the British heavily relying upon allied Indian nations for their military operations in the North American theater. Some of the tensions between American colonists and their home government in London can be traced back to British military commanders' observations that Indian military forces aided the war effort against the French much more effectively than the colonial militias.

During its war for independence, in the late eighteenth century, the United States engaged in the European practice of treaty making and forging military alliances with Indian nations. Before heading to France to secure European allies, Benjamin Franklin visited the Iroquois League in hopes of securing a military alliance with some or all of the member nations of this regional power. This practice continued through the young nation's formative years. The foreign relations, or international law, era is considered to have lasted until 1830. The later part of this period is marked by expansion through war on the part of the U.S. government, supplemented by treaties for land cessions, trade agreements, and military alliances.[2]

DOMESTIC DEPENDENT NATIONS

The case of *Cherokee Nation v. Georgia* (1831) marked the transition from international law to the period of domestic dependent nations, as defined by the Supreme Court of the United States. One of the "civilized" Indian peoples that had largely adapted to living near expanding non-Indian populations, the Cherokee Nation, found itself besieged by the State of Georgia. The Cherokee Nation had developed a written language, a written constitution, a European electoral style of government, and a national newspaper in the Cherokee and English languages. Cherokees modeled their lives after their European neighbors and accepted a reduced land base to live on in exchange for the false promise that they would be left in peace. In the decade before *Cherokee Nation v. Georgia*, the Cherokee Nation achieved greater material success than many of its non-Indian neighbors. When gold was discovered in Cherokee national territory, the State of Georgia stepped up its aggression against the Cherokee Nation as part of its continuing attempts to dispossess the Cherokees of their lands. The Cherokee Nation responded by bringing an original action before the United States Supreme Court as a foreign nation.

Chief Justice John Marshall found himself in a difficult situation. If the Supreme Court accepted jurisdiction of this case between a foreign government and a state, and ruled against Georgia's aggression, as the legal standards of civilized peoples would require, the authority of the court would be jeopardized. The hostile chief executive, Andrew Jackson, would likely seek to undermine or render impotent any ruling against Georgia's aggression. Rather than face the potential of a decision that might be ignored by the federal executive, Marshall described the Cherokee

Nation as a "domestic dependent nation," thus denying the court jurisdiction, as the action was not between a foreign nation and a state.[3]

Marshall, while denying Indian nations status as foreign nations, used the Doctrine of Discovery to establish, under U.S. law, the unenforced right of Indian nations to occupy, as domestic dependent nations, the land Indians believed had been theirs since the beginning of time. The aggression of the State of Georgia and the executive branch could not be checked by the limited legal rights of land occupation that Marshall had tried to protect for indigenous populations. The period of domestic dependent nations was marked by forced removal and relocation of Indians, including the Cherokee "Trail of Tears."[4]

Together with *Johnson v. M'Intosh*, an 1823 land title precedent that the later cases relied upon, *Cherokee Nation v. Georgia* and *Worcester v. Georgia* created the theoretical foundations for situating indigenous peoples in the legal system of the United States. The three cases are known today as the Marshall Trilogy. Operating under a modified form of the Doctrine of Christian Discovery, *Johnson* established the legal notion that simply discovering indigenous peoples granted ownership to the discovering Christian European power of the underlying title to the lands Indian peoples lived on. This gave the discovering power the exclusive right to buy or take by "just war" lands the indigenous peoples continued to have the legal right to occupy. As Indian nations did not own the lands they occupied and could sell their land rights only to the discovering power or its successor in law (as the United States was to Great Britain after independence and to France after the Louisiana Purchase), Indian nations were not fully sovereign foreign nations but domestic dependent nations, with the United States standing as their guardian (in theory but rarely in practice), as Marshall determined in *Cherokee Nation*. In *Worcester*, Marshall affirmed the supremacy of the U.S. government in Indian relations and the states' powerlessness over Indians and the internal affairs of sovereign Indian nations. This was the established legal theory, even if historical practice did not necessarily conform to it.[5]

In that era, the Alabama Supreme Court challenged federal supremacy in Indian affairs and exemplified the aggressive support of some state governments for forcibly removing Indian populations. In addition to Georgia, other states enacted similar repressive measures violating Indian sovereignty; Alabama took measures as draconian as those taken by Georgia in its assault on Indian rights and sovereignty. The courts in southern states engaged in legal arguments that twisted or ignored precedent and adopted positions on the history of treaty making and conquest that were unsupported by the historical record. Legal scholar Tim Alan

Garrison has concluded that the southern judiciary abetted the illegal and unjust assault on indigenous rights by providing legal cover that filled the vacuum left by the non-enforcement of *Worcester*.[6]

The era of domestic dependent nations involved a long period of transition. For the initial decades of this period, the Indian nations of the Southwest were not under any claim of jurisdiction by the United States, still being part of the Spanish, French, or Mexican claims to European dominion, depending on the year. The treaty-making process remained in place until 1871. Over this period the U.S. government pressured Indian nations to remove from the East and cede land, and it used negotiation or force to reduce indigenous landholdings to smaller and smaller reservations. Making attempts to limit the indigenous population to reserves in less violent ways, the federal government moved the Indian Office from the Department of War to the Department of the Interior in 1849. By the late nineteenth century, the U.S. government was using Indian reservations—which many in the non-Indian population initially intended as places for indigenous peoples to retain self-government—as tools for the destruction of Indian cultures, religious freedom, and self-governance.[7]

ALLOTMENT AND FORCED ASSIMILATION

As the domestic dependent nation period was coming to a close and the U.S. government was about to embark on a more aggressive set of policies designed to wipe out indigenous governments, religions, and cultures, the first books by non-Indians seeking to reform Indian policy appeared. There is a long history of non-Indian objections to official U.S. Indian policies, and the last decades of the nineteenth century saw the first publication of more widely read dissenting opinions. In 1881 Helen Hunt published her descriptive exposé *A Century of Dishonor: A Sketch of the United States Government's Dealings with Some Indian Tribes*, one of several books from this era exposing the poverty and disease on reservations.[8]

The assault against indigenous culture and sovereignty began one of its more aggressive phases with the allotment policy. In 1887 the U.S. Congress passed the Dawes Act, which called for transforming economic life on reservations by extinguishing traditional indigenous property-management methods and instituting European-style private property through individual ownership of allotments. Each head of an indigenous household was to receive 160 acres of land and was expected to become a farmer.[9] "Surplus" land was to be made available for use by the non-Indian population. In the period of allotment, land held by the indigenous population shrunk from 138 million acres to 48 million acres, with

20 million acres of the land retained being semiarid or desert.[10] The allotment process was piecemeal and rolling, hitting different reservations and different parts of reservations at different times. Some reservations avoided allotment altogether. Thus a complex legacy of landownership and checker-boarded Indian lands remains to this day. (With checker-boarding, plots of land alternate between Indian and non-Indian ownership, with Indian ownership further complicated by differences in communal, family, and individual ownership.)

During the era of allotment and assimilation, Indian reservations were ruled by Indian agents of the federal government. As part of the policy of the destruction of indigenous religion and culture, the federal government supported Christian missionary boarding schools that were intended to prevent the transmission of indigenous religion and culture to the next generation. It was during this period that resistance to these repressive policies grew among both indigenous and non-Indian people. Non-Indians who hoped to secure constitutional protections for Indian religious freedom worked to get the 1924 Citizenship Act passed. This act conferred upon American Indians U.S. citizenship, whether they wanted it or not. Though initiated by those seeking to promote Indian religious freedom, the act has been viewed by some as another avenue with which to force the indigenous population to abandon it culture in favor of that of the European immigrant population.[11]

Opinions differ as to what ultimately drove the policies of allotment and assimilation. Some have focused on the role of ethnocentric social scientists in shaping public and congressional opinion by presenting the indigenous population as lacking the mental capacity to duplicate white culture, and therefore needing neither land nor education. Others believe that economic considerations, rather than intellectual forces, drove Congress to loosen restrictions on the alienation of allotted lands. This view finds that rather than being guided by moralistic administrators, the Indian bureaucracy conducted its policies in compliance with the economic interests of the settler population over the interests of the indigenous population it was purportedly serving. In any event, the shift in rationalization for white supremacy from cultural concerns to racial concerns had the ironic consequence of a loosening of educational standards and reducing the dedication of the federal government to forced assimilation. This change in rationalization for white supremacy provided indigenous culture some breathing room to survive.[12]

THE INDIAN NEW DEAL

The year 1934 marked the next major shift in federal Indian policy with passage of the Indian Reorganization Act (IRA), or Indian New Deal. Championed by

John Collier, a cultural pluralist named commissioner for Indian affairs, the IRA was an attempt to reverse the policy of governmental, religious, and cultural destruction of indigenous societies. The IRA promoted the adoption of Indian governments modeled on European American political forms. Collier ended Bureau of Indian Affairs (BIA) policies that criminalized indigenous cultural practices and instituted a revolving development fund to promote economic growth on reservations. Allotment, while already largely abandoned due to indigenous resistance, was repudiated as a policy.[13]

Indian reactions to the IRA's process of creating European-style governments were as varied as the conditions of Indian peoples. Many indigenous groups on the brink of social destruction, such as the Washoes, were able to restructure and revive under IRA governments. The Blackfeet Nation, whose traditional form of government had disintegrated, was already operating with the Blackfeet Tribal Business Council, which lobbied on behalf of Blackfeet people, and this de facto government simply became the legal Blackfeet government. Other Indian nations with surviving traditional governments, such as the Hopis, found the IRA government to be in direct competition with their traditional forms of organization, so adoption of IRA governments caused new political divisions within Indian societies. The Navajo Nation most famously is a rare instance of successful resistance to the imposition of an alien government on an indigenous nation.

TERMINATION

After the Second World War, federal policy changed yet again. The termination era brought a renewed assault on indigenous sovereignty. The federal government sought to terminate federal services that provided economic support to indigenous peoples, eliminate tribal governments, and destroy any independent existence of indigenous peoples in the United States. In 1946 the U.S. government started the Indian Claims Commission (ICC) to provide financial redress for lands illegally appropriated (under U.S. law) from indigenous peoples by the federal government. The ICC was a special administrative court designed to examine historical claims against the U.S. government for the illegal or unconscionable dispossession of indigenous peoples from their lands in the lower forty-eight states. It was not empowered to return lands under any circumstances. Highly conservative in its approach, the ICC was intended to last only a decade but was not concluded until the late 1970s. The designers of the termination policy intended the ICC to lay to rest outstanding claims and to clear the path to end the separate political and cultural identity of Indian communities. To further this end, indigenous people were offered financial incentives to leave reservations and move to urban areas. Additionally, Public Law 280 provided states with the power to take full criminal jurisdiction over Indian lands while mandating the extension of state criminal jurisdiction in some locations, including all of California. In 1953 Congress passed legislation allowing for the removal of federal recognition of and services to Indian nations. The federal government terminated the political and legal existence of 109 Indian groups between 1954 and the early 1970s.[14]

During the 1950s the study of American Indians underwent something of a revival. In 1950, no history department in the United States offered Indian history as a major field of study for graduate students, and no department offered even a single undergraduate course in the topic. The ICC created a demand for expert testimony, and this need revived the field of western Indian history.[15] As the termination process revived the study of Indian history, it also revived indigenous efforts to preserve their religions, cultures, and political sovereignty.

The 1960s saw the rise of Red Power and Indian militancy, including the Hopi traditionalist movement and Blackfeet activism. In 1968 the American Indian Movement (AIM) was founded. In 1969 Indian activists, calling themselves Indians of All Tribes, seized Alcatraz Island, justifying their actions with treaty provisions stating that unused federal installations were to be returned to local Indian people. In 1972 AIM and more mainstream Indian organizations participated in a cross-country caravan known as the Trail of Broken Treaties. This event ended with an unplanned occupation of BIA headquarters in Washington, DC. The occupation ended peacefully through negotiations. Among other concessions, the U.S. government agreed to pay the fares of the occupiers to return home. In 1973 AIM occupied a church in Wounded Knee, South Dakota, an event known as the Second Wounded Knee. Vine Deloria Jr.'s *Custer Died for Your Sins* (1969) and N. Scott Momaday's *House Made of Dawn* (1968) are important works of the era and provided some of the first Indian voices addressing Indian history and issues.[16]

SOVEREIGNTY AND GOVERNMENT-TO-GOVERNMENT RELATIONS

The Indian activists were not without allies: dissidents in the non-Indian community who did not support the policies of their government. After decades of struggle, non-Indian American society changed in many ways. In the early 1970s, U.S. president Richard Nixon admitted, "The American Indians have been oppressed and brutalized, deprived of their ancestral lands, and denied the opportunity to control their own destiny."[17] In the face of the new Indian militancy, the Nixon administration reacted with both a carrot and a stick. J. Edgar Hoover's COINTELPRO, a counterintelligence program designed to suppress dissent across the United States, sought to disrupt AIM activities by means both legal and illegal. Just as it had previously targeted leftist organizations, the civil rights movement, the antiwar movement, and the Black Panther Party, the FBI used COINTELPRO to try and destroy the Indian civil rights movement. Many Indian activists died under mysterious circumstances in the early 1970s, and AIM was rendered largely impotent by a series of unfounded criminal cases brought against members, mixed in with a few that might have had some basis in fact and law.

Among the less deadly actions of his administration, President Nixon renounced termination and ushered in what is known among scholars as the era of renewed Indian sovereignty or government-to-government relations. These changes were part of a series of liberal reforms initiated by the Nixon administration, including the 1969 National Environmental Policy Act. NEPA required creation of an environmental impact statement whenever policy decisions would have significant environmental impacts. When policy decisions were found to have significant impacts on cultural and religious sites, the law incorporated consultation with Indian peoples into the procedures for creating environmental impact statements. The Nixon administration also undertook reforms that promoted government-to-government relations between Indian governments and the United States. Both Indians and official governmental policy supported this new era of self-determination. The federal government ceded control of more and more functions to Indian governments. The policy gained formal standing as law in 1975 with passage of the Indian Self-Determination and Education Act.[18]

Indian activists pushed for more reforms and greater self-determination, and 1978 saw the passage of two landmark pieces of legislation that addressed Indian rights. The U.S. Congress passed the Indian Child Welfare Act in 1978, in part to address widespread abuses on the part of state child services agencies that placed Indian children in non-Indian homes for both foster care and adoption.[19] That same year saw Congress pass the American Indian Religious Freedom Act (AIRFA). This law changed the official stated policy to one of preserving and protecting religions of the indigenous peoples of the land. AIRFA provides for consultation with Indian political and religious leaders when governmental actions might impact Indian sacred sites, but it provides no substantive protections, as discussed in detail below.

INDIAN SACRED SITES AND THE LAW SINCE 1978

The 1980s and 1990s saw a marked reaction against Indian sovereignty and religious freedom as the United States Supreme Court challenged the new trajectory of Congress and the executive branch. The attack on Indian sovereignty will be examined in detail in chapter 6, but an examination of the struggles over religious freedom in the eighties and nineties will be necessary to understand the case studies of the following chapters. As examined in more detail below, the United States Supreme Court effectively ended any hopes for substantive constitutional protections for indigenous religious freedom with *Lyng v. Northwest Indian Cemetery Protective Association* (1989) before turning to end any substantive constitutional protections for the free exercise of religion for all in the United States with *Employment Division v. Smith* (1990).[20] In these decisions the court undermined what little remained of the "official" policy of the federal government to respect and protect indigenous religions, as enunciated in the American Indian Religious Freedom Act of 1978. For its part, Congress acted to protect religious freedom in the United States and in 1993 passed the Religious Freedom Restoration Act (RFRA) in response to the *Smith* decision. The late twentieth and early twenty-first century was a time of increased executive attention to strengthening and clarifying the consultation process required by the Indian Religious Freedom Act of 1978 and expanding possibilities for protecting Indian sacred sites by congressional amendments to existing historical preservation laws.

Continuing the general trend of increased executive and legislative respect for Indian religious concerns, Congress also acted to bring a modicum of respect with regard to Indian graves and the long-buried dead. In November 1990, Congress passed the Native American Graves Protection and Repatriation Act (NAGPRA) to bring under control the ghoulish practice of non-Indian scientists digging up ancient Indian gravesites and using the human remains as specimens for their experiments. Both NAGPRA and the American Indian Religious Freedom Act required administrative consultation when Indian religious and cultural concerns were implicated in administrative actions. In 1992 Congress amended the National Historic Preservation Act such that sites of religious and cultural significance to Indian peoples became eligible for inclusion as "traditional cultural properties" on the National Register of Historic Places. Strengthening the consultation process, President Bill Clinton issued Executive Order 13,007 in 1996. This order called on administrative agencies to avoid adverse impacts and to maintain the physical integrity of public lands of cultural significance to Indians while making it clear that such a policy shift created no new legal cause of action for those who believed their religious freedoms were being trampled. The order was supplemented by Executive Orders 13,084 (1998) and 13,175 (2000). The first directed the National Park Service to develop regular policies for consultation and communication with Indian officials, and the second expanded the requirement to other agencies.[21]

FREE EXERCISE OF RELIGION AND INDIAN SACRED SITES

Legal questions regarding American Indian religious beliefs, practices, and cultural rights often involve a complex interaction between administrative law, constitutional law, and congressional statutes. Many sites of religious and cultural significance to Americans Indians are located on land owned and operated by the U.S. government, under U.S. law. The federal government of the United States claimed ownership of this land and for more than a century placed much of it in national forests, parks, and other federal lands. This places many sites of cultural, religious, and historical significance to Indians under management of the executive branch through various federal agencies, including the Forest Service, the National Park Service, and the Bureau of Land Management. When these agencies formulate and implement land management policies, they often impact places of historical, religious, or cultural importance to Indians. In addition, many Indian nations explicitly retained rights, such as access for hunting, fishing, logging, gathering, or more explicit religious uses, on lands they were forced to part with. Many agency actions have harmed or destroyed Indian sacred sites, and agencies have a history of violating retained treaty rights. As agency actions are government actions, for a time many wanted to call upon First Amendment provisions protecting the free exercise of religion and the American Indian Religious Freedom Act to protect sacred sites from agency actions.

By contrast, federal administrators have occasionally curtailed some land uses to protect and preserve Indian sacred sites, and in these instances, some outside interests claimed that either protecting or merely educating the public about sacred sites amounted to an unconstitutional establishment of religion. These interests argued that First Amendment prohibitions against government establishment of religion should require agencies to implement policies that would harm or destroy Indian sacred sites when recreational or economic interests were harmed by respecting Indian sacred sites. What emerged from legal struggles of the late twentieth and early twenty-first century was broad discretion for administrators in how they implemented and formulated policies that impacted Indian sacred sites. The Free Exercise Clause did not protect sacred sites, and the Establishment Clause did not prevent their protection.

In the last decades of the twentieth century, the general trend has been for the legislative and executive branches of the federal government, in the face of growing Indian protest, to end the more overtly destructive Indian policies and support greater Indian sovereignty and cultural rights (the end of termination, greater sovereignty over social services, the Indian Child Welfare Act, the American Indian Religious Freedom Act, and the Native American Graves Protection and Repatriation Act). By contrast, the courts have departed from their more traditional role of being the only limited source of protection for Indian interests within the federal government to a position many have seen as one of outright hostility.[22] As shown below, the U.S. Supreme Court recently refused to recognize any constitutionally protected religious freedom rights of American Indians when those rights might interfere with agency discretion in the management of U.S. public lands.

Congress has found that the myriad number of rules and regulations necessary to manage a modern bureaucratic society are impossible to create by individual legislative enactments. In addition, Congress has decided that certain levels of expert knowledge are necessary to evaluate which rules and regulations might be best for any particular circumstance. Thus Congress delegates the essentially legislative power of rule making to administrative agencies within the executive branch. Constitutionally, Congress is required to provide clear guidelines and definitions under which these administrative agencies promulgate rules and make decisions, and there must be some administrative process by which those potentially adversely impacted may appeal an administrative decision to the administrative body. Administrative rule-making agencies may further be directed by executive orders from the president, guiding policy formation and agency decisions.

Appellate review by the courts comes after administrative appeals are exhausted, but the grounds for review by the courts are limited. The courts have given great deference to administrative decisions, and only administrative actions the courts found to be "arbitrary, capricious, an abuse of discretion, or otherwise not in accordance with the law" were set aside by judicial review[23]—the theory being that the understanding and expertise of administrative bodies are superior to that of the courts. Only the most openly faulty decisions are to be overturned.

AMERICAN INDIAN RELIGIOUS FREEDOM ACT

Further complicating this process of administrative appeals are decisions that might have been "otherwise not in accordance with the law." A claim that an administrative decision violated a protection of religious freedom or unlawfully established religion would be a claim that the decision was not in accordance with the law. Until the 1930s, the official policy of the U.S. government was to suppress the practice of indigenous religion with administrative penalties that effectively criminalized Indian religions and culture. The Indian Reorganization Act ended this policy, and in passing the American Indian Religious Freedom Act in 1978, Congress claimed to reverse the policy in favor of protecting indigenous religions and religious freedom. This act made protection and preservation of the inherent rights of American Indians to their beliefs the stated policy of the U.S. government.[24]

The American Indian Religious Freedom Act placed three duties on administrative agencies. First, agencies were to evaluate policies and procedures with the aim of protecting American Indian religious freedom. Second, the law required federal agencies to consult with Indian groups regarding proposed agency actions. Third, agencies were to refrain from prohibiting access to religiously and culturally significant sites of Indians and refrain from prohibiting possession and use of religious objects or the performance of religious ceremonies. The Hopis and Navajos brought the first challenge to a Forest Service decision on religious freedom grounds under AIRFA with *Wilson v. Block*. In this case, the Forest Service approved the first major expansion to the Snowbowl ski resort on the San Francisco Peaks, a place of deep religious significance to many Indian peoples, including the Hopi and Navajo Nations. The appellate court for the District of Columbia in 1982 determined that so long as Indian peoples had been consulted, as they had in the process of approving the proposed expansion, the government was free to ignore Indian concerns and take whatever action adverse to Indian interests it pleased.[25]

The arguments on the Senate floor in favor of AIRFA made it clear that the act provided no substantive rights. Subsequent litigation has plainly established that AIRFA provides merely a procedural requirement for consultation. The courts ruled that AIRFA did not provide a basis for review of the decisions of administrative agencies, even if those decisions could arguably be shown to be arbitrary, capricious, or an abuse of discretion with regard to preserving and protecting Indian religions. While the law, along with later legislation and executive orders, created substantive consultation requirements, as long as the Forest Service provided access to religiously and culturally significant sites, the law provided no basis for judicial review of administrative decisions. Some have characterized the act as nothing more than empty verbiage.[26]

THE FIRST AMENDMENT DOES NOT PROTECT SACRED SITES ON FEDERAL LANDS

Lyng v. Northwest Indian Cemetery Protective Association (1989) demonstrated conclusively that the United States Supreme Court would not protect any substantive religious rights on public lands with either AIRFA or the Constitution. A remote stretch of land in northwestern California is of the highest cultural and religious significance to the Yurok, Karok, and Tolowa Nations. After engaging in consultation with Indian interests, the Forest Service formulated several options regarding two roads in an area being logged. Despite Indian complaints, the Forest Service chose the most destructive option through the most sacred part of the area, dividing sacred sites viewed as indivisible by Indian religious practitioners. After an initial injunction, the first two appeals courts sided with the indigenous practitioners and found that the proposed Forest Service action would create an undue burden on the religious freedom of the affected tribes and would violate First Amendment protection for the free exercise of religion. The United States Supreme Court took the appeal and in 1989 issued its opinion reversing the lower courts and allowing the Forest Service to go forward with the proposed action.[27]

Justice Sandra Day O'Connor wrote the opinion for the majority of the Supreme Court, finding that the consultation with affected Indians had taken place, as required by the American Indian Religious Freedom Act and other statutes. Most interestingly, the court noted and agreed with the Forest Service assessment that the proposed road was a grave threat to the impacted Indian cultures. The road would "virtually destroy the Indians' ability to practice their religion." The Supreme Court ruled that this destruction of Indians' ability to practice their religion was properly constitutional as the actions of the government on lands it claimed to own violated no cognizable rights under the Constitution.[28] As O'Connor wrote:

> The Government does not dispute, and we have no reason to doubt, that the logging and road-building project at issue in this case could have devastating effects on traditional Indian religious practices.... Even if we assume that we should accept the Ninth Circuit's prediction, according to which the G-O road will "virtually destroy the Indians' ability to practice their religion," the Constitution simply does not provide a principle that could justify upholding respondents' legal claims.[29]

Further illuminating O'Connor's opinion is its relationship to Supreme Court free exercise jurisprudence at the time. In *Wisconsin v. Yoder* (1972), the high court ruled that a state law that "unduly burdens the practice of religion" without a "compelling interest," even though it might be "neutral on its face," would be unconstitutional. The majority ruling in *Lyng* was that federally authorized road building and timbering on federal lands including American Indian religious sites did not burden Indian religious practice at all—at least within the intendment of the Free Exercise Clause of the First Amendment. By holding that the land policies of the Forest Service in *Lyng* constituted no burden at all, the court bypassed entirely existing standards requiring a compelling interest to justify an undue burden on indigenous religion or any other religion.

Justice William Brennan, dissenting from the court's decision, articulated quite clearly the practical impact of the decision on Indian religious freedom, the American Indian Religious Freedom Act, and Indian cultural survival. I quote Brennan at length to provide the full nuance of the implications of the court's decision:

> Today, the Court holds that a federal land-use decision that promises to destroy an entire religion does not burden the practice of that faith in a manner recognized by the Free Exercise Clause. Having thus stripped respondents [the Yurok, Karok, and Tolowa Tribes] and all other Native Americans of any constitutional protection against perhaps the most serious threat to their age-old religious practices, and indeed to their entire way of life, the Court assures us that nothing in its decision "should be read to encourage governmental insensitivity to the religious needs of any citizen." I find it difficult, however, to imagine conduct more insensitive to religious needs than the Government's determination to build a marginally useful road in the face of uncontradicted evidence the road will render the practice of respondents' religion impossible. Nor do I believe that respondents will derive any solace from the knowledge that although the practice of their religion will become "more difficult" as a result of the Government's actions, they remain free to maintain their religious beliefs. Given today's ruling, that freedom amounts to nothing more than the right to believe that their religion will be destroyed. The safeguarding of such a hollow freedom not only makes a mockery of the "policy of the United States to protect and preserve for American Indians their inherent right of freedom to believe, express, and exercise their traditional religions," it fails utterly to accord with the dictates of the First Amendment.[30]

The Supreme Court's opinion was not the final act in the *Lyng* case. While the *Lyng* decision made it quite clear that the U.S. government may use land it claims title to as it pleases, the majority opinion clearly stated that the Constitution did not prohibit the U.S. government from considering the impact on indigenous religion. Furthermore, the court encouraged accommodation that would minimize the disruptions that concerned Indian peoples. The Clinton administration, acting within the court's suggestion to accommodate religious concerns, moved the road of marginal utility with a six-mile detour.[31]

EMPLOYMENT DIVISION V. SMITH

In *Employment Division v. Smith* (1990), the United States Supreme Court explicitly abandoned its long-held standards regarding the free exercise of religion. Previously the standard had been that when laws of general applicability were found by the courts to penalize, directly or indirectly, religious practice, the government action was then examined to see if the measure forwarded a compelling governmental interest. If it did not, the governmental action was unconstitutional as applied. In *Smith*, the United States Supreme Court abandoned this precedent and upheld the application of an Oregon law that forbade the use of peyote under any circumstances, including religious use. The Supreme Court acknowledged that the statewide ban on peyote use infringed upon the religious beliefs of Al Smith, a member of the Native American Church, but refused to apply the rest of the established test, instead finding that generally applicable laws were constitutional, even if they substantially burdened the free exercise of religion.[32]

Al Smith, from whom the case takes its name, has been described as a "twentieth century Indian Everyman" and was born in 1919 at Modoc Point, Oregon. Smith, a Klamath Indian, often went by his "restaurant name" of Red Coyote. Though his grandparents were fluent in the Klamath language, they did not teach the language to Smith for fear it might hold him back in life. Unquestionably a full-blooded Indian by appearance, Smith would use the name Red Coyote when he waited for a table at a restaurant. When this name was called, he knew he would not disappoint those who looked up to see.[33]

The fortunes of Smith's life closely followed the changing Indian policies of the twentieth century and the fortunes of the Klamath people. At age seven he was forcibly sent to a brutal Catholic boarding school. There he resisted, falsely telling the nuns that he had already been baptized. He regularly ran away from the school. In the 1930s he moved to a Bureau of Indian Affairs boarding school in Nevada. At first he was out of place among the Paiutes who made up most of the school population, but he won his place among the students by stealing large quantities of homemade alcohol from a local and sharing it with the other students.[34]

Smith was an alcoholic at the same time the Klamath Nation hit its low point. The Klamath Nation was among those first selected for termination in the 1950s. Smith, a Klamath without a nation, entered Alcoholics Anonymous in 1957 and began working the program. At first he ran into difficulty, as the program was very much based in protestant Christianity and his only experience with Christianity was as an oppressive force he had previously fought against. Smith sought out

Indian religious practices and educated himself. Ultimately he was able to make the AA program work for him and remained sober after 1957.[35]

As Indian resistance to termination became both a political resistance and a religious revival, Smith revived his life in professional and religious ways. He became a successful addiction counselor with a specialty in helping Indian people cross the cultural gap to make the Alcoholics Anonymous program work for them. Smith continued his own religious awakening into the 1970s, participating in Indian religious ceremonies and learning more. In 1977 Smith adapted the AA method to work with the needs of the practitioners of Indian religions.[36]

The 1980s saw the restoration of the Klamath Nation, and the Douglas County Council on Alcohol and Drug Abuse Prevention and Treatment (ADAPT) hired Smith. After years of protest, a portion of Klamath National Forest was returned to the Klamaths. The Klamath Nation and reservation were restored in 1986. Smith started to work for ADAPT because of the treatment center's goal of better serving Indian clients.[37] Soon Smith came into conflict with his employers over the Native American Church and their sacramental use of peyote.

The Native American Church was an Indian innovation created to keep religious activities alive in the face of government repression during the period of allotment and forced assimilation. American Indians have been using peyote for at least ten thousand years for religious purposes, and in the 1880s, Indian peoples blended Christian rituals and theology in with traditional peyote ceremonies. The Native American Church incorporated in 1918 and added talk of Jesus in ceremonies to try and escape government attempts to wipe out indigenous religions. The Native American Church spread and grew. It was not always welcomed by Indian groups, but the religion had positive impacts on many. Scientific studies from the 1970s showed that active members of the Native American Church who partook of the sacrament of peyote had better recovery rates than other drug and alcohol abusers.[38]

While not a member of the Native American Church in 1983, Smith knew that participation in the church was a successful path to recovery for many Indians, and he clashed with ADAPT administrators over the issue. ADAPT policies followed the prominent belief in recovery circles that only through total abstention from substance use can recovery be maintained. That year a fellow employee participated in Native American Church ceremonies and partook of peyote. That employee was fired, and Smith protested vigorously. As Smith continued to clash with management, it altered ADAPT policies to make it clear that partaking in peyote, even for religious reasons, was grounds for immediate termination.[39]

A local congregation of the Native American Church invited Smith to partake in its ceremonies in 1984. Smith informed ADAPT of his plan to participate in church sacraments over the weekend. When he returned on Monday, ADAPT fired Smith. Smith said of his actions, "You go to church, and then you get terminated. It is a continuation of being put down, to my people and our religion not being recognized by you newcomers. They just riled me up to the point where I'm ready for a fight."[40]

Terminated, Smith applied for unemployment benefits. ADAPT challenged the validity of the claims, stating that Smith was fired for good cause. Smith and another terminated employee appealed and won at every level, up to and including the Oregon Supreme Court. The lower courts all applied the compelling interest test and found that religious use of peyote could be accommodated. The Oregon Supreme Court found that the legal status of peyote in the state was irrelevant and that there was no state interest in denying unemployment compensation to those terminated for religious conduct. The United States Supreme Court agreed to take the case in 1987.[41]

In 1989, when the *Smith* case went to oral arguments before the Supreme Court, the controlling precedent was *Sherbert v. Verner*. In this employment case, working on Saturdays conflicted with the religious practices of a Seventh Day Adventist. In this case, the Supreme Court established a test to determine whether or not a generally applicable law impermissibly violated First Amendment religious freedom rights. When religion is infringed upon, the government must show that it has a compelling interest to do so and that the law is narrowly tailored to carry out the compelling interest. At no point in the proceedings did the State of Oregon or Smith and his allies challenge the validity of the *Sherbert* compelling interest test. The attorneys for both Oregon and Smith confined their arguments to the terms of the compelling interest test, simply arguing that the test was or was not met by Oregon's law.[42]

Justice Antonin Scalia delivered the opinion of the court in 1990 and abandoned the compelling interest test, even though no one involved in the case had briefed or argued for such a drastic change in religious freedom jurisprudence. Overturning almost thirty years of precedent, the majority of the court ruled that generally applicable laws that did not specifically target religion did not violate the Free Exercise Clause of the First Amendment. In his opinion, Scalia noted, by making reference to the *Lyng* case, that the Supreme Court had previously departed from applying the compelling interest test to laws where the central tenants of the religious beliefs of an individual were burdened by a law of general applicability. Scalia ignored thirty years of successfully balancing religious interests against societal interests with the *Sherbert* test when he wrote, "It may be fairly said that leaving accommodation [of religious belief] to the political process will place at a relative disadvantage those religious practices that are not widely engaged in; but that unavoidable consequence of democratic government must be preferred to a system in which each conscience is a law unto itself or in which judges weigh the social importance of all laws against the centrality of all religious beliefs."[43]

Justice O'Connor, author of the *Lyng* decision, agreed with the outcome of the majority's decision, but in her concurring opinion she argued that *Lyng* was different because it regarded how the U.S. government used its own land and that in applying the prior compelling interest test to Smith, the same results would be achieved.[44] O'Connor was quite disturbed that the majority endorsed an opinion that had as an unavoidable consequence the disfavoring of minority religions, which Scalia admitted his extremist transformation of religious freedom jurisprudence accomplished.[45]

The dissenting opinion in *Smith* would have applied the compelling interest test and found religion unconstitutionally burdened. Brennan wrote, "I do not believe the Founders thought their dearly bought freedom from religious persecution a 'luxury,' but an essential element of liberty—and they could not have thought religious intolerance 'unavoidable,' for they drafted the Religion Clauses precisely to avoid that intolerance."[46]

The reaction to Scalia's opinion, which offended many beyond those who traditionally supported Indian religious freedom, was relatively quick. This reaction of a broad coalition was due to the immediate recognition of the wide-ranging threat to religious freedom in the United States that the *Smith* decision presented. Many saw Scalia's opinion as an attack on core values that mainstream Americans thought were foundational to their national identity. Scalia's opinion threatened more than simply the religious freedom of American Indians. Shortly after Scalia's opinion was delivered, Amish exemptions from having to place silver reflectors on their buggies in Minnesota ended; Jews and Hmong were forced to allow autopsies they found religiously offensive; Presbyterian and Lutheran churches lost their cause of action against the federal government, which had sent covert agents into their churches to spy on the sanctuary movement; and people realized that general meat-handling regulations could potentially prevent the preparation of kosher foods.[47]

THE RELIGIOUS FREEDOM RESTORATION ACT

The national reaction to this threat to more than just indigenous religious freedom grew. Several people publicly accused Scalia of eliminating religious freedom in the United States, and opponents accused him of trying to use a drug-use dispute to eliminate all claims of infringement of religious freedom from the courts. Politicians acted quickly to introduce a bill into Congress to reverse Scalia's decision. Though the bill was held up for a couple of years, by 1993 the Religious Freedom Restoration Act had broad support. Supporters of the law included the American Jewish Congress, the Mormon Church, the Southern Baptist Convention, the National Council of Churches, the National Conference of Catholic Bishops, People for the American Way, the Traditional Values Coalition, and the American Civil Liberties Union.[48]

The Congress of the United States passed the Religious Freedom Restoration Act of 1993 in direct response to the *Smith* case. The law prohibited the government of the United States in all cases from substantially burdening the religious freedom of any person, unless that burden promoted a compelling governmental interest and the interest was achieved in the least restrictive means possible. The protections provided to religion in this act go beyond the prior standards overturned by *Smith* in that the test is to be applied in *all* cases where religion is burdened (previously there had been numerous exceptions for the military, prisons, and public lands, and there was some investigation into whether or not the belief in question was central to religious exercise) and any compelling governmental interest must be achieved *in the least restrictive means possible*. Despite these obvious expansions beyond the former protections, with the exception of the Ninth Circuit Court of Appeals, federal appellate courts have consistently found prior exceptions to the compelling interest test from pre-*Smith* case law to be exceptions to the compelling interest test mandated by RFRA when Indian religious freedom is involved.[49]

While RFRA was deliberately crafted to be ambiguous on the use of peyote for religious purposes, proponents of Indian religious freedom continued to lobby Congress and obtained protections for Indian uses of peyote. In 1994 Congress passed a law exempting registered members of Indian nations from state and federal criminal prosecution for the use, possession, or transport of peyote for traditional religious purposes. The law also directly addressed the *Smith* case by prohibiting the denial of any benefits because of traditional peyote use. Native American Church congregations differ in their policies regarding allowing non-Indians to participate in services, but the law permits only registered tribal members to use, possess, or transport peyote.[50] Again, the other branches of the U.S. government moved to counter the overt attacks on religious freedom by the United States Supreme Court, often mistakenly believed to be the protector of rights in the U.S. legal system.

Even with the advent of RFRA, there remained much debate as to the proper extent of protections afforded indigenous religious sites on public lands. While RFRA explicitly overturned *Smith*, the statute itself made reference to precedents that predate *Lyng*. Some commentators have argued that *Lyng* did not properly apply the substantial burden on religion test as applied in these precedents, as Scalia claimed in *Smith*. Those who hold this position argue that, by Scalia's reference to *Lyng* in *Smith*, *Lyng* was similarly overturned by RFRA. The majority in the Ninth Circuit case would later hold a contrary opinion and state that *Lyng* was still the controlling precedent with regard to management of public lands. Thus, for the Ninth Circuit Court of Appeals, any action that destroys indigenous religion, short of coercing a party to act contrary to its religious beliefs, was a legally proper act under the laws and Constitution of the United States.[51] The Ninth Circuit opinion in *Navajo Nation v. Forest Service* is examined in detail in chapter 2.

MANAGEMENT OF SACRED SITES: ESTABLISHMENT OF RELIGION CONCERNS

At the end of the twentieth century, with the advent of the American Indian Religious Freedom Act of 1978, practitioners of indigenous religions and Indian governments sought greater protection for sacred sites on public lands. This led to increased judicial discussion of fears that the government might act to unconstitutionally support Indian religions. These articulated fears of the U.S. government suddenly reversing policy and endorsing Indian religions were issued by the courts apparently with no intentional irony (or sense of history, context, or reality). With Indian challenges to administrative decisions that harmed or jeopardized the integrity of sacred sites, judges began to muse that if administrators protected Indian sacred sites in ways Indian peoples wanted, that would unconstitutionally establish Indian religion. With the beginning of the consultation process in the 1980s there emerged the occasional case where administrators acted to protect Indian sacred sites, diverging from the long history of hostility and indifference to indigenous religious and cultural concerns. Some who found their activities limited by administrative decisions protecting sacred sites brought suit, claiming that protecting Indian sacred sites violated the First Amendment by establishing religion. In some cases, against better judicial practice, judges entered into hypothetical musings about protective procedures that were not before the courts, creating a string of opinions claiming that more vigorously protecting Indian sacred sites would impermissibly establish religion.

The historical cases below set the contours for the state of First Amendment establishment law as it relates to the protection of sacred sites. This information is necessary for understanding two of the case studies in this book. The first case involves Bear's Lodge, more popularly known as Devils Tower (owing to a non-Indian mistranslation of the location's name), the first national monument recognized in the United States and a location for religious ceremonies since time immemorial. The second case examined is highly representative of changes taking place in public lands management over the last decades of the twentieth century and involves Rainbow Bridge, a sacred place to Navajos and others. The National Park Service ignored Navajo pleas to more respectfully manage the site in the early 1980s, only to later turn to the Navajos for assistance in formulating plans to rehabilitate the area at the end of the century. What emerged from these cases was a trail of problematic comments not relevant to the logic of the decisions. In these comments, the courts speculated that limiting access to sacred sites to protect or preserve them in accord with Indian religious beliefs would violate the constitutional ban on the establishment of religion. A court engaging in such idle speculation on issues neither briefed by the parties nor before the court in the current case is an example of a dictum. Such opinions that have no bearing on the disposition of the case before the court are widely considered to be of little to no legal weight. This trail of problematic dicta repeated the unsupported opinion that administrative bans on access to public lands to protect sacred sites would amount to government establishment of religion. Opponents of management plans at Cave Rock would later offer a compromise based on a Devils Tower (Bear's Lodge) climbing management plan that had caused the creation of some of the problematic dicta. When recreational users of public lands found their access curtailed at Cave Rock and Badger-Two Medicine, their lawyers planned their arguments around this judicial language.

BEAR'S LODGE

Bear's Lodge, more commonly known as Devils Tower (owing to a non-Indian mistranslation of the name of the location), has a most fascinating origin in Kiowa cultural traditions. Long ago, in what would later become the northeast corner of Wyoming, seven young girls of the Kiowa Nation strayed from camp. Soon they found themselves being chased by bears. They sought refuge on a rock, maybe three feet in height. One of the girls prayed for the rock to take pity on them. The rock was moved by her prayers and began to grow, pushing the girls out of reach of the bears. The bears jumped and scratched at the sides of the growing rock, leaving long distinct lines along its columnar shape. The girls then ascended to the sky and became the seven stars of the Pleiades cluster. Today the Kiowa and other Indian nations refer to this iconic location as Bear's Lodge.[52]

Bear's Lodge has long been a place of significance for both indigenous and non-Indian peoples. In the modern era, Bear's Lodge was located in Lakota territory before annexation by the U.S. government. Bear's Lodge plays a role in many indigenous religions, including those of the Crows and Cheyennes, as well as the Kiowas and Lakotas. For centuries Bear's Lodge served as a place for religious ceremonies that required solemnity and solitude, including Sun Dances and vision quests. While the U.S. government sought to eliminate indigenous religion during the period of forced assimilation and outlawed Sun Dances, President Theodore Roosevelt declared Devils Tower to be the first national monument under the 1906 Antiquities Act.[53]

As recreational climbing grew in popularity in the United States, the increased presence of climbers disrupted both religious services at Bear's Lodge and the environmental integrity of the site. Only 312 climbers visited in 1973, but by the 1990s, more than six thousand climbers visited annually. Over the years, climbers established 220 climbing routes and placed some six hundred bolts in the rock face of Bear's Lodge. In the 1980s a tourist climbing industry arose; professional guides took amateur climbers on excursions at the site. Many, including National Park Service personnel entrusted with managing the site, were not aware of the religious significance of the place. Climbers would remove prayer bundles, photograph people engaged in worship, and approach people who were praying or fasting. Climbers also disrupted religious ceremonies with their hammering, shouting, and climbing. By 1992 the National Park Service recognized that climbing was having significant negative impacts on animal habitats and natural resources and that a climbing management plan needed to be created.[54]

The National Park Service initiated a consultation process for creating a climbing management plan, designed to reach consensus among interested parties. The Park Service created a working group with representatives from the climbing community, environmental organizations, local government, and interested American Indian communities. Initially groups were completely at odds with one another. In the first working group meetings, participants expressed their maximalist goals. Climbers wanted few or no restrictions on access, while Indian representatives called for a ban on all climbing, declaring the practice to be a desecration of a sacred place. Park Service administrators attempted to foster cross-cultural communications and were aided in this by the communication skills of Elaine Quiver.[55]

Initially not an official representative of any Indian group, Elaine Quiver of Pine Ridge, South Dakota, emerged as a leader. She was instrumental in bringing the working group to consensus. Quiver demonstrated that she could clearly explain the positions of Indian elders to outsiders in terms they could understand. Quickly all parties came to agree that some form of preservation program was necessary. Climbers feared a ban on climbing and tried to describe climbing as a religious experience. Through the process, Indian interest groups remained united on the position that a mandatory climbing ban for the month of June was necessary, as that was the most crucial month for religious ceremonies, but it was also the busiest month for climbing. Quiver and other Indian leaders returned to their communities and learned that many Indian people felt that a voluntary climbing ban would be much more meaningful to them. If climbers voluntarily abstained from climbing in June, it would be seen as an expression of respect for Indian religions and culture.[56]

The climbing management plan that emerged from the working group bore no resemblance to the maximalist positions of any group. The expansion of areas for climbing would stop; no new routes would be permitted. Existing climbing equipment would be camouflaged, and no new climbing bolts would be placed; existing ones would be replaced only to preserve safety. Bear's Lodge would be closed to climbing during raptor mating season. The climbing community and the Park Service were to encourage climbers to abstain from climbing in June. To facilitate this last part, the Park Service planned to stop issuing commercial permits to guides for that month. The stated goal of the plan's cultural education components was to have the June voluntary climbing closure reach 100 percent compliance. If ethical suasion through the education program failed to do the job, the Park Service would revisit the issue of a mandatory closure.[57]

In many ways, the approach of the National Park Service in formulating a climbing management plan for Bear's Lodge was emblematic of broader changes in federal public lands management. In 1994 President Clinton signed an executive memorandum that reiterated the obligation of the federal government to work with Indian governments as sovereigns and that required departments and agencies to consult with Indian governments to the greatest practical extent in matters that impacted Indian interests. Executive Order 13,007, issued in 1996, required federal land managers to accommodate Indian use of sacred sites and to avoid adversely impacting places of religious significance to indigenous peoples.[58]

While the working group had come to consensus, commercial climbing guides took issue with the climbing management plan and in 1995 both challenged the plan and sought an injunction against implementation of the ban on the issuance of commercial permits in June. Working with the Mountain States Legal Foundation, climbing interests challenged cultural education programs, the voluntary June climbing closure, and the ban on June commercial permits on the grounds that the Park Service was engaged in the unconstitutional establishment of religion. They immediately requested a preliminary injunction against the June permit ban.[59]

Judge William F. Downes of the U.S. District Court for Wyoming issued an injunction preventing the ban on June commercial guide permits from going into effect in a highly questionable legal opinion. Rather than engage in any substantive analysis of precedent in the Tenth Circuit Court of Appeals, Downes based his decision on dicta from a religious freedom case in which the Navajo Nation challenged Park Service management of Rainbow Bridge National Monument as desecrating a sacred place to the Navajos. The case of Rainbow Bridge is examined in more detail below, but in that 1980 case, the Tenth Circuit Court of Appeals speculated that the request by the Navajos to exclude everyone year-round from Rainbow Bridge, except for religious services, might run afoul of the constitutional prohibition against religious establishment. Downes's order also failed to distinguish the fact that the climbing management plan merely called for a temporary periodic cessation of commercial permits, and the order failed to acknowledge that many places managed by the federal government, such as Arlington National Cemetery, Ebenezer Baptist Church in Georgia, Bethesda Baptist Church in Pennsylvania, and Annunciation Chapel in Alaska, were regularly closed for European religious services. Ultimately the issue was never fully litigated, as the Park Service withdrew the ban in 1996.[60]

Despite this initial legal failure, and serious reasons to question Downes's partiality, the Park Service, Indian interests, and their allies succeed in defending the remaining parts of the climbing management plan from claims that it was an impermissible establishment of religion. After the initial injunction and the subsequent removal of the June permit ban, Downes berated government attorneys for wasting government resources and expertise on the case. Downes told them, on the record, that the resources would have been better spent on programs diverting the Indian youthful offenders he saw in his court from crime and alcohol rather than on activities to preserve Indian culture. Despite his misgivings about the propriety of the use of government resources to defend the case, Downes found that the plaintiffs lacked standing and that the cultural education aspects and voluntary June closure did not establish any religion in violation of the First Amendment of the U.S. Constitution.[61]

By the 1990s, establishment jurisprudence was a muddled affair. Contemporary critics felt that Downes was not engaging in proper analysis in his decisions. While making mention of the then nominally controlling case, *Lemon v. Kurztman*, 403 U.S. 602 (1971), Downes never engaged in the three-part analysis recommended by *Lemon* in his decision for the preliminary injunction. The *Lemon* test examines whether or not a government action (1) has a secular purpose, (2) advances or inhibits religion, and (3) fosters excessive government entanglement with religion. With *Lee v. Weisman*, 505 U.S. 577 (1992), Justice Anthony Kennedy stressed that the key element to be considered was coercion. Justice O'Connor instead suggested that endorsement of religion was key, as determined by examining the purpose and effect of the alleged establishment of religion and that this was the controlling test for the Tenth Circuit. Contemporary commentators felt that Downes should engage in some form of *Lemon* analysis in determining whether or not any part of the climbing management plan served to establish any of the various Indian religions considered in the Park Service plan.[62]

When the issue of the validity of the climbing management plan returned to Downes for final disposition on the establishment claims, he applied the *Lemon* test, modified by O'Connor's endorsement test, which had become the test within the Tenth Circuit. In the analysis, Downes examined the purpose and effect of the voluntary closure. He found that the purpose of the voluntary closure was to allow for the accommodation of Indian religions, not to promote them. He found that the effect of the voluntary closure was not, as the climbing guides claimed, coercion preventing them from climbing. Downes then examined the level of entanglement the government had with religion and found there was minimal government involvement with religion in this program.[63]

While Downes ruled that the voluntary closure was not the establishment of religion, in dicta he reiterated his opinion that a ban on climbing would serve to establish religion. Misreading precedent, Downes quoted a dictum from the 1980

Rainbow Bridge case, *Badoni v. Higgins*, stating that a free exercise of religion claim cannot be used to prevent the normal use of an area.[64] Here Downes again ignored the fact that the government often closed public places for religious services and that the normal historic use of Bear's Lodge was for religious services, not climbing. This twice-repeated dictum about permanent closures unconstitutionally establishing religion would concern Forest Service planners later at Cave Rock and give hope to climbers seeking to continue climbing at the most sacred of Washoe places, as examined in more detail below.

The guides and their legal allies appealed Downes's decision to the Tenth Circuit Court of Appeals but found no relief. Indian organizations solicited friend of the court briefs from Christian and Jewish religious organizations to add a broad moral force to their defense of the management plan. Though the Tenth Circuit ultimately affirmed Downes's decision in 1999, the unanimous opinion of the court only partially adopted Downes' reasoning. The Tenth Circuit agreed that various plaintiffs lacked standing to challenge parts of the plan, but the court also determined that climbers and guides lacked standing to challenge the voluntary closure. The court reasoned that while the Park Service stated that it might contemplate an involuntary closure sometime in the future, the current plan, which merely urged climbers to refrain from climbing in June out of respect for others, was not a current harm that was actionable in court. The potential threat of a mandatory closure was too remote, and the Tenth Circuit never revisited the issue of the management plan serving to establish religion, as the climbers and guides had not alleged any actual harm. Thus they lacked standing to seek relief from the courts on all aspects of their claims.[65]

In the initial years after implementation of the climbing management plan, the voluntary closure was highly successful. The United States Supreme Court refused to take the case on appeal. Initially climbing in June dropped by 79 percent from preplan average use. Climbing guides remained a permanent economic interest whose livelihoods were in some part dependent upon encouraging people to not respect the June closure of Bear's Lodge. In June 2004 the climbing use of Bear's Lodge was only 69 percent less than preplan averages, and 55 percent of the 2004 climbers were led by paid guides.[66]

RAINBOW BRIDGE

Long ago, a Navajo hero god was hunting when he was caught in a flash flood in what is now southern Utah. He faced certain death by drowning, but then Sky

Father intervened and cast a rainbow for him to run across. Later the rainbow turned to stone; this Rainbow Bridge remains to this day. Rainbow Bridge is the world's largest natural bridge. It spans 278 feet. It is 290 feet high, 33 feet wide, and 42 feet thick at the top of the arch. Located in the middle of Navajo territory, Rainbow Bridge remained remote and unpublicized to the outside world until 1909.[67]

While located inside Navajo territory, Rainbow Bridge is of religious significance to several indigenous religions. The Hopis understand Rainbow Bridge to be where the Snake Clan first dropped into this world. Rainbow Bridge is the remnant of a rainbow swinging around to strike Navajo Mountain and dropping the Snake Clan of the Hopis into this existence. In addition, the Paiutes and other Indian peoples have historical connections to Rainbow Bridge and believe it is a place of religious significance. For many, it is impermissible to pass beneath Rainbow Bridge without saying the proper prayers.[68]

The history of U.S. management of Rainbow Bridge is in many ways emblematic of the changes in public lands management of Indian sacred sites in the twentieth century. During the assimilation period, when the U.S. government sought to eradicate Indian religions, in 1910 President William Howard Taft issued Proclamation 1043, unilaterally declaring the 160 acres surrounding Rainbow Bridge to be a national monument. In 1916 the National Park Service took over management of the site. Construction on Glen Canyon Dam finished in 1963, during the era of termination, and the Colorado River began to flood the monument site, forming Lake Powell. By 1977 the water beneath Rainbow Bridge was more than twenty feet deep. The creation of Lake Powell increased tourist traffic to the site significantly.[69] No one even consulted Indian peoples as to their thoughts on how to manage the sacred site.

As the U.S. government switched to government-to-government relations and the 1978 American Indian Religious Freedom Act brought hopes that consultation requirements and an "official" policy of protecting Indian religions might bring some protections to Indian sacred sites, the actions of federal land managers of Rainbow Bridge and the courts again disappointed the Navajos. The U.S. government had drowned the gods of practitioners of traditional Navajo religion and denied them access to sacred sites with the growth of Lake Powell. Many felt that the government-permitted tourist traffic completely desecrated Rainbow Bridge. Practitioners of traditional Navajo religion brought suit against the government, complaining that the drowning of their gods and the presence of tourists violated Navajo rights to the free exercise of religion. In *Badoni v. Higgins*, the Tenth Circuit

Court of Appeals ruled in 1980 that the presence of Lake Powell did burden Navajo religion but that operation of Glen Canyon Dam was a compelling governmental interest sufficient to outweigh consideration for Navajo rights.[70]

The *Badoni* court, in its consideration of the tourist issue, was somewhat cavalier in its analysis and created dicta that would cause Downes problems in the 1990s, as discussed above, and administrative concerns in the management decisions for Cave Rock, as discussed below. While the Navajos objected to the presence of all tourists, they particularly complained of the disorderly and often drunken conduct of tourists, which prohibited their ability to engage in religious ceremonies in peace. Without specifically identifying whether or not the particular permitted conduct was a burden on Navajo religious practitioners, the court determined that existing Park Service regulations were sufficient to deal with drunk and disorderly persons and that the Navajo could apply for permits for park closures like other groups. Most problematic to posterity was the court's dictum regarding a total ban on tourists. Without engaging in any analysis of existing case law on the establishment of religion, the court simply stated that a total ban on tourists would clearly violate the constitutional prohibition on the establishment of religion.[71]

As with other cases, such as management of the San Francisco Peaks, the Navajos were unable to find satisfaction through the American Indian Religious Freedom Act, but the Park Service managers of Rainbow Bridge National Monument quickly changed their opinions and wanted greater input from Navajos by 1985. Increased boat access across Lake Powell to Rainbow Bridge proved problematic in short order. In 1955 merely one thousand outsiders visited Rainbow Bridge. By 1974 that number had increased to fifty-five thousand. By 1986 the number was sixty-five thousand, or about 270 visitors a day. By 1995 the number had ballooned to 346,000. By 1985 the visitors were problematic. Vegetation was trampled and destroyed, litter became a problem, erosion and soil loss proliferated, visitors defaced petroglyphs, and rocks were covered with graffiti. In 1985 the Park Service recognized the need to reorganize management of the site. Officials wanted to improve relations with the Navajo Nation and obtain its assistance in managing and protecting the site. The Park Service consulted Navajos and other Indian groups in formulating a new management plan.[72]

The Park Service issued its draft environmental impact statement for a new general management plan (GMP) in 1990 and in 1993 issued a final plan, designed to both respect Indian religious concerns and rehabilitate the environment of Rainbow Bridge. The GMP included a program to rehabilitate trails, eliminate tourist-created trails, and maintain a cement paved trail from Lake Powell docks to Rainbow Bridge viewing areas; a program to discourage the use of informal trails; and a program to rehabilitate native species of plants and to close some areas for revegetation. Most important to the Navajos and other concerned Indian groups was Park Service inclusion of an educational program designed to improve awareness of the sacred character of the place in the eyes of practitioners of indigenous religions. As part of this program, signs, park materials, and park rangers would ask that visitors refrain from walking under Rainbow Bridge out of respect for traditional Indian religious beliefs.[73]

After implementation of the plan, a visitor named Earl DeWaal went to Rainbow Bridge and loudly complained about the cultural education program. DeWaal reportedly demanded the right to go anywhere in the park and became verbally abusive to park rangers. DeWaal vocally complained that the signs informing the public of the sacred character of the national monument were all lies created by a conspiracy involving Indians and environmentalists. He reportedly used the word "Injun" in his loud complaints and finally left after other visitors asked him to leave.[74]

DeWaal joined the Natural Arch and Bridge Society and other, less belligerent parties in a lawsuit challenging the validity of the cultural awareness portion of the general management plan in 2000. The plaintiffs accused the National Park Service of engaging in the establishment of religion merely by educating the public about Indian religious concerns and asking visitors to respect those beliefs by voluntarily abstaining from walking under Rainbow Bridge. Judge Bruce S. Jenkins for the District Court of Utah, Central Division, issued his opinion in 2002.[75]

While Jenkins dismissed many of the plaintiffs' complaints against the Park Service for lack of standing, he did conduct a substantive establishment analysis regarding the cultural program of the GMP. By 2002 the Tenth Circuit Court of Appeals was using the *Lemon* test, as modified by Justice O'Connor, as the standard test for determining if a governmental action does in fact serve to establish religion. This variant examines the purpose and effect of the government action and then examines if the government has become too entangled in religion. With regard to the Rainbow Bridge cultural awareness program, Jenkins found that the purpose of the program was to educate and inform. When considering effect, the court considered what effect the program would have on a reasonable and aware observer. Jenkins determined that the cultural program could not possibly have the effect of leading a reasonable and aware observer to believe that the Park Service had adopted a religion. As to entanglement, Jenkins determined that the program merely called for new signs, a new website, and new brochures and that this, considering the nature of the work of the Park Service in managing sites, could not be considered entanglement. Jenkins went further and commented that the cultural awareness program merely made the area more conducive to worship by Americans Indians and that the American Indian Religious Freedom Act of 1978 required the consultation of Indian religious communities in creating management plans. Though the determination of Jenkins fully supported the GMP, Jenkins added to the growing list of cases that failed to engage in a substantive analysis of an involuntary ban on activities at an Indian sacred site and opined in a dictum that a ban on travel under Rainbow Bridge "could possibly" violate constitutional prohibitions on the establishment of religion.[76]

Perhaps remaining belligerent to the end, Earl DeWaal, joined by only one other visitor to Rainbow Bridge, appealed Jenkins's decision to the Tenth Circuit Court of Appeals. The appellate court found that the remaining plaintiffs had suffered no injury in fact. The court affirmed the dismissal on the grounds that the cultural program and request to not walk under Rainbow Bridge in no way injured the plaintiffs and that they lacked standing to challenge the GMP.[77]

EXECUTIVE AND LEGISLATIVE ACTION

Entering the twenty-first century, the courts provided wide latitude for administrative agencies regarding the management of sacred sites, but with several statements that agencies might not be able to prohibit use of sacred sites by non-Indians to protect those places. Essentially, the First Amendment placed no limitations on agency discretion so long as agencies consulted Indians in accordance with the law. While none of the courts ruled on fully briefed and argued challenges to mandatory bans on uses of Indian sacred sites that protected the sacred quality of those sites, several judges stated that hypothetical involuntary bans would violate the Establishment Clause. In the first decade of the twenty-first century, this issue would finally be settled, as seen in the case of Cave Rock, below.

As the new millennium started, there was cause to be hopeful despite the lack of constitutionally protected religious freedoms in the United States. The executive and legislative branches of the U.S. government had taken positive steps to respect indigenous religions and offered some respect for indigenous religious sensibilities. In 2009 President Barack Obama ordered agencies to report on their compliance with these orders. The 2008 Farm Bill expanded protections for confidential information regarding sacred sites from Freedom of Information Act requests.[78] At the end of 2016 the Obama administration approved a modified version of the proposal of five Indian nations to create a new national monument in Utah, Bears Ears. The year 2017 began with a new president taking power in the United States. President Donald Trump had a record of open hostility to Indian interests and a Congress willing to destroy Indian cultural sites for foreign corporate interests, as explained in the case of Oak Flat in chapter 5.

A SELF-DETERMINATION MODEL FOR ANALYSIS AND SOLUTIONS

Lloyd Burton, in his 2002 book, *Worship and Religion: Culture, Religion, and Law in the Management of Public Lands and Resources*, explained, in part, the growing political acceptance of Indian religious views of the land by non-Indians. Burton identified a growing diversity and appreciation for nature in the non-Indian populations of the United States. He noted that in many cases, including *Lyng*, Christian and Jewish groups offered briefs in support of protecting Indian sacred sites on public lands as part of protecting religious freedom. Burton concluded that *Lyng*, *Smith*, and sacred site cases keep us locked in a fruitless rights-based dialogue that places Indian rights at the bottom of concerns. Burton identified a significant historical shift in practitioners of mainstream European religions in the United States and noted that support for Indian rights and religious perspectives was on the rise. For Burton, the historic struggle exists in the non-Indian community, with such groups as the Mountain States Legal Foundation engaged in a war against pluralism by attacking the cultural education elements of the Bear's Lodge climbing management plan. The cultural education program was a threat to European cultural hegemony over the Americas. Burton identified negotiation as not always being possible, as the forces against pluralism often are interested in complete domination and subjugation. A potential path forward for Burton is to better use national parks and monuments as classrooms for educating people about the rich cultural diversity in the United States.[79] Burton's perspective is that the pertinent struggle is not simply of one culture against another but a deeper struggle over values in the European American community. Will non-Indians accept the universal aspiration for freedom and self-determination or will they demand cultural hegemony under some form of European American culture?

With the expansion of legislative and executive actions offering regularized consultation and new options for protection through designating sites as traditional cultural properties, there is no reason to believe that differences in religious perspectives fundamentally prevent non-Indians from understanding and respecting the views of others. One need only look at the efforts of non-Indians to protect sites of historical and cultural significance to understand that notions of sacred places are not so alien to the European mind.

Some have characterized a fundamental cultural difference in perspectives on land that may create a barrier to cross-cultural understanding. Indian religions have a great deal of diversity, but some commonalities set Indian religions apart from most religions of European populations. For many Indians, religion is a way of life. To study the history of an Indian religion is to study the totality of an Indian group's art, culture, economics, music, dress, and politics. Religion is a community-centered way of life that includes animals, the land, and the spirits of the dead. In the late nineteenth and early twentieth century, U.S. government suppression of the Lakota religion, which was centered on a community that included both living and dead, was particularly distressing to the Lakota, who commented that the "white man" harassed their people even in death.[80] This encompassing religious experience differed significantly from the general experience of non-Indian populations from the late nineteenth century to today. Generally, those of European origin came to conceive of religion as something separable from other aspects of life and based in core beliefs and behaviors that are distinct from the customs and practices of any particular society.[81]

Indian religious perspectives, by contrast, tend to see the land and the bounty of nature as being part of the greater community of people. These contrasting perspectives can be discerned by differing answers to the question "Does the land belong to me or do I belong to the land?" In most Indian religions, people belong to the land and their beliefs about their origins and cultural interactions with the land and nature are part of religious practice and observation. Another way to contrast the general perspectives is to compare the origin stories of different religions. Most Indian religions see Earth as the mother and origin of the people, an important part of the larger spiritual community, while Europeans have a story about being expelled from the natural world into a world of struggle and torment. The lives of many European religious practitioners are in conflict with Earth. Many Indian religions stress the responsibility of the individual to the community, including the land. By contrast, liberal Christians brought to North America the notion of individual property rights responsible to no one. As legal scholar Brian Edward Brown characterized it, "Land exists in a condition of servitude; it ultimately belongs to someone who enjoys control over the allocation of resources contained within its boundaries."[82]

Like Indian cultures, non-Indian cultures are not monolithic and are constantly changing. While the liberal, capitalist view of land and notions of western

European cultural supremacy may now dominate the legal and economic cultures of the United States, change over time has occurred, as Burton has noted. Even at the darkest period of U.S. history, when the government sought to destroy indigenous societies, religions, and cultures, the people of the United States were not completely beholden to the notion that places existed only for economic exploitation. Some accepted the notion that places had noneconomic values in culture. The dominant culture of the United States is capable of appreciating places for their cultural value, and with the growth of the environmental outlook Burton appreciates, the non-Indian peoples of North America have the intellectual tools necessary for cross-cultural communication and appreciating the different perspectives of Indian societies.

The non-Indian mainstream population of the United States has found at least two places to be of such cultural significance that many have called them sacred and sought their federal protection. While the definition of "sacred" is contested by some, these are places removed from ordinary life by extraordinary patterns of action. These patterns are not necessarily religious in origin but have political or cultural significance. On the fiftieth anniversary of the Japanese attack on the U.S. military base at Pearl Harbor, Hawaii, there was a great deal of controversy surrounding the National Park Service handling of an exhibit and celebrations. Many were concerned that the National Park Service would desecrate the wreckage of the USS *Arizona*, going so far as to call is a "national shrine."[83] Practitioners of European religions were among those who identified the site of the wreckage as a shrine and called for it to be treated with special reverence.

In 1893 the federal government used the power of eminent domain to force the purchase of privately owned land that was part of the Gettysburg battlefield. Privately owned land was converted to public ownership to protect this "sacred ground." A unanimous Supreme Court upheld the use of eminent domain to convert private property to public property because the land in question touched "the heart and comes home to the imagination of every citizen, and greatly tends to enhance his love and respect" for the nation.[84] Practitioners of European religions have had a sense that certain places are of more importance than others for cultural reasons for at least a century. They understand that these sacred places can be desecrated by human action and should be protected over the values of property as dictated by liberal capitalism. Though it should be noted that while the Supreme Court recognized the power of Congress to protect sacred places such as Gettysburg, there has never been a constitutional requirement that places sacred to non-Indian populations be protected from desecration.

While there are significant differences between Indian religions and settler religions and how they conceptualize the significance of place, some places within the cultural lives of non-Indians have near-religious significance and take on a sacred character. Many in non-Indian communities have viewed it as intolerable to allow these places to be desecrated and have approved or called for action by the federal government to protect these places. While the U.S. Constitution offered no protection for sacred places, or a broader sense of religious freedom after *Smith*, the Supreme Court has interpreted the Constitution as not preventing the federal government from acting to protect even Indian sacred sites.

The difficulty arises, then, not from a different sense of the primacy of private property or individual rights over the protection of sacred space but instead from a widespread lack of understanding among those who claim property rights, such as the federal government. This lack of understanding leads to a lack of respect for places sacred to peoples finding themselves under the political and military domination of others in their homelands. Congress and the executive branch have been more sensitive to desires of the non-Indian population to protect their sacred sites because they share the same cultural understanding of the sacred qualities of these places. The non-Indian population has the capacity to respect Indian people but lacks the knowledge, understanding, and education to do so.

As the non-Indian population has become more civilized and its representatives in the executive and legislative branches have become more receptive to respecting indigenous sovereignty, cultures, and religions, the most aristocratic branch of government has left its more traditional role of being the only refuge for indigenous interests and has become markedly anti-Indian. The executive branch previously penalized indigenous cultural practices and the legislative branch actively sought to destroy indigenous society, but through struggle and organizing, combined with the development of pan-Indian awareness, indigenous interests have pressed those two branches of the non-Indian government to announce that their official policies are to protect indigenous religion and culture and to require a fair hearing of indigenous concerns when government action will adversely impact Indian religion and culture.

As administrative agencies offered more and more protection to Indian sacred sites, a wave of cases entered the courts. In these cases, corporate and business interests attempted to challenge administrative decisions as violations of the First Amendment prohibition on the establishment of religion. Consistently, the courts found the administrative decisions of agencies to be in compliance with the federal government's special trust responsibility to American Indians and furthering the policy goals of the American Indian Religious Freedom Act.[85] The current study moves beyond this purely legal framework and examines the strengths and weaknesses of the administrative consultation process that emerged at the turn of the twenty-first century and evaluates suggestions to strengthen protection for Indian sacred sites for the future. Perhaps most importantly, the individual historical contexts of the Indian nations involved in the cases will be examined with enough information to provide a basic understanding of the significance of the sacred places to the practitioners of a particular indigenous religion.

This study will use a synthesis of approaches to the understanding of indigenous sovereignty and its relation to the legal and constitutional protection of Indian sacred sites. In the first instance, the international law principle that all peoples are entitled to self-determination is accepted here. Additionally it is assumed that the various indigenous peoples of the world are "peoples" under the meaning of international law, though it should be noted that acceptance of this principle is not yet international consensus. In this regard, something needs to be done to address the alarming trajectory of the United States Supreme Court and the unchecked plenary power of Congress as they both threaten Indian sovereignty and any future of meaningful self-determination. The essence of self-determination is the ability to self-define relations to other peoples and a recognition of indigenous nations' inherent sovereignty.[86]

This study explicitly adopts a universalist approach to indigenous sovereignty. This approach is both essentialist and pragmatic. Some have argued that universalist concepts have been used to rationalize colonialism. This book argues that rather than forcibly imposing allegedly universal European cultural values on the people of the world through military force and conquest, the better approach is to accept the universal human aspiration for freedom and self-determination, both collectively and individually. Collective self-determination does not need to be at the expense of individual freedom, and the political and cultural histories of many indigenous peoples point to this fact (as do the rare moments in Western history where such arrangements existed for short periods of time). Following the lead of legal theorist Raymond Cross, the current work views freedom as both a means and an end and acknowledges the importance of providing individuals and peoples the conditions necessary to act as agents in their own lives while positing freedom as essential to a human existence. Erich Fromm, in his analysis of Marx's concept of humanity, identified freedom as the essence of humanity. At the heart of the difficulties humanity faces is alienation. According to Fromm, alienation for Marx was that "man does not experience himself as the acting agent in his grasp of the world, but that the world (nature, others, and he himself) remain alien to him. They stand above and against him as objects of his own creation. Alienation is essentially experiencing the world and oneself passively." For Fromm, this was the same problem created by idolatry: "Instead of experiencing himself as the creating person, he is in touch with himself only by the worship of the idol." Thus the goal of social organization is the abolition of alienation and the realization of the ideal of freedom in the positive sense of exercising creative possibilities.[87] This study accepts the conceptualization of development as expanding the abilities and possibilities in freedom of both individuals and peoples.

Cultural and religious self-determination are crucial aspects necessary for expanding human freedom. Cross and others acknowledge that meaningful cultural and religious freedom are part of the positive expression of freedom as the development of human societies. Pragmatically, Huffman, Miller, Begay, Cornell, Jorgenson, Kalt, and a host of others have shown that development, in all senses, does better under conditions where indigenous peoples are provided resources to manage as they see fit (see chapter 6). Thus self-determination as an expression of a less (or non)alienated social organization will have both economic and cultural benefits. Applying these universal values of freedom, it becomes clear that indigenous societies need more freedom to develop as they choose and relate to other cultures in ways they find beneficial. Those seeking to assist the growth of this freedom must make available the tools indigenous people feel are necessary to best develop their freedom in their preferred ways. As many indigenous sacred sites are found outside the current territorial confines of Indian nations, concepts of extraterritorial sovereignty will have to be considered in any analysis of conditions. For practical implementation of cultural self-determination, Indian sovereignty will likely have to be extended beyond the territorial boundaries of reservations rather than be curtailed or eliminated altogether.

This study takes the position that freedom and self-determination are positive values that should be extended and improved in practice for the lives of all peoples, including indigenous peoples. In recent decades, these norms have become more and more accepted by the legislative and executive branches of the U.S. government, as well as by the international community through such measures as the 2007 United Nations Declaration on the Rights of Indigenous Peoples. Yet the United States Supreme Court has become more hostile to these notions of freedom and equality. From this tension in branches of the U.S. government, the consultation process has emerged. The following case studies examine the details, successes, and limitations of the legal contours of the consultation process for federal management of Indian sacred sites at the turn of the twenty-first century. Acknowledging the dynamics of congressional plenary power and Supreme Court hostility to the emerging international consensus on indigenous rights, this study looks to what can be learned from consultations of the early twenty-first century to gain insights into what needs to be considered to protect the cultural and religious self-determination of Indian peoples as the central portion of North America moves toward eventually becoming a plurinational society.

2 THE ARIZONA SNOWBOWL RESORT AND THE HOPIS

The San Francisco Peaks are known to the Hopis as Nuvatukyaovi, and for those who practice the traditional Hopi religion, Nuvatukyaovi has been the most important of sacred places since time immemorial. In the mid-nineteenth century, the U.S. government claimed ownership of the San Francisco Peaks, and it incorporated Nuvatukyaovi into the national forest system in 1907. In the early twentieth century, the U.S. government allowed a ski resort to be built on Nuvatukyaovi. The U.S. Forest Service decided in 2002, in consultation with the owners of the ski resort, Arizona Snowbowl Resort Limited Partnership, that the ski season on the San Francisco Peaks needed to be regularized by construction of the infrastructure necessary for artificial snowmaking. The Forest Service began the required consultation process with Indian communities. In 2005 the Forest Service approved the upgrade for the Snowbowl ski resort, including artificial snowmaking with reclaimed sewage effluent.

The Hopis, environmentalists, activists from the greater community of northern Arizona, and other Indian nations protested the Forest Service decision and sought to prevent implementation of the plan in federal court. The federal court in Prescott, Arizona, joined the various lawsuits of the Navajos, Hopis, environmental groups, and individuals on July 8, 2005. *Navajo Nation v. United States Forest Service*, as the case was titled, was the first case to test the limits of the Religious Freedom Restoration Act of 1993 as it applied to actions taken by the Forest Service that desecrated indigenous sacred sites. The litigation efforts of the Hopis and other Indian nations met with failure as the District Court of Arizona and the Ninth Circuit Court of Appeals ruled that the types of harm suffered by the Indian plaintiffs were not the types contemplated by the Religious Freedom Restoration Act. The potential for legal remedy ended when the United States Supreme Court refused to review the case on June 8, 2009.[1]

This is a case where existing financial interests with significant high-level contacts with Forest Service administrators initiated the administrative decision-making process. The consultation process that followed was not designed to bring parties together in dialogue; instead consultation was a formality to be overcome by many involved. Arizona Snowbowl Resort (ASR) personnel had daily interactions with Forest Service administrators, and ASR owners desired to increase the value of their investment and ongoing for-profit operation of the ski resort, which pushed administrators to consider expanding the existing infrastructure to include snowmaking with reclaimed sewage effluent. Former interior secretary Bruce Babbitt contacted Forest Supervisor Nora Rasure on behalf of ASR to assure her that the courts would support any decision, including a decision to desecrate Indian sacred sites.[2]

Despite the almost procedural approach some Forest Service administrators took to the consultation process, Hopi political and religious leaders were able to inform Forest Service staff as to the nature and depth of their concerns. While Rasure ultimately approved the expansion in 2005, the consultation process successfully educated administrators as to the concerns and perspectives of the Hopis and other Indian groups. This case demonstrates the ability of the consultation process to bridge cultural gaps in understanding, even when administrators have strong reasons to be resistant. Unfortunately, it also demonstrates the lack of substantive protections for Indian sacred sites under the Religious Freedom Restoration Act.

HOPI RELIGION

Hopi religious life was quite diversified long before Hopi contact with European explorers, and this diversity was due to organizational structures of Hopi political and religious life. Hopi politics were organized in decentralized village structures spread over three different mesas. Each village had its own government, and there was no overarching national Hopi government. Religious life was, and continues to be, further diversified, as the Hopis are organized into matrilineal clans. Each clan was responsible for keeping and performing different religious ceremonies. With no written language to create definitive sacred texts, traditional Hopi religion and prophesies were transmitted by oral means. Traditional Hopi religion, legends, stories, and myths varied historically by locality and clan, and this diversity continues to this day. Despite these differences, there was and continues to be a recognizable common religion among the Hopi people.[3]

Despite being one of the most studied and written-about peoples, the Hopis have always guarded their religious privacy. Hopi traditional religion is based on knowledge gained through secrecy and initiation. The Hopi term *utihi'i* is more than a simple translation of "sacred." It also means that the sacred thing in question cannot be shared or revealed to those not eligible to receive it. Among Indian peoples, the Hopis led the claim that the notes and records of anthropologists are the cultural property of Indian peoples, and they have demanded the end of academic research on Indians. Some Hopis desire to prevent all publications on Hopi culture, even those based on secondary sources. The interpretation of the central prophecy of the return of the Pahaana, or white elder brother, has been the source of much differentiation and disagreement among Hopis. This prophecy says that when the Hopis have strayed from the ways of the deity Maasaw, the Pahaana will return from the East. The Hopis will then adopt the ways of the Pahaana, there will be a purification, and Maasaw will reclaim what is his. Over time, differing Hopi political groupings have used variations of this and other Hopi prophesies, as well as interpretations of prophesies, to assist with achieving their political ends. The Hopis believe that Maasaw lives on the Peaks with the kachinas. Hopi society was based upon matrilineal clans, and the clans have a spiritual covenant with Maasaw. Hopi children are introduced to the kachinas at their naming ceremonies. All Hopis are expected to visit the Peaks during life, and they go to the Peaks when they die.[4]

The kachinas were and continue to be of central importance to the Hopis, in the promulgation of the Hopi way of life from generation to generation. The Hopis have several religious societies. All Hopis belong to one of the kachina societies, but all members of kachina societies do not necessarily belong to another religious society. The kachinas come from the Peaks to visit Hopi villages around February each year and stay at kivas, underground rooms for religious ceremonies. The kivas are opened by the kachinas each year. The kachinas perform songs and dances for the Hopi people every year when they live in the villages for a time. These songs and dances are the central method for teaching morals and the Hopi way of life to succeeding generations. During their visits, the kachinas give gifts to children. Many Hopis fear that without belief in the kachinas, the Hopi way of life will pass from Earth.[5]

The Hopis view the water of the San Francisco Peaks as intricately linked to the identities of the kachinas. The Hopis live in an arid region and are dependent on rainfall for growing corn, which is also of cultural significance to them. The kachinas take the Hopi prayers for water back to the Peaks after their visits. The kachinas deliver "good moisture" from the Peaks for farming. Some view the kachinas themselves as the rain and clouds. Water is central to the Hopi way of life. To the Hopi, water is life, and the kachinas bring this life from the Peaks. Hopi religious practitioners view the artificial making of snow from any source as dirty. Some see the making of artificial snow on the Peaks as irreversibly contaminating the Hopi source of life.[6]

HOPI HISTORY

The Hopis have a tradition, stretching back at least to the seventeenth century, of protecting their culture from outside domination. The first known reference to the Hopi people in western European documentation is by the Spanish, from 1539. As the Spanish extended their influence over what became known as the Southwest, they spread their control over the various Pueblo peoples, including the Hopis. In 1680 the Hopis participated in the Tewa-led Pueblo Revolt. This indigenous rebellion successfully expelled Spanish rule from the region. Spanish influence slowly crept back in, and the Hopis reacted in 1692 by destroying one of their own villages. The village of Awatavi had allowed Spanish missionaries to return. In response, the Hopis destroyed the village and scattered the population among other villages. Hopi isolation effectively ended about 1850. From that time to the present, there are records of European contact with Hopis no less frequently than once per year.[7]

As the non-Indian population continued to encroach upon the neighbors of the Hopis, the Navajos in turn encroached upon Hopi lands. In response to the crowding of Navajos onto Hopi lands, on December 16, 1882, the U.S. government, by executive order, declared the boundaries of the Hopi "reservation" to be a rectangle. The Hopis found themselves surrounded by Navajos on three sides. The boundary was somewhat arbitrary, more in line with profiting settler administrators than providing a practical boundary between the Navajos and Hopis. The rectangle excluded approximately one hundred Hopis and included three hundred Navajos.[8]

In 1890 Hopi land was surveyed for the purposes of allotment. Hopi land was held collectively by clans at the time. All Hopi village leaders opposed allotment.

The U.S. government's attempts to force individual allotments of land on the Hopis ended in 1912. This program of forced assimilation failed, as there was not enough water in the region to support individual allotments. There were continuing unresolved land issues with the Navajos, and the Hopis continued their opposition. Allotment was meant to force Indians to become agricultural settlers, but the Hopi way of life was already grounded in agriculture, particularly the growing of corn, and the practical reality of agriculture in arid Hopi lands was that it required a flexibility in planting that individual allotments were incapable of accommodating.[9]

From the late nineteenth century and into the 1930s, the Bureau of Indian Affairs actively sought to suppress Hopi religion. In its administration of the Hopi Nation, it promulgated rules that outlawed the practice of indigenous religion. One component of the U.S. government's continued efforts to eradicate indigenous culture and religion was the adoption of compulsory schooling for Indian children at Christian missionary schools. The U.S. government attempted to implement a policy of forced schooling upon the Hopi beginning in 1892. In the 1920s, the BIA tasked agents with collecting information on Hopi religious ceremonies, dances, and practices that would prove the "pornographic" nature of these practices. BIA superintendent Robert Daniels favored the Navajos in disputes, persecuted conservative Hopis, and, in an attempt to bolster the decontextualized propaganda collected by the agents, actively prevented outsiders from accessing any but his supporters within Hopi lands. During this period, Indian agents demanded the presence of ceremonial leaders when they were needed elsewhere for traditional religious ceremonies in a deliberate attempt to further disrupt and suppress the religious lives of the Hopi people.[10]

Hopi opposition to the policy of forced schooling in the late nineteenth and early twentieth century was widespread. The U.S. government arrested many Hopis and had to rely upon military personnel several times while trying to enforce schooling decrees and forced allotment. Open warfare between the Hopi public and U.S. troops was barely averted. In 1899 the most militant resisters of U.S. policies formed their own village and maintained a 90 percent boycott rate in opposition to compulsory schooling. The U.S. government Indian agent at the turn of the century has been described as "violent" and "temperamental." His repressive orders extended to using force against Hopi males to make them comply with his edict prohibiting long hair.[11]

Hopis were able to circumvent Daniels's attempts to cut them off from the outside world, and with the aid of translators and sympathetic non-Indians, they worked to publicize the extent of BIA repression and the deliberate misrepresentations of Hopi culture. The Indian Welfare League, a nongovernmental organization based in the non-Indian community, took up the Hopi cause in the 1920s. This marked the Hopis' first major use of outsiders as allies to protect indigenous cultural practices and religious freedom. The struggle to protect Hopi religious expression culminated in the 1924 Citizenship Act, which granted U.S. citizenship to all Indians in the United States. The hope was that citizenship would extend the religious freedom sections of the Bill of Rights to Indian religious expression, though some Hopis opposed the measure for fear it would lead to their cultural destruction in less direct ways. By 1927 the Navajo presence had come to surround the entire Hopi reservation.[12]

Complex Hopi traditional governmental forms still existed in Hopi lands in the 1930s. At the time, the Hopi had no central government. Each village had a government based upon the Hopi clan structure. Individually, clan identity was prominent in Hopi life. The clans were the holders of particular ceremonial homes, offices of ritual authority, and land. While there were clan leaders, any particular village had several clans with differing ceremonial responsibilities, and each clan had its own leaders. Each village leader, known to the Hopis as a *kikmongwi*, was the leader of the clan that had founded the village. Kikmongwi were limited in their authority to maintaining the integrity of ceremonies controlled by their clans. Kikmongwi were further limited in the amount of authority they had to deal with family issues outside their own clans or with interclan rivalries.[13]

In 1934 U.S. policy suddenly shifted with passage of the Indian Reorganization Act. New BIA superintendent John Collier tasked anthropologist Oliver Lafarge with implementing a new constitution for the Hopi people. Working for Collier and the BIA, Lafarge wrote the constitution and bylaws of the Hopi Tribe. Lafarge attempted to provide a constitution based upon how power actually worked in Hopi land.[14]

Lafarge's constitution contributed to growing Hopi political divisions and ignored the political traditions of the Hopi people, causing political difficulties that continue to the present day. The constitution Lafarge wrote provided for each village to have a great deal of autonomy and called upon villages to create their own constitutions. The constitution failed to account for the Hopi form of direct democracy and decision-making, which was alien to European electoral politics. Lafarge felt that the local provisions of his constitution reflected the actual political organization of Hopi life. But that portion of the new constitution was vague and did not address how to represent villages that failed to ratify local constitutions. Conflict over interpretation of this portion lasts to this day. In addition, those villages without kikmongwi were to have elections, which was a foreign concept to the Hopis. Traditionally the Hopis engaged in a more participatory form of democratic decision-making: matters were discussed until a general mood dominated and general opinion had moved overwhelmingly in one direction. Continued opposition would then be expressed by abstention.[15]

Most alien to Hopi organization was the creation of a national Hopi central government made up of representatives selected by each village. The representatives had to be certified by kikmongwi. Until that time, the Hopis had no overarching national government; the village had been the largest Hopi political unit. The organization of the new national Hopi government relied upon grafting new political and secular powers onto the kikmongwi, who had hitherto been responsible only for the religious and ceremonial stewardship of villages. Lafarge justified these constitutional powers for the kikmongwi, since he saw the Hopis as "a pure theocracy." Conceptually, a national Hopi government was more difficult since the Hopi tradition considered it morally wrong for anyone to claim to represent the Hopi people. Hopi sovereignty was practically nonexistent in Lafarge's constitution; every tribal council resolution required the approval of the Indian agent superintendent.[16]

The Indian Reorganization Act required a 30 percent turnout for the vote to approve the proposed constitution, but Hopi abstention prevented any broad sense of legitimacy from attaching to the new Hopi tribal government. Local BIA officials claimed that there was a 50 percent participation rate based upon what are now highly disputed population statistics. Hopi tradition was to abstain from that which they viewed as illegitimate, and most Hopis abstained from the vote for ratification. Many Hopis made attempts to fully understand the meaning of the words of the proposed constitution but gave up such efforts and rejected it out of hand when they learned the proposal came from Washington. Lafarge informed Collier that the vote should be taken as a widespread rejection of the constitution, since he felt that no amount of explaining to conservative Hopis could bring them to understand that boycotting the vote was not the same as voting against the constitution in the eyes of the BIA. The constitution was implemented in 1936.[17]

A significant change the constitution brought to Hopi society was to transform the religious and ceremonial positions of the kikmongwi into positions of political rivalry. Those kikmongwi allied with conservatives boycotted the tribal council and refused to certify any representatives to the national body. Further tensions developed as members of the general population began to criticize kikmongwi for stepping outside their traditional roles and interfering in secular affairs. Entire villages boycotted participation in the IRA constitution in the name of Hopi tradition.[18]

While most Hopis boycotted the IRA referendum and other votes involving the IRA government, it was later revealed to the general population that the constitution bound the Hopi Tribal Council to agreements with the U.S. government and the Navajos regarding highly unpopular land reorganization in disputed territories under Navajo occupation. This revelation ended what little Hopi support for the new tribal government existed. The widespread lack of popular support contributed to the collapse of the Hopi Tribal Council in the early 1940s.[19]

In the 1940s the Hopi traditionalist movement, a resistance moment, came to some prominence. Often in conflict with both the U.S. and the IRA government, the traditionalist movement was never a formal organization but more of a loose affiliation of Hopis with different backgrounds working together for similar goals. The movement had a diverse leadership that included Christian Hopis, college-educated Hopis, and low status village members who spoke only Hopi. The movement never had any formal organization, budget, or consistent and systematic campaign. People dropped in and out of the traditionalist movement. In addition to providing new prophesies, formulating new interpretations of prophesies, and bringing their message to a wider audience, the traditionalists broke with tradition in claiming that anyone could prophesy or interpret prophecy.[20]

Ideologically, the traditionalists stood for six broad principles. First, the U.S. government has no legal right of authority over the Hopis because the Hopis never signed any treaty with the United States recognizing its existence. Second, the U.S. government and missionaries have no right to pressure the Hopi people to assimilate into or acculturate to the settler society. Third, the Hopi tribal government has no authority beyond that granted by traditional leaders. Fourth, only traditional leaders, including the kikmongwi, are to be recognized as legitimate Hopi leaders. Fifth, public works, mineral leasing, and other potentially beneficial projects can be sanctioned only in accordance with prophecy and the prophecy predicting the end of Hopi life if material benefits are accepted by those who have previously rejected them. Finally, the search for Pahaana is imperative.[21]

In 1951 the IRA government of Hopi land was finally revived. The BIA pushed for revival of the Hopi Tribal Council to facilitate three of its ends: to accept the latest Navajo–Hopi rehabilitation act (an act of U.S. Congress to provide development aid); to hire an attorney to file a claim before the Indian Claims Commission (an action rejected by the traditionalists); and to approve mineral leases on Hopi land. Not surprisingly, the Hopi Tribal Council's legitimacy was still contested by many Hopis in 1951.[22]

Throughout the 1950s, the traditionalist movement became more apocalyptic in its prophesies. The traditionalists also began to characterize Maasaw as a more general, godlike figure, often conflating him with the Great Spirit and stating Maasaw was a god for more than just the Hopi. In 1955 the traditionalists opposed a proposed BIA permitting system for livestock. Traditionalists led the call to boycott and not comply with the process. Adherence to this boycott forced the BIA to accept the continuation of Hopi traditional practices in the raising of livestock, without the permitting process. In 1958 the traditionalists made their first public request to address the UN General Assembly regarding their apocalyptic prophesies.[23]

In the 1960s the traditionalists increasingly came into conflict with both the Hopi Tribal Council and the U.S. government. During the rise of pan-Indianism and renewed Indian militancy of the decade, the traditionalists had a major success in achieving conscientious objector status for all Hopis initiated into kachina societies. The year 1963 saw the publication of Frank Waters's *The Book of Hopi*, which was widely decried as a horribly inaccurate account of Hopi tradition. The publication of this book attracted great numbers of hippies to Hopi land. The traditionalist movement welcomed them, but the tribal council passed a resolution in 1967 calling for the expulsion of hippies. While the resolution was never acted upon, traditionalists denounced it as illegitimate.[24]

Throughout the 1970s the traditionalists continued to garner support in the world outside Hopi land while continuing to lose support among the Hopis. During this time, the traditionalists opposed mineral leasing and took the unpopular stand against bringing public utilities to the Hopis. Traditionalist opposition to utilities was based upon their opposition to economic dependency on the outside world. This opposition ended with the advent of locally operated solar power.[25]

In the wake of the Nixon administration's change in Indian policy to one of renewed sovereignty and government-to-government relations, the Hopi Tribal Council took concrete steps to protect the sovereignty and cultural integrity of the Hopi people. In 1972 the tribal council established Hopi-run courts, displacing those run by the BIA. New Hopi laws required that Hopi tradition be given the weight of precedent before Hopi courts, beginning a distinctly Hopi legal system.[26]

Generally the Hopi people have historically demanded the return of most of northern Arizona. This claim continued to be pressed, even though the Indian Claims Commission lacked the power to return land. In 1976, when the commission returned a settlement of $5 million to compensate the Hopi Nation for the illegal seizure of northern Arizona, the traditionalists led a movement to boycott the referendum to accept the settlement. Ninety percent of the Hopi people boycotted the vote. The tribal council concurred and voted to not accept the award, demanding the return of their lands in place of monetary compensation.[27]

While the 1980s brought a significant decline in the Hopi traditionalist movement, with the deaths of many of its aging leaders, the vitality of Hopi traditional religion continued to increase. While the movement had died out by the middle of the 1990s, there are now more practitioners of the Hopi religion than in 1983. Initiations to kachina societies have increased since the Second World War, and the Hopis have increased the number of kachina ceremonies performed.[28]

As the interpretation of prophecy changed over generations, the Hopis adapted kachina ceremonies and dances to their changing circumstances. Many Christian Hopis returned to the kachina ceremonies, partaking in them as social and cultural occasions. The kachinas are of prehistoric origin and are a central part of continuing Hopi cultural survival. Though Hopis have often bitterly disagreed among themselves on the forms and methods of preserving the Hopi way of life, the major Hopi factions have all espoused protection of Hopi culture. Despite these differences, the Hopis have historically been united in near unanimity in the need to keep Nuvatukyaovi pure. But the practice of many Hopis boycotting the Hopi Tribal Council continues to this day. Two villages refused to certify representatives to the council in 2008.[29]

The partisans of the tribal council and traditionalists each claimed to be representing and protecting Hopi culture and sovereignty. Those supporting the traditionalists claimed it was that movement that pushed the tribal council to support Hopi sovereignty and culture. Some claim that the traditionalist movement died out in part because of the partial institutionalization of many of its values. One Hopi Mennonite in the 1990s said, "We are all traditionalists out here."[30] With the return of Christian Hopis to the kachina ceremonies, this was surely true to a large extent. Despite their divisions, the traditionalist movement and the council agreed upon opposition to the first major Snowbowl expansion, proposed in 1977.

THE ARIZONA SNOWBOWL RESORT AND ITS EXPANSION, 1962–2005

When Franciscan missionaries first saw the San Francisco Peaks, located just north of modern-day Flagstaff, Arizona, they were so impressed that they named them for their founder, Saint Francis, who taught that the beauty of the landscape was a direct manifestation of a higher power. The surrounding Indian peoples recognized the Peaks to be located within the territory of the Havasupais. The Havasupais served as the caretakers of the Peaks for indigenous nations that held them to be culturally and religiously significant. The Peaks are religiously and culturally significant to at least thirteen American Indian peoples. The Navajo Nation, Havasupai Tribe, White Mountain Apache Nation, Yavapai-Apache Nation, Hualapai Tribe, and Hopi Tribe are among these thirteen and were later plaintiffs in the suit to stop the Forest Service–approved expansion on religious freedom grounds. In 1898 the executive branch of the U.S. government designated the Peaks as the San Francisco Mountain Forest Reserve. In 1907 the reserve was incorporated into the Coconino National Forest.[31]

In the 1930s, a Flagstaff skiing club used an old cabin on a lower prairie of the Peaks as a base camp. In 1937 the U.S. Forest Service built a new base camp consisting of a small cabin higher on the mountain. At the time, the official policy of the BIA was to suppress and prohibit indigenous religions. Expression of Indian religions was punished with criminal penalty.[32]

Over these years of changing Indian policies of the federal government and growing Indian resistance to attempts to destroy Indian cultural identity, the skiing facility in the San Francisco Peaks remained little changed. Until 1958, the only device present to aid skiers was a mechanical towrope. In 1958 a Poma lift was installed, and in 1962 a single chairlift was installed at the small skiing facility. In the context of growing Indian resistance to the policies of termination and the increase in militant resistance to cultural destruction, both the Navajo and Hopi peoples protested the expansion of facilities in 1962.[33]

In April 1977, the Forest Service granted a permit to run the Snowbowl facility to Northland Recreation Company (NRC). In July of that year, the company submitted a master plan for expanding the skiing facilities on the San Francisco Peaks. On February 29, 1979, the supervisor of the Coconino National Forest approved a plan to clear 777 acres on the San Francisco Peaks for skiing, a smaller area than NRC had initially requested.[34]

Opposition to the expansion among Indian peoples of the region was widespread. Not only were the traditionalists and the Hopi government unified in their opposition, the Navajos, who continued to be in a long-standing border dispute with the Hopis, joined the Hopis in their opposition. In April 1977 the U.S. Forest Service issued a permit to NRC to expand the ski resort area. The Snowbowl facility, as the resort had come to be known, would undergo a substantial alteration on the western shoulder of the Peaks. The facility would be expanded to 777 acres, an increase of 223 percent in the area opened to skiing. The Forest Service plan allowed for five chairlifts, dining facilities for more than nine hundred, eight acres of parking, and expanding and paving the small dirt road to the facility.[35]

Local Indian groups found the proposed expansion offensive. Practitioners of traditional Navajo religion saw the ski resort as a cancer growing on their living god, the Peaks. Hopi practitioners viewed the expansion as an insulting trivialization and commercialization of the sacred home of the kachinas, spirits of central cultural importance. The Hopis viewed the Peaks as their most important religious shrine. The Hopis and Navajos took their complaints regarding the proposed expansion to the regional forester in charge of the Coconino National Forest. The traditionalist Hopis and their opponents on the Hopi Tribal Council were united in their opposition to the project. Upon review, the regional forester determined that the Snowbowl could never be made into an outstanding sports area and reversed the Forest Service decision, maintaining the status quo.[36] The Forest Service prepared an environmental impact statement for the project as required by the National Environmental Policy Act. It stated in part: "It is obvious, however, that no amount of development would make the Snowbowl into a topnotch area; nor will the expansion approved by the Forest Supervisor or even the permittee's larger proposal provide for all the demand. Where then is a good place to cut off development? I have concluded that a good cut-off place is somewhere near the present size."[37]

In turn, Northland appealed that decision to the chief forester of the U.S. Forest Service. Chief Forester R. Max Peterson reinstated the Snowbowl development plan on December 31, 1980. On March 2, 1981, the Hopi Tribe and the Navajo Medicinemen's Association filed suit in federal court to stop the 777-acre expansion. Characterizing the adverse impact as merely "spiritual disquiet," the court ruled that while mental and emotional anguish might indeed be caused by the proposed expansion, there was nevertheless no constitutional rights infringed upon. The coalition of Navajos and Hopis appealed the decision on grounds that the proposed expansion violated the American Indian Religious Freedom Act. The federal court of appeals for the District of Columbia, the highest court to take the case, ruled that AIRFA merely required consultation and consideration. Federal agencies, the court decided, need not defer to Indian religious interests. The court also said that if the decision did not restrict Indian access to a place, Indian religious practices were not burdened in a way protected by AIRFA. The expansion went forward, though NRC did not expand to the full 777 acres approved in the proposal.[38]

THE NEXT EXPANSION OF THE SNOWBOWL SKI RESORT

The Arizona Snowbowl Resort Limited Partnership purchased the Snowbowl facility in 1992 for $4 million. Historically the Snowbowl resort was dependent upon natural snowfall, and throughout the 1990s and early new millennium, the facility found its operable days per season varying wildly from year to year: 1992–93: 130 days; 1995–96: 25 days; 1997–98: 115 days; 2001–2: 4 days: 2004–5: 139 days.[39]

Forest Service personnel were in daily contact with representatives of the Snowbowl facility. Conversations between Forest Service personnel and Arizona Snowbowl Resort regarding an expansion were under way when lifelong Forest Service employee Gene Waldrip became ranger for the Peaks ranger district in 1999. Waldrip entered the ongoing discussions regarding what could be done to improve the carrying capacity of the resort.[40]

Ranger Waldrip, who personally used the Snowbowl facilities with his family, felt the area lacked the necessary infrastructure to support the number of skiers who visited. The infrastructure was twenty years old and had not kept up with the increase in demand for use of the facility. Members of Waldrip's immediate family, including his wife, had been involved in skiing accidents at the facility. Another concern Waldrip had was the lack of snow play areas in the region. Whenever it snowed, the public used areas near the Snowbowl facility as improvised snow play areas.[41]

Normally, when approving such a large-scale expansion, the Forest Service, like any other governmental agency, is required to create an environmental impact statement (EIS). But Waldrip and ASR contemplated pushing their envisioned expansion through a series of small improvements without public input and with an abbreviated consultation with Indian interests. In places where American Indian cultural and religious sites were involved, AIRFA, NAGPRA, and other laws and regulations required consultation with Indian peoples who might be adversely impacted by Forest Service action. After consulting with ASR, Waldrip felt that much of what was being proposed by the resort could be accomplished by a series of small piecemeal projects. Waldrip's scheme was to issue a series of categorical exemptions for each stage of the contemplated expansion. Categorical exemptions had a simplified environmental assessment process as well as much more limited requirements for consultation with Indian interests. Most appealing to Waldrip and ASR was the fact that a categorical exemption was not a decision that could be appealed. Ultimately, Waldrip and ASR abandoned this path for expanding

Snowbowl, as Waldrip felt the political climate required public participation in the EIS consultation process.[42]

Snowbowl publicly claimed that without snowmaking, warmer weather and shorter skiing seasons would require the closing of the facility as financially unviable. Snowbowl made a formal request in 2002 to begin artificial snowmaking at the facility using Class A+ reclaimed water from the City of Flagstaff. Class A+ is the highest purity rating for treated sewage effluent, which consists of waste discharged by households, businesses, and hospitals. The proposed expansion of Snowbowl included approximately 205 acres of snow-making coverage with reclaimed sewage water; a 10 million-gallon reservoir for the reclaimed sewage water near the top terminal of the existing chairlift; construction of a pipeline between Flagstaff and Snowbowl for the reclaimed sewage water, with booster stations and pump houses; construction of a three thousand- to four thousand-square foot snowmaking control building; construction of a ten thousand-square foot guest services facility; an increase in skiable acreage to 205 acres (an approximately 47 percent increase); thinning trees on 47 acres; and 87 acres of grading, stumping, and smoothing. The initial proposal included the building of night lighting on the Peaks. As part of negotiations for formulating the expansion, ASR agreed to include a snow play area as a quid pro quo for the Forest Service's support for artificial snowmaking.[43]

Waldrip met with Snowbowl representatives in formulating the proposal. He met with the former secretary of the interior Bruce Babbitt in 2002. At the time, Babbitt worked as an attorney for the Arizona Snowbowl Resort Limited Partnership. He would later send Waldrip's superior a memorandum arguing that the courts uphold any decision to approve the proposed expansion if faced with legal challenges from Indian peoples on religious freedom grounds. Waldrip saw the goals of the proposal as twofold. First, the proposed action was to provide a consistent skiing season so that ASR could remain economically viable. Second, by bringing the terrain in line with demand, safety would be improved. Before any public comment process had begun and before any other alternatives had been created or considered, Waldrip was in favor of the proposed expansion of the Snowbowl facility.[44]

Waldrip and those supporting the proposed expansion were aware of the history of opposition to the Snowbowl resort by Indian peoples and hoped to avoid problems similar to those of the previous Snowbowl expansion by including Indian nations in the process. Waldrip was also aware that the National Historic Preservation Act, NAGPRA, and other statutes and regulations required this consultation. The Forest Service opened up government-to-government discussions with thirteen Indian nations, including the Hopis and Navajos, by sending notice by letter in June 2002, three months prior to the beginning of general public notice.[45]

Waldrip personally met with the Hopis on Hopi land and saw his mission as an opportunity to convey information and personally talk with Hopi people. He admitted to first learning of the importance of the Peaks and the kachinas to the Hopis in the consultation process. As he had already decided to support the expansion, Waldrip did not change his opinion regarding the project upon learning of the nature of Hopi concerns. Internal Forest Service memorandums indicated that Waldrip's perspective drove the immediate goals of the consultation with the Hopis and other Indians. The primary goals were not learning of Indian concerns but fulfilling the letter of the law and blunting the anticipated Indian opposition to a decision that had already been made in the formulation of policy goals.[46]

The tribal consultation plan for the Arizona Snowbowl upgrade, dated June 5, 2002, lists among the key messages Forest Service representatives were to articulate:

- We think [the proposed expansion is] a good idea, and we already know you don't approve of it, but Snowbowl is there & isn't going away.
- Is NOT an expansion—is an "upgrade" within the scope of the 1980 court decision.
- *Upgrade cannot be done without snowmaking.*[47]

This internal memorandum also enumerated the Forest Service's objectives for the consultation. Among those reasons included in the June 5, 2002, memorandum:

- Provide basic information about the proposal—what it is, what it is not.
- Are there any additional tribal concerns we don't already know about.
- Keep the process moving along expeditiously.[48]

Despite these plans to inform Indians of the need for the project and to keep things moving, Waldrip noted that this particular proposal of the Forest Service generated more Indian opposition than others.[49]

While the ultimate decision for approving the proposal did not reside with Waldrip, he had already made up his mind to support the proposed expansion and was involved in the consultation process from the beginning. As discussed below, not every member of the Forest Service unreservedly supported the Snowbowl expansion with its inclusion of snowmaking with reclaimed sewage effluent. After consultation with indigenous religious practitioners and receiving comments from the public, Waldrip recognized that the proposed expansion was an adverse action on a traditional cultural property, but he reiterated that the Forest Service may take adverse actions so long as the proper consultation process has been followed.[50] The evidence here strongly suggests that Waldrip and elements of the Forest Service were only interested in following the required consultation process so that they could take the adverse action they had already decided upon, in consultation with ASR.

Heather Cooper Provencio, the Forest Service zone archaeologist for the San Francisco Peaks and Mormon Lake, had a very different opinion of the proposed action and made an attempt to explain the religious and cultural importance of the Peaks to Forest Supervisor Nora Rasure. Provencio had started her position as zone archaeologist in January 2002, years after Waldrip had been in conversation with ASR.[51]

Prior to becoming zone archaeologist, Provencio served as district archaeologist for the Black Mesa Ranger District of the Apache-Sitgreaves National Forests for seven years. With a master's degree in anthropology from Northern Arizona University, Provencio was the lead member of the interdisciplinary team in charge of cultural consultation with Indian governments and tribal members. Outside her professional life, Provencio had visited Hopi land and viewed kachina dances.[52]

In her position as zone archaeologist, Provencio edited a memorandum of understanding that formed a formal agreement between the Forest Service and the Hopi government regarding cultural consultation. The document included a confidentiality agreement about Hopi cultural sites. Respecting Hopi religious sensitivities on issues of privacy, the Forest Service agreed to keep locations of Hopi sacred sites confidential and to release the information only on a need-to-know basis. It was among her responsibilities to see that confidential information regarding Hopi cultural sites was kept out of any EIS. Provencio served as the lead editor on the cultural section of the EIS for the proposed expansion for the Snowbowl resort.[53]

Much like Waldrip, Provencio was aware of the lawsuit that had followed the 1980 Forest Service approval of the first major Snowbowl expansion. She was careful to document each step in the consultations with Indian governments because of Forest Service concerns that a similar lawsuit would challenge the decision regarding the proposed expansion of the Snowbowl facilities. When the Forest Service initially informed Indian governments regarding the proposed expansion, Provencio offered to hold meetings with them. These meetings began in September 2002 and included the Hopi Cultural Resource Advisory Task

Force. Provencio personally met with Hopi people and government officials at public meetings in Hopi lands once a month during the consultation process.[54]

Provencio anticipated Indian opposition to the project. This anticipation was based upon her prior knowledge of the proposal's impact on Indian cultural resources combined with her knowledge of the thirty years of history the Forest Service had in consulting with Indians in the area through both submissions of written comments and public meetings. Provencio consulted with Indian governments before the general public because she wanted them to know they were important to the process and she hoped they would become involved in creating alternatives that might mitigate the adverse impact of the proposed expansion on Indian cultural resources. Throughout the consultation process, Provencio found virtual unanimous Indian opposition to the Snowbowl facility.[55]

In May 2003, Nora Rasure became supervisor for the Coconino National Forest. Rasure was the one ultimately responsible for approving expansion of the Snowbowl facility and the use of reclaimed sewage effluent in artificial snowmaking. Employed by the Forest Service for more than a quarter of a century, she had received her bachelor of science degree in forestry from the University of Illinois at Urbana-Champaign in 1980. That year she worked for the Forest Service a youth conservation core crew leader. Over the decades she served as forester, fire prevention and fuels management officer, staff officer for recreational land minerals programs, district ranger, and finally deputy forest supervisor in the Coronado National Forest before being promoted to forest supervisor in charge of the Coconino National Forest. Though she was not forest supervisor before Waldrip decided to support the project and had no input in formulating the goals memorandum regarding the necessity of the project, Rasure personally participated in meeting with Hopi people as part of the consultation process after she became supervisor in May 2003.[56]

After the initial consultation process, the Forest Service released a draft EIS in February 2004, making it available for public comment. The consultation process and other public meetings had brought a few alterations to the proposals of the Forest Service. The draft EIS included three alternative proposals. The first was to do nothing. Including such an alternative was a legal requirement so that the other proposed alternatives could be compared to taking no action. Alternative two, the Forest Service's preferred alternative, was the expansion detailed above, including the creation of artificial snow made with reclaimed sewage effluent, but with the proposed night lighting removed. Alternative three was developed by the Forest Service in response to the consultation process. The Forest Service had received many comments in opposition to the artificial snowmaking and the use of reclaimed sewage effluent. Alternative three removed both the snowmaking and the snow play area but was otherwise identical to proposal two, the Forest Service preferred alternative. The snowmaking and snow play were removed as a group because ASR supported the snow play area only if it received approval of snowmaking in return.[57]

In response to the consultation process and public feedback, the Forest Service removed the construction of night lighting from the preferred alternative. The Yavapai-Apaches had concerns regarding the night lighting, but it was the concerns of the non-Indian population in Flagstaff that served as the primary motivation for Waldrip to support dropping the night lighting from the project. Waldrip noted that Flagstaff was the first International Dark Sky City and that there was much local sensitivity to the issue of darkness. Thus it was not socially acceptable to have night lighting in Waldrip's view because of non-Indian opposition to night lighting. The Forest Service was faced with protests by the Dark Skies Coalition and gave in to these demands, as the night lighting was not necessary to meet the proposal's goals of extending the ski season.[58]

The Forest Service made the draft EIS available for public comment for sixty days, an extension of thirty days over the legally required minimum, and expected heavy Indian opposition. Interdisciplinary team leader Heather Provencio expected Indian comments to be in opposition to the proposed preferred alternative. Provencio met with most of those involved in the ongoing comment and consultation process, including with the Hopi cultural preservation officer. She also met with the Hopi Cultural Resource Advisory Team. Outside of the government-to-government consultation process, Provencio met with Bill Bucky Preston, a traditional Hopi religious practitioner and future plaintiff in the lawsuit in opposition to the proposed expansion. Provencio met with Preston as an interested person, outside of her official consultation with the Hopi government.[59] Preston later filed suit to stop the expansion and testified extensively at the trial.

Throughout, Provencio found Indian concerns to be consistent. She found the comments on the draft EIS to be consistent with what she knew to be Indian opposition to the project. Before the consultation process began, Provencio was well aware that the central importance of the Peaks to the Hopis and Navajos was well documented. The Forest Service carried out the consultation and comment process despite being well aware of Indian objections to the project because it was required to do so by law. Provencio had hoped Indian leaders would provide feedback and alternatives to minimize cultural damages.[60]

Provencio personally assessed for the Forest Service the three proposed alternatives of the draft EIS and determined that all had adverse impacts on Indian cultural resources. Not surprisingly, her assessment determined that alternative one had the least impact; that the preferred option, alternative two, had the greatest impact; and that alternative three would be somewhere in between. Many tribal members supported no action. Provencio found virtual unanimity in Indian opposition to the very presence of the Snowbowl resort and tried to communicate this opposition to Waldrip and Rasure. Provencio's experience in the consultation process was that many tribal members supported absolutely no action, option one of the draft EIS.[61]

As the deadline approached for a final decision by Rasure, she called Provencio in for a meeting. Sometime in late 2004 or early 2005, the women had a two-hour meeting to discuss the potential fallout of whatever decision the Forest Service might ultimately make. In the course of the two hours, Provencio discussed the state of the law with Rasure. Provencio later testified that she felt Rasure was struggling with the decision. Provencio was sensitive to the religious and cultural concerns of the various Indian peoples and informed Rasure that she preferred alternative three, the expansion without snowmaking and snow play. In the course of the conversation, Provencio specifically discussed Hopi beliefs and concerns with Rasure. They discussed the Hopi belief that the Peaks are the source of life, that Hopi spirits of the dead travel to the Peaks, and that these spirits bring rain from the Peaks to Hopi lands.[62]

Though Provencio felt as if Rasure had really listened to her and she felt valued as an employee and for her perspective, she was ultimately disappointed by the final decision. When Provencio saw the final record of decision, as approved by Rasure, she was "concerned" and "disappointed" that the various Indian concerns had not been "adequately addressed." At trial, Provencio was sure to make the distinction between "considered" and "addressed." While she felt the concerns of various Indian religious practitioners had not been addressed in a way Indians would have liked and she "was disappointed with the decision," she felt that "the final decision describes that they [the concerns of tribal members] were considered. I think the Record of Decision shows that, that those concerns were considered."[63]

While Provencio, in her professional capacity as head of the interdisciplinary team and Forest Service anthropologist, opposed the inclusion of snowmaking in the proposed expansion of the Snowbowl resort, sentiment among Forest Service employees was divided. The final decision fell to Rasure. She was personally involved in the consultation process once she came on board as forest supervisor in May 2003. As part of the consultation process, Rasure met with Hopi governmental leaders. In addition to meeting with Provencio for two hours, in preparation for her final decision, Rasure personally reviewed all six thousand to eight thousand comments on the draft EIS.[64]

Whereas Provencio had a preexisting understanding that the Hopi would view the proposed expansion as having a deeply negative impact on their most sacred of places, Rasure felt she gained a sense of how others viewed the Peaks from her experience with the consultation process. Rasure felt that as part of the consultation process, the Hopi people had shared their innermost feelings with her and that she had come away with a deeper understanding of what the Peaks mean to the Hopi people.[65]

Despite this, Rasure later testified that she became focused on alternative two, the full expansion with snowmaking with reclaimed sewage water, in December 2004. She stated that she made her ultimate decision with great difficulty. In her review of comments, Rasure found all oral comments from the consultation process to be in opposition to the preferred alternative, based upon Indian cultural and religious concerns. Rasure testified at trial that she tried hard to come up with a decision that would meet the needs of the ski area and skiers while being considerate of the interests of Indian peoples:[66]

> As a Forest Manager, I think I pride myself on being able to manage the natural resources and to also work with people to respect their interest, to manage for their interests, and try to come up with solutions that meet both our needs. And while I mentioned earlier that I shared many values with the Native Americans, and I appreciate that, that we both care about the natural resources, it was very difficult to pick a decision that I knew would, as some of them described, it would hurt them, because that's not my intention.[67]

Despite these professed attempts to find some method of managing the resources under her supervision that would respect the needs of both the Arizona skiing community and the religious interests of tens of thousands of people, Rasure approved alternative two because it was the only one that met the needs of the project and was consistent with the forest plan and laws.[68]

The goals of the proposed project Rasure referred to can be found in the record of decision: "1) to provide a consistent and reliable operating season, and; 2) to improve safety, skiing conditions, and recreational opportunities by bringing terrain and infrastructure into balance with existing demand."[69] While the use of reclaimed sewage water gave Rasure pause in approving the expansion, she felt there needed to be changes to improve safety and to maintain the viability of the area as a skiing resort, as described above. Rasure felt the variable snowfall on the Peaks had been a problem and that snowmaking was necessary to improve skiing in the area and maintain the economic viability of the resort. Rasure recognized that the snowmaking was a concern to the Hopis and others but that snowmaking was common.[70]

While Rasure admitted that snowmaking with reclaimed sewage water was not a common occurrence on Forest Service land, she reasoned that she could evaluate the snowmaking only in terms of whether it was common or uncommon. Ignoring the fact that there was near unanimity among Indian groups that the Peaks were an indivisible whole and a sacred place that would be desecrated by the production of artificial snow anywhere on them, Rasure reasoned that the project area was but 1 percent of the forest and that none of the ski area was used for ceremonial purposes.[71] "I looked at it from the perspective of how common is snowmaking in terms of an activity that occurs," she testified at trial. "Snowmaking occurs on other mountains. Snowmaking occurs at other ski areas. It is a normal activity."[72] Rasure stated that she prided herself on considering the interests of others, including Indian religious practitioners. She stated that the details of alternative two gave her pause, particularly the snowmaking and use of reclaimed sewage water. Provencio also testified that this decision appeared to be a difficult one for Rasure. Rasure stated that her intent was not to hurt those who viewed the use of reclaimed sewage water and snowmaking on the Peaks as religiously offensive and personally hurtful. But ultimately she felt that the stated need, which was formulated by Waldrip and ASR years before she became forest supervisor, could be met only by alternative two and that the means to meet that need, while religiously offensive to a minority of those within the United States, were quite commonly used and "normal."

Nowhere in the process did anyone in Forest Service state that there was a consideration of whether or not the alleged need for a consistent ski season in any way justified the potential harm to the various Indian religious interests. To the contrary, the primary concern appeared to be whether or not the proposed action was consistent with the law and forest plan. The record of decision, in its stated reasoning, indicated that so long as it was legal, desecration of Indian sacred sites could not prevent the approval of alternative two because of the way the question was framed:

Some tribes requested that Alternative 1, the no action alternative, be selected. Alternative 1 does not address the purpose and need for the project. Alternative 1 may still have adverse effects to the cultural resources, even with the implementation of the MOA [memorandum of agreement]. In addition, since Alternative 1 does not resolve the significant needs associated with long term operation of the ski area, other proposals could be expected in the future. Alternative 3 was designed to address the most significant issue of using reclaimed water for snowmaking. Alternative 3 addresses some needs of the ski area; however, it does not address the critical need of providing for a consistent operating season. Most commenters supported either Alternative 1—no action, or Alternative 2—the selected alternative; there was little support for Alternative 3.[73]

If meeting the goals of providing a consistent ski season was necessary for acceptance of any alternative, the decision was made before the consultation process began by the framing of the need. Rasure had no choice but to accept alternative two, since any alternative selected had to provide for the needs of ASR to have a consistent ski season. There is no indication in the record that anyone in the Forest Service asked if providing marginally better ski facilities in the northern Arizona desert in any way outweighed the real pain that would be caused to indigenous religious practitioners or the significant threat to the survival of their religions. If Rasure insisted upon meeting policy goals, the framing of the question by Waldrip and ASR in the years before Rasure took over as supervisor determined the outcome of the consultation process before it ever began. Rasure signed the record of decision on the final EIS and amended the forest plan on February 18, 2005.[74]

HOPI RESISTANCE TO THE EXPANSION

Upon learning of the proposed expansion and the plan to artificially make snow with reclaimed sewage effluent, Hopi government officials and private individuals began to voice their concerns. Public events and protests were coordinated with other Indian peoples as well as local and national activist organizations. Hopi people worked with the Save the Peaks Coalition, the Sierra Club, the Center for Biological Diversity, and the Flagstaff Activist Network in demonstrations and other events. The Indian group Youth for the Peaks provided information to the public through use of the internet and Myspace.[75]

Early in the consultation process, the *Arizona Daily Sun,* an allegedly liberal

Flagstaff newspaper, printed a staff editorial that denigrated indigenous religion and fueled local racism against Indians. Indian activists and allies in Flagstaff flooded the paper with comments and protested the paper's stand. The editors of the paper met with representatives of those complaining of its position and irresponsibility. Nine days later the paper published an apology and pledged a commitment to balanced coverage in the future. The paper admitted that its omissions both misled and offended its readers and noted that the experience had shown them "that real racism against native peoples is alive and well in Flagstaff."[76]

On February 2, 2004, the day the Forest Service announced that it favored expansion of the Snowbowl facility with artificial snowmaking in the draft EIS, practitioners of indigenous religions founded the Save the Peaks Coalition. This coalition, which included members of local non-Indian communities, grew to more than two hundred members in the first eight days of its existence. Favoring alternative one, the no action alternative, the coalition organized marches and prayer vigils to raise awareness and encouraged people to produce comments on the draft EIS urging the Forest Service to adopt alternative one. Coalition members stressed in their public outreach that the no-action alternative was the best compromise as it allowed skiing, which was already offensive to most local indigenous religions, to remain while preventing further destruction and desecration of sacred places.[77]

Before consultation with indigenous religious practitioners and receiving comments from the public, Gene Waldrip recognized that the proposed expansion was an adverse action on a traditional cultural property, but he reiterated that the Forest Service could take adverse actions as long as the proper consultation process had been followed. In the course of the consultation process, Bill Bucky Preston spoke with Forest Service personnel and stated they left him feeling as if they were not listening to anything the Hopis had to say. Preston stated that he felt the Forest Service officials had already made up their minds to approve the expansion with artificial snowmaking.[78]

NAVAJO NATION V. FOREST SERVICE

The Hopis immediately objected to the proposal of the Forest Service to make artificial snow with reclaimed sewage effluent on Nuvatukyaovi and worked both inside and outside legal avenues to try and prevent the desecration of their most sacred of places. After exhausting the administrative appeals process, the Hopis filed suit in the U.S. District Court for Arizona in 2005, with the first case testing whether or not the Religious Freedom Restoration Act protected places sacred to Indians on public lands. In 2006 the district court ruled that the harm the Hopis and other Indians would suffer as a result of the Forest Service approval of snowmaking with reclaimed sewage water was not the type of harm that was protected by RFRA. The Hopis and their allies appealed this decision to the Ninth Circuit Court of Appeals and first met with success in 2007, when a three-judge panel of the Ninth Circuit ruled that Hopi religion was impermissibly burdened by the approved snowmaking. The full Ninth Circuit reheard the case and overturned the three-judge panel decision. In 2008 the full Ninth Circuit determined that the harms the Hopis and other Indians would face were not those that fit within the meaning of "substantial burden on religion" as intended by Congress in RFRA.[79]

The Navajo Nation filed its complaint against the Forest Service on June 17, 2005, before the United States District Court of Arizona in Prescott, Judge Paul G. Rosenblatt presiding. The complaint challenged the Forest Service decision on religious freedom, environmental, and other grounds. On July 8, 2005, the case was consolidated with several others, including the complaints of the Havasupai Tribe, White Mountain Apache Nation, Yavapai-Apache Nation, Hualapai Tribe, Hopi Tribe, and various individuals, and was designated the lead case. Rosenblatt concluded that the only issue he could not determine on summary judgment was the religious freedom claims of the indigenous religious practitioners. The district court held an eleven-day bench trial before issuing its opinion. Practitioners of indigenous religions and their allies carried on demonstrations in opposition to the proposed expansion of Snowbowl facilities outside the courthouse in Prescott.[80]

The attorneys for the plaintiffs worked for a nonprofit organization dedicated to promoting Indian sovereignty and served as assistant counsel within the Hopi government. One was a member of the non-Indian community with an interest in and dedication to Indian concerns. Lynelle K. Hartway, assistant general counsel for the Hopi government, was lead counsel for the Hopi government in court. Hartway had received her BA from the University of Michigan and her law degree from the University of Wisconsin–Madison. She was admitted to the bar in Arizona in 1999. Howard M. Shanker of Tempe, Arizona, represented the Navajo Nation, White Mountain Apache, Yavapai-Apache Nation, Center for Biological Diversity, Flagstaff Activist Network, and Sierra Club. Shanker had received his law degree from Georgetown University in 1989. He had worked for the Justice Department and attended law classes at Georgetown at night. He had served three years on the National Environmental Justice Advisory Council in the Clinton administration. His specialties included environmental and Indian law. DNA Legal Services, a nonprofit legal services firm for the Hopi and Navajo reservations—dedicated to providing legal aid and promoting Indian sovereignty—provided counsel for the Hualapai Tribe, plaintiff Nora Nez, and Bill Bucky Preston.[81] Though the trial was conducted with each counsel serving their clients, attorney for the Navajo Nation and later congressional primary candidate Howard Shanker took the lead for the plaintiffs in statements to the press and oral arguments before the various courts.

HOPI TESTIMONY AT TRIAL

At trial, Hopi political and religious leaders informed the court of their concerns regarding the use of reclaimed sewage effluent in snowmaking on the Peaks. The district court's opinion that nothing in the proposed expansion would prevent the Hopi from carrying out any particular acts or ceremonies was accurate in the short term, but the Hopi religion placed moisture brought from the Peaks by the kachinas at the center of Hopi life. Hopi leaders predicted that artificial snowmaking with reclaimed sewage water would cause profound mental and spiritual harm of such significance that both Hopi religion and Hopi culture could be destroyed.

Despite prior predictions that the initial expansion of the Snowbowl resort in 1983 would have devastating impacts on their religion, the Hopis admitted that their religion had not changed since 1983 and that now there were in fact more practitioners of the Hopi religion than in 1983. It was also clearly established in testimony before the district court that the Hopi were not excluded from going to the Peaks for a wide variety of religious purposes, though one traditional practitioner, Bill Bucky Preston, appeared unhappy about the necessary permitting process.[82]

The Hopis view their religion as a largely private affair and were uncomfortable talking about it with outsiders. Certain elements of their religion they do not even discuss among themselves.[83] The district court and the defendants, the U.S. Forest Service and the Arizona Snowbowl Resort Limited Partnership, appeared to largely respect this reluctance of the Hopi to speak of their religion. There was discussion at trial of an agreement regarding this need for privacy and keeping testimony confidential. Thus, while the intent of this section is to explain some degree of the psychic harm the Hopis expected to be caused by the proposed Snowbowl expansion, many religious details were left out in the testimony at trial, so only vague explanations will be possible.[84] The information on Hopi religion and culture found below is a synthesis of the testimony of several Hopi religious practitioners, from two different days of the trial. The testimony was delivered by Preston; Hopi religious leader Leigh Kuwanwisiwma; director of the Hopi Cultural Preservation Office of the Hopi government, Emory Sekaquaptewa, a former chief justice of the Hopi appellate court, anthropology professor at the University of Arizona, and kachina expert, and Antone Honanie, a Hopi silversmith and maker of kachina dolls.

Honanie was born in 1973. He was a member of the Water Clan and became a member of a kachina society at age twelve. Honanie worked as a self-employed silversmith and carved kachina dolls. A speaker of the Hopi language, he lived at Kykotsmovi, Third Mesa, on the Hopi reservation. Residents of this village belonged to only kachina societies, historically having split from the village of Old Oraibi to avoid turmoil among the leadership of other religious societies. The founders of Kykotsmovi had deliberately retained only kachina societies and left the other religious societies out of their new village.[85]

There is little information regarding Preston in the legal record. He was a native speaker of the Hopi language and felt more comfortable speaking in Hopi, though he spent some of his education in English-language schools. Preston was a Hopi religious figure, but in keeping with the Hopi tradition of not sharing information to the uninitiated, he refused at trial to divulge the identity of his position within Hopi religious societies, other than to say he held a significant position. Preston had been initiated into the religious societies as a youth and was a member of the Bamboo, Eagle, and Sun Clans. He refused to discuss at trial the specific responsibilities of the clans he belonged to. He spoke to the Forest Service interdisciplinary team as a concerned individual and became a plaintiff in the lawsuit challenging the Forest Service's approval of the proposed expansion with artificial snowmaking.[86]

Leigh Kuwanwisiwma represented the Hopi government throughout the trial. He had been initiated into a kachina society at age eleven, as part of the Clan of Greasewood of Bavavi, Third Mesa. For fifteen years he served as director of the Hopi Cultural Preservation Office. His work included interfacing with outside agencies and working within Hopi land to preserve the Hopi language. He was the chief government official in charge of relations with the U.S. federal government on cultural matters. His background was in business, and he had a nonacademic background in archaeology. Kuwanwisiwma also served as assistant director of the Hopi Health Department. As part of his cultural preservation work, he regularly consulted with Hopi elders, including getting input from female leaders in informal meetings on cultural affairs.[87]

Emory Sekaquaptewa was known as the Noah Webster of the Hopi language.

He had a long and distinguished career both within the Hopi nation and without. The records of his birth are inconsistent. Hopi records place his birth in 1927; U.S. records in 1928. Sekaquaptewa celebrated his birthday on December 28, preferring the Hopi birth year, but reluctantly used the U.S. recorded date for legal purposes. He was raised in Hotevilla, Third Mesa. Sekaquaptewa was the first Indian to attend West Point. He served two years in the United States Air Force and graduated from Brigham Young University in 1953. He was the first Hopi to receive a law degree from the University of Arizona and was the founding chief justice of the Hopi appellate court. In the last years of his life he worked at the University of Arizona as an applied research anthropologist and taught Hopi language courses. In 1998 he published the first Hopi–English dictionary, *Hopi Dictionary/Hopiikwa Lavaytutuveni: A Hopi-English Dictionary of the Third Mesa Dialect*. The dictionary has more than thirty thousand entries with pronunciation guides. His awards include the 1989 Arizona Indian Living Treasure Award, University of Arizona's 2004 Bureau of Applied Research in Anthropology Lifetime Achievement Award, the 2007 Byron S. Cummings Award, and the Heard Museum's 2007 Spirit of the Heard Award. An expert on kachinas, Sekaquaptewa was a native speaker of the Hopi language and a member of the Eagle Clan. He died on December 14, 2007.[88]

Taken together, the testimony of Hopi witnesses Preston, Kuwanwisiwma, Sekaquaptewa, and Honanie conveyed the critical areas of Hopi faith and belief relevant to their case. They conveyed that the San Francisco Peaks are of central importance to the Hopis because they are the home of Maasaw and the kachinas. The kachinas are of central importance to the survival of the Hopi way of life since their songs are the main method of transmitting cultural values from one generation to the next. Water is of central cultural importance to the Hopis, as they have historically lived in a desert and have been dependent on rainfall for their survival. The Hopis believe that rainfall is brought to them from the Peaks by the kachinas. Practitioners of Hopi traditional religion believe that the artificial creation of snow from any source is unclean. The Hopis believe it is imperative that the water of the Peaks be kept pure, since it is the source of life, brought to them by the kachinas. The testimony the Hopis presented went on to explain the devastating cultural, spiritual, and emotional impacts they expected the expansion with artificial snowmaking would rain down upon the Hopi people.

In explaining his objection to the proposed expansion, Kuwanwisiwma said:

> Particularly, the making of artificial snow, which is so adverse to the fundamental beliefs of the Hopi people in relation to Kachina and what the Peaks

mean to us; and compounding it is the use of recycled wastewater to make artificial snow.... The making of artificial snow is so contrary to what the beliefs of the Hopi people are about, what the Katsina [kachina] beliefway [sic] is all about, and what the mountain represents to us. And the Hopi depend a lot on how we have a relationship in both tangible and intangible ways with the Katsina spirits and petitioning of the Katsina and our prayers that they act as messengers to take to the Peaks and to bring us moisture, bring us rain.[89]

Preston testified that no person had the power to purify water and that the use of wastewater on the Peaks would be destruction:

> The reclaimed water is destruction. It will contaminate all that is there and all the surroundings, because as a Hopi person, I was taught and I believe no matter what it is, you have a spirit. To me they're alive. This is why I can communicate with them. Stillness with myself makes me understand who they are and how much it's destroying them. And by using reclaimed water, that's total destruction. It will never be the same.[90]

On the situation facing the Peaks in general, Preston, at times with the help of an interpreter, said:

> It has already hurt me a lot. Right now sitting here my spirits are very low. My mind is confused. My heart is broken and confused. This is why I chose to come here, because I need to speak for the powerful Nuvatukyaovi. I need to show the mountain that I am doing my job, although it's very hard and difficult for me to express my feelings, because nobody can see ... how life is at Hopi and all the surrounding world.... I am sad. Our life is all broken up. It's already broken up. Nobody cares who we are. No one has respect for us. I guess we're nobody. Nothing is complete. I am very sad.[91]

A good deal less emotionally, Sekaquaptewa described the impact of the proposed expansion on the Hopi people:

> I think this undermines the faith of the Hopi people in their belief in the Katsinas [kachinas] and the place where they are seen or—where they are in their belief dwell on these mountains and would tend to diminish the strength of this faith.... When that—when young—younger generation of Hopi begin to lose faith, the Kachina religion will soon be a performance for performance sake.... It would no longer be a religious effort in behalf of all the people, and thus undermine the integrity of the Hopi religion as

we know it today.[92]

Kuwanwisiwma explained that snowmaking on the Peaks would cause devastating mental harm to the Hopi people. He said of the snowmaking, "It's a defilement. It violates spiritual law as far as our belief into the Peaks and the Katsina."[93] He further explained: "It defiles the sanctity of the Peaks. It defiles the spiritual character of the Peaks, of what they stand for. It basically creates an emotional burden for the Hopi people because of this defilement. It affects our psychology. It contributes to the burden of negative emotion, which is part of what the results are when it's defiled in this manner."[94]

The Hopis felt that this defilement of the Peaks had a significant possibility of destroying Hopi cultural identity. With the desecration and pollution of the mountain, the sacredness of the kachinas might be brought into question or even destroyed. The kachinas are central to the Hopis in teaching religious and cultural values to their children. The destruction of this central religious belief would possibly destroy the central means of cultural reproduction of the Hopis.

The Hopis provided no evidence at trial that the proposed action of the Forest Service would sanction or penalize the practice of the Hopi religion, certainly not in the same way the federal government did when it sent indigenous religious practitioners to prison in the late nineteenth and early twentieth century.[95] Throughout the trial, when asked by attorneys how their religion would be burdened by the proposed Snowbowl expansion, the Hopi practitioners replied in the psychological, emotional, and spiritual terms quoted above. Given the centrality of water, the kachinas, and the Peaks to the Hopi religion, the significance of the mental harm was not exaggerated.

The Forest Service acknowledged that the proposed expansion, including the use of snowmaking with reclaimed sewage effluent, would have an adverse impact on the cultural concerns of Hopis and other Indian peoples. The Hopis argued that this particular set of adverse impacts could destroy not only their religion but also their entire culture and way of life. The official policy of the U.S. government was to preserve and protect the religions of Indian peoples, as stated in the American Indian Religious Freedom Act, yet the Forest Service approved the proposed expansion and the courts of the U.S. government have found no legal remedy available to the Hopis for the harms of this acknowledged adverse impact.

RELEVANT FINDINGS OF THE TRIAL COURT
REGARDING THE HOPIS

Judge Paul Rosenblatt of the Arizona District Court concluded that the Forest Service had followed the proper procedures and that harms the Hopis would suffer as a result of the Forest Service approval of artificial snowmaking were not the kind prohibited by the Religious Freedom Restoration Act. Rosenblatt determined that the Hopis had been properly consulted in the decision-making process of the Forest Service, and the testimony at trial amply supports this conclusion. The eleven-day bench trial was conducted in the United States District Court of Arizona in Prescott. Rosenblatt acknowledged that the proposed expansion would have a negative impact on the Hopis' "frames of mind" and that the production of artificial snow would impact them "emotionally." He concluded that the Hopis "presented no evidence that Snowbowl upgrades would impact any exercise of religion related to the Kachinas or the Kachina songs. The Kachinas have continued to come to Hopi villages since the establishment of Snowbowl in the late 1930s, and since the Forest Service approved the expansion of Snowbowl in 1979." He found that the "the Hopi Plaintiffs provided no evidence that the decision would impact any religious ceremony, gathering, pilgrimage, or any other religious use of the Peaks." Based on the above factual conclusions, the trial court ultimately decided that "Plaintiffs have failed to demonstrate that the Snowbowl decision coerces them into violating their religious beliefs or activities. . . . Plaintiffs have failed to present any objective evidence that their exercise of religion will be impacted by the Snowbowl upgrades."[96]

The responses to Rosenblatt's decision were quite predictable. Forest Supervisor Nora Rasure applauded the judicial opinion, which reaffirmed her decision as to a valid use of a national forest, and she expressed her hope that the Forest Service could continue work with Indian interests so that "the Peaks retain as much value to the tribes as possible." Indigenous members of the Save the Peaks Coalition denounced the decision as a miscarriage of justice. Members of the Flagstaff Activist Network pledged to use all legal means necessary to fight the decision and shifted protest efforts to the Flagstaff City Council in the hope of stopping the sale of reclaimed sewage effluent to the Snowbowl facility by the City of Flagstaff. Jeneda Benally of the Save the Peaks Coalition, Navajo punk band Blackfire, National Native American Honor Roll Society, and a former Flagstaff Indian Days powwow princess noted that the "Nazi regime" was meticulous in its adherence to legal principles while it destroyed religious and ethnic minorities. Northern Arizona University anthropology professor Miguel Vasquez commented, "It's OK to screw the Indians. You've just gotta make it sound good."[97]

THE APPELLATE DECISIONS

On January 11, 2006, the District Court of Arizona issued its final opinion in the case of *Navajo Nation v. U.S. Forest Service*. In its findings, the court concluded that there had been no burden placed upon the religious practices of the various indigenous plaintiffs. The plaintiffs appealed to the Ninth Circuit Court of Appeals. Oral arguments were held on September 14, 2006. On March 12, 2007, a three-judge panel from the Ninth Circuit, composed of William A. Fletcher, Johnnie B. Rawlinson, and Thelton E. Henderson unanimously reversed the decision of the trial court and found that the Religious Freedom Restoration Act expanded protections for religious freedom in the United States beyond those of the Constitution and the prior standards in *Lyng*. Writing for the court, Fletcher further found that not only was religion burdened but that the Forest Service did not have a compelling reason for doing so.[98] While the Ninth Circuit Court later took the uncommon move of meeting en banc to overturn the three-judge decision, the decision is worth examining because, unlike the Forest Service in formulating the goals to be met by the proposed expansion, the Ninth Circuit considered whether the policy goals of the Forest Service were substantial enough to justify the harm to the indigenous religions and their followers.

The decisions of the Ninth Circuit Court of Appeals—both the three-judge panel and the full court—were additionally complicated by the lack of clear Supreme Court precedent on the application of legal protections for Indian religious concerns on public lands. While the *Lyng* opinion stood as precedent that directly denied any form of constitutional protection to followers of Indian religions when the government acts on land it purports to own as public lands, the Justices of the Supreme Court could not agree on how to interpret the reasoning behind that opinion. In *Smith*, Justice Antonin Scalia cited *Lyng* as an example of the court's departure from the compelling interest test that the Supreme Court finally abandoned with *Smith*. Justice Sandra Day O'Connor strongly protested this interpretation and replied, in her concurring opinion in *Smith*, that *Lyng* did not apply the prior test because the action was on public lands and stood as an exception to the application of the compelling interest test. The justices of the Supreme Court of the United States had no agreement as to what exactly the *Lyng* case stood for.

The decision of the full Ninth Circuit Court was incoherent, confused, and unsound, but this does not necessarily mean that the ultimate conclusion of the majority was legally "incorrect." The better and more coherent opinion came from the dissenting judges from the three-judge panel. The central issue the court wrestled with was the definition of the term "substantial burden" as found in the

Religious Freedom Restoration Act of 1993. Congress did not define "substantial burden," and this left the court to determine what the intent of both houses of Congress was in the use of the words as they applied to religion. While there are general rules of statutory construction, it is completely possible to use those rules to formulate a definition of "substantial burden" consistent with the approach of either the majority or the dissent. The majority's presented decision was incoherent and unsupported by the case law, but this is not to say that better reasoning for their position did not exist. The trial court in the case of the Standing Rock Sioux and the Dakota Access Pipeline would later provide that more coherent interpretation of the law.

The outcome of this case was entirely dependent upon interpreting what Congress meant by a "substantial burden" upon religion. The Forest Service acknowledged that the approved action would be an adverse action on the cultural interests of the Hopis. The testimony at trial revealed that this adverse impact would be significant, and the Hopis argued that it would destroy their entire way of life, both religious and cultural. This admission of adverse action by the Forest Service would have been legally significant only if the adverse action was also a substantial burden upon the religion of the Hopis (or other Indian plaintiffs). If the adverse action was indeed a substantial burden upon the religion of Hopi people, then the protections of RFRA would be implicated. If this adverse action was not a substantial burden on religion, then the action could not violate any legal rights and the analysis would stop there.

After the decision of the three-judge panel on March 12, 2007, environmentalists, supporters of Indian interests, and many activists in the Flagstaff area praised Fletcher's opinion, while Eric Borowsky, managing owner of the Arizona Snowbowl Resort Limited Partnership, denounced the position of the Hopis and other Indian nations as hypocritical. Bill Bucky Preston linked many ills of the day, including local forest fires and the war in Iraq, on the continuing disrespect shown to the San Francisco Peaks and stated that these difficulties were warning signs of what everyone would suffer if sacred places were not respected. Hopi chairman Ben Nuvamsa noted that even snowmaking with potable water would be a problem for the Hopis.[99]

Borowsky's denunciation of the Hopis and other Indians was joined by the Flagstaff Chamber of Commerce, and while the denunciation was logically untenable, it served to increase the level of animosity and conflict between the differing sides of the dispute. Borowsky's claim that the Hopi political position on Snowbowl "is nothing short of hypocritical" completely ignored a simple fact that is true of all cultures and religions: different places have differing significance and value. Borowsky dismissed Hopi protests over the desecration of the Peaks because the Hopi government was concurrently involved in leasing Hopi lands to Peabody Coal for strip mining operations.[100] Many supporters of the Snowbowl ski resort joined Borowsky in these nonsensical and inaccurate denunciations. Borowsky characterized the concerns of the Hopis as environmental rather than religious or cultural and made no acknowledgment that Nuvatukyaovi is the *most* sacred of places to the Hopis. Borowsky's argument did not acknowledge that there are places not necessarily appropriate for every activity. For example, while one may love playing soccer, one can also recognize that plowing over the historic Gettysburg battlefield to build a soccer pitch is perhaps not the most respectful or culturally sensitive thing to do. Every culture recognizes different places as being appropriate for different activities. Yet Borowsky called on the Hopis and their supporters to oddly be against all land development and usage or none, regardless of place.

Positions were reversed in the wake of the decision of the full Ninth Circuit Court of Appeals on August 8, 2008. Borowsky expressed his pleasure with the opinion. Preston stated, "It's never going to go our way, no matter what kind of government it is, when there's money involved." Taking the lead in public statements for the attorneys working for the various plaintiffs, Howard Shanker noted, "As the law stands now, Native Americans have no process in place and no recourse to protect sacred sites." Dick Wilson, lead plaintiff from the 1980 suit to prevent the first major Snowbowl expansion, *Wilson v. Block*, expressed his regret and resignation at the failure of court to protect Indian sacred sites. A coalition that included the Anglican Church in the United States, the Presbyterian Church, and Catholic nuns joined the plaintiffs in urging the United States Supreme Court to review the case. Upon the failure of the Supreme Court to do so, attorney Robert Greene, on behalf of that coalition of Christian religious interests, stated, "[T]his will make it very difficult for all sort of religious people to protect religious rights. The remaining step for the tribes and their supporters is to see whether the Interior Department can or will reconsider their approval."[101]

THE PANEL DECISION OF THE NINTH CIRCUIT

Judge William A. Fletcher authored both the panel decision and the strident dissent to the opinion of the full Ninth Circuit. Originally the case was considered by a three-judge panel before a hearing en banc. Such a hearing was traditionally held before all the judges of an appellate court, but the Ninth Circuit had twenty-eight judges, so departing from tradition, eleven judges composed a panel en banc for this district. The decision of the three-judge panel, as well as the dissent for the rehearing en banc, relied on the same reasoning: dictionary definitions of "substantial" and "burden" would place the harm suffered by the Indian plaintiffs squarely within coverage of the Religious Freedom Restoration Act. Fletcher, a Rhodes scholar, had worked in the Office of Emergency Preparedness of the executive branch of the U.S. government from 1970 to 1972. After obtaining a law degree from Yale in 1975, he clerked for Justice William J. Brennan Jr. of the United States Supreme Court. He became a law professor at the University of California–Berkley in 1977 and coauthored a textbook on civil procedure.[102] In 1992 Fletcher ran the northern California segment of Bill Clinton's successful run for the office of president of the United States. Clinton appointed Fletcher to the Ninth Circuit Court of Appeals in 1999.

In the initial three-judge panel opinion, the Ninth Circuit Court of Appeals noted the various religious harms the plaintiffs demonstrated, focusing on the Hopi, Navajo, Havasupai, and Hualapai Indians. Writing the unanimous opinion of the court, Fletcher noted that the making of artificial snow with reclaimed sewage effluent would render unclean and unusable necessary components for different religious ceremonies of the Hualapais, Havasupais, and Navajos. While unhappy with the mere presence of the ski resort, some Navajos viewed the resort as a scar on the body of their holy place; the injection of this new poison would completely corrupt that body. Similarly, the Hualapai collected water and plants from the Peaks for use in religious ceremonies. The presence of treated sewage effluent on the Peaks would contaminate these items necessary for religious ceremonies. For the Havasupai, the treated sewage effluent on the Peaks would undermine the integrity of their sweat lodge purification ceremonies and lead to the end of those ceremonies. Fletcher also noted the concerns of the testimony examined in detail previously in this essay, including the fear that "the contamination by effluent would fundamentally undermine their entire system of belief and the associated practices of song, worship, and prayer, that depends on the purity of the Peaks, which is the source of rain and their livelihoods and the home of the *Katsinam* spirits."[103]

Fletcher ruled that the nature of the burden placed upon the Hopis and other indigenous religious practitioners by the making of snow with reclaimed sewage effluent fit within the expanded protections of the Religious Freedom Restoration Act, and the court found that the religious freedom of the various Indians had been substantially burdened. As the next part of the required analysis, Fletcher examined whether or not the Forest Service had a compelling interest to pursue in approving alternative two, the expansion of the Snowbowl resort with snowmaking from treated sewage effluent.[104]

Fletcher concluded that a substantial burden had been placed upon religion but found that this burden did not forward any compelling governmental interests. He wrote for the court, "We are unwilling to hold that authorizing the use of artificial snow at an already functioning commercial ski area in order to expand and improve its facilities, as well as to extend its ski season in dry years is a governmental interest 'of the highest order.'" The court did note that Arizona Snowbowl Resort had claimed that the variability of the season had caused it difficulty, but it responded that ASR had paid $4 million for the resort in 1992 and had made no showing that it was in any danger of going out of business: "[T]he evidence in the record does not support a conclusion that the Snowbowl will necessarily go out of business if it is required to continue to rely on natural snow and to remain a relatively small, lowkey resort. The current owners may or may not decide to continue their ownership. But a sale by the current owners is not the same thing as the closure of the Snowbowl."[105]

Judge Fletcher went further and noted that even if the Snowbowl facility were to completely close, saving it as a ski resort would not be a compelling governmental interest:

> Even if there is a substantial threat that the Snowbowl will close entirely as a commercial ski area, we are not convinced that there is a compelling *governmental* interest in allowing the Snowbowl to make artificial snow from treated sewage effluent to avoid that result. *We are struck by the obvious fact that the Peaks are located in a desert. It is (and always has been) predictable that some winters will be dry.* The then-owners of the Snowbowl knew this when they expanded the Snowbowl in 1979, and the current owners knew this when they purchased it in 1992. . . . Even if the Snowbowl were to close (which we think is highly unlikely), continuing recreational activities on the Peaks would include "motocross, mountain biking, horseback riding, hiking and camping," as well as other snow related activities such as cross-country skiing, snowshoeing, and snowplay [second emphasis added].[106]

As to the second need discussed in the record of decision, safety, the court found that there had been no showing that skiing in Snowbowl without the expansion was unsafe. Again, even if the area were unsafe, the court determined, "[T]his safety concern is not a compelling interest that can justify the burden imposed by the Snowbowl's expansion." The court was specifically addressing the alleged safety concerns created by the lack of a snow play area. The Forest Service had traded support for snowmaking for ASR support of a snow play area, but "[e]ven assuming that the safety concerns motivating the creation of the snowplay area are a compelling interest, we do not agree that inducing a commercial ski resort, which is not the source of the danger, to develop a snowplay area as a quid pro quo for approval of the resort's use of treated sewage effluent is the least restrictive means of furthering that interest."[107] Thus the court determined that there was no compelling interest and that even if safety were a compelling interest, there were less restrictive means of protecting those interests than approving snowmaking with treated sewage effluent.

Against well-established precedent, the attorneys for ASR argued that if the Forest Service were to accommodate indigenous religious concerns by not allowing the making of artificial snow with reclaimed sewage effluent, the Forest Service would be engaging in the unconstitutional establishment of religion. Fletcher took a scant few paragraphs to dismiss such an argument and noted that the Supreme Court had repeatedly held that the Constitution "affirmatively mandates accommodation, not merely tolerance, of all religions, and forbids hostility toward any." Fletcher noted that the federal government was not required to act with callous indifference toward religion and that accommodation of religion was to be sought. Interestingly, Fletcher made no reference to the American Indian Religious Freedom Act in stating it was the official policy of the federal government to protect and preserve indigenous religions. This was likely because AIRFA had no substantive protections to offer. Finally, the court noted, again, that even if the Snowbowl resort was *removed*, this hardly would establish religion, as other activities religiously offensive to Indians (just markedly less offensive and burdensome) would still be conducted on the Peaks.[108]

The three-judge panel finally noted that the use of treated sewage effluent on the Peaks was a significant and severe burden on indigenous religious practitioners. It wrote, "To get some sense of equivalence, it may be useful to imagine the effect on Christian beliefs and practices—and the imposition that Christians would experience—if the government were to require that baptisms be carried out with 'reclaimed water.'" The full Ninth Circuit Court of Appeals did not agree. It accepted the case for rehearing en banc to clarify the Ninth Circuit's position on what constitutes a substantial burden to religion.[109]

THE DECISION OF THE FULL NINTH CIRCUIT COURT OF APPEALS

Arizona Snowbowl Resort and the Forest Service appealed the decision of the three-judge panel to the Ninth Circuit Court of Appeals for rehearing en banc. The Ninth Circuit accepted the case for rehearing en banc, and oral arguments were presented on December 11, 2007. The court en banc delivered its opinion, overturning that of the three-judge panel, on August 8, 2008.[110]

The majority of the judges on the Ninth Circuit Court of Appeals joined with Judge Carlos T. Bea, author of the opinion. After preliminaries, Bea simply stated that "substantial burden" was a legal term of art chosen by Congress. For the Ninth Circuit, this term of art required the government to either prohibit or condition a benefit upon violation of a principle of a complainant's religion before there could a finding that a "substantial burden" had infringed upon religion. Bea wrote, "Where, as here, there is no showing the government has coerced the Plaintiffs to act contrary to their religious beliefs under the threat of sanctions, or conditioned a governmental benefit upon conduct that would violate the Plaintiffs' religious beliefs, there is no 'substantial burden' on the exercise of their religion."[111] As there was no substantial burden upon religion, the substantive analysis of the facts ended with that decision.

Bea then provided a policy argument that was ahistorical, was factually muddled, and misrepresented the arguments of those who disagreed with him.

> Were it otherwise, any action the federal government were to take, including action on its own land, would be subject to the personalized oversight of millions of citizens. Each citizen would hold an individual veto to prohibit the government action solely because it offends his religious beliefs, sensibilities, or tastes, or fails to satisfy his religious desires. Further, giving one religious sect a veto over the use of public park land would deprive others of the right to use what is, by definition, land that belongs to everyone.[112]

This policy argument did not address the issues or harms the Indian plaintiffs were seeking to have redressed. In characterizing the harm, Bea did not address the expected inability of Navajos and Hualapais to perform ceremonies in the future because of the loss of key ingredients. Nor did he address the potential destruction of the entire Hopi culture; nor the potential loss of Havasupai sweat lodge ceremonies. Instead Bea characterized the expected harm as merely one involving "the Plaintiffs' subjective spiritual experience. That is, the presence of the artificial snow on the Peaks is offensive to the Plaintiffs' feelings about their religion and will decrease the spiritual fulfillment Plaintiffs get from practicing their religion on the mountain." He argued that the use of artificial snow made with reclaimed sewage waste merely "decreases the spirituality, the fervor, or the satisfaction" of the complaining Indians.[113]

The dissent, written by Fletcher, was particularly bitter. It went as far as to state that the reasoning of the majority "is not just flawed. It is perverse." The dissenting opinion called for the effect on religion to be the important consideration rather than the particular mechanism by which religion might be burdened. In disagreeing with the perspective of Bea and the majority, the dissent stated that the term "substantial burden" was not defined in the Religious Freedom Restoration Act; nor did it ever appear in the case law that the majority alleged supported its much narrower definition of the term. Fletcher suggested that the common dictionary definitions of "substantial" and "burden" be adopted. The facts of this case would then support a finding of substantial burden upon the religions of the Indians in violation of RFRA, the dissent reasoned.[114]

The central contention between the dissent and the majority was the definition of "substantial burden." The dissent reasoned that the term was undefined and that dictionary definitions of "substantial" and "burden" easily included the types of harms being brought to the religious practices of the various Indian plaintiffs by the making of artificial snow with reclaimed sewage effluent. The majority reasoned that references in RFRA to prior case law implied that Congress intended "substantial burden" to be defined in prior case law, despite the fact that the phrase never appeared in prior cases of the Supreme Court. The majority found *Lyng* to be directly on point and denied the plaintiffs any form of claim to a cognizable burden on their respective religions.[115]

Most problematic in the reasoning of Bea and the majority was their reliance on an interpretation of *Lyng* at odds with the interpretations of both Justice Scalia and Justice O'Connor. Recall that in *Smith*, Scalia and O'Connor had disagreed over the reasoning in *Lyng*. Scalia, in the majority opinion of *Smith*, stated, "[W]e declined to apply *Sherbert* analysis [the compelling interest test] to the Government's logging and road construction activities on lands used for religious purposes by several Native American Tribes [in *Lyng*], even though it was undisputed that the activities 'could have devastating effects on traditional religious practices.'"[116] Implicit in this interpretation of *Lyng* is the notion that Indian religions would in some way be harmed or burdened by the destruction of sacred sites (for if the free exercise of religion was not in any way infringed, the court would not be abandoning the compelling interest test).

O'Connor disputed Scalia's interpretation of her opinion in *Lyng*, but her interpretation also contains an implicit burden on religions of Indian practitioners.

O'Connor insisted that the compelling interest test did not apply to how the government used or disposed of government land, as uses of government property by the government are exceptions to the compelling interest test.[117] Thus for neither Scalia nor O'Connor did *Lyng* stand for the proposition that land use that harms Indian religious practices and sensibilities can never be a burden on religion. To the contrary, implicit in their reasoning was the view that Indian religion *was* burdened by the proposed road in *Lyng*.

Each of the contradictory readings of *Lyng* by justices of the Supreme Court rendered the position of the majority of the Ninth Circuit Court of Appeals impossible. Scalia argued that religion was burdened in *Lyng*, but the Supreme Court abandoned the compelling interest test. RFRA later restored the compelling interest test and expanded it. Thus the trial court should have applied the compelling interest test, as required by RFRA, to the burdens placed on Hopi religion. O'Connor argued that there was an exception to the compelling interest test when it came to federal land use, but RFRA clearly stated that the compelling interest test was to be used in *all* cases. Thus RFRA directly overturned either interpretation of the *Lyng* precedent the Supreme Court offered. To carry their argument, the majority of the Ninth Circuit was forced to disagree, and Bea in the opinion created a third understanding of *Lyng* that was directly contrary to the positions of both Scalia and O'Connor. Bea read *Lyng* to mean that Indian religion cannot be "substantially burdened" by rendering the religion impossible to practice through desecration and destruction of sacred places. Thus, for Bea and the majority of the Ninth Circuit Court of Appeals, RFRA offered the Hopis and others no protection from the adverse action approved by the Forest Service.

The Hopis and other Indian plaintiffs appealed the decision of the Ninth Circuit to the Supreme Court of the United States. On June 8, 2009, the United States Supreme Court declined to take the case for consideration. This left the decision of the Ninth Circuit Court of Appeals interpreting "substantial burden" on religion to not include the desecration of holy sites as the relevant precedent, denying the Hopis and others relief on religious freedom grounds.[118]

Was the decision of the majority correct, despite its unsupportable interpretation of case law? The issue before the court was: What did the U.S. Congress mean by "substantial burden" on religion? With such cases, there always can be competing interpretations of what undefined terms in legislation might mean. The Religious Freedom Restoration Act did not define the term, and there certainly existed a better-reasoned argument than that of the majority in the Ninth Circuit, one that does not directly contradict Scalia's and O'Connor's interpretations of Supreme Court precedent.

Nothing should be read into the refusal of the Supreme Court to rehear the case. While the decision was left to stand by the Supreme Court, there are any number of reasons the court might not have taken the case, including waiting for a conflict with another jurisdiction in interpretation or simply hoping Congress might act to clarify matters. Given the natural tendency of courts to avoid any decision that might increase their caseloads, that decision, which narrows the scope of "substantial burden" and keeps litigation over federal land use to a minimum, will most likely remain the "correct" understanding as reasoned by the courts, until shown otherwise by an additional act of Congress.

A more philosophical interpretation of the bitterness of the case recognizes that the dispute between Fletcher and Bea was at its core about whether or not to include Indians as part of the community. As issues of congressional intent regarding nuance of meaning are rarely clear-cut, any judge faced with this case had two broad options. First, as Judge Fletcher did, one could relate to the Hopis as human beings who were faced with a very real harm that made a mockery of the stated policy of the U.S. government to preserve and protect Indian religions. This human perspective acknowledges that decent people do not desecrate the most holy of places of others to provide a regular ski season to a profitable low-key ski resort that can never be a great ski resort. From this perspective, any plausible interpretation of the definitions of "substantial" and "burden," such as those found in dictionaries, would have been the correct approach.

Contrary to this perspective was one that denied history and hampers the larger community's ability to heal the wounds of the past.[119] There can be any number of motivations for such an orientation, but none of them would be to treat the Hopis as decent human beings would. Vine Deloria suggested more than one potential answer: the supremacy of material interests over religious concerns in an increasingly secular society, a general hostility to Indians, or a desire to maintain the supremacy of the state over all matters of conscience. Added to this, as mentioned above, one cannot overlook the natural tendency of the courts to want to reduce their caseloads in the face of an overburdened court system. This provided motivation to interpret legislation in such a way as to reduce one's own work.

What these and other possible underlying motivations for the decision of the majority had in common was their inability to face and take responsibility for the adverse action against Hopi religious concerns. The majority of the Ninth Circuit never engaged in any examination of the adverse action against the Hopis because the law, as they constructed it, prevented them from doing so. The Ninth Circuit majority used policy and law to provide cover for any responsibility for treating the Hopis indecently, in a manner that was quite similar to that of Forest Supervisor Rasure.

MEANING AND IMPACT OF THE PEAKS CASE

The decision of the Forest Service to desecrate the Hopi sacred mountain and the Ninth Circuit's decision to narrowly interpret the meaning of "burden" under the Religious Freedom Restoration Act have had several lasting impacts. First, they have undermined the trust and working relationship between Indian governments and the Forest Service. Second, this interpretation of the law has effectively removed Indian sacred sites from any form of statutory or constitutional protections. The power to decide the fate of Indian sacred sites on public lands was left to the discretion of federal administrators. This left the Forest Service with the knowledge that it had a great deal of discretion when it comes to management of sacred sites.[120]

The case also stands as a stark example of how Forest Service administrators were able to fully comply with the consultation process and still take an adverse action against a sacred site. The Forest Service managers framed their management goals in such a way that the only possible answer was to engage in actions that adversely impacted an Indian sacred site. Well aware of prior Indian protest, these administrators managed to fully comply with consultation requirements and the decision-makers even came to understand Hopi religious concerns in full. This example demonstrates that government officials can desecrate sacred sites as they please, as long as they fully understand that is what they are doing. Indians are left no recourse to the law.

This is also a case where the administrative decision was driven by the financial interests of a well-connected corporation. The Arizona Snowbowl Resort hired the former secretary of the interior as its attorney. He contacted forest administrators while formulating policy and pressured the forest supervisor to approve ASR's plans. As seen below, when corporate interests are not driving the proposed policy changes that trigger the consultation process, outcomes more favorable to Indian concerns were obtainable. The consultation process in the case of the Peaks was able to teach Supervisor Rasure of the importance of the mountain to the Hopis and others and to cross any cultural divide. Absent well-connected corporate pressures, the outcome may have differed.

3 CAVE ROCK AND THE WASHOE TRIBE OF NEVADA AND CALIFORNIA

In the 1980s, the National Park Service was quickly overwhelmed by the sudden rise of recreational rock climbing at Bear's Lodge (Devils Tower). In the 1990s the National Forest Service was similarly caught without a management plan after highly skilled climbers discovered the challenges of Cave Rock, the most sacred of places to the Washoe people. Unlike at Bear's Lodge, no professional climbing guides made their living at Cave Rock. But Cave Rock offered the most challenging climbs in North America, with a unique view of Lake Tahoe below it. Cave Rock had a long history of alterations by the U.S. government, with the Transportation Department blasting tunnels through the rock below the main cave in 1931 and 1957. Despite this adversity, Cave Rock remained a place of religious significance and spiritual power for the Washoe.

Unlike the management of the San Francisco Peaks, the Forest Service initiated a series of meetings with both climbers and interested Washoe Indians in 1998 to create some form of mutual agreement and creative compromise for management of Cave Rock. For the Washoes, Cave Rock remained a powerful portal between worlds, and many felt the well-being of all the world was put at risk when anyone but shamans visited the site. The Washoes found the continued intimate contact of climbing to be much more concerning and dangerous than the transit of vehicles or the visits of picnickers to lower portions of the site.

Although the parties were unable to reach a compromise, the consultation process had a profound impact on many climbers in attendance. When the climbing organization, the Access Fund, initially moved to portray the Washoes as selfish and privileged, members condemned the organization and prevented it from engaging in any openly ethnocentric or racist attacks on the Washoe people. A large number of climbers went as far as to endorse leaving Cave Rock to the Washoes to enjoy alone.

When, in a narrow decision, the Forest Service ultimately moved to ban all climbing at Cave Rock to preserve the physical and cultural integrity of the site, the Access Fund challenged the decision in the courts. Relying on dicta from previous cases involving Bear's Lodge and Rainbow Bridge, the Access Fund claimed the decision unconstitutionally established Washoe religion. Ultimately the courts affirmed the decision of the Forest Service, finally clarifying that federal administrators had wide latitude to protect places of cultural and religious significance to Indian nations, including permanently banning certain recreational activities.

THE WASHOE PEOPLE

The Washoe Indians of California and Nevada have lived for centuries along Lake Tahoe. Cave Rock, a mountain along the lake's eastern shore, holds unique religious and cultural significance for the Washoe people. Lake Tahoe is considered the center of the Washoe world. Historically, the Washoes were a peaceful people, living, between the Paiutes of Utah and Indians of California, on the eastern edge of the Sierra Nevada in the Great Basin. Traditionally, the Washoes traded with Paiutes and Indians of California, with Washoe lands serving as a trade route between the regions.[1]

The traditional economy of the Washoes was based upon seasonal movements to engage in hunting, fishing, and gathering. Gathering piñon nuts and *waju* seeds was a central part of the Washoe economy. The gathering of waju seeds differentiated the Washoes from their Paiute neighbors, with whom they frequently traded. The name "Washoe" is derived from "waju." The Washoes fished at Lake Tahoe, and the hunting of bears was of religious significance.[2]

The Washoes had no traditional national government, but custom and informal hunting bands served as the basis for coordinated military action in the rare times of war with their neighbors. The Washoes were divided among four regional groups, and people tended to identify with their regional group. These four groups came together at Lake Tahoe during the fishing season, with fishing and gathering rights ruled by custom. Generally, custom maintained the peace, which included the practice of the wealthy giving to those who were not well-off. Any leadership positions, among hunting parties or at other times, were temporary and based upon merit.[3]

War was not a national affair for the Washoe people. When fighting did occur, usually with Paiute groups, the temporary leaders of informal hunting groups had to rally people to support the cause of the fight in question. At times, for larger conflicts, small hunting groups formed alliances to work in concert to engage in warfare. The Washoes did not fight at close quarters but instead used hunting bows as their primary weapons. Battles rarely lasted as long as one day and often ended when one side or the other ran out of arrows. The Washoes were skilled bowmen; a firsthand report tells of soldiers being able to regularly hit a man at five hundred yards.[4]

WASHOE RELIGION

While the Washoes had temporary economic and political leadership based on merit, they had no religious leaders among their traditional shamans and doctors. Traditional Washoe religion holds that certain people are called to be shamans or doctors through power acquired in dreams. Spirits use dreams to call members of the community to become shamans, who then have supernatural power. This power is acquired involuntarily, and it is not hereditary. Both men and women can be called to become shamans. Washoe custom held that shamans were to use their powers for the good of the community, but this was not always the case.[5]

While imbued with supernatural powers, shamans were viewed with ambivalence in Washoe communities. Washoe shamans had no political power, as the general populace viewed them with a certain amount of distrust. The powers of Shamans could be used for both good and bad. Shamans could use their powers to bring misfortune or illness. In addition, shamans served as the traditional source of medical care within Washoe communities. They traded their healing powers within the traditional economy and customarily demanded payment before they provided any healing services.[6]

Historically, Cave Rock was a place of great power to practitioners of the traditional Washoe religion, and before the arrival of non-Indians to Washoe territory, only shamans were permitted to go to Cave Rock. Shamans carried out secret rituals there. Those following traditional Washoe religion also believe that otherworldly creatures use Cave Rock as a portal to enter Washoe territory. Cave

Rock's power is thought to be considerable. The Washoe permitted only shamans to visit Cave Rock because misuse of this great power was a threat to the safety of individuals and communities.[7]

Traditional Washoe religious beliefs include common origins for the world and its natural features. In the Washoe religion, the world has passed through five different stages of existence, with each stage serving as a habitation for different creatures. The current world of contemporary Indian peoples was the fifth habitation. Within this fifth habitation, the Washoes have two contradictory origin stories, and traditional practitioners largely found this to be unproblematic. The first creation story involved Creation Mother. Creation Mother scattered the seeds of a cattail around the Tahoe Lake region. This scattering of seeds then created the Washoes, Paiutes, and the Indian peoples of California. The second origin story involved Creation Man as the driving force behind creation of the Washoe people. In this story, Creation Man creates the Washoes, Paiutes, and Indians of California by separating his three sons to prevent them from quarreling.[8]

While multiple stories explain the presence of the Washoes in the Lake Tahoe region, the origin of significant natural features of the region are tied directly to Cave Rock and the supernatural beings that travel through the portal within Cave Rock. Water Beings are gray humanoid creatures about one and a half feet tall with long flowing black hair that floats above the ground. Water Beings are also boneless creatures that are cold and damp to the touch. They are not of this realm and travel to any part of Washoe lands through a portal in Cave Rock.[9]

Water Beings are creatures of great power. Washoe religion holds that once, long ago, Damalali, the short-tailed weasel and younger brother to the much wiser long-tailed weasel, Pewetsoli, was foolish enough to take a Water Being captive. The Water Being threatened to flood the entire world if Damalali did not free him. Damalali was unconvinced, and the Water Being began to flood the world. Damalali let the Water Being go and the flooding stopped, but Lake Tahoe and the other lakes within Washoe lands remained.[10]

Together, the Water Beings and Cave Rock are of central importance to Washoe cosmology. The Water Beings are seen as the source of power for shamans in this world. The Washoes believe that shamans commune with spirits in a secret cavern within Cave Rock. This cavern, and the portal the Water Beings use to travel into this world, are of significant power, so it is dangerous for anyone other than shamans to enter Cave Rock.[11]

Water Beings continued to be a significant presence in the religious world of traditional Washoe practitioners even after the entry of non-Indians into their lands and the disruption of traditional sacred places. Washoe religion has incorporated interactions with non-Indians into its traditions. For instance, tradition says that around the turn of the twentieth century, a white man fishing in Lake Tahoe accidentally caught a Water Being and was unaware of what he had caught. The Water Being ended up being placed in the San Francisco Aquarium. Water Beings are powerful, and deliberately catching one imperils the safety of the entire world. The captured Water Being that was placed in the San Francisco Aquarium eventually escaped, causing the 1906 San Francisco earthquake in the process.[12]

ADAPTATION AND SURVIVAL

Just as the Washoe religion grew to include new stories involving the non-Indians who encroached upon Washoe lands, the Washoe people adapted and changed their lives to face new challenges brought by the influx of settlers into their lands. The Washoes first discovered European Americans in the early 1840s, but it was the Donner Party that left the first lasting impression. The ill-fated Donner Party became trapped in the snow inside Washoe territory in 1846. The Washoes observed from a distance and left deer and nuts for the trapped settlers to eat. The Washoes became aware the Donner Party engaging in unconventional means to ingest nutrients, and this shaped Washoe perceptions of white people for generations. Whites were incorporated into the Washoe list of creatures that ate human beings, along with mountain lions, bears, wolves, and coyotes. So white people entered Washoe culture as fearsome man-eating creatures to be avoided or tricked, and never directly confronted.[13]

By 1858 only about one thousand non-Indians had encroached on Washoe land. Numbers changed significantly with the discovery of silver. East of Washoe territory, the discovery of the Comstock Lode brought many more non-Indians to Washoe territory. The new squatters took over Washoe lands as they pleased, expanding farms, ranches, and mines in the area. Whites tended to simply take what they wanted, and the Washoes generally offered no violent resistance. Unlike their Paiute neighbors, who went to war with the United States, the Washoes never entered into any treaty with the United States. Because of aggressive behavior by incoming settlers, the Washoe called white people became *mushege*, the same word used for fierce animals or ill-tempered men. The mass influx of non-Indian immigrants to Washoe lands severely disrupted the lives of the Washoes and undermined the traditional Washoe economy.[14]

The expansion of ranching in Washoe territory was largely detrimental to the Washoe economy. Cattle, horses, pigs, and sheep quickly monopolized the best lands for traditional Washoe gathering of food. The Washoes also found that poaching these animals led to violent reprisals from settlers. The Washoes quickly abandoned the practice of killing the animals for food.[15]

Nearby mining created a growth in the need for lumber and charcoal, and this had devastating impacts on the Washoe economy over the long term. At first the expanded demand for lumber provided short-term employment for some Washoes, as piñon trees were harvested. Before long, Chinese laborers replaced the Washoes as workers in the lumber industry. With the quick expansion of the nearby mining industry, the need for lumber was high, and overlogging by companies employing Chinese labor soon eliminated most of the piñon trees. This destruction of a crucial traditional food source created among many Washoes a long-standing prejudice against people of Chinese ancestry; the Washoes blamed Chinese laborers for the destruction of the piñon forests.[16]

In the face of the destruction of their traditional economy, many Washoes turned to other traditions to survive. While some Washoes scavenged through the trash of non-Indian settlers, others asked wealthy settlers for economic assistance. Washoe culture had no prohibition on asking the wealthy for assistance, and it was traditional for the well-off among the Washoes to provide material assistance to those in need. In the face of the great material wealth of the new settlers, the Washoes thought it was perfectly reasonable to seek assistance. Coming from a much different tradition, the settler population looked down on the Washoes for this behavior and for not fighting for their lands, as their neighbors the Paiutes had.[17]

With the development of commercial fishing in Lake Tahoe in 1859, many Washoes moved to enter this new industry. Commercial fishing quickly expanded in the region, spreading to every stream in Washoe territory. The Washoes fought to protect their access to traditional fishing grounds and defended them with fistfights when necessary. For a short time many Washoes were quite successful in commercial fishing, but overfishing quickly depleted the stocks. In 1880 regulations outlawed all fishing in streams that fed Lake Tahoe. The Washoes generally ignored these regulations and local settlers tended to not care, as they also hated fishing regulations. But by the early twentieth century, most Washoes had given up fishing at Tahoe because there were insufficient fish to catch.[18]

The nature of leadership in the Washoe communities also began to change after the influx of non-Indian settlers. By the 1850s the Washoes had adopted the habit of calling community leaders "captains," though settlers sometimes referred to them as "kings." Claims of leadership over Washoe groups evolved over time, with men claiming to have, for example, an ancestor who had served as a leader of a rabbit hunt group. This marked a departure from the traditional practice of temporary leadership based solely on merit.[19]

With the influx of settlers, no treaty recognizing a Washoe land base, and no reservation, the Washoes almost became a people with no land, but the 1887 Dawes Act, so harmful to other Indian nations, provided the beginning of formal recognition of Washoe landholdings. While the Dawes Act was being used so destructively to force other Indian nations into individual allotments and to remove "surplus" land from Indian control, the act recognized legal Washoe control over a small amount of land with poor irrigation and little game.[20] In 1893 the Washoes used the terms of the Dawes Act to reacquire eighty-seven thousand acres of land. Later the Washoes lobbied Washington, under the leadership of Gumalanga, also called Captain Jim, and regained control of culturally significant land where piñon nuts grew. In the 1900s the Washoes moved into permanent settlements for the first time. The poor land returned to the Washoes was not sufficient to support them, and the U.S. government provided $10,000 for them to purchase more land in 1916. In 1917 a rancher returned forty acres to the Washoes as a donation, providing the land base for Sagetown. The Washoes were able to purchase another 795 acres in 1938.[21]

New political challenges arose with the creation of an Indian Reorganization Act government in 1937. While the Washoes had landholdings, they had no formal reservation to draw people together and lived in scattered communities. The new IRA government clashed with traditional leaders for control of Washoe communities. With the advent of the termination policy, federal recognition for those Washoe people living in California ended in 1953.[22]

WASHOE SHAMANS AND THE NATIVE AMERICAN CHURCH

While political changes created new challenges for the Washoes, the greatest threat to the place of shamans in Washoe society was the spread of the Native American Church, sometimes called the Peyote Cult by anthropologists of past generations. In 1932 Lone Bear first introduced the ways of the Native American Church to the Washoes. Some trace the spread of the Native American Church among the Washoe people to the efforts of Washoe Ben Lancaster in 1936. Others credit the preaching in 1936 by Franklin York, another Washoe Indian, with the rapid spread of the new religion among the Washoes.[23]

The Native American Church was well suited to spread among the Washoes as its practices meshed with much of traditional Washoe cosmology. Use of peyote brought visions to members of the Native American Church. Traditional Washoes believed that power came from dreams, and peyote-induced visions tapped into the same source of power as traditional dreams. Native American Church practitioners also claimed to have healing powers similar to those of Washoe shamans, but they adhered to the belief that their powers could be used only for good, as opposed to the shamans, whose power could be used to both heal and harm. Also appealing, the Native American Church claimed that use of peyote as a sacrament prevented Washoe shamans from harming people.[24]

The Native American Church also took political and economic positions that the Washoe people welcomed. While sacramental use of peyote protected people from the potential harmful uses of power by shamans, those seeking healing turned to Native American Church healers because they accepted only voluntary donations for their services. Washoe shamans continued their traditional practice of demanding payment for their services upfront, and the need for their services was undercut by church healers. The church also opposed the use of alcohol. This was a welcome position, as many Washoes viewed alcohol use as deeply harmful. By 1939 the presence of the Native American Church among the Washoes had spread to such a degree that disruptions in the Washoe community began to appear.[25]

Unhappy with the undermining of their livelihood, position in society, and spiritual powers, the shamans rallied and organized to drive the Native American Church from the Washoe community. While also having economic concerns, the shamans were most alarmed by the claims that peyote use could eliminate their spiritual powers. The shamans engaged in a campaign of accusing members of the Native American Church of practicing sorcery. The shamans also publicly claimed that peyote use caused madness. By standing united, the shamans were able to largely expel the Native American Church from Washoe communities, but some felt that this was their final victory and that adherence to Washoe traditional religion and respect for shamans was permanently on the decline.[26]

HENRY RUPERT

While some in the twentieth century concluded that traditional Washoe society was in decline and U.S. government officials thought the Washoes were soon to be an extinct people, Henry "Moses" Rupert revitalized declining shaman practices by merging them with some Western medical practices and a broader cosmological view. Rupert linked the source of the power of shamans to the sources of spiritual powers of other religions around the world. Rupert also served as chief informant for the major ethnographic study of the Washoe people, and it is his historic connections to Cave Rock that were key in leading the Forest Service to determine that Cave Rock should be restored to the condition it was in 1965, the year of Rupert's death.[27]

Powerful dreams came to Henry Rupert at a young age. Rupert's mother worked as a servant to a white family when he was born in 1885. As a child, Rupert dreamed of bears and as a young man dreamed that his powers would come from water, connecting him in the spirit realm to the Water Beings. At an early age, his uncle Welewkushkush served as his mentor. Welewkushkush was highly regarded for his prowess as a shaman, and Rupert witnessed his uncle cure several people. Rupert gained the nickname Moses when he was caught in a flash flood. The water reportedly parted, leaving Rupert unharmed. Moses Street in Carson City, Nevada, is named for Rupert.[28]

In 1894 the U.S. government forced nine-year-old Rupert to attend the Carson Indian School. The Carson School was part of the system of boarding schools designed to remove Indian children from their families, religions, and languages in an effort to "uplift" them by forcing them to adopt Western cultural ways, including some form of Christianity and exclusive use of the English language. Rupert ran away on his second day at the school. The Nevada Indian Agency retaliated by arresting his parents. The policy at the time was to incarcerate parents until a child returned to school. Rupert returned but tried to run away two more times before eventually giving up.[29]

In 1898 Rupert committed to the path of becoming a shaman, despite the Bureau of Indian Affairs banning such religious practices. That year Rupert dreamed of the Rain Boss. This dream confirmed to the young man that his primary power source was water and he was to become a shaman. Rupert graduated from the Carson Indian School at age eighteen and traveled to Reno for work. While the boarding school had tried to suppress Rupert's shamanistic destiny, he did learn the skill of typesetting at the school. He found work as a typesetter for the *Reno Evening Gazette*.[30]

At the same time, Rupert continued his spiritual evolution. By age twenty he had mastered the skill of hypnotism. Rupert worked with his uncle for a time. In 1907 his uncle sent him to seek guidance from Beleliwe, who was widely known among the Washoes for having great powers. Beleliwe quickly recognized Rupert's power and encouraged him to become a shaman. That same year, Rupert healed his first patient. This woman was the mother of a good friend and had been unable to be cured by Western medicine. News spread quickly that Rupert had healed a formerly intractable illness.[31]

During his early years as a healer, Rupert encountered visions that motivated him to expand the Washoe understanding of the sources of spiritual power in the universe. He dreamed of meeting Hindu spirits. After this experience, Rupert believed that all beings drew power from a common pool of energy, regardless of race, culture, or ethnicity. In this new understanding, the Hindu spirits drew upon the same power as the Washoe beings and spirits.[32]

Rupert met resistance to his new revelations from more conservative Washoe practitioners. In 1909 a Washoe man suffering from typhoid sought out Rupert, still a novice shaman, as a last resort. Rupert was able to heal the man. Despite these impressive early successes in using spiritual power, some Washoe shamans were unhappy with Rupert's expanded perspective. Rupert incorporated a study of Western medicine as part of his expanding knowledge. In 1910 Rupert suffered from persistent joint pain. Welewkushkush warned Rupert that this pain was a result of him studying Western medicine and other religious perspectives.

Rupert further broke with tradition by marrying a Northern Paiute woman. While such marriages were not unheard of, they were still highly discouraged by conservative Washoes. In 1916 the federal government returned land to the Washoes to form the Carson Colony. Rupert moved there in 1924. At the Carson Colony, Rupert and his wife obtained land. They engaged in a profitable business raising strawberries and turkeys and lived together until her death in 1933.[33]

After the death of his wife, Rupert returned to more concentrated work on expanding Washoe cosmology. He developed a theory of ethereal waves that connect every living thing to the spirit world. According to this theory, the spirit world is part of a three-layered cosmology. Humans can access the spirit world through dreams. The healing powers of shamans and others, according to Rupert's understanding, came from the third layer of the spirit world. This world, which Washoe shamans could access in dreams, was the same source of miracles and power in other religions, including the healing and miracles of Jesus, according to Rupert's expanded Washoe cosmology.[34]

Rupert never advertised his healing abilities, but he became known by many around the world. Throughout the 1950s, Rupert continued to meld Western healing practices with his expanding understanding of Washoe cosmology, which connected the source of Washoe power to powers of other religious traditions. As his understanding of Washoe cosmology as being inclusively connected to other religious traditions evolved and as inclusion of Western medicine in his practices expanded, Rupert visited the secret places of great power in Cave Rock. By the 1960s, people from near and far were coming to Rupert for healing. One of these visitors was a traditional Hawaiian healer. This healer provided Rupert access to a Hawaiian healing spirit that Rupert called upon in his later activities.[35]

THE CHANGING ROCK

A volcano formed Cave Rock some three million years ago. The Washoe people named it De'ek Wadapush, which translates literally as "standing gray rock." Settlers passing through the area in the 1800s left markings and graffiti that the National Historic Register later found to be of archaeological significance. An aboriginal trail along the eastern shore of Lake Tahoe passed Cave Rock. As settler travel increased between 1858 and 1863, this trail was expanded to connect Carson City and Virginia City.[36]

The road along Cave Rock was steep and proved to be an impediment to the transport of heavy mining loads, leading to a series of improvements to the transport infrastructure. A trestle road constructed along the lake side of Cave Rock was sufficient to accommodate the heavier traffic. The U.S. government later incorporated this impressive and expensive road into Highway 50 in 1925.[37]

Traffic increased and expanded as tourism at Lake Tahoe grew, motivating drastic alterations to the Cave Rock area. In 1931 the Forest Service highway fund allocated $86,000 to construct a highway beneath Cave Rock, including a 151-foot tunnel through the rock itself. No representatives from the Forest Service contacted any Washoes regarding the project. At the time, the Washoe people were fragmented and had no government the United States recognized.[38]

As time passed, casinos and ski resorts grew up around Lake Tahoe, leading to further road upgrades. As more tourists flocked to the attractions, expanding the tourist season year-round, planners determined that a second tunnel would be necessary to accommodate tourist traffic. As with the first tunnel, no one consulted the Washoes or their government. Construction on a second tunnel began in 1956. The 410-foot tunnel was completed in 1957. Practitioners of traditional Washoe religion believed that those who misuse Cave Rock put themselves and others at risk, especially those engaged in prolonged contact with Cave Rock. The construction of the second tunnel was plagued by injuries, mishaps, and accidents.[39]

Initially, many Washoes viewed the blasting of the tunnels through Cave Rock as a serious threat, but the roads through and near the rock now have different meanings to both the Washoe and non-Indian populations. For the Washoes, the transportation tunnels came to represent, by the end of the twentieth century, the resilience of Washoe culture and its ability to adapt and survive. The unique proximity of highways from four different engineering periods of U.S. history made Cave Rock eligible for designation as a historic transportation district in 1997.[40]

In 1970 the Washoe people won a claim against the United States in the Indian Claims Commission. As part of a failed push to terminate Indian governments, the United States had created the commission to settle land disputes regarding the vast territory it admitted it had no legal claim to. As the Washoes had no treaty relations with the U.S. government and simply found all their lands taken from them, the commission determined that the Washoes were entitled to a $5 million settlement. The commission based its findings on the 1862 value of the lands seized.[41]

THE CLIMBING OF ROCKS

The second half of the twentieth century saw the rise of a new recreational sport, rock climbing. Sport rock climbing began in the 1950s and grew in popularity, spreading across the United States. Around 1988 recreational climbers discovered Cave Rock. They began to create climbing paths along the rock face, with permanent bolts forced into the rock for safety measures. Rock climbing quickly grew in popularity at Cave Rock, and as early as 1993, authorities considered issuing regulations, as they feared the proliferation of climbing would lead to permanent destruction of the rock face. The climbing community created its own guides to the climbing paths, including community-created names, many of them vulgar and offensive.[42]

Despite the propensity of some to create vulgar names for climbing paths, the climbing community also included a strong contingent of "leave-no-trace" climbers. These climbers felt that respect for the environment was part of the quasi-spiritual experience of their sport. They called for restraint in the sport and respect for the environment. They published guides that urged limiting the expansion of new climbing paths to only those that significantly differed from existing paths and taking extra efforts to preserve the quality of climbing sites. In 1997, the leave-no-trace faction called for climbers to leave alone sites that faced damage or destruction and further called for climbers to leave Indian sacred sites in peace. These climbers noted that climbing sacred sites "shows disregard for early Americans."[43]

DAN OSMAN

Dan Osman was one of the leaders who developed Cave Rock for climbers. Osman was of mixed European and Japanese ancestry; he had a Japanese paternal grandparent. He dedicated his life to climbing-related activities. A skilled and well-respected climber, Osman survived on a meager income from climbing-related sponsorship deals. Drawn to other dangerous activities such as street racing, Osman often did not have the money to pay fines related to his activities, which did not always comport with the law. One of his closest friends was a doctor, and Osman frequently paid his medical bills with free equipment from his sponsors, which the doctor accepted in lieu of monetary compensation.[44]

Osman was a daredevil whose quest for greater challenges brought him to Cave Rock in the early 1990s. He was attracted to the most difficult climbs in the world and would engage in such activities as free-climbing the most difficult rock faces. The climbing difficulty rating system ranks the most difficult climbs as 5.15. In 1990 Osman spent months creating paths along Cave Rock, with ratings of 5.12 and 5.13. Osman took months to make the paths because he refused to rappel down the peak to put in safety bolts. Instead he climbed from the bottom, attaching new bolts as he went. This was his way of respecting climbing traditions. While working to create the most difficult route at Cave Rock, Osman fell and required months of recuperation before he could climb again.[45]

During his recovery, Osman created the most invasive alterations to Cave Rock since the 1957 highway tunnel below the main cave. With the quick proliferation of climbing, the floor of Cave Rock had become quite littered. Osman cleaned up the refuse and then began the laborious process of hauling boulders and hundreds of bags of cement to the cave floor. Osman created a floor for the main cave, paved with flat stones, and arranged boulders to serve as benches. Other boulders were arranged to serve as belaying points for those providing safety to climbers. Osman built a low rock wall and steps into the cave. The look was elegant, and his efforts had the impact of attracting even more climbers to Cave Rock.[46]

Just as Osman was reaching the pinnacle of climbing celebrity, he changed the focus of his endeavors. Inspired by the rush he received from falling during climbs, Osman reasoned that greater excitement could be achieved by controlled jumps from high places. He shifted the focus of his activities to releasing commercial videos of himself jumping off heights in scenic areas. He even did extreme jumps for advertisements. He produced a video of himself cartwheeling off Cave Rock and falling, only to be caught by a rope just as he hit the waters of scenic Lake Tahoe.[47]

Concerned with the proliferation of climbing and the unapproved "improvements" at Cave Rock, the Forest Service issued a temporary order closing Cave Rock to all climbing. Dan Osman joined other climbers in organizing a resistance to this closure in February 1997. The first meeting of the climbers working with

Osman was dominated by ignorance and misinformation. The climbers repeated unfounded rumors that the Forest Service planned to trade Cave Rock to the Washoe people for a piece of more valuable land. Some repeated the mistaken belief that the Washoes had long ago sold Cave Rock and the vicinity for a penny an acre and had no legal claims to the lands. Osman claimed that Cave Rock was a spiritual place for the climbers as well and went as far as to question the validity of Washoe claims to having any real spiritual connection to the place. Osman said he felt that if the Washoes simply understood the spiritual significance of the place to climbers, some form of accommodation might be reached.[48]

While the discussions regarding how best to manage Cave Rock continued and the temporary closure came to an end, Osman continued his thrill-seeking jumps, to deadly effect. In October 1998, after the end of the temporary closure, Osman planned a jump in Yosemite National Park. After setting up his gear, he was delayed by two weeks in jail for failure to pay fines related to several vehicle violations. Fearing the Forest Service might confiscate his equipment, Osman returned to Yosemite upon release and impulsively altered his setup to push his jump to more than one thousand feet. This last-minute change caused part of the apparatus to snap, and Osman fell to his death in November 1998. Five days later, two hundred people gathered to spread his ashes over Cave Rock and Lake Tahoe, where he had pioneered some of the most difficult climbing routes in North America.[49]

FOREST SERVICE MANAGEMENT OF CAVE ROCK

Until December 1994, no one was entirely sure who was in charge of Cave Rock. The Nevada Department of Transportation and the Nevada State Parks Department each had management responsibilities in the vicinity. Some thought that crucial portions of Cave Rock were privately owned. Though inquiries in December 1994 indicated that Cave Rock was under Forest Service jurisdiction, this was not confirmed until a title search was completed in 1998.[50]

Partially in response to Executive Orders 13,006 and 13,007, which called for further protections for historic sites, traditional cultural properties, and sacred sites and for land management by government agencies to avoid adverse impacts on Indian sacred sites, the Forest Service began to develop a plan for managing Cave Rock under its newly discovered managerial duties. Brian Wallace, chairman of the Washoe Tribe of Nevada and California, reiterated the significance of Cave Rock to traditional Washoe religion and ongoing Washoe objections to the continuing adverse impacts to Cave Rock, including but not limited to rock climbing. As part of this process, the Forest Service determined that Cave Rock could be nominated to the National Register of Historic Places.[51]

In 1997 Robert Harris, the outgoing forest supervisor for the Lake Tahoe Basin Management Unit, who had begun his work at the Forest Service as an engineer, issued an order temporarily closing Cave Rock to climbing. The closure was to be in place for the minimum time necessary to develop a comprehensive plan for managing Cave Rock. The closure was met with immediate protest. In February of that year, Dan Osman met with climbers to organize their opposition. The Access Fund, an organization that lobbies and initiates lawsuits on behalf of maintaining access to public sites for climbers, immediately contacted the new forest supervisor, Juan Palma. The Access Fund threatened the Forest Service with a lawsuit if the ban was not lifted.[52]

To step up its campaign to protect climbers' access to Cave Rock, the Access Fund attacked the Washoe people directly in an editorial in its newsletter, but the Access Fund met with resistance from its own membership. Attempting to portray climbers as victims, the newsletter piece called the Washoes selfish and accused them of picking on climbers. Powerful, selfish Indians were creating false religious claims to deny climbers their rights, the Access Fund tried to assert. This ploy to spread ignorance and hate to further a political agenda was met head-on by resistance from members of the Access Fund itself. The climbing community by 1997 had a strong leave-no-trace contingent. Like-minded members of the Access Fund denounced the fund's anti-Washoe editorial, called claims that climbers were powerless victims of Indian plots "ludicrous," and noted that the Indian communities of the United States had been brutally mistreated by U.S. policies for centuries. Some quit the Access Fund over the newsletter editorial. Others condemned the comments as "imperialist garbage."[53]

Despite opposition to the demonizing of the Washoe from within its own ranks, the Access Fund was still able to get the climbing ban lifted, well before any management plan could be devised. The Access Fund flooded the Forest Service with negative comments and appealed the closure order to the Western Regional Office of the Forest Service. Access Fund attorneys contacted the Forest Service and threatened a lawsuit if the involuntary ban on climbing was not immediately lifted. In their communications, Access Fund attorneys relied upon dicta from the Bear's Lodge case. Unrelated to that case, the court had opined that a hypothetical mandatory closure to protect religious interests might not comport with the Establishment Clause of the Constitution. To avoid a lawsuit, the Forest Service removed the mandatory climbing ban after just three months.[54]

In the meantime, the Washoe continued to press the U.S. government to improve their economic and cultural conditions. In 1997 President Bill Clinton hosted the Lake Tahoe Summit in an effort to keep Lake Tahoe and the surrounding area environmentally healthy and economically thriving. Washoe chairman Brian Wallace argued for the inclusion in the summit of the Washoe people, as the historic guardians of Lake Tahoe and the surrounding region. At the summit, Wallace and Clinton came to an understanding: the president would support a Washoe bid to manage the Meeks Bay Resort and Marina. Ultimately the Forest Service issued a twenty-year special-use permit for the Washoes to manage the area, after the normal bidding process. Forest Supervisor Palma finalized the order in 1997.[55]

Once the complete climbing ban was lifted, Palma had to institute an interim management plan until a final plan could be formulated. Palma's interim plan called for a ban on all new safety bolt placements in Cave Rock. In addition, climbers would be encouraged to voluntarily abstain from climbing out of respect for the Washoes.[56]

Those looking to maintain climbing access to Cave Rock challenged the Forest Service judgment that Cave Rock could be placed on the National Register as a traditional cultural property. They claimed that the tunnels had destroyed the value of Cave Rock as a traditional cultural property and that even if Cave Rock was a traditional cultural property, rock climbing did not adversely impact it. In 1998 the National Register determined that Cave Rock was a traditional cultural property and that rock climbing was adversely impacting it. In addition, Cave Rock was eligible for listing as a historic transportation district since roadways from four distinct engineering periods of U.S. transportation history were present in and about Cave Rock. Crucial to the eligibility of Cave Rock as a traditional cultural property were the historic activities of Henry Rupert and the cultural and religious significance of Cave Rock to the Washoe people.[57]

CONSULTATION

Early in 1998, Palma organized the mandatory consultation process as a way to bridge the gap between the Washoe people and the climbing community. Palma had a business management degree from Oregon State University and a master's degree in environmental sciences from the University of Nevada. He had previously worked as a budget officer, administrative officer, district manager, and deputy forest supervisor. The Forest Service organized five meetings for members of the public, including climbers and the religious and political leadership of the Washoe community, from January to May. The Forest Service sought to use the initial meetings to gather information and facilitate discussion as part of the consultation process. Personally, Palma indicated that he felt the climbing community needed to be better educated as to the concerns of the Washoe people. The first of the consultation meeting was held on January 22, 1998, bringing climbers and Washoe people together to begin the search for some form of management compromise for Cave Rock. Twice as many people as expected attended, about evenly split between climbers and Washoes. Jean McNichols, a descendant of Henry Rupert and caretaker of Cave Rock, presented the central Washoe position: the Washoe opposed any recreational use of Cave Rock. Terry Lilienfield spoke for the climbers and tried to stress the respect for Cave Rock that climbers held. She stressed the willingness of the climbers to find common ground with the Washoes.[58]

This first consultative meeting ended in what the Forest Service viewed as a success. While Palma was not present until the third meeting, his goals for the first meeting were to introduce the participants to the collaborative process and to share perspectives among the interested groups. The meeting included small discussion groups where the participants focused on sharing their concerns and expressing their ideal outcome for Cave Rock.[59]

The second meeting was held on March 10 and continued the dialogue among the interested parties. It included a presentation by Forest Service archaeologist John Maher about the eligibility of Cave Rock for the National Register of Historic Places. Maher took the assembled participants through the reasons for Cave Rock's eligibility for inclusion on the National Register as a traditional cultural property and addressed the fact that rock climbing was an ongoing adverse impact that endangered the site's integrity. After Maher's presentation, those assembled broke into groups to answer questions as to why Cave Rock was special to different groups and the problems these groups might encounter under a new management plan[60]

The organization of the proceedings began to concern many Washoes at this point. Some participants noted that only one of the five questions addressed Washoe concerns, while the remaining four either covered the concerns and perspectives of climbers. The meeting summary delivered to participants did not alleviate these concerns. The summary omitted Maher's assessment of the negative impacts of climbing on the traditional cultural property and emphasized the willingness of climbers to compromise to almost any extent to retain access to Cave Rock. The summary also emphasized that climbers did not understand why they were being singled out for exclusion among the site's many recreational users. It ignored Maher's assertion that climbing threatened the integrity of Cave Rock—despite Maher's role as Forest Service archaeologist.[61]

In the midst of the collaborative process, the climbers met on their own on March 3, 1998, to formulate a compromise that they hoped might alleviate Washoe concerns. The climbers created a plan based upon the Bear's Lodge (Devils Tower) management plan. Their proposal called for greater climber responsibility in trash management, camouflaging existing safety positions, and signage that explained the importance of the area to the Washoes and asked people to be respectful. The climbers also planned to ask the creators of climbing paths to change the vulgar and offensive names. The plan called for urging climbers to voluntarily vacate Cave Rock during the most sensitive times, even though unlike Bear's Lodge, Cave Rock does not have a season when people visit for ceremonies. The climbers also agreed to leave when Washoes arrived to use places at the site, as long this happened fewer than six times a year. But if the Washoes began asking for privacy every day, the agreement would have to be reopened.[62]

When presented with this proposed compromise, Brian Wallace did not respond positively. He found the Bear's Lodge compromise to be a poor fit for Cave Rock. He noted that many groups found Bear's Lodge to be a sacred place, while only the Washoes saw Cave Rock as the center of their cosmology. Further, the proposed compromise did not acknowledge the crucial differences between Washoe religion and the traditions and beliefs underlying the compromise at Bear's Lodge. Many participated in ceremonies at Bear's Lodge that they preferred be conducted in private, while only shamans were permitted to visit Cave Rock. When confronted with the accusation that the climbers were willing to compromise and the Washoes were not, Wallace replied that 177 years of compromise were enough for the Washoes.[63]

The third collaborative meeting, on March 17, 1998, nearly saw the collapse of the process. Already unhappy that the framing of the process appeared to favor the climbers, the Washoes were further distressed when a display was created with the two most extreme positions at opposite ends: full access for the climbers, and full closure for the Washoes. This display was presented as starting points for finding some compromise between these positions. The Washoes felt that by asking everyone to find a compromise in the middle, the presentation was both calling for the Washoes to abandon their position and painting them as obstructionist. Matters took a turn for the worse when the next phase of the meeting was a Forest Service presentation of climbing techniques featuring pictures of climbers active on Cave Rock.[64]

During a break, the Washoes conferred as to whether or not they would simply walk out of the meeting. They requested equal time to present their views, and though it was not on the agenda, the Forest Service allowed Wallace to address the participants. With no time to prepare, Wallace was able to speak for twenty minutes. He explained that even talking of these matters was difficult for the Washoe people. He stressed their belief that Cave Rock was sacred and that there could be no way to partially honor the holy place. He stated that the Washoes felt it was unfair to ask them to compromise their cultural values. At the end of the meeting, the Forest Service polled the participants as to their feelings regarding continuing the process. All but one Washoe felt there was no point in meeting again for further discussion, while the climbers were more evenly split.[65]

Despite their concerns with the process, Wallace and others attended the fourth meeting, on April 9, where the Forest Service set out the goal of finding a creative solution. The climbers reiterated their goal of working with the Washoes to find some compromise. Chairman Wallace reiterated the Washoe position that they were happy to share ideas but that the importance of Cave Rock was such that no compromise was possible. Wallace gave voice to the emerging Washoe belief that the Washoes were being portrayed as uncompromising when they refused to agree to further destruction.[66]

While the Washoes again presented their position, the final collaborative meeting, on May 27, 1998, more highlighted the division within the climbing community. Washoe elder Ruth Abbie spoke of the Great Spirit giving this land to the Washoes and the government of the United States coming along, taking everything, and building tunnels through Cave Rock without even consulting the Washoes. She said she felt as if speaking during this process was as useful as speaking in the wind. Aaron Silverman, a climber from Reno, spoke in support of the Washoe position and stated that there were plenty of other climbing opportunities in the area. He had participated in the previous meetings and expressed his feeling that it was ridiculous to even consider recreational climbing to be worthy of opposing Washoe cultural concerns. Leaders from the climbing community were quick to disagree with Silverman and noted that the beauty near Lake Tahoe was unlike that of any other climbing opportunity and that the uniquely high difficulty ratings could be found nowhere else. Silverman's position represented the emerging influence of the leave-no-trace movement, and other climbers began to call for Cave Rock to be left to the Washoes. Despite the difficulties, Palma declared the process a success, as he had gathered a great deal of information regarding all the parties' positions and he would be able to make an informed decision.[67]

THE DRAFT ENVIRONMENTAL IMPACT STATEMENT

After the initial consultation process, interested parties kept lobbying Forest Supervisor Palma. Chairman Wallace wrote to reiterate many of the positions the Washoes had expressed at the collaborative meetings. Wallace added that many Washoes found it offensive that some climbers appeared to presume the right to climb Cave Rock while ignoring the much deeper connection the Washoes had had to Cave Rock for a much longer time. He also stated that recreational climbing was not like religion. An attorney for the Access Fund, Paul Minault, argued in a letter that the roads through Cave Rock had already completely desecrated the site, thus Washoe positions were unsupportable. He accused the Washoes of demonizing climbers and said the Washoes were merely claiming Cave Rock as a trophy of their resurgent power.[68]

With the continued input from interested parties, in January 1999 Palma issued a draft environmental impact statement with a preferred alternative that favored the position of the Access Fund. The preferred alternative was nearly identical to the compromise proposal of the climbers based on the voluntary management plan for climbing at Bear's Lodge. The draft EIS considered five alternatives that ranged from no action to exclusive Washoe use of Cave Rock, with two different plans to phase out rock climbing over several years. The preferred alternative limited and managed climbing in familiar ways. There were to be no new climbing routes and no new climbing bolts. Existing safety gear was to be camouflaged, and a small number of routes were to be eliminated, not for consideration of the Washoes but for the safety of the automobile traffic nearby. All proposed alternatives were to include an educational component, with signs and brochures about the cultural significance of Cave Rock.[69]

Early that year, Palma conducted further consultation and public comment meetings regarding the proposed action of the draft EIS. He met with Washoe chairman Wallace, the vice chair, the Washoe cultural resources coordinator, tribal council members, and twenty-five members of the Washoe public, ranging in age from eight to eighty. At the meetings, the Washoes expressed their displeasure with the proposed action. Palma conducted a further public comment meeting in February 1999, and twenty members of the public attended to discuss the preferred action management plan.[70]

The public comment period continued in written form, and while the Access Fund attorney wrote to express support for the preferred action of the Forest Service, many prominent commentators expressed their displeasure with the plan to merely limit climbing at Cave Rock. Don Kilma, writing for the Advisory Council on Historic Preservation, noted that the draft EIS itself acknowledged that climbing would have continued harmful impacts on the traditional cultural property. Kilma urged the Forest Service to protect the rock face from further damage by climbing, and he reminded the Forest Service that protecting a traditional cultural property was a secular purpose and would not be an unconstitutional establishment of religion. The Nevada State Historic Preservation Office complained that the continuation of climbing would damage the traditional cultural property of Cave Rock and expressed concerns for the cumulative effects of continued climbing. Former forest supervisor Robert Harris, who had initiated the previous temporary closure to climbing, wrote to object to the preferred action on several grounds. Harris said that the preferred alternative did not comply with the general forest plan's requirement to protect cultural sites; nor did it comply with the laws protecting heritage resources. Harris complained that the preferred alternative would have significant and cumulative adverse impacts on the cultural site by allowing climbing to continue, and he noted that similar climbing opportunities were readily available nearby.[71]

In addition to written comments from official sources, the Washoes and their allies complained of the proposal to allow the continuation of rock climbing. The Progressive Leadership Alliance of Nevada, a social justice coalition, wrote to complain that continued rock climbing would hurt the religious experience of Washoe people and noted that there were about 150 climbing areas in the vicinity of Lake Tahoe but that Cave Rock was the only place of central religious significance to the Washoes. Wallace reiterated Washoe complaints and added that the draft EIS was objectionable because joint management of Cave Rock by the Washoe government and the Forest Service was not considered.[72]

During this period of comments, in July 2000, Maribeth Gustafson became the new supervisor for the Lake Tahoe Basin Management Unit. Juan Palma had moved to a job with the Bureau of Land Management as a ranger in Oregon shortly after he had issued the draft EIS. Gustafson was a nineteen-year veteran of the Forest Service. She had graduated from San Diego State University in 1980 and had previously served as a resource officer, a district ranger, and an assistant forest manager.[73]

FINAL ENVIRONMENTAL IMPACT STATEMENT

Forest Supervisor Gustafson took her decisions regarding the completion of the final environmental impact statement seriously and brought a fresh set of eyes to the issues. Gustafson personally reviewed all the materials involved. In addition, she met with Washoe officials and religious leaders.[74] She issued the final EIS in October 2002 after considerable revision.

After Gustafson made her review, she totally changed direction from the previously preferred alternative. The final EIS included a new preferred alternative that was much closer to the Washoe position. This new, sixth alternative specifically focused on the protection of the historical and cultural character of Cave Rock. The final EIS noted that the top priorities of the Lake Tahoe Basin Management United forest plan were first to protect water quality, second to protect threatened and endangered species, and third to preserve significant cultural resources. The final EIS noted that the overall Forest Plan had a goal of enhancing traditional cultural properties and the plan made no mention of climbing (except with regards to limiting climbing to protect falcons). The new preferred alternative was to restore Cave Rock to its conditions at the end of 1965, well before climbing began.[75]

The final EIS explained that Cave Rock would be restored to conditions of 1965 because that was the year Washoe shaman Henry Rupert had died. The statement identified Rupert's involvement in Cave Rock as being crucial in making the area a traditional cultural property. It noted Rupert's contributions to synthesizing new Washoe traditions and his significance in working with ethnographers, as well as his activities at Cave Rock.[76]

The final EIS proposed several immediate changes and management policies to restore Cave Rock to 1965 conditions. The Forest Service expressed the intention to remove the paved floor added by the late climber Dan Osman. The final EIS also called for an immediate closure of Cave Rock to all climbing and the removal of all climbing bolts. The Forest Service would also undertake remedial efforts to restore the rock face and remove all graffiti in the cave and tunnels made after 1965. There would be further restrictions on any activities not consistent with the site prior to 1965.[77]

APPEALS PROCESS

While the final EIS called for an immediate ban on climbing and remedial efforts, the implementation of the new preferred alternative was delayed for another five years by appeals. Climber Terry Lilienfield and the Access Fund immediately appealed Gustafson's decision. On November 5, 2003, Deputy Regional Forester Kent P. Connaughton upheld the decision. At that point, Lilienfield abandoned any further appeals, but the Access Fund took the appeal to the federal district court at Reno. On January 8, 2005, Judge Howard McKibben issued his ruling from the bench, stating that while he may have not have made the same decision, all laws and policies had been complied with and that the decision by Forest Supervisor Gustafson comported with the First Amendment.[78]

The Access Fund continued its fight to the Ninth Circuit Court of Appeals and met with no success at the last court to consider the case. The appeals in this case were based upon motions for summary judgment, with no additional evidence presented at the trial court. The Access Fund challenged the new management plan for Cave Rock on the grounds that the Forest Service was unconstitutionally establishing the Washoe religion by banning all climbing to protect a place of religious importance to the Washoes. The argument of the Access Fund relied heavily on dicta of cases from Rainbow Bridge and Bear's Lodge that opined that permanent involuntary closures of sites to accommodate religion might not be in compliance with the Establishment Clause of the First Amendment. In cases involving summary judgment, the court revisits the issue using its own judgment, considering the facts in the best possible light to the losing party, here the Access Fund.[79]

While all three judges of the panel concurred in the outcome, Judge M. Margaret McKeown wrote the opinion for the majority. There she engaged in a detailed analysis of the claim that the management plan established religion. McKeown first noted that the standards of the United States Supreme Court had become muddled in recent years and that the Supreme Court rarely engaged in any significant entanglement analysis at that time. Despite this lack of coherence by the top court, the Ninth Circuit engaged in a modified *Lemon* test, examining the purpose and effect of the government action while giving some consideration to the issue of entanglement of government in religious affairs.[80]

McKeown first determined that the climbing ban at Cave Rock had a secular purpose. She noted that Cave Rock was a cultural, historical, and archaeological monument, eligible for listing on the National Register of Historic Places. This eligibility, she continued, was not based on religion but on the historic and ethnographic records, which just happened to also have religious components. Climbing impacts the eligibility of Cave Rock for such listing, and thus there was a secular purpose for the ban. McKeown went on to note that there was a long history of government action protecting places of cultural and historic value that were also religious sites, including the National Cathedral in Washington, D.C., the Touro Synagogue in Rhode Island (the oldest standing synagogue in the United States, established in 1763), and the Sixteenth Street Baptist Church in Birmingham, Alabama.[81]

McKeown then examined the effect of the management plan and again found no violation of the Establishment Clause. Here McKeown examined whether or not the effect of the plan was to send a message of religious endorsement or disapproval. In coming to her conclusion, she noted that the final management plan contained a wide range of activities that were religiously offensive to practitioners of traditional Washoe religion and that the Washoes consistently expressed that their preferred outcome was to close Cave Rock to all recreational visitors, not merely to ban climbing. McKeown found there to be no "specter of favor" and noted that a benefit to a particular religious perspective was not an endorsement of that religion.[82]

McKeown briefly addressed the issue of entanglement, finding none, and spent more of her analysis addressing the arguments of the Access Fund that relied upon dicta from the Rainbow Bridge and Bear's Lodge cases. As to government entanglement with religion, McKeown commented that the Forest Service simply carrying out its traditional oversight responsibilities did not constitute entanglement. The Access Fund had stressed the arguments of Judge William F. Downes, from his preliminary injunction against the initial ban on climbing in June at Bear's Lodge, and highlighted dicta of the Tenth Circuit Court of Appeals with regard to the Navajo desire to ban all tourists from Rainbow Bridge. While noting that these cases were outside the Ninth Circuit, having merely persuasive value, and the opinions expressed were contained in nonbinding dicta, further diminishing their relevance, McKeown distinguished the situations. The climbing ban in the case of Cave Rock was to protect a culturally and historically significant site, while the hypothetical bans at Rainbow Bridge and Bear's Lodge would have been to protect the religious solitude of those engaging in worship.[83]

In response to the confusion created by the Supreme Court with *Van Orden v. Perry*, Judge J. Clifford Wallace concurred in the decision of the majority, but he would have used a different rationale. *Van Orden* was a confused Supreme Court opinion in which a majority of the court agreed that a monument on the Texas State Capitol grounds containing a version of the Ten Commandments, including both Christian and Jewish iconography, did not violate the First Amendment prohibition on the establishment of religion, but a majority could not agree on the analysis to be used. While some in the Supreme Court would still use a version of the *Lemon* test, similar to that used by McKeown, Wallace wrote that the better course was to use the test used by the largest group in the *Van Orden* plurality. This test considers two separate components or faces. One is the nature of the nation's history and the other the nature of the monument. Wallace found that here Cave

Rock had both historical and religious significance, as some of the justices had claimed the Ten Commandments had in Texas. As Cave Rock has both cultural and historic value, as well as religious value, protecting it from the adverse effects of climbing comported with the requirements of the First Amendment.[84]

The Forest Service began the rehabilitation of Cave Rock, once it secured the necessary funds, in 2009. That year, the recovery began in earnest with the removal of the climbing bolts and their metal sleeves. Workers then filled in the holes to restore the rock face. One worker noted that some of the bolt holes contained water that would have quickly destroyed the surface of Cave Rock. A six-person crew using jackhammers took four and a half days to remove the paved floor that climber Dan Osman had put in. They removed thirteen thousand pounds of debris. A worker who was a former climber himself noted that a vast majority of the climbers he encountered were happy for the Washoes.[85]

MEANING AND IMPACT

The case of Cave Rock and the Washoes demonstrates both the strengths and the weaknesses of a consultation process when used by administrators without a preconceived agenda. The Forest Service became aware of the dangers that rock climbing posed to the integrity of Cave Rock and brought the Washoes together with climbers to learn from one another and try to formulate a compromise. The process adopted by Forest Supervisor Palma educated not only Forest Service officials as to the interests and feelings of the Washoes but also the climbing community. Rather than treating the consultation process as a formality to comply with, the administrators of the Lake Tahoe area purposefully used the process to bring people together and promote understanding. While at times contentious, the process facilitated dialogue and education.

The educated climbing community proved to be an important ally of the Washoes in public discussions regarding access to Cave Rock. The initial inclination of Access Fund leaders was to play on public ignorance of the history of Indian affairs and concerns and to demonize the Washoes as selfish. This was quickly met by opposition within the climbing community, forcing the Access Fund to portray the Forest Service as the enemy in the case. By the end of the consultation process, other climbers came to side with the Washoes in calling for Cave Rock to be left to them.

The resulting court case again affirmed the wide discretion of federal administrators in formulating policy for the management of Indian sacred sites. Previous cases had considered hypothetical closures of public lands to protect Indian sacred sites. These cases did not engage in full Establishment Clause analysis, but the judges speculated that mandatory closures of public lands to climbing would establish religion. Here the appellate court determined that protecting the integrity of sites of traditional and cultural significance to Indians that are also sacred sites was a legitimate secular purpose of government, noting that both Christian and Jewish religious places had been protected and managed for some time by the federal government.

The Cave Rock record demonstrates just how narrow the Washoe victory was. Forest Supervisor Palma appeared to indicate that he would have approved the management plan based on the Bear's Lodge ban on new climbing routes. But Palma was replaced by Gustafson just before the final decision on the climbing management plan needed to be made. Gustafson reviewed the record and decided to alter the proposed plan significantly, with a total ban on climbing as the most effective method for protecting and managing the traditional cultural property. The plan did leave Cave Rock open to uses such as hiking, which the Washoes were not entirely happy with. In history, events happen only once, so it is mere speculation, but had Palma stayed in his position just a little longer, the outcome here may have been very different. Provided there is consultation, administrators have wide discretion to desecrate or to protect.

4 BADGER-TWO MEDICINE AND THE BLACKFEET NATION

In the early twenty-first century, managers of Lewis and Clark National Forest in Montana identified a need for a new plan to manage both off-road and road-traveling motor vehicles. The Forest Service brought the neighboring Blackfeet Nation into the required consultation process, and administrators quickly learned that they were woefully unaware of existing Blackfeet treaty rights and religious interests in the Badger-Two Medicine portion of the forest. Rather than delay the entire project or rush decision-making, the Forest Service separated the planning process for Badger-Two Medicine for further consultation in 2007.

Initially the Forest Service was inclined to ban all motor vehicle travel from Badger-Two Medicine, but additional consultation with the Blackfeet modified the plan. While the Blackfeet wanted to protect the solitude of Badger-Two Medicine, like many non-Native hikers and horseback riders, the Blackfeet had other interests beyond religious solitude. When in 1895 the Blackfeet parted with Badger-Two Medicine, they were rather unwilling sellers. Afraid the land would be taken if they did not sell, the Blackfeet ensured the retention of hunting, logging, and access rights in the treaty of sale. In 2007 the Blackfeet pushed to have a small number of motor vehicle roads left intact so that members could use the land for hunting and logging, and to provide better access to sacred sites for the elderly and disabled.

This case demonstrates the ability of the consultation process to deliver on Indian demands through its educational powers. Complicated by Indian treaty rights, the consultation process served as a mechanism to educate Forest Service administrators lacking a preconceived agenda and allowed for the full protection of Indian rights and interests in the management plan. The consultation process also allowed greater compromise and the building of intercultural community connections; the Blackfeet agreed to open up sections of the reservation to provide new recreational opportunities for snowmobile enthusiasts displaced by the closing of Badger-Two Medicine to off-road motor vehicle travel. A court challenge affirmed once again the wide discretion federal administrators have in crafting policies protecting Indian religious concerns and treaty rights.

BLACKFEET RELIGION

Traditional Blackfeet religion places humanity as part of a wider community that includes a myriad of other-than-human persons, including geographic locations. This larger family of persons encompasses animals, plants, rocks, land, natural processes, powerful deities, and the dead. The Blackfeet do not divide other-than-human persons, or *naahks*, into supernatural and natural categories. Because parts of the ecosystem are found among the family of naahks, many places are of sacred character. The Great Spirit, Great Mystery, or Good Power is omnipresent, giving every place and thing some form of sacred character.[1]

Old Man Na'api and Old Woman, two other-than-human persons in the Blackfeet family, appear in many significant religious stories of the Blackfeet, such as the story of the creation of humanity and the story of Blackfeet lands. Na'api and Old Woman emerged to create humanity out of mud. Old Man set the boundaries of Blackfeet lands and warned the people that trouble would come to them if they let others trespass or invade. Some Blackfeet believe that commercial encroachment can profane the sacred nature of their lands.[2]

The Blackfeet are a people of the Sun Dance, which is central to their religious practices. The son of Feather Woman and Morning Star was first known as Star Boy. For a transgression of his mother, Star Boy was exiled to Earth with a scarred face; he then became known as Poia. The girl Poia loved rejected him because of his scarred face. But Poia did the first Sun Dance and healed his body, winning the affection of the girl. Then Poia shared the Sun Dance with the Blackfeet to restore health to the people. The Blackfeet do the annual Sun Dance in his honor and to restore health.[3]

The Sun Dance, together with the medicine lodge, are key religious practices of the Blackfeet, requiring seclusion in the wilderness. Central to these practices are dreams induced after days of fasting. For the most fervent, the fasting and subsequent dreaming induced by the Sun Dance and medicine lodge must be performed in isolated wilderness settings.[4]

Many religious Blackfeet sites are found in and around their traditional homelands, of which the contemporary Blackfeet Reservation makes up only a small portion. The Blackfeet call the Rocky Mountains the "Backbone of the World." The Backbone of the World once was the western edge of Blackfeet territory. The wilderness area on the edge of the mountains, Badger-Two Medicine, is home to many deities, including Cold Maker, Wind Maker, Medicine Elk, Medicine Wolf, and Medicine Grizzly. Today the lands of Badger-Two Medicine, seen as one territory by the Blackfeet, are controlled by the U.S. Forest Service and the National Park Service; these lands have been arbitrarily divided between the two agencies by a highway. Much of the territory remained wilderness into the early twenty-first century and was the location of many significant religious happenings involving naahks. The Blackfeet named the places of the region after Poia, Morning Star, Sett Pine, and other nonhuman persons. These sites and their names were of such significance to the Blackfeet that they protested the renaming of sacred places in 1915.[5]

One of the religious stories of Badger-Two Medicine involves the sacred origin of the birch tree. Careless Na'api's food was stolen by Bobcat. The angered Na'api blamed his nose for failing to warn him about Bobcat's presence and burned it. Anguished, he called upon Cold Wind to soothe his pain, but the wind was so strong that Na'api was almost blown away. He was saved by a birch tree. Grateful for the tree's assistance, Na'api gave the birch adornments and made it the most beautiful of all trees.[6]

A tale of assistance by other-than-human persons explains why Badger-Two Medicine is a sanctuary for wolves. The Crow Indian Nation captured a Blackfeet woman by the name of Itsapichpaupe. The Crows took her hundreds of miles away, but a kindly Crow woman helped Itsapichpaupe escape so she could return home. Exhausted after the long journey, she met Wolf in Badger-Two Medicine and asked for his pity and aid. Moved by the Blackfeet woman's plight, Wolf helped carry Itsapichpaupe home. The Blackfeet have since had a prohibition against killing wolves and believe that any gun used to shoot a wolf will never shoot straight again.[7]

Perhaps of even more consequence to the survival of the people, Badger-Two Medicine is the source of all romance among the Blackfeet. Long ago, camps of women and men lived apart but visited for mating. On one occasion, the chief of women was not looking her best. She chose Na'api, but he rejected her because other comelier ladies were available. The angry chief of women told the other women what happened, and they agreed that no one would go with Na'api. The chief of women then returned to him, after cleaning up and looking her best. Na'api became quite interested in the chief of women, but she and all the other women rejected him. Na'api became quite angry because no one would mate with him. So the chief of women turned Na'api into a pine tree at the edge of the plains, where the mountains begin. The Blackfeet believe that the undisturbed natural beauty of this place, located in Badger-Two Medicine, keeps all Blackfeet romance alive.[8]

HISTORY OF THE BLACKFEET NATION

The Blackfeet Nation is composed of three bands, once united by a common language and religion but now divided by the border between the United States and Canada. The Kianaas, Piikanis, and Siksikas are alternatively known by the English versions of their names: the Bloods, Muddy River Indians, and Black-footed People. The entire nation came to be known by the name of the Siksika band: the Black-footed People. After their permanent division into Canadian and U.S. segments, the northern group came to be called the Blackfoot Nation while the segment in the United States became the Blackfeet Nation.[9]

Blessed with a favorable strategic position, the Black-footed People hunted buffalo over a large territory reaching from what is now Canada to the middle of the contemporary United States. The Backbone of the World, the Rocky Mountains, served as the western boundary of Blackfeet territory. To the east, the Blackfeet were bordered by several Indian nations deeply hostile to European expansion, which provided the Blackfeet with a buffer against non-Indian incursions. The Blackfeet freely traveled from the central United States to Canada as one nation until after 1870, when the Blackfeet/Blackfoot, U.S./Canadian division became permanent.[10]

In the 1670s, as French traders encroached upon the Hudson Bay region, the Blackfeet experienced their first taste of globalization. Trading with their Indian neighbors, the Blackfeet quickly obtained European manufactured tools and weapons in this period of indirect trade. Obtaining horses through the Nez Perce Indians, the Blackfeet were convinced by them that horses were creatures that had emerged from the water. Before 1750, the Blackfeet fully integrated horses, guns,

European tools, and other goods obtained in trade with their Indian neighbors. Horses and European weapons were integral in buffalo hunting and war. By 1750 the Blackfeet economy was dependent on the international trade of European goods. The Blackfeet used European pots, kettles, and other manufactured metal goods in daily life. To remain effective, their military relied on the international arms trade.[11]

After 1750 the Blackfeet began to engage in direct trade with European powers, and the next hundred years tended to be a prosperous time. From 1750 to 1850 the Blackfeet had no formal diplomatic relations with any European powers (or their successor states). No missionaries or settlers tried to penetrate Blackfeet territory, and the Blackfeet had no need of European treaties. Fur traders actively discouraged both missionaries and settlers, since these groups hurt the fur trade with Indian nations.[12]

European demand for beaver pelts increased, and while some nations neighboring the Blackfeet altered their economic patterns to accommodate this demand, the Blackfeet largely did not alter their economy. The Blackfeet economy remained centered on the buffalo hunt, and their society was more stable than that of their neighbors. The Crees and Assiniboines altered their economies to produce more beaver pelts for French trade. But this proved highly disruptive to Cree and Assiniboine social life. By contrast, the Blackfeet did not alter their economy to supply the growing European demand for beaver pelts. Instead the Blackfeet allowed the Crees and Assiniboines to hunt beaver in Blackfeet territory. In this period of direct trade with European powers, the Blackfeet exported buffalo coats, pemmican, and, to a lesser extent, wolf skins. In return, the Blackfeet imported kettles, guns, ammunition, and other metal tools.[13]

During the period of direct trade, the Blackfeet remained healthy and prosperous. They expertly managed the buffalo hunt, never engaged in overhunting, and could have maintained their economy indefinitely if not for European encroachment and the subsequent reduction of their hunting lands. Since they were buffalo hunters, their ample diet largely consisted of meat. With their economy centered on the buffalo, the Blackfeet were often able to avoid the worst impacts of European diseases, as they would quickly scatter into small groups at the first sign of illness. Though this practice usually mitigated the impacts of plagues, the Blackfeet were still devastated by a smallpox epidemic in 1781.[14]

The Blackfeet were often at war with their neighbors and were intolerant of whites who tried to make claims on their lands. They raided neighbors for horses—first adjacent Indian nations and later Canadian and American towns.

The Blackfeet also took female captives as part of their warfare. Due to a mix of losses suffered in war and female captives, Blackfeet society tended to have a ratio of four women to every three men.[15]

Conditions changed quickly for the Blackfeet in the decades after they established diplomatic contact with the United States and Canada in 1850. The Blackfeet entered into the Fort Laramie Treaty with the United States in 1851. Policy makers in the United States used the treaty to push the Blackfeet and their neighbors to become farmers, though the region was not favorable to the practice. An 1855 treaty with the United States formally defined the extent of Blackfeet territory and allowed the United States to place forts in these lands and to cross the nation with roads. The northern section of the Black-footed People did not enter into a formal treaty with the Canadian government until 1877.[16]

The continuing invasion of Canadian and American immigrants quickly tore apart traditional Blackfeet society. Bootleggers illegally exported alcohol to the Black-footed People in both Canada and the United States. These criminals encouraged Blackfeet people to steal horses to trade for alcohol. In January 1870, when Blackfeet society was already suffering the impacts of the alcohol trade, settlers retaliated violently, angered by the constant horse theft. Compounding the series of misfortunes, the Blackfeet were hit by another smallpox outbreak. Though the Blackfeet tried to peacefully reconcile, the U.S. military killed 173 Blackfeet (mostly women and children) at the January 23, 1870, Baker Massacre. In the face of this series of difficulties, the government and council of the Blackfeet Nation collapsed.[17]

Unlike many of his contemporaries, John Wood, the Indian agent for the U.S. government, took effective steps to help the Blackfeet recover from their difficulties. Wood supported the reconstitution of the Blackfeet Tribal Council and encouraged the Blackfeet to draw up laws to govern their shrinking territory. Wood also oversaw a significant reduction in crime on Blackfeet lands when he was finally able to suppress the illegal alcohol trade in 1876.[18]

In the face of continuing encroachment from settlers, the Blackfeet sent diplomats to the 1874 Cypress Hill Conference called by the Lakota Nation. The Lakotas intended to form a coalition of nations for coordinated military resistance to U.S. expansion. Conference attendees called for wiping out white people. In response to the call for unified military action, the Blackfeet withdrew from the conference.[19]

After the conference, the Lakotas and their allies engaged in a military campaign against the United States without the Blackfeet Nation, but the U.S. government made no differentiation between allies and enemies in response. After the Lakotas and their allies destroyed U.S. general George Armstrong Custer's forces at the Battle of the Little Bighorn, the United States uniformly banned breach-loading weapons for Indian nations, even those that had remained out of the conflict. Recognizing that the Blackfeet had remained at peace with the United States, Agent Wood did not enforce the ban in Blackfeet territory, and a steady supply of illegally imported rifles continued through Canada.[20]

With the ability to keep their weapons, the Blackfeet were able to continue hunting through the 1870s, but cattle ranchers began to aggressively usurp Blackfeet territory, further disrupting their already crippled economy. In 1864 gold fever and invading miners hit Montana. Throughout the 1860s and 1870s, settlers regularly attacked and killed Blackfeet without repercussions. In the 1870s, as mining towns became more developed, settler cattle ranching expanded heavily. Blackfeet hunting was further curtailed by the presence of ranches that invaded reservation territory. Canadian settlers permanently separated the northern and southern portions of the Black-footed People in 1877.[21]

In the face of pressure from ranchers and their constant conflict with the Blackfeet, the United States unilaterally expelled the Blackfeet from half of their treaty lands, further endangering the economic conditions of the Blackfeet people. Their economy was in shambles. Exports dwindled. Lands available to hunting were insufficient to support the people. Some Blackfeet had transitioned to cattle ranching, despite the U.S government's insistence that the Blackfeet become farmers. In 1882 the U.S. Congress cut funding for food support to the reservation. The result was food rationing, which was entirely inadequate. Contemporary prisoners of the Russian czar were allotted twice as much food as the Blackfeet were expected to live on. Major John Young, the new Indian agent for the Blackfeet reservation, resorted to appeals to private charity to try and meet the food needs of the Blackfeet people.[22]

The winter of 1883–84 was horrific. With their economy destroyed, the Blackfeet faced massive hunger. Conditions worsened as the Cree Indian Nation raided Blackfeet territory. Despite pleas to Washington for assistance, the winter was marked by famine and starvation. The few successful Blackfeet ranchers had their enterprises wiped out as the cattle were eaten to hold off starvation. Even with such drastic measures, five hundred Blackfeet starved to death before the end of the winter. Young resigned as Indian agent in protest over the continuing cruel conditions suffered by the Blackfeet. The U.S. government finally delivered emergency rations to prevent further starvation in 1885.[23]

With Blackfeet society shattered, Washington moved to push greater changes on the Blackfeet. As part of the policy of aggressive forced assimilation, the United States granted the Methodist Church jurisdiction over the reservation for religious conversion and schools, but the Methodists made no efforts to establish missions or schools there. Some Blackfeet children were removed to Catholic boarding schools, and there were several deaths in the first class. Fearing their children would die at such institutions, the Blackfeet successfully kept their children from the schools. As part of the related policy of allotment, the U.S. government, under pressure from ranchers, determined that 17.5 million acres of the Blackfeet Reservation was surplus land. It was sold for twenty-nine cents an acre. The Indian Claims Court would later rule that the land was worth eighty cents an acre. In 1891, 83 percent of Blackfeet depended on government rations for survival; in the same year, the railroad cut through the reduced Blackfeet Reservation.[24]

TREATY TRANSFER OF BADGER-TWO MEDICINE AND RETAINED RIGHTS

Throughout all these difficulties, the Backbone of the World and Badger-Two Medicine remained part of recognized Blackfeet territory. In 1895, however, with the Blackfeet again on the verge of starvation, the Bureau of Indian Affairs, on behalf of miners convinced that there was gold to be found, demanded further land concessions from the Blackfeet. Miners gave the name Mineral Strip to a large portion of the Blackfeet Reservation, including Badger-Two Medicine. The BIA united with the covetous miners and pushed the Blackfeet to sell the western portion of their reservation. At the time, Blackfeet funds were running out. The people were again on the verge of starvation.[25]

Despite fear of famine, negotiations over the latest land demands by the United States were contentious; the Blackfeet secured several conditions as part of the sale of their western territories. Backed into a corner, the Blackfeet felt it would be impossible to keep the miners away with the U.S. government demanding a sale on their behalf. Many Blackfeet feared another deadly famine without additional funds to obtain food. Yet the Blackfeet were reluctant to give up rights to religiously significant land. When U.S. negotiators complained of the Blackfeet reluctance, Little Dog replied that the Blackfeet did not ask the United States to sell its lands. Many were bitter about and wary of repeated U.S. violations of previous treaties. Ultimately the sale was approved, but on the conditions that the Blackfeet retained the right to hunt, fish, harvest lumber, and have continual access, so long as the areas remained public lands of the United States.[26]

Not long after the contentious land sale, prospectors quickly determined that there was no mineral wealth within what had been the western portion of the Blackfeet Reservation. Rather than return the land, the U.S. government combined the property with lands taken from the Flathead Indian Nation. In 1897 the U.S. government created the Lewis and Clark Forest Reserve.[27]

Before the beginning of the twentieth century, the Blackfeet economy partially revived when the U.S. government ended insistence that the Blackfeet become farmers. Perhaps because non-Indians surrounding the Blackfeet Reservation had created cattle ranches rather than farms, the U.S. government relented in its demands that the Blackfeet adopt farming as a necessary change to their national economy. As a result, some Blackfeet began to make a living as cattle ranchers on the reservation.[28]

In 1910 the United States violated the terms of the sale of the western lands when it began to deny the Blackfeet access to portions of Badger-Two Medicine. The U.S. government delivered portions of Badger-Two Medicine and the Lewis and Clark Forest Reserve to the National Park Service, creating Glacier National Park. The new park banned all hunting, except for a limited number of permits for whites. Park administrators also prevented Blackfeet access to the land. The Blackfeet immediately protested that they had given up only mineral rights and had retained access for hunting and other purposes. They ignored the orders of the National Park Service and continued to exercise their reserved rights. The Park Service began arresting Blackfeet exercising their treaty rights in 1912.[29]

While considerable lands had previously been sold as surplus, the U.S. government did not begin full-scale allotment of Blackfeet properties until 1911. As the land was parceled out to individual members of the Blackfeet Nation, the government declared another 156,000 acres to be surplus. This included the best grazing land in the remaining Blackfeet holdings, land connected to an expensive irrigation system that the BIA had required the Blackfeet pay for, and territory connected to considerable water rights. The Blackfeet immediately began to organize against the plans to sell off the most valuable portions of their remaining territory.[30]

With allotment, new political and economic divisions developed between full-blooded and mixed-blood Blackfeet. While technically referring to the relative racial mixture of Blackfeet genetic heritage, the distinction became more political and economic over time. Mixed-bloods were those oriented toward European ways and willing to leave behind traditions. More traditional, or full-blooded, Blackfeet often faced intimidation at the hands of whites; mixed-bloods were willing to work with whites. Some mixed-bloods worked with whites to obtain private sales of the best allotted lands. Full-bloods were the first to oppose the sale of the designated surplus.[31]

Divisions between the mixed- and full-blooded Blackfeet also represented growing economic divisions. With continued growth of the Blackfeet cattle industry, a small number of mixed-blood Blackfeet became quite wealthy. This newfound wealth eluded many. By 1915 less than 2 percent of the Blackfeet Nation owned more than 85 percent of all cattle. By contrast, the leading cause of death among full-blooded Blackfeet in 1914 was starvation. Full-blooded Blackfeet became the political voice of those left behind by the changing reservation economy.[32]

THE BLACKFEET TRIBAL BUSINESS COUNCIL

With their traditional government gone, a new Blackfeet organization emerged to become the de facto government of the nation: the Blackfeet Tribal Business Council. The BTBC was founded in 1915 to lobby on behalf of the growing Blackfeet business interests. The group pressed the BIA for higher grazing lease rates on communally held lands. In December 1915, the BTBC came to agree with the full-bloods that the sale of lands designated as surplus would be a further economic blow to their already struggling economy. The council leadership voted to oppose selling. In 1922 the BTBC adopted a charter that provided every enrolled member of the Blackfeet Nation the right to vote for council members. The political and economic conflicts continued between the full- and mixed-blood segments of the Blackfeet people, but now these conflicts played out in contested elections for representation on the BTBC.[33]

Throughout the 1910s and 1920s, the BTBC was in constant conflict with the BIA, which held considerable power over economic matters on the Blackfeet Reservation. Oil exploration and development quickly became lucrative in Montana, and the BTBC pressed for oil leases to obtain new revenues for tribal members. The BIA favored providing leases to individual allottees, at the expense of collective tribal economic interests. The BIA then renewed the push for agricultural development, despite the repeated failure of past attempts. The BTBC pressed to have higher grazing rates on tribal-owned lands and a tribal herd for collective income. The BIA generally opposed attempts at collective industry, even preventing the opening of a Blackfeet store that the BTBC hoped would eliminate the price gouging members faced at white-owned businesses. The BIA prevented the council from borrowing on tribal assets to gain credit to create a Blackfeet oil well. The most significant success of the BTBC's first decade was the opposition to selling lands the government designated as surplus.[34]

As the Blackfeet clashed with the BIA over economic affairs, the Blackfeet continued to skirmish with the National Park Service over treaty and land rights.

In 1919, after a harsh winter posed a significant setback to the nascent Blackfeet cattle industry, the Park Service pressed to take more land from the Blackfeet. The Park Service wanted the BIA to stop parceling out individual allotments so that it could buy Blackfeet lands on the border with Glacier National Park in one purchase from the BIA. The Park Service sought to push the growing Blackfeet cattle industry farther from Glacier National Park, where cattle occasionally wandered. For their part, the Blackfeet exercised their treaty rights, in violation of Park Service regulations, and continued to hunt and fish as they pleased, though faced with continued arrests by Park Service officials. The Blackfeet presented petitions demanding recognition of their reserved rights. Little Chief explained the Blackfeet position: "We sold to the U.S. government nothing but rocks only. We still control the timber, grass, water, and all the big or small game or all the animals living in this [sic] mountains." When the National Park Service asked the BIA the extent of the rights retained by the Blackfeet, the bureau reported that the Blackfeet had no retained rights to the lands in Glacier National Park.[35]

Expanding tourism at Glacier offered no relief to the Blackfeet. The park began leasing lands to the Great Northern Hotel in 1929. The hotel hired a small number of Blackfeet to use as props in a tourist attraction (an exhibit of the soon-to-be-extinct Blackfeet Indians) but otherwise relegated Blackfeet to menial, out-of-sight jobs. The Blackfeet continued to exercise their rights in Glacier National Park, and the Park Service continued to arrest them for violations into the 1930s.[36]

In the two decades before the Great Depression, BIA management of the Blackfeet Reservation was a parade of corruption, incompetence, and malfeasance. Betraying any pretense to managing Blackfeet property for the improvement of the Blackfeet people, the agency administered affairs for the benefit of local whites and the bureaucrats themselves. Two hundred thousand acres of the best allotted Blackfeet lands were lost to whites before 1929 by duplicitous manipulation. Blackfeet were at times forced to take private title against their will and were then pressured to sell the land to whites. Collusion between Indian agents, clerks, and whites coveting Blackfeet land resulted in practices such as fraud and debt manipulation to force allottees into selling. The land the Blackfeet kept in collective ownership was similarly managed for the benefit of local white businesses. Retained Blackfeet lands were among the best for grazing cattle in Montana; the agency charged well-below-market rates for grazing leases to white ranchers.[37]

Blackfeet funds were rarely used for the benefit of the people. The Blackfeet Agency spent a large portion of assets on buildings and agency automobiles. The agency paid local white businesses more than $1 million for shoddy workmanship for an irrigation project on land unsuitable for farming. The agent in charge of the Blackfeet Reservation personified both the incompetence and the corruption of this management when he could not tell congressional investigators how many of his own sheep were grazing on Blackfeet lands. He was only able to guess that the number was between fifteen hundred and eight thousand.[38]

In the face of agency mismanagement and corruption, Joseph Brown emerged as the Blackfeet Tribal Business Council leader. He pushed for greater Blackfeet control and involvement in managing economic resources. Brown was a successful rancher and politician. His formal education had ended in eighth grade, but he hired tutors once he was a successful businessman. As part of his interests in continued education, Brown was an elected member of the Glacier County School Board. The Blackfeet, bitter over constant mismanagement and the irrigation project specifically, pushed for more power over their financial resources. The BTBC tried to negotiate oil leases in the 1930s, but the agency refused to approve them, favoring leases for individual allottees. The council pushed for better terms on the oil leases they could get approved, but this was met by conspiracy among oil companies, who refused to do business with the Blackfeet. Brown pushed for tribal management of the irrigation project, and the use of Blackfeet workers in the project and at local BIA offices. The BTBC sought to create a national Blackfeet oil company and cattle herd. While the local Indian agent preferred pushing allotment in the early 1930s, as opposed to collective Blackfeet projects, the council obtained greater input in business issues.[39]

THE INDIAN REORGANIZATION ACT

When John Collier promoted the Indian Reorganization Act in 1934, the Blackfeet were among the most active in debating the provisions and making recommendations for modifications. Blackfeet leaders participated in hearings and discussions on the proposed law in Rapid City, South Dakota. The suggestion that the Blackfeet could take over BIA functions was highly popular among all Blackfeet, as long as the reservation remained protected from state laws and taxes. The Blackfeet split over the proposal of recollectivization of allotted lands, as some Blackfeet businessmen wanted to keep their private holdings. These Blackfeet complaints induced Collier to make the recollectivization portions of the act voluntary.[40]

Most Blackfeet were highly supportive of the Indian Reorganization Act, and Blackfeet leaders pressed Congress to support the proposed law. Leaders spoke before congressional committees on the incompetence and corruption they faced with BIA mismanagement and argued in favor of the bill. Joe Brown confronted the ugly racism of arrogant members of Congress who accused him of not understanding the proposed law.[41]

Collier's proposal had language supporting Indian self-determination, provisions for Indian courts, and support for higher education opportunities. Congress stripped all these provisions from the bill and changed the educational focus to vocational training. Congress eliminated the proposal for development grants, changing them into loans, but it did increase money for a revolving credit fund intended for promoting Indian businesses created by the law.[42]

Eager to end decades of mismanagement with more control over their economic and political affairs, and craving access to credit for business development, the Blackfeet favored even the weakened version of the bill. The final version of the IRA disappointed Blackfeet leaders, but even with its deficiencies, the Blackfeet overwhelmingly supported the law.[43]

Before and after passage of the Indian Reorganization Act, the Blackfeet Tribal Business Council, serving as the de facto government of the Blackfeet for more than a decade, was the focal point for Blackfeet debate. Of key concern to many was the IRA provision that the United States recognize Indian governments organized under the new law. These new governments could then access the development assistance of the act. Traditionally, Blackfeet society had been much more decentralized, and some distrusted the central authority of the BTBC. The majority of those aligned with the full-blooded Blackfeet wanted restoration of the traditional tribal council. However, in the course of the debates, a consensus emerged. It favored a centralized government based upon the Blackfeet Tribal Business Council.[44]

Immediately the Blackfeet began to test the limits of sovereignty they could exercise under the reorganized relations with the BIA. The Blackfeet proposed a constitution with clear provisions stating that the BIA and Department of Interior had no power to supervise BTBC decisions. The bureau agent's protests proved futile. The Blackfeet also retained the right to determine their own membership standards in the new constitution. It also contained provisions allowing the Blackfeet to end supervision of their affairs. During the debates over adoption of the IRA and the new Blackfeet constitution, Glacier National Park urged the BIA to deliver it more lands. Reorganized relations with Indian nations meant that such deals required Blackfeet consent, and Joe Brown rejected the sale, stating, "I would rather be a respected citizen of my people than to be a dog in the Indian service."[45]

With the implementation of the IRA, the Blackfeet Nation was able to better direct its economic development and provide much-needed economic growth to the reservation. The first BTBC elections under the new constitution took place in

1936, with 85 percent turnout. The BTBC quickly took over many governmental functions, including resource management, appointing game wardens, and creating courts. BTBC management revitalized ranching. Many took advantage of the new IRA revolving credit fund. Traditional women organized sewing groups, with IRA credit, to create homemade goods for the tourist trade. The BTBC started several construction projects, including a sawmill in 1937.[46]

Even with these initial successes, the Blackfeet Nation continued to be divided along economic class lines and the balance between long-term investment and the short-term survival of its poorest members. The continuing full-blood/mixed-blood divisions among the Blackfeet remained largely economic. Unlike other reservations, Blackfeet lands were not marred by mixed-blood-driven cultural repression targeting more traditional Indians. Those most economically suffering, and their traditional allies, participated in the BTBC electoral process. The Blackfeet Indian Welfare Association (BIWA), a political organization primarily concerned with the short-term survival of the poorest, put forward a slate of candidates in 1938 and largely swept the elections. Mae Aubrey was among the BIWA candidates and was the first woman elected to the BTBC.[47]

As political fortunes shifted in Washington, the Blackfeet worked for greater autonomy, even while Congress sought to meddle more in Indian affairs. In 1945 the Blackfeet were the first Native group to point out the needless administrative duplication of the BIA. They called for a full withdrawal of the BIA from Indian governance. In stark contrast, the 1949 Congress placed statutory limitations on the amount of funds IRA governments could withdraw from their accounts, hindering BTBC development plans for the reservation. In 1950 the BTBC hired Felix Cohen, author of the *Handbook of Federal Indian Law*, as its legal adviser in continuing struggles with the BIA.[48]

Washington signaled the changing policy direction of Indian affairs by naming Dillon Myer Indian affairs commissioner in 1950. Myer had overseen Japanese internment during the Second World War and now brought to his administration the same disrespect of Indian rights as he had of the rights of U.S. citizens of Japanese ancestry. Myer encouraged placing Indian children in white foster homes. He would soon prove to be the most interventionist and repressive Indian commission since the nineteenth century, as he repeatedly moved against Blackfeet expressions of national sovereignty.[49]

Myer directly intervened to undermine the authority of the BTBC. In 1950 he turned to a group of traditional Blackfeet who felt the current BTBC policies were hurting their economic well-being. Myer had them propose, on his behalf, a series of amendments to the BTBC constitution that would have expanded BIA powers and BIA oversight of the council. Myer pushed for a referendum on these proposed amendments, even after the same traditional leaders entered into dialogue with the BTBC, asking for their proposal to be dropped.[50]

Working with Felix Cohen, the mixed-blood and full-blood factions of the Blackfeet people united in their opposition to BIA policies of forced Americanization and termination of tribal existence. Dillon Myer accused Cohen of being a communist, but an FBI investigation turned up nothing. While the U.S. government moved to terminate Indian governments in the 1950s, the Blackfeet and Cohen's other clients were never scheduled for governmental termination. In the midst of this growing conflict between the BIA and the BTBC, the courts awarded the Blackfeet Nation funds based on outstanding claims against the U.S. government, but the United States deducted the costs of several BIA buildings on the reservation from its payment. In retaliation, the BTBC seized the BIA buildings and expelled the BIA officials.[51]

In the meantime, the BTBC, in conversation with the full-blood opposition, created its own set of proposed amendments to the BTBC constitution. On May 9, 1952, the BIA and the BTBC each organized competing referendums. Then each denounced the other for conducting an illegal and unconstitutional referendum. In the face of the confusion, neither group garnered enough votes to be meet the turnout requirements to validly amend the Blackfeet constitution.[52]

As federal policies moved away from Indian self-determination, government and business interests increased their discrimination. Glacier National Park moved to eliminate all visible presence of the Blackfeet people from the park outside of Blackfeet-themed tourist attractions. Then Glacier reduced the number of Blackfeet employed in the tourist attractions. Locally, the Blackfeet commonly faced businesses with signs proclaiming that dogs and Indians would not be admitted or that Indians would not be served.[53]

Into the 1960s and 1970s, the Blackfeet continued to promote their economic and political interests, locally and nationally. In 1969 Blackfeet member Chief Old Person was elected president of the National Congress for American Indians, a leading Indian rights organization. In 1972 the Blackfeet opened the first pencil factory west of the Mississippi River and saw a shift as young people began to return to the reservation. That same year, Chief Old Person initiated discussions with Arizona State University to open Blackfeet Community College. Also in

1972, the Montana State Constitution was amended to include Article X, stating the educational goal of Montana to maintain Indian cultural integrity.[54]

Attempts to exercise rights reserved in Badger-Two Medicine and other lands sold in 1895 had dropped off in the 1950s and 1960s. In the 1970s, the Blackfeet renewed efforts to protect these reserved rights. In 1973 Blackfeet member Woodrow L. Kipp refused to pay the entrance fee to Glacier National Park. The Park Service cited him for this violation. Kipp challenged the citation in federal court. Referring to the rights reserved by the Blackfeet people in the 1895 sale agreement, Kipp won his challenge. The reserved rights of the Blackfeet were finally recognized by the U.S. government.[55]

Into the late 1970s and 1980s, the Blackfeet continued to take the lead in improving opportunities of themselves and all Indians. The Blackfeet founded the National Tribal Employment Rights Organization in 1977. This organization helped Indians find training opportunities and employment across the United States. In the 1980s, Blackfeet Community College grew and the Blackfeet managed the expansion of Head Start programs on the reservation.[56]

Throughout the latter part of the twentieth century, the BTBC made several cooperative agreements with the State of Montana. In 1965 the state negotiated a settlement of contentious water rights rather than litigate with its Indian neighbors as other states had. In 1981 Montana passed the State-Tribal Cooperative Act, paving the way for government-to-government agreements on collection of taxes and delivery of social services. By 1988, the BTBC had more than forty separate agreements with Montana, covering social services, taxes, and more.[57]

Despite the Blackfeet's improving relations with the state in the 1980s, the federal government moved to exploit oil resources in the sacred lands of Badger-Two Medicine. The Forest Service conducted an environmental assessment in 1981, enabling the Bureau of Land Management to issue oil and gas leases the following year. The environmental assessment declared that the proposed oil drilling would have no significant impact on the quiet and solitude necessary for Blackfeet religious practices; a schedule for drilling would be posted, and those performing religious ceremonies could move farther up the mountains to get away from disturbing sounds. The federal government issued several leases to energy companies, and drilling was approved to start in 1985.[58]

Public reaction to the leases put a hold on the drilling permits. The Blackfeet Nation and the public protested. The Blackfeet and others appealed the administrative decision to issue the permits, and these appeals delayed the beginning of drilling until 1993. In 1993 the secretary of the interior suspended the drilling permits, pending congressional action. In 2004 the Blackfeet Nation and Blackfoot Nation of Canada issued a joint statement reiterating the central importance of Badger-Two Medicine to practitioners of the traditional Blackfeet region.[59]

In response to the public outcry, Congress passed legislation to partially protect Badger-Two Medicine. Senator Max Baucus of Montana proposed legislation that would prohibit issuing any new oil or gas drilling leases for Badger-Two Medicine. Tax incentives were provided for companies giving up existing leases. Congress passed the proposed legislation as part of the Tax Relief and Health Care Act of 2006. Five companies took the offer and surrendered their drilling permits in 2010, but several others did not.[60]

The Solenex Company instead pressed its claims to one of the outstanding leases, despite continuing opposition by the Blackfeet and environmental groups. In 2013 Solenex sued the Interior Department to revive the stalled appeals process and act on its outstanding 1985 application for a drilling permit. Many Blackfeet, in alliance with several environmental groups, petitioned to intervene in the case. In 2014 they called for the Interior Department to cancel the lease, based in part on faulty conclusions of the original environmental assessment. In July 2015, Judge Richard Leon issued an order commanding the Department of the Interior to produce a timeline for all remaining portions of the administrative process. In response, the secretary of the interior, Sally Jewell, canceled the Solenex leases. The Mountain States Legal Foundation appealed on behalf of Solenex, but on March 17, 2016, the Bureau of Land Management also canceled the leases, determining that the Solenex lease violated the National Environmental Policy Act and the National Historic Preservation Act.[61]

Blackfeet leader Elouise Pepion Codell provided national leadership on a host of Indian economic issues, including the largest settlement of Indian claims by the U.S. government. Codell had revived the Blackfeet National Bank and expanded it into the Native American Bank Corporation. She had helped to create the Native American Community Development Corporation to facilitate the creation of new Indian businesses. In 1996 Codell had filed a lawsuit against the United States for failure to sufficiently manage and account for BIA trust accounts. This case was ultimately settled for $3.4 billion in 2010.[62]

In the twenty-first century, the Blackfeet have taken significant steps to protect and preserve the survival of their culture. In 2000 there were 27,104 enrolled members of the Blackfeet Nation. There were 85,750 people of Blackfeet ancestry;

1,356 people were then known to speak the Blackfeet language. In 2010 the Blackfeet language was taught in the public schools of Browning Montana, at Blackfeet Community College, and at private language immersion schools.[63]

EMERGENCE OF RECREATIONAL OFF-ROAD MOTORIZED TRAVEL

When in 1906 the U.S. government created Lewis and Clark National Forest out of portions of the Blackfeet and Flathead Reservations, including the sacred places of Badger-Two Medicine, regulations regarding a motorized travel plan were unnecessary. As motor vehicle technology changed and advanced, the new challenges required management plans to protect forests around the country. Up to the 1960s, the Forest Service placed no restrictions on motorized travel in Lewis and Clark National Forest. This changed in 1964 with the Wilderness Act. The Forest Service designated parts of Lewis and Clark National Forest as wilderness, limiting some forms of travel. Badger-Two Medicine was never designated as wilderness because of the reserved rights of the Blackfeet to hunt and harvest lumber in the area. In 1972 President Richard Nixon ordered the Forest Service to develop the first travel plan for the Rocky Mountain Ranger District of Lewis and Clark National Forest. The Forest Service completed the plan in 1976. The plan called for 620 miles of roads and trails in the district, including within Badger-Two Medicine. The Forest Service updated the travel plan in 1984; the coverage of roads and trails was reduced, as more of the district had been designated as wilderness in 1977. The plan was again updated in 1988, at the same time all-terrain vehicles (ATV) were increasing in popularity and use on Forest Service lands.[64]

By the twenty-first century, the travel plan for the Rocky Mountain Ranger District, including Badger-Two Medicine, had several problems. The 1988 plan was complex and confusing, with twenty-four different types of restrictions. Maps delineating the regulatory areas had errors and created a great deal of confusion for visitors. Inadvertent violations became common, and tourists were understandably angry. The 1988 plan had not contemplated ATV traffic and regulations; a new management plan needed to account for the impacts of this form of motor transport. In 2001 the Forest Service issued the Three State Order, encompassing all Lewis and Clark National Forest and ending all off-road travel for wheeled motorized vehicles (such as ATVs). This order did not impact the more limited snowmobiling. The Three State Order limited wheeled motorized traffic to existing roads and trails. Adding to the existing confusion and conflict was a significant increase in public demand for nonmotorized recreation such as hiking and skiing. Many seeking nonmotorized travel alternatives preferred their recreation not to be disrupted by the sounds of motorized recreation. In 2005 the Forest Service issued a service-wide rule limiting all motorized travel to designated roads, with local flexibility to allow for some snowmobile traffic in specified areas.[65]

In response to the Three State Order, the Rocky Mountain Ranger District of Lewis and Clark National Forest created an interdisciplinary team to study and formulate a new travel management plan for the district, including Badger-Two Medicine. The study investigated how to ensure the long-term protection of forest natural resources and recreation. It examined how to best protect fish and wildlife, provide erosion controls, protect resources, promote safety, and reduce conflicts between users. The interdisciplinary team issued its proposed plan in August 2002. It had evaluated the impacts of ATVs and snowmobiles in the district and proposed to simplify and clarify travel and vehicle access rules while reducing conflict between users and diminishing the negative effects of motorized vehicle use in the forest.[66]

After issuing the proposed travel management plan for the Rocky Mountain District, including Badger-Two Medicine, the Forest Service embarked upon the required consultation process. The proposed travel plan significantly reduced motorized travel in Badger-Two Medicine but made provisions for continued ATV use on one trail loop and for some snowmobile use in that area. While the interdisciplinary team had held ten open houses to scope the views of the public in formulating the proposed plan, formal consultation with the Blackfeet Nation did not begin until October. On October 10, 2002, Forest Service officials met with the Blackfeet Tribal Business Council and the Blackfeet Cultural Committee to schedule three open houses on the reservation. Four additional open houses were conducted outside Blackfeet territory. The Forest Service extended the comment period beyond the statutory minimum, to January 2003, to allow interested Blackfeet members to comment on the proposed plan.[67]

Through the course of the initial consultation process, the interdisciplinary team and the Forest Service became aware of significant public and Blackfeet concerns, and they adjusted the proposal for the draft environmental impact statement considerably. The growing interest of vocal elements of the public in nonmotorized travel, including horseback riding, hiking, and biking, compelled the Forest Service to consider closing all trails to motorized traffic. Consultation with the Blackfeet educated the Forest Service as to the extent of their reserved treaty rights in Badger-Two Medicine and the necessity for solitude. This led to contemplation of a plan that would close all roads and trails to motorized travel and end snowmobiling in Badger-Two Medicine.[68]

Despite the concerns expressed by Blackfeet tribal members, the proposed preference of the 2005 draft EIS merely reduced ATV and snowmobile use in Badger-Two Medicine. All proposed alternatives in the draft EIS called for the elimination of all motorized, wheeled cross-country travel, in compliance with the 2001 Three State Order. As far as Badger-Two Medicine was concerned, the preferred alternative included areas available for motorcycle travel, ATV travel, and seasonal snowmobile use.[69]

The Forest Service issued the draft EIS in 2005 and again modified plans after the period of public comment. The Forest Service held eight open houses and received some thirty-five thousand comments on the draft EIS.[70] Ultimately the Forest Service abandoned the preferred alternative from the draft EIS and issued no single preferred alternative for the Rocky Mountain Ranger District as a whole. The 2007 final EIS was a mix of the alternatives, with the final decision for some areas delayed.[71] After consideration of continued concerns of Blackfeet members, the Forest Service deferred a final decision for Badger-Two Medicine until it had further consultation with Blackfeet interests.[72]

This further consultation brought more alterations to the travel management plans, and it was another two years before the Forest Service issued a record of decision for a plan for Badger-Two Medicine. Comments from the general public overwhelmingly supported further separation of motorized and nonmotorized recreational travel in the forest. A "vast majority" of comments stressed the need for quiet trails and supported full closure to any motorized travel. In response to the public desire for quiet trails, the Forest Service considered closing all of Badger-Two Medicine to all motorized traffic, whether on- or off-road, including a ban on all snowmobiling, but ongoing talks with Blackfeet interests modified the plan, as the Blackfeet did not favor a total ban on motorized travel.[73] Further consultation brought small but significant changes to the management plan.

The Blackfeet stressed their opposition to all snowmobile travel in Badger-Two Medicine but urged limited motor vehicle access to facilitate their treaty rights. While religious ceremonies require solitude for their effectiveness in the view of practitioners of traditional Blackfeet religion, the Blackfeet Nation retained access to Badger-Two Medicine for both hunting and harvesting lumber. The Blackfeet requested that a small number of roads remain open to provide access for exercising their treaty rights. The Blackfeet argued that motor vehicle access would also allow elders to reach trailheads for access to sacred sites and that others could more easily engage in hunting and lumber harvesting. Throughout, Blackfeet members consistently opposed motorized travel on trails and snowmobiling in Badger-Two Medicine, but they offered to open up nearby portions of the Blackfeet Reservation to snowmobile travel to offset the lost recreational area.[74]

The final travel management plan for Badger-Two Medicine reflected the desired outcome for practitioners of traditional Blackfeet religion, even in the face of strong public support for closing the entire area to all motorized travel. The final plan increased the nonmotorized areas of Badger-Two Medicine from 51 percent to 92 percent. The plan left 182 miles of trails motor-free. A small number of roads would remain open to licensed motorized vehicles (cars and trucks) for a limited season each year, from July 1 to November 1, to allow public access to trailheads, including Blackfeet exercising their treaty rights.[75]

Despite the small number of comments in favor of continued snowmobile access and motor trail access, twenty-six people filed appeals challenging the record of decision for the Badger-Two Medicine travel management plan. While some of these appeals included members of the Blackfeet Nation expressing concerns for their continued treaty rights, several challenges suggested that the travel management plan violated the constitutional prohibition against the establishment of religion. After reviewing the relevant materials, Jane L. Cottrell, the appeal deciding officer, followed the recommendation of the appeal reviewing officer and dismissed the internal appeal on June 18, 2009. Ten of the appellants, including the Montana Trail Vehicle Riders Association, the Capital Trail Vehicle Riders Association, and Montanans for Multiple Use, took their appeal to the United States District Court for the District of Montana, Great Falls Division. The Glacier-Two Medicine Alliance, Montana Wilderness Society, and the Wilderness Society joined the United States Forest Service as defendant-intervenors in the case.[76]

Judge Sam E. Haddon for the Great Falls Division disposed of the remaining issues on January 20, 2011, finding, in part, that the travel management plan for Badger-Two Medicine did not violate the Constitution of the United Stated by improperly establishing religion. Haddon applied the three-part *Lemon* test in his decision and relied heavily upon the *Access Fund v. USDA* decision involving Cave Rock from 2007. Haddon found that there were a host of secular purposes in banning off-road travel, including benefits to air quality, water quality, soil quality, and fish and wildlife habitat. With regard to effect, the judge determined that "an informed and reasonable person" could not perceive the government action was endorsing a traditional Blackfeet religious perspective. As to entanglement,

Haddon found that the government was merely involved in its typical management role for public lands.[77]

After some small consideration of further action by those interested in off-road vehicular recreation, the district court opinion was the final legal opinion in the case. An appeal was initially filed with the Ninth Circuit Court of Appeals. This appeal was voluntarily dismissed in late October 2011.[78]

IMPACT AND MEANING

There are several superficial similarities between the cases of the Badger-Two Medicine travel management plan and the Cave Rock management and rehabilitation plan, but their differences demonstrate the significance of the Badger-Two Medicine case. In both cases, administrators did not come to the consultation process with preconceived plans. Rather, administrators were faced with new administrative needs or mandates. The administrative changes were not being advanced by a for-profit enterprise to increase its financial reward (while desecrating Indian sacred sites). Administrators used the consultation process, for both Cave Rock and Badger-Two Medicine, to formulate plans and search out compromises, instead of considering them as necessary hurdles for carrying out a preconceived policy. Thus administrators were open to looking for solutions that could accommodate indigenous interests.

The differences in the cases stem from the differences in the history of the Blackfeet and Washoe Nations. For the Blackfeet Indians, Badger-Two Medicine was a place of religious significance, visited for religious ceremonies and solitude. In addition, the Blackfeet retained substantive rights to access, hunt, and harvest lumber in the same treaty by which they unwillingly parted with the land. Also, Blackfeet interests did not fully coincide with the maximal objectives of environmental concerns and those seeking solitude; some roads were kept so that the elderly and disabled could better access sacred sites and to facilitate other treaty rights to make use of the land. So while the Washoes obtained significant protection of Cave Rock (they remain unhappy with the hiking and picnicking), the Blackfeet obtained all they could, within the limits of the administrative purview of the Forest Service. The Blackfeet Nation also showed its willingness to work with its neighbors by opening up parts of the reservation to recreational snowmobiling to offset recreational use excluded from Badger-Two Medicine. Under the right circumstances, when federal administrators do not have a preconceived agenda, the consultation process can potentially produce agreements that protect Indian sacred and cultural sites.

5 FOUR NATIONS AND FIVE CONTROVERSIES IN INDIAN RELIGIOUS FREEDOM

This chapter examines five cases that do not quite follow the administrative pattern traced in the previous chapters. None of these cases involve decisions of the Forest Service, but all are relevant to the federal administrative and consultation process as it developed in the early twenty-first century. All five cases directly involve Indian religious self-determination and complications related to federal administrative procedures. Two involve the Bureau of Land Management and the Quechan Indian Nation of southern California. One involves sites sacred to the Western Apaches of the San Carlos Reservation in Arizona that were unilaterally removed from Forest Service and consultation protections. One involves treaty rights protecting off-reservation religious practices of the Makah Nation and the demands of racist environmentalists, outside the mainstream of the environmental movement, insisting that these treaty rights be subjected to federal administrative analysis and approval, even as federal officials supported Makah treaty and religious rights. The final case involves the Army Corps of Engineers approving the permit that allowed the Dakota Access Pipeline to pass beneath the sacred water of Lake Oahe, north of the Standing Rock Sioux Reservation.

First we look at the Makah Nation of Washington and its attempts in the late twentieth and early twenty-first century to revive their religious and cultural practice of killing and eating whales. Whaling was so important to the Makahs that they made sure to explicitly retain the right to hunt whales in the Neah Bay Treaty of 1855, when they ceded the bulk of their interior lands to the United States. On their own initiative, the Makahs gave up whaling when they realized the threat of extinction, well before the U.S. government banned whaling. The Makahs approached the federal government for assistance in obtaining a quota of whales to hunt in 1997, well after the whale population had rebounded. After engaging in a successful whale hunt in 1999, the Makahs were confronted by a small number of environmentalists who made common cause with politicians hostile to Indian rights. These opposing forces engaged in a shameless campaign against the Makahs based on lies and counting on the ignorance of the public. It culminated in the demand that Makah religious and treaty rights be subject to the administrative procedures of the Marine Mammal Protection Act of 1972.

The second and third cases examined here regard the Quechan Nation and its struggles to protect sacred places in lands adjacent to their reservation that are managed by the Bureau of Land Management (BLM). In both of these cases, the Quechans succeeded, but in one case they were welcome allies of environmentalists; in the other, environmentalists soundly condemned the Quechans as opponents of progress for seeking to protect their rights and cultural heritage. In the first case, the Quechans worked with environmentalists to challenge a proposal by a Canadian corporation to mine for gold among their sacred places. Once the BLM and the State of California placed significant regulations on mining operations to mitigate damages, the Canadian corporation challenged these actions as violating its rights under the North American Free Trade Agreement (NAFTA). The Quechans appealed to the NAFTA mediation tribunal for leave to file briefs as an interested third party, and in 2009 the Quechan Nation became the first indigenous nation permitted to submit briefs to a NAFTA tribunal. In the other case, the BLM simply refused to conduct any consultation with the Quechans before approving a solar power project. As the Quechans challenged the failure of federal administrators to engage in the required consultation, many condemned the Quechans for standing in the way of environmental progress.

The fourth case examined here also involves lands managed by the Forest Service, but the case demonstrates one of the key weaknesses with the current administrative regime regarding Indian sacred sites on public lands. Apache Leap and Oak Flat are of deep cultural, historic, and religious significance to the San Carlos Reservation Apache people, with religious ceremonies still carried out there. The federal government had placed these Apache lands in the Tonto National Forest and protected them from mining. But in 2014, congresspeople from Arizona slipped a rider into a must-pass military appropriations bill at the last moment, giving Oak Flat and Apache Leap to an Anglo-Australian mining corporation. A former lobbyist for the corporation circumvented any protection a consultation process might have provided Apache interests by giving title to the land to said corporation (in exchange for land elsewhere).

The fifth case is the most recent and most widely publicized. The controversial Dakota Access Pipeline, while built almost exclusively on private land, outside of regulatory concerns, required approval from the Army Corps of Engineers for every time it crossed a federally controlled waterway, such as the Missouri River. The pipeline crossed the Missouri under Lake Oahe less than half a mile upstream from the Standing Rock Sioux Reservation. The Standing Rock Sioux have substantial retained rights in Lake Oahe and areas that would be severely impacted by a leak or spill from the pipeline. The Sioux challenged the regulatory approval on a host of legal grounds, including the Religious Freedom Restoration Act. As of winter 2018 they had found only limited success on grounds that the environmental assessment did not sufficiently consider the potential impacts of leaks and spills on the treaty rights of the Standing Rock Sioux.

THE MAKAHS AND WHALING

The Makah Indian Nation is located on the Pacific coast of the United States, and whaling has been a central part of Makah economic and religious existence for centuries. Archaeological studies of Ozette Village reveal that the area near the Makah capital of Neah Bay, in modern Washington State, has been continuously inhabited for more than two thousand years. Since time immemorial, the Makahs have hunted whales for sustenance. Whales are also central to Makah culture and religion. Makah religion tells of instances when humans transformed into whales. When whale hunting, Makah hunters traditionally offered prayers to the whale to both flatter it and to cajole it to turn toward the beach. After a successful hunt, the whale was recognized as an honored guest that sustained the village, and entire villages would sing the praises of a whale that had given itself to the community.[1]

After meeting representatives of the United States in 1855, the Makahs sought to protect the place of whaling in their society, as it was both an economic necessity and of central cultural importance to them. Pressed by the United States to give up vast portions of their inland holdings, the Makahs agreed to do so in exchange for goods and supplies, including the advanced whaling equipment and technology of the United States. The Makahs were confident they could continue to survive on a reduced land base, as the ocean was the source of their sustenance. In the 1855 Treaty of Neah Bay, the Makahs agreed to abandon the practice of slavery and freed their slaves. So important was whaling to the Makahs that they insisted on the explicit statement that they retain their whaling rights in the treaty with the United States. The Makahs were the only Indian nation to specifically reserve the right to hunt whales in a treaty with the United States. The United States never delivered the promised whaling equipment and shorted the Makahs on the other promised supplies.[2]

The Makahs faced hardships similar to those faced by other Indian nations when the U.S. government turned to the policy of forced assimilation. The U.S. government disrupted the traditional Makah government, forcibly rearranged property rights, and suppressed the Makah language. The federal government supported the removal of Makah children to distant boarding schools. In the face of government suppression of their religious and cultural life, the Makahs resisted by shifting their holidays and ceremonies to coincide with the political and religious holidays of the Christians trying to eliminate their religion, as other Indian peoples had.[3]

Through the difficult decades before 1927, the Makahs continued their practice of whaling, until commercial whaling threatened the existence of the gray whale. As stocks of the large water mammal dropped precariously low, the Makahs voluntarily stopped whaling in 1927. Facing the potential extinction of many whale species, the United States banned whaling in 1937. The United States joined the International Whaling Commission (IWC) when it was created in 1946, retaining a quota for subsistence whale hunts for indigenous peoples of Alaska.[4]

The international program to preserve whales was highly successful, at least for the gray whales the Makahs hunted. In 1993 the U.S. government removed gray whales from the list of endangered species. In 1994 gray whales were at carrying capacity, with some twenty-six thousand in existence. Gray whales began to die because they lacked sufficient food for their populations. In the face of the rebounded gray whale population, the Makahs approached the U.S. government about obtaining a quota from the IWC for hunting for sustenance and cultural purposes.[5]

With the tradition of whaling still within living memory, the Makahs had kept related skills alive into the 1990s. In July 1995, a whale landed on shore in Makah territory. One hundred and fifty Makahs descended upon the creature and, under directions of elders, quickly butchered the whale. The Makahs used old recipes to cook the meat.[6]

The U.S. government, in part because of retained Makah rights in the Treaty of Neah Bay, made arrangements to obtain a whaling quota for the Makahs from the IWC. But U.S. negotiators encountered difficulties at the commission and made arrangements with Russia to have the Makahs share the existing whaling quota of Siberian Natives rather than seek an entirely new quota. By 1997 the United States had secured international permission for the Makahs to harvest up to twenty gray whales over a five-year period. Under this agreement, no extra whales would be killed; the Makah simply obtained a share of the existing quotas.[7]

Makah leaders hoped that the revival of the whale hunt would help revitalize the Makah Nation, which faced high unemployment, poverty, and drug use. Makah leaders hoped this cultural revival would bring the community together. While some elders believed that a truly traditional hunt could not be revived, 85 percent of the Makah people supported the hunt. The Makahs consulted with Inuit whaling experts in putting together their hunt. Traditional hunts had been conducted by specific whaling families, but the Makahs created the Makah Whaling Commission to select the team for the hunt. Family and political rivalries continued, and the animosity between hunting team captain Wayne Johnson and harpooner Theron Parker initially caused difficulty in preparations. An eight-man team led by Johnson set out with a traditional boat, handmade paddles, and a handheld harpoon wielded by Parker for the whale hunt in 1999. The U.S. government required that the whale be killed mercifully, with a shotgun blast to the head once the beast was landed. While the Makahs had considered using parts of the whale for traditional economic purposes, such as food and oil sales, the United States required they use the whale only for food.[8]

Once the general U.S. public learned of the intentions of the Makahs, the reaction in one sector was vile, violent, and grotesque in the extreme. While no major international environmental groups protested the Makah whale hunt, smaller, attention-seeking groups with dubious connections to racist causes rushed to condemn and attack the Makahs. While the Makahs were supported in their efforts by other indigenous nations, the response of elements within the non-Indian community was violent. Indian children received death threats. Non-Indians sold and displayed bumper stickers that read, "Save a Whale, Kill an Indian." Activists opposed to whaling tried to physically disrupt Makah training and practice, causing collisions and finally requiring the United States Coast Guard to impose and enforce a five-hundred-foot exclusion zone around the Makah hunting team.[9]

Most vile of those seeking to undermine Makah sovereignty was Paul Watson, who acted for the cameras for nearly a decade before becoming the central subject on the Animal Planet reality television program *Whale Wars*. Greenpeace had expelled Watson in the 1970s, and he went on to found the Sea Shepherd organization. Described by writer, director, and creator of *South Park* Trey Parker as "an unorganized incompetent media whore who thought lying to everyone was okay as long as it served his cause" and as "a smug, narcoleptic liar with no credibility," Watson made alliances with politicians with no interests in whale preservation who hoped to use the issue of Makah whaling to undermine legal recognition for Indian treaty rights. Watson publicly endorsed the position that misleading the public was acceptable to promote his political agenda, and he repeatedly pushed the lie that the Makahs intended to sell whale meat to the Japanese. Once the Makahs succeeded in their 1999 whale hunt, Watson commented, "American whalers managed to blast a whale out of existence in American waters on the pretext of cultural privilege."[10]

Success in overcoming opposition to the hunt, and success in the hunt itself, had beneficial outcomes for the Makah Nation. Most felt the vile racist opposition helped unite the Makah people. Some Makahs noted that the whale fed both the stomachs and the spirits of the Makah people. The Makahs placed the skeleton of the killed whale on display in the Makah Culture and Research Center in Neah Bay.[11] The Makahs also learned that many of their "liberal friends" were not really committed to political and cultural self-determination. As Makah Tribal Council chairman Ben Johnson said the next year in the face of continued protests, "'Liberals' seem always to want to fit Indians into a safe, acceptable ideal of the noble savage, and are uncomfortable when modern methods can be adopted to achieve ancient aims. Times change and we have to change with the times. They want us to be back in the primitive times. We just want to practice our culture."[12]

While the Makahs were able to succeed in their 1999 hunt and tried, but failed, in 2000, whale preservation groups and activists turned to the courts in their attempts to deny the Makahs their cultural and political self-determination, as well as their freedom to exercise religion. Initially, animal rights activists challenged the legitimacy of the whale hunt on grounds that the U.S. government did not issue an environmental impact statement before obtaining the Makah quota. The courts agreed and prevented the Makahs from conducting another hunt until an environmental assessment was conducted. Once the Makahs and the U.S. government overcame this hurdle, the animal rights activists put forward the argument that the rights retained by the Makahs from the 1855 Neah Bay

Treaty were subject to the Marine Mammal Protection Act (MMPA) of 1972 and thus a more extensive environmental assessment had to be carried out by the National Marine Fisheries Service of the National Oceanic and Atmospheric Administration (NOAA).[13]

In 2002 the Ninth Circuit Court of Appeals, in a confused opinion, decided that Makah treaty rights were subject to the MMPA. Under the United States Constitution, treaties are the supreme law of the land, and in 1995 Congress amended the MMPA to specifically say that the act did not abrogate any Indian treaty rights. Indian legal issues can be complicated, with many competing tests, and courts have been known to apply the wrong test to obtain the desired results. In the Makah whaling case, rather than examine whether or not Congress had intended to abrogate Makah treaty rights, the court applied a test used by the U.S. Supreme Court for determining whether or not Indian hunting and fishing treaty rights might be subject to state, *not federal*, regulations for the narrow purpose of preventing the extinction of the resource.[14]

To reach the conclusion that Makah treaty rights were subject to the MMPA, the Ninth Circuit Court of Appeals had to engage in some fanciful speculation. For Indian hunting and fishing treaty rights to be subject to state (not federal) regulations, the regulations must be necessary to prevent extinction, not merely to conserve the resource. The court opined that if the Makahs were not subject to the MMPA, despite all the evidence to the contrary, then the Makahs could possibly decide to hunt the gray whale to the brink of extinction. The court also worried that if the Makahs were allowed to hunt whales without being subject to the MMPA, other Indian nations might try to exert the right to hunt whales as well, despite the Makahs being the only nation holding such reserved treaty rights.[15] As there were some twenty-six thousand gray whales in the world, the court's claimed worries of extinction were particularly fantastical. Only under such absurd hypothetical situations would it be necessary to protect a species that was then at its carrying capacity with the additional regulatory scrutiny of an environmental impact statement crafted by the National Marine Fisheries Service.

After more than a century of much greater adversity than simply working with more government bureaucrats, Makah leaders refused to give up and immediately began working with NOAA officials to create a new request for a permit to harvest gray whales. In 2005 the Makah Indian Nation formally submitted a proposal for harvesting gray whales to NOAA. Unhappy with delays, in September 2007, five Makah citizens killed a gray whale without regard to the laws, regulations, or traditions of the Makah Nation. NOAA issued an initial draft environmental impact statement in 2008 but withdrew it in 2012 when additional scientific data became available. After another three years of consideration, another draft EIS was issued in February 2015.[16]

The current Makah proposal takes into consideration the many regulations of the MMPA. The proposal limits the hunting season to five months, from December to the end of May, and provides for an average of four gray whales harvested a year, with no more than five in any given year, over a six-year period. The proposal would limit the number of whales the Makahs might unsuccessfully attack and makes provisions for actions to be taken if whales outside the large gray whale population might suffer attack instead. The NOAA analysis covers several variants on the plan to thoroughly explore options, but it offers no preferred alternative. Instead NOAA is waiting to combine comments with its analysis before making a final decision.[17]

When giving up their lands, the Makahs felt that whaling was so significant to their culture and economy that they specifically reserved the right by treaty. They had federal administrators as allies in their quest to exercise their religion, but even this could not prevent liberal imperialists from infringing on their religious and economic freedoms. While major environmentalist organizations did not oppose the Makahs, racist environmentalists made common cause with those looking to undermine Indian sovereignty and self-determination. Watson's lies were able to take hold because of the deep ignorance of the non-Indian public as to the foundational history of their own country. Unaware that the range in diversity in Indian cultures has always been greater than the range of cultural diversity in Europe, the general American public often becomes outraged when Indians do not live up to their liberal environmentalist fantasies and prejudices. In addition, non-Indian education has failed to teach even the basic notions of freedom—that religious freedom must exist for things that others do that you do not like. Otherwise, as racist environmentalists demonstrated, one does not believe in religious freedom.

THE QUECHAN NATION AS ENVIRONMENTAL HEROES AND VILLAINS

The Quechan people place the origin of humanity as part of the unfolding of the potential of an infinite universe. For Quechans, time is infinite and without beginning. Kwikumat and Blind Old Man were the first creatures to actualize the potential of reality and emerge from primordial waters. Kwikumat went on to create the first Quechan, Marxokuvek, and several nonhuman people, including Coyote, Raven, and Cougar. Kwikumat and Blind Old Man then had sexual intercourse to create Kumastamxo. Kumastamxo was also quite powerful and created the sun, stars, and vegetation of the world. All Yuma-speaking people were created in historic Quechan territory at Avikwaame, or Spirit Mountain.[18]

Traditional Quechan religion is a religion of dreams, visions, and potential for the accumulation of spiritual power. Spiritual power could be obtained by contacting Kumastamxo in dreams. The spirits of the dead, including Kwikumat and Kumastamxo, dwell in Indian Pass at Anaimtapoi, located in traditional Quechan territory. *Kwoxots*, the traditional national political leaders of the Quechans, were called to public service by visions in dreams, which delivered spiritual power to them.[19]

While the Quechans had no formal church structure or hierarchy in traditional life, kwoxots obtained their prominence through a mix of public service and spiritual power. Once someone was called to service by powerful spiritual visions, the person had to act on that call by volunteering to take on the responsibilities and duties of leadership. Such leaders held sway only as long as they had the confidence of the people. Competence was their real source of authority, and if they lost the support of the people, they were no longer leaders.[20]

Unlike their neighbors, the Quechans had a national identity with a unitary leadership as early as 1604, but actual political power resided in the people, as decision-making was based on consensus. Occasionally in Quechan history there was more than one kwoxot at a time. Often kwoxots publicly struggled with each other for leadership, but on occasion they worked cooperatively. Kwoxots had no authoritarian power to command obedience. Their authority originated in their spiritual power, wisdom, and generosity. Villages had their own leaders, known as *pipa taxa*, or "good for the people." These local leaders tended to have less spiritual power than kwoxots, but some could heal. Others were nice, generous, and wise and gave good advice. The Quechan military leadership was separate from the political leaders, and the top military commander was known as the *kawanami*. This distinction was again based in competence, but also in bravery.[21]

Perhaps because the Quechans had a central national leadership, unlike their neighbors, they led a powerful alliance of eight nations. The Quechan League formed in response to dislocations caused by the Spanish slave trade in Indian peoples. The Quechan League successfully protected the freedom of the Quechan people and lands from Spanish and later Mexican military forces for three hundred years. The United States militarily defeated the Quechans in 1852. In 1853 the local

U.S. military commander deposed the traditional leadership of the Quechan Nation and imposed a new kwoxot, over public protests by the Quechan people.[22]

Now incorporated by force into the expansionist United States, the Quechan Nation faced a series of dislocations similar to those of hundreds of other Indian nations. The president of the United States declared Quechan territory to be limited to lands on the eastern shore of the Colorado River, but in response to vocal Quechan protests, the president changed the location to the western shore of the Colorado River, leaving the Quechan some forty-five thousand acres of land in the southeastern corner of California. Once the United States began the policy of allotment, altering indigenous landholdings to reflect its own economic ideology, local government agents forged paperwork, making it appear that the Quechan people approved the plan to parcel out their land into private holdings and sell the "surplus." While the Quechans were fortunate to have none of their retained lands leave the period of government "trust," and thus had none of their remaining lands lost, the United States sold off some 80 percent of the 1884 reservation land as "surplus." The Quechans were already unhappy about being forcibly separated from their children by the U.S. policy of forced assimilation through boarding schools. Quechan leaders urged widespread resistance to the policy as the Quechan learned of the physical abuse their children suffered at the schools.[23]

With the change in policy by the U.S. government during the Great Depression, Quechan cooperation with U.S. policies did not markedly increase. The Indian Reorganization Act provided for indigenous nations to form European-style governments with elected officials. Many Quechans resisted efforts to produce an IRA government, and a constitutional committee, organized by the Bureau of Indian Affairs and made up of younger Quechan representatives, merely adopted the model BIA constitution with little alteration. After losing the first referendum to adopt the IRA constitution, the BIA held a second election in 1936. There the constitution was approved by merely thirteen votes in face of low voter turnout. Even with indications that the BIA wanted the formation of a new Quechan government more than the Quechan people, the first tribal council took office in 1937. It immediately clashed with the BIA over attempts to exercise its authority. The Quechan IRA government attempted to pursue policies designed to promote Quechan economic interests, but the BIA opposed them at every turn. As the BIA strong-armed the Quechan Tribal Council, public participation in the electoral process dropped off and voter turnout fell further in the 1940s.[24]

In the early 1970s, the Quechan Tribal Council pressed the U.S. government for the return of all lands from the 1884 reservation that were then in the legal possession of the federal government. As part of its ongoing Indian Claims Commission complaint, the Quechan government demanded that land be returned to the nation, rather than monetary compensation for the taken lands. The Nixon administration was receptive to the proposal and drew up plans to return twenty-five thousand acres. The proposed land transfer fell apart as the Watergate scandal consumed the Nixon administration.[25]

Without returning Quechan land, the U.S. federal government continued to manage Quechan sacred sites on federal property in Indian Pass and much of Imperial County, California, through the Bureau of Land Management. While parts of the land had been mined, and there remained outstanding claims to mineral rights, most of the land remained undisturbed. The lands contained numerous sites of religious, cultural, and historic significance to the Quechans that were eligible for designation as traditional cultural properties. There were archaeological sites dating back more than twelve hundred years. These sites include dance circles created by historical leaders of the Quechan, petroglyphs, and the Running Man geoglyph. Indian Pass was the spiritual resting place for Quechan dead. Several sacred mountains were also found in the area. These included Avikwaame, also known as Spirit Mountain, where Quechan leaders and healers obtained spiritual power in dream travel.[26]

The Quechan Nation as Environmental Heroes

In 1994 the Canadian corporation Glamis Imperial submitted a proposal with the Bureau of Land Management so it could act on its mining claims. The proposal called for an open-pit gold-mining operation using heap leach processing. It would disturb some fourteen hundred acres of Imperial County, including Indian Pass. The proposal called for several shafts to be dug. The deepest of these would have been 850 feet deep. The proposal did not provide for refilling the open pits once mining was completed. Glamis planned to leave a thirty-story-high debris pile instead.[27]

Glamis Imperial did not have the best record as an international corporate actor. It had no public environmental or human rights policies. Glamis was not a member of the Mining Association of Canada or the International Council on Mining and Metals. Both organizations had standards for sustainable mining and relations with indigenous peoples. While Glamis brought litigation regarding mining regulations before the NAFTA arbitral tribunal, communities in Central America complained of the environmental harms and human rights violations of Glamis operations.[28]

In preparing the draft EIS and final EIS for the Glamis mining proposal, the BLM first became aware of the extent of Quechan interests in Indian Pass and the surrounding lands, and took measures to protect places culturally and religiously significant to the Quechan Nation. In 2000 the BLM conducted a study and removed the Indian Pass area from eligibility for any future mining claims. In January 2001 the BLM rejected the Glamis mining proposal, charging that it would cause irreparable harm to Quechan sacred and cultural sites. When a new presidential administration took over, the new secretary of the interior, Gale Norton, reversed the BLM decision and approved the mining proposal in November 2001.[29]

The Quechan Nation and its many allies protested the approval of the mining project and took steps to hinder the damage the mine would have on Quechan cultural sites. The National Congress of American Indians, California governor Gray Davis, both California senators, the California congressional delegation of twenty-nine House members, the California State Legislature, and others protested the reversal of the BLM decision to reject the mining proposal. In response, in 2003 the California State Legislature passed a law requiring the backfilling of any mines to mitigate environmental damage.[30]

Unhappy with the new California regulations requiring rehabilitation of the landscape, Glamis filed a complaint against the United States under Chapter 11 of NAFTA. This provision allowed foreign corporations to file claims against member governments for unfair or unequal treatment. While Glamis complained of excessive federal delays in approving the gold mine proposal due to consideration of Quechan cultural concerns, its central argument was that the new California regulations were directed specifically at Glamis as a Canadian corporation and were a regulatory taking, as the mining project would cost considerably more to conduct. The Quechan Nation requested that the NAFTA tribunal accept its nonparty submissions for consideration in the arbitration in 2005. The Quechan Nation was the first indigenous nation to have briefs accepted for consideration by a claims dispute tribunal authorized under NAFTA.[31]

In 2009 the NAFTA claims tribunal denied any claim to damages by Glamis and considered the importance of protecting indigenous sacred sites in its opinion. With regard to the alleged regulatory delays, the tribunal found that consideration for indigenous sacred places was a legitimate and predictable operation of government. With regard to the claim that the California regulations were a taking, the tribunal found that the mining project could still be profitable, only less so, and that mitigating the damage to indigenous sacred and cultural sites was a legitimate purpose. With regard to the claim that Glamis was targeted for regulation as a Canadian corporation, the tribunal found that the California regulation may have been triggered by the approval of the Glamis mine proposal but that the law was generally applicable and could potentially apply to other future mining operations.[32] Glamis had been defeated, and the Quechan Nation stood as a hero alongside its environmentalist allies. Worthy of note was the tribunal's reliance on emerging standards of international law regarding the rights of indigenous peoples, including the United Nations Declaration on the Rights of Indigenous Peoples of 2007.

The Quechan Nation as Environmental Villains

In 2008 Tessera Solar Limited Liability Corporation approached the BLM about producing a solar complex on federal lands near the Quechan Reservation. This proposal required leasing sixty-five hundred acres of land upon which to build thirty thousand solar collectors. This land contained hundreds of archaeological and religious sites, some containing human remains, of significance to the Quechan people. Many of the sites would potentially be destroyed by the proposed solar project. These were the days of the 2008 economic meltdown, and Tessera Solar hoped to qualify for federal funds under the American Recovery and Reinvestment Act. The BLM began an expedited process to complete approval of the project, as the project would lose its eligibility for federal stimulus funds if it did not begin before the end of 2010.[33]

The leaders of the Quechan Nation became aware of the project, and the Quechans notified the BLM of the requirement to consult with them on a government-to-government basis. The Quechan Historical Preservation Office initiated first contact between the Quechan Nation and the BLM by sending the BLM a letter in February 2008. This letter informed the BLM that the solar project endangered cultural, religious, and historical sites of significance to the Quechan people and requested a meeting. The BLM did not reply, and the Historical Preservation Office resent the letter the next month. The Quechans repeatedly requested government-to-government consultation and private meetings, and informed the BLM that the project plan had not identified what historic and cultural sites might be impacted. In response, the BLM merely invited Quechan leaders to bring their information to meetings designed for general public comments.[34]

The planning process of the BLM in no way included consideration of Quechan sacred and cultural sites. In June 2010, the BLM admitted that it had no maps inventorying sites that might be impacted by the proposed solar complex. The

BLM went ahead and issued the final EIS in July 2010 without meeting with any representatives of the Quechan government. The Quechan Nation objected to the completion of the final EIS without any consultation with their representatives. On October 4, 2010, the BLM director signed the Imperial Valley Solar Project record of decision, approving the plan. On October 13, 2010, Secretary of Interior Ken Salazar signed off on the project. The first meeting between Quechan leaders and the BLM took place on October 16, 2010, three days after the final approval of the project.[35]

The record left by the BLM clearly indicated no consideration for efforts to mitigate any damage to sacred sites and archaeological treasures, in addition to a total lack of consultation with the Quechan Nation. The project threatened hundreds of archaeological sites, and the BLM did not even have a map of these sites. The EIS went so far as to admit that the project could wholly or partially destroy all archaeological sites in the project area.[36]

Faced with a total disregard by the BLM for the legal requirements of consultation when projects might impact places of cultural or religious significance to Indian nations, the Quechan Nation turned to the federal courts and received the sought relief. On October 29, 2010, the Quechan Nation filed a complaint with the federal court for the Southern District of California, demanding a preliminary injunction. On December 13, the district court heard oral arguments. Two days later the court delivered a written opinion issuing a preliminary injunction, as the Quechan were likely to win on a full consideration of the merits on the issue of consultation.[37]

Judge Larry Alan Burns explained in his opinion that the law and regulations clearly required government-to-government consultation when a proposed action might impact Indian cultural and religious sites and that the government had in no substantive way engaged in such consultation. The court noted that government-to-government consultation was required at the earliest possible time in the planning stages and required much more than merely inviting the Quechans to collect their own information and bring it to a meeting designed for general comments on the draft EIS. Burns also noted that the Quechans had put the BLM on notice that this consultation was required as early as February 2008. The court went on to take to task the government's pleading practice, complaining that it was not good form to simply file page after page of documents without explaining the significance of any particular document and expecting that "the court will sift through them."[38]

While the Quechan Nation was able to prevent the destruction of its sacred sites by a poorly planned project, the press was largely incapable of understanding the subtleties of the issues and portrayed the Quechans as blocking progress and environmental protection. A "storm of media criticism" against the Quechans followed their victory. The press seemed incapable of understanding that the Quechan objections came from the BLM's failure to consult with their officials and the lack of consideration for any effort to mitigate damage or destruction to archaeological, cultural, and religious sites. Had the consultation taken place, the Quechans could have helped identify the most significant sites, and a plan that could have either protected or minimized the damage to those sites may have been designed. Instead the press condemned the Quechans for not being stewards of the environment and for placing their traditions over the environmental well-being of all. Some felt it was their place to lecture the Quechans on their cultural and economic interests and condemned the Quechans for building a casino to deal with their economic needs but being traditional only when it came to the proposed solar project.[39]

The Quechan cases illustrate several important points. First, it is easier to be heroes to ignorant liberal environmentalists when your political goals match their ill-informed opinions. Second, the court in the solar complex case demonstrated that the consultation process must involve something more than an invitation to bring concerns to a public meeting and must take place at a government-to-government level. Third, people are deeply ignorant of Indian concerns and were easily misled into conflating complaints about lack of consultation with opposition to the solar project as such. Fourth, many non-Indians continue into the twenty-first century to feel it is their place to tell Indians what their traditions should be.

Finally, the Quechan involvement in the NAFTA arbitration tribunal demonstrates several disturbing trends in U.S. law. The Quechans, in their brief, brought up the emerging international consensus regarding protecting the rights of indigenous peoples, including the United Nations Declaration on the Rights of Indigenous Peoples. While the tribunal accepted the protection and preservation of indigenous cultural and sacred sites as a legitimate concern of government and a predictable cost of business, this acceptance of such emerging international law standards serves only to highlight the move against such standards by the courts of the United States. In addition, the tribunal's decision serves to highlight that foreign corporations have more avenues for seeking protection of their financial interests than the indigenous peoples of the United States have for protecting their cultural and religious interests. The NAFTA tribunal permissively allowed the Quechan Nation to file a brief as an interested third party. Alone, the Quechans would have had no standing to protect their interests before the international arbitration body. In U.S. courts, Quechan arguments regarding the emerging international consensus about the rights of indigenous peoples would almost certainly have been ignored.

APACHE LEAP AND OAK FLAT

Federal managers of public lands must meet a series of requirements when operating with Indian sacred sites. The federal government cannot prevent Indian access to such places. When carrying out decisions, such as assessing the impacts of proposed mines or massive solar farms, managers of public lands must substantively consult with Indian nations and religious leaders about how the proposed actions will impact sacred sites. While the Forest Service has never been under any obligation to protect sacred places consistent with Indian desires, the service has become quite skilled at conducting substantive meetings at the earliest stages of planning, in a manner consistent with U.S. laws and regulations.

Alternatively, if the United States Congress simply privatizes public lands encumbered with executive prohibitions against mining, Indian rights to consultation and access have no legal protections.

The traditional religion of the Western Apaches is in many ways similar to religions of other Indian peoples. The Western Apaches view the universe as a living entity. They view bears, snakes, and lightening as creatures of spiritual power. The Apaches view the yellow pollen of cattails as charged with benevolent energy, and many carry pollen with them. The Western Apaches believe in *gaans*, or mountain-dwelling spirits, which come to visit their lands during ceremony times. Much like the Hopis and kachinas, the Western Apaches have people dress up as gaans, in hoods and masks, for religious ceremonies.[40]

Unlike many of their neighbors, the Western Apaches placed the celebration of female power in a position of prominence in their ceremonial life. The Western Apaches did not have a fear of abstract female power. They did not require women to leave camps while menstruating. Celebrating when young women achieved puberty was a major public ceremony before the time of contact with European powers. Among extended family groups, the puberty ceremony was the central ritual. After the years of the suppression of religion, the Western Apaches enthusiastically revived the female puberty ceremony and carried it out in the most sacred of their places, Oak Flat, located in the southeastern part of Arizona, in the Tonto National Forest, not far from the San Carlos Reservation, where most Western Apaches now live.[41]

The Western Apaches were and continue to be one of several Apache groups with similar languages organized in matrilineal clans. A husband would move to join his wife's clan, and the wife was considered to be the owner of their dwelling. The different Apache groups did not form a single cohesive nation, in the minds of the Apaches, but were groups with their own interests and traditions.[42]

The Western Apaches developed a slightly different economy after the introduction of horses and made few changes in their political traditions. Eastern Apache groups expanded their buffalo hunting with the introduction of horses, while the Western Apaches remained agricultural but significantly supplemented their hunting and farming with raiding on neighbors. The Western Apaches had a strong tradition of distributing wealth among extended family members, including the tradition that the sister of the wife of the assistant to the hunter who killed a deer had first pick of the meat. Status was obtained through generosity and sharing. The Apaches generally did not have lasting formal political leadership. What leaders did exist, the Apaches elected them to lead for specific short-term tasks.[43]

As the Spanish expanded their invasion of Mexico, they came into contact with the various Apache peoples and sought to extend their sovereignty over the Apaches. The Spanish were never able to commit the military resources necessary to subdue the Apaches, and wiping them out was impossible. The Spanish turned to the strategy of trying to contain the Apaches by building a northern string of military garrisons, but containment proved impossible. Apache raiding parties moved quickly, and they easily outmaneuvered the Spanish military to raid Spanish villages within their reach.[44]

Access to Spanish technology, resources, and equipment altered the economy of the Western Apaches, but it did not alter their resistance to Spanish authority. As Western Apaches raided Spanish villages for supplies, they found those villages were a better source for the necessities of life. While never completely abandoning agriculture, the Western Apaches became dependent on raiding Spanish villages for materials. Sometimes the Western Apaches negotiated peace with some Spanish villages and even traded with them. Never did any Apache group recognize the sovereignty of the Spanish Empire or the later Mexican Republic over their territory and lives.[45]

The ongoing conflict between Mexico and the Apaches became considerably more violent when Mexican officials adopted policies intended to exterminate the Apaches. The governors of the Mexican states of Chihuahua and Sonora each offered bounties for the scalp of any Apache, man, woman, or child. Anglo-American bounty hunters entered Apache lands in the 1830s and 1840s and regularly attacked Apache villages while men were away. Finding large numbers of women and children massacred, Apache raiding parties retaliated by increasing the ferocity and violence of their attacks on Mexican villages. In response the Apaches began killing more in raids and took more captives, including children, to forcibly integrate into their families.[46]

When the European power claiming sovereignty over Apache lands shifted from Mexico to the United States, Apache relations with the United States were initially peaceful. Cochise, a leader among the Chiricahua Apaches, negotiated a peace treaty with the United States. This treaty offered the generous concession of allowing U.S. mail transports safe passage through Apache territory. By 1860 the United States had largely withdrawn any presence from Apache territory.[47]

Apache–U.S. relations quickly deteriorated into war at the beginning of the U.S. Civil War. In 1861, with regard to a Mexican captive, U.S. Army lieutenant George Bascom called upon Cochise and other leaders to negotiate a solution to the situation. Acting in bad faith, Bascom seized Cochise and the other diplomats. Cochise quickly escaped, and the Chiricahua Apaches declared war on the United States, pulling the Western Apaches into the war as part of an alliance of several Indian nations.[48]

The United States had other concerns in the region as well. Both the United States and the separatist Confederate States of America claimed the New Mexico territory as their sovereign territory. U.S. leaders suspected that the local Anglo-American populations sympathized with the separatists and sent a large military contingent to establish U.S. sovereignty over the territory in 1862.[49] This military presence quickly ran afoul of the Apaches looking to protect their territory and sovereignty.

While the United States intended this military presence to impress separatist sympathizers, the Apaches found the military presence in their sovereign territory to be an affront and attacked. In the ensuing battle, for the first time Apache forces encountered a fully supplied European military with the latest artillery technology. After this encounter, many Apache leaders acknowledged that military defeat was inevitable, but they decided to fight on, preferring liberty and death over slavery.[50]

While the Apaches fought on, the invaders from the United States sought to speed the Apache people to the end of their existence. In 1863 President Abraham Lincoln carved out a portion of the New Mexico territory and created Arizona.

The Arizona Territorial Legislature met for the first time in 1864. Among its first resolutions was a call to exterminate the Apache people.[51]

Determined to fight to the bitter end, Apache forces conducted a guerrilla struggle, raiding Anglo-American settlements for supplies and retreating to mountains they knew much better than the invaders. Though Apache soldiers had long before incorporated firearms into their military and hunting operations, they remained proficient in usage of the bow and arrow. By judicious use of the bow as a stealth weapon, the Apaches continued the fight for liberty through the decade, and some struggled on into the 1880s.[52]

The U.S. military was able to defeat the various Apache resistance groups only by employing Apache scouts. After the subduing of the separatist forces, the U.S. military returned to Apache lands in force. Even then, the U.S. Army relied upon Apache scouts to hunt down Apache hiding places. Here the lack of national identity hurt Apache groups. The various Apache groups still had their own rivalries and jealousies, and the United States hired scouts from one Apache group to hunt down resistance fighters from other Apache groups. Scouts often took the U.S. military past their own kin and provided the locations of other Apache peoples.[53]

As the U.S. subdued the region by force, many Western Apaches, preferring death to capture, threw themselves from a cliff in the 1870s. This cliff, located near Oak Flat, was later named Apache Leap Cliff and was incorporated into the Tonto National Forest. By 1871 the United States had forced all Apache groups onto five separate reservations. U.S. forces confined the Western Apaches to the San Carlos Reservation, which was composed of the worst of the formerly expansive Western Apache territory. At first, the reservation was run as a prisoner of war camp with regular roll call. The occupiers required everyone to have tags about their necks, identifying which group they were with and their number in the group.[54]

Initially, Oak Flat was part of the San Carlos Reservation, but the U.S. government separated it in 1886. In 1905 Oak Flat was turned into public lands. Later it was part of Tonto National Forest. Throughout it remained a place of religious significance to the Western Apaches and a place where the Apaches conducted puberty ceremonies.[55]

The Western Apaches continued to resist military occupation and U.S. attempts to force them to conform to Anglo-American culture. In 1881 Noche-do-Klinne started a religious revival that, while preaching peace, prophesied the return of great military leaders, such as Cochise. The U.S. military killed Noche-do-Klinne in a botched arrest attempt. To prevent a general uprising, the local military commander exercised considerable restraint in the face of the violent Apache reaction to the killing. Some Chiricahua and Mimbres Apache were located in the San Carlos Reservation, and in 1886 the great Chiricahua leader Geronimo led a breakout from the reservation. By the end of the decade, most attempts at military resistance to the occupation had come to an end. But even with the relative peace, the Western Apaches remained so resistant to U.S. policies that in the decades that followed, U.S. officials found it necessary to place Apache children in chains to prevent them from escaping when the government forcibly removed them to boarding schools.[56]

In the early 1920s, Arizona farming and mining interests pressed for the creation of the Coolidge Dam, a project that would flood the best farmlands of the San Carlos Reservation. While the United States was engaging in a policy of religious suppression and forced acculturation at the time, theoretically policy makers imagined such cultural repression as beneficial for the Western Apaches. To gain approval for the dam designed to benefit Anglo-American interests in Arizona at the expense of Apache farmlands, Arizona farmers claimed the dam would provide much-needed jobs to Western Apaches as well as provide irrigation for poor Pima Indian farmers.[57]

In 1935 the Western Apaches adopted an Indian Reorganization Act government, and this new government pressed claims to lands on the eastern edge of the reservation the Apaches had been removed from in 1896. Federal authorities had taken the land for gold mining but had never legally transferred title. By 1941 ranchers were squatting on the land. Rather than remove the ranchers, the BIA approved leases. It took until the 1980s for the Western Apaches to regain full control of the land.[58]

The 1980s were a period of revival for the Western Apaches. Their recalcitrance to forced assimilation had left 75 percent of their population retaining fluency in their language, with some twelve thousand speakers living on the San Carlos Reservation. Female puberty ceremonies had nearly been wiped out in decades past, but they returned in the 1980s and were enthusiastically embraced by the Western Apache population. Western Apache performances of gaan dances returned to festivals that lasted for days. Many found a new synthesis of traditional religion and evangelical Christianity as their preferred religious life. Owls are symbols of death for practitioners of traditional Western Apache religion and are well-known to speak Apache fluently (but are incapable of speaking English). One woman in the 1960s reported that an owl that spoke to her in Apache. The owl advocated on behalf of the Christian religion.[59]

Western Apache difficulties with Anglo-American immigrant communities continued. The concentrated Apache population of the San Carlos Reservation was a concern of political leaders in Arizona. In 1980 Arizona politicians decided to split the reservation among three different congressional districts, each with a majority non-Indian population. After an action brought by Indians under the Voting Rights Act, the district borders were altered, and Arizona redistricting and voter access regulations were placed under the supervision of the federal government.[60]

The Oak Flat region of the Tonto National Forest had been coveted by mining corporations doing business in Arizona as early as 2005. Oak Flat, throughout the history of the San Carlos Reservation, remained a place of religious significance to the Western Apaches and an important location for puberty ceremonies. Nevertheless, the Australian–British company Resolution Copper, a subsidiary of Rio Tinto, wanted access to the copper beneath the ground. Problematic for mining access, President Dwight Eisenhower had closed Oak Flat to mining in 1955. The Nixon administration had reaffirmed the closure of that part of the Tonto National Forest in 1971. Resolution Copper lobbied Arizona legislators to sell the corporation the Oak Flat area, but attempts dating back to 2005 failed; Congress did not support transferring public lands to a private foreign corporation for copper mining.[61]

Resolution Copper continued to press the issue, and its investment in politicians finally paid off in December 2014. Former Rio Tinto lobbyist Jeff Flake, then a senator for Arizona, introduced a rider to the Defense Authorization Act, a must-pass military spending bill, at the last moment. Supported in this move by the other Arizona senator and a recipient of Rio Tinto campaign contributions, John McCain, the rider authorized the transfer of full title to Apache Leap, Oak Flat, and the surrounding twenty-four hundred acres of the Tonto National Forest to Resolution Copper in exchange for fifty-three hundred acres of land that Resolution Copper had already mined. McCain defended the act as necessary for national security. The rider required an EIS to be completed before the land transfer but also included provisions stating that no matter what the EIS might report, the transfer of title would go through sixty days after completion of the environmental assessment.[62]

The Western Apaches were outraged by this privatization of their historical, cultural, and religious sites inside the Tonto National Forrest and quickly gathered allies in their opposition to this land transfer conducted without any public debate. Before the end of 2014, seventy Indian nations had denounced the proposed land transfer. Western Apaches began an occupation of Oak Flat, stating that they would not move until the land transfer was undone. Activists from the group Apache Stronghold began a caravan across the country, and members toured with rock legend Neil Young. Activists including Nizhoni Pike, a young Apache woman who had had her puberty ceremony at Oak Flat, opened Young's concerts and explained to attendees the importance of Oak Flat and what the U.S. government had done with it. By July 2015, six hundred thousand people had signed a petition calling for the return of Oak Flat to public ownership and an apology to the Apache people. It is worth noting that the same Access Fund that opposed protecting Cave Rock is among the many recreational and environmental allies of the San Carlos Apaches.[63]

Resolution Copper reached out to the residents of the San Carlos Reservation. The company sent representatives to speak with the public on the reservation and held an open house. Company representatives claimed to be willing to work with the Apaches to protect culturally and religiously significant places. The company explained that the underground mining would cause massive surface subsidence, creating a two-mile-long, one-thousand-foot-deep crater, but would have no impact on ground or surface water, as was required by law. Company representatives stated that they planned to protect Apache Leap and to provide access to Oak Flat "as long as it is safe to do so, and we expect access will continue for a number of decades."[64]

Not satisfied with merely having access to one of their most sacred and culturally important places for some unspecified number of years as determined by a distant foreign corporation, the Western Apaches of San Carlos Reservation continue their quest for more allies. In the summer of 2015, Arizona representative Raul Grijalva introduced a bill that would overturn the proposed land transfer. With growing bipartisan support for the repeal, Senators Bernie Sanders of Vermont and Tammy Baldwin of Wisconsin introduced a companion bill in November 2015.[65]

Matters took an almost surreal turn when Oak Flat was nominated to the National Register of Historic Places (NRHP) as a traditional cultural property in mid-2015. While placement on the NRHP would merely require a more detailed environmental assessment, politicians, including those who supported giving Oak Flat to a private foreign corporation, bitterly complained that the legally proper notice was somehow deceptive; the reactionary commentary outlet the *Daily Caller* characterized the nomination as an attempt by the federal government at a "stealth land grab." The obvious hypocrisy seemed completely lost on those worshiping at the altar of private power. During the period of nomination, some Western Apaches questioned the claims that Oak Flat had a history of sacred importance (noting that there were no traditional songs or stories of the importance of Oak Flat) without mentioning the historic significance of nearby Apache Leap. Oak Flat, which is also sacred to practitioners of the Yavapai-Apache religion, as their gaan spirits emerge from Oak Flat, was ultimately listed as a historic place by the National Park Service on March 4, 2016. Those familiar with the legal requirements widely understood the listing to have no impact on the ultimate transfer of Oak Flat to Resolution Copper, barring further congressional action. As of this writing, Congress has not passed a bill to stop the stealth land grab by Resolution Copper. In December 2017 the Forest Service approved the final management plan for the Apache Leap Special Management Area. The environmental assessment found that the activities of Resolution Copper would have no significant impact on Apache Leap. While these activities include tunnel making, the activities are primarily in support of mining in Oak Flat, which is not covered by the protections of the special management area.[66]

While providing no avenue for relief in the courts, the privatization of Apache sacred and cultural sites is in obvious violation of the new standards of international law regarding the rights of indigenous peoples. Article 19 of the Declaration on the Rights of Indigenous Peoples states: "States shall consult and cooperate in good faith with the indigenous peoples concerned through their own representative institutions in order to obtain their free, prior and informed consent before adopting and implementing legislative or administrative measures that may affect them." The second paragraph of Article 32 states: "States shall consult and cooperate in good faith with the indigenous peoples concerned through their own representative institutions in order to obtain their free and informed consent prior to the approval of any project affecting their lands or territories and other resources, particularly in connection with the development, utilization or exploitation of mineral, water or other resources."

The 2015 Defense Authorization Act is a violation of international law. The law gave Oak Flat and Apache Leap to a corporation for the purposes of mining. The U.S. government did not consult any elected official of the various Apache governments, or any other Apache. Thus Article 19 was violated, as the land transfer impacts the Apaches. Article 32 was violated because a traditional cultural property of the Western Apaches and the Yavapai-Apaches was privatized for the purposes of mining without the consultation of the Apaches.[67]

The consultation process regarding the management of public lands, mandated by the Indian Religious Freedom Act and strengthened by later executive orders, offers no protection to Indian sacred sites when Congress gives sacred sites to private corporations to destroy as they please. The unilateral privatization by the

U.S. of indigenous sacred sites without consultation violated the provisions of the United Nations Declaration on the Rights of Indigenous Peoples requiring consultation with indigenous peoples as to the disposition of their traditional sacred sites. While a tribunal under NAFTA will take notice of the changing norms of international law, there is yet no indication that any part of the U.S. government, be it the executive, legislative, or judicial branch, has any intention of even pretending to conform the management of indigenous sacred and cultural sites to the new requirements of international law.

THE STANDING ROCK SIOUX AND LAKE OAHE

The Standing Rock Sioux Reservation is one of the remnants of the Great Lakota Nation, which once ranged from Canada to Texas and as late as 1877 encompassed all of present-day South Dakota and portions of what are now its neighboring states. The Lakotas are an alliance of seven bands that make up the Council of Seven Fires. After the United States seized land from the Lakotas, in 1889 it created the Standing Rock Reservation, with a large population of Hunkpapas, the people of Sitting Bull. Today the Standing Rock Sioux Reservation straddles the border between North and South Dakota, sitting east of the sacred Black Hills.[68]

For centuries, the Lakotas, known to the French as the Sioux, maintained a nomadic society based on buffalo hunting. Their neighbors the Ojibwes called the Lakotas the Naddewasioux, or "little enemy." The French, upon meeting the Ojibwes, shortened the name to the Sioux. Economic life generally improved when the Lakotas integrated horses to their hunting around 1680. The Lakotas found themselves pushed westward by the Ojibwe Nation, which had more secure supplies of European weapons. In turn, the Lakotas pushed their neighbors the Shoshones and the Crows farther west.[69]

The Lakotas held places to be of religious significance and viewed humanity as kin of nonhuman peoples, including animals and spirits. The Lakotas are a people of the Sun Dance and believe in Wakantanka, an unseen omnipresent power. The Black Hills are the sacred center of the Lakota world, and the sacred pipe is brought there for ceremonies. The Standing Rock that gives the reservation its name is believed by some to have been left by the Arikawa people when they lived in the area, but the Lakotas believe it to have religious significance. The Lakotas believe that long ago, a young woman was jealous of her husband's second wife and she refused to follow him, so she was turned into the Standing Rock of Standing Rock Reservation.[70]

Life changed rapidly for the Lakotas in the nineteenth century. The Lakotas encountered the Lewis and Clark expedition in 1804, but little came of the meeting, as good translators were not available. During the North American portion of the last stages of the Napoleonic Wars (the War of 1812), the Lakotas allied with the British Empire against the United States. Regular trade was established with the United States when steamboats traveled up the Missouri River in 1837. This in turn caused a smallpox epidemic that year. The Lakotas signed twenty-six treaties with the United States between 1815 and 1868. By the mid-1800s the Lakota population was about fifteen thousand.[71]

With a history of constantly violating treaties with its neighbors, the United States approached eight nations of the Great Plains and sought another peace treaty in 1851, negotiated at Fort Laramie. The treaty called for recognized borders and peace between the nine nations. The Council at Horse Creek, as the Lakotas called the treaty gathering, also agreed to safe passage for people from the United States along the Oregon Trail, or the Shell River Trail as it was first known to the Lakotas. The Lakotas would later mockingly call the Oregon Trail the "Holy Road" because of its importance to the United States and the swath of death it created through Lakota lands. In exchange for this right-of-way, the United States would provide annual payments in supplies and foods for fifty years (though when the U.S. Congress ratified the treaty, it announced the intention to break it and stop payments after only ten years). Peace between the Indian nations did not last long.[72] For the Lakotas, peace with the United States did not last much longer.

Fort Laramie was located in what is now the state of Wyoming, and in 1854 the United States violated Lakota territory in response to the destruction of a cow. A cow belonging to a Mormon migrant had wandered into a Lakota camp. The cow was killed and eaten. The owner demanded that the U.S. military get his cow back. Conquering Bear attempted to negotiate a peace after the incident, offering horses worth much more than the sickly cow, but the owner refused to accept the generous offer of compensation. The United States used the incident as a pretense to attack the Lakotas, first by Lieutenant John Gratten, a self-professed hater of Indians, who used artillery to attack Lakota camps in 1854.[73]

The escalation in aggression by the United States left a lasting impact on the young Jiji Kin, who would later be the great military leader Crazy Horse. In 1855 General William Harney attacked the camp of Little Thunder. Harney's troops mutilated and massacred civilians, including women and children, earning him the name Woman Killer from the Lakotas. Before he was given the name Crazy

Horse, the young Jiji Kin was among the first to find the mutilated corpses of General Harney's victims.[74]

By the 1860s Crazy Horse has become a great leader among the Lakotas. Many Lakota leaders were elected, such as Sitting Bull, but others were called to lead by example by their dreams. Crazy Horse was such a thunderdreamer, a person called to sacrifice ego for the people. Such a person was a *wica*, or "complete person," who embodied the virtues of generosity, courage, fortitude, humility, and wisdom. As part of this calling, Crazy Horse never participated in the Lakota tradition of *waktoglakapi*, or the telling of one's victories. He left that to others.[75]

Crazy Horse quickly came to understand the way of war for the United States. Crazy Horse became familiar with the unchecked violence of the U.S. military, whose army did not distinguish between military targets and civilians in battle. Crazy Horse saw the carnage left by the Woman Killer at Little Thunder's camp. Crazy Horse lost a friend among his Cheyenne allies, Yellow Woman, at the Sand Creek Massacre. Crazy Horse felt the United States did not understand that war was about courage and honorable victory. He saw the United States as interested only in killing and as measuring victory by body count alone. Fighting had continued with the United States on and off over the decade, but Crazy Horse led Lakota troops in the decisive 1866 battle the Hundred in the Hands. For this battle, Crazy Horse lured the bulk of U.S. forces out of Fort Kearny (built in open violation of existing treaties) into an ambush. Crazy Horse's victory was the worst defeat the United States had suffered, to that point, in western North America.[76]

The United States sued for peace, and the Fort Laramie Treaty of 1868 granted favorable terms to the Lakotas. From the Lakota perspective, the war was a total victory. The 1868 peace treaty established the boundaries of the Great Sioux Reservation to forever include the Black Hills. The United States pledged to pay for schools, doctors, mills, and blacksmiths for the Lakotas, and no whites were to enter the Powder River country. Article 12 of the treaty prohibited future land sales by the Lakotas unless the treaty was signed by three-quarters of the Lakota adult male population. The Lakotas retained extensive hunting rights on lands off the reservation. The U.S. government was forced to abandon Fort Kearny. (Red Cloud's men burned it down immediately upon its vacation.) The great leader Sitting Bull never recognized the treaty but instead kept to the west and maintained the peace.[77]

While the Lakotas saw the peace treaty as a total military victory for them, the United States used the time to regroup and plan for future invasions of Lakota territory. Almost immediately the United States violated the treaty and engaged in economic warfare by trying to exterminate the buffalo, the central pillar of the Lakota economy. Red Cloud requested that Sitting Bull make peace. The buffalo were disappearing, and the economy was slowly being destroyed by the encroaching United States. The payments made to the Lakotas under the treaty were in substandard rations and goods, as corrupt Indian Bureau agents profiteered. The Lakotas grew weaker, and the railroad encroached on their lands in violation of the 1868 treaty. By 1873 the Sioux returned to hit-and-run attacks on rail construction sites, and the United States was unhappy that no progress had been made in "civilizing" the Lakotas.[78]

As the aggression of the United States escalated, the resistance of such leaders as Crazy Horse and Sitting Bull increased. In 1871 the U.S. Congress unilaterally declared the treaty-making period to be at an end. Rather than treaties ratified by the Senate, simple acts of legislation would now be the defining instrument of U.S.–Indian relations. In 1874 General George Custer conducted a scientific expedition into the Black Hills and widely circulated that gold had been found there. Illegal immigrants from the Unites States entered to desecrate the Black Hills and take the gold along what the Lakota called the Thieves' Road. Crazy Horse conducted silent attacks on the invaders, killing entire camps of miners with his troops. With the invasion of the United States and its clear determination to seize the sacred Black Hills, Lakota leadership was divided. Red Cloud agreed that a sale of the Black Hills would be best, as the United States would simply take whatever it wanted by force, but Sitting Bull and Crazy Horse were determined to fight. The United States opened up negotiations, but Lakota leaders refused to sell the Black Hills even when the U.S. troops put guns to the heads of Lakota diplomats. The diplomats present at the "negotiations" only signed when the United States threatened to deport the entire Lakota population to Oklahoma by force. The fraudulent negotiations, which made no pretense of obtaining the consent of three-quarters of the adult male Lakota population, caused Sitting Bull and Crazy Horse to harden their determination to resist the invasion of their national territory.[79]

During these escalating hostilities, Sitting Bull called for unity in opposition to the invasion from the United States. Crazy Horse and Sitting Bull worked together, with Crazy Horse serving as the military leader. The Lakotas united with their Northern Cheyenne allies in 1876. Crazy Horse commanded the combined troops in a series of battles designed to prevent U.S. attacks on civilian women and children. On June 25, 1876, this culminated in the Battle of Greasy Grass, known as the Battle of the Little Bighorn in the European world. Crazy Horse was able to gain the upper hand, in part, because he knew the United States understood death and killing as its measure of success in battle.[80]

The United States reacted strongly to this defeat and sent reinforcements. President Ulysses S. Grant expanded the military campaign to include all Sioux, regardless of whether they had previously been peaceful. Congress cut off all food aid to the Lakotas, even those who had already surrendered. The ultimatum was delivered: sell the Black Hills or starve.[81]

Dealing with constant economic and military warfare, Crazy Horse and Sitting Bull were faced with difficult decisions. Economic warfare had destroyed the buffalo, but alternative game remained abundant. Crazy Horse's troops could survive indefinitely on the remaining game, but his soldiers were constantly engaged in battles with the United States, defending Lakota women and children from massacre. This caused a shortfall in food, and ammunition was running short as well. Some counseled hiding the civilian population, thereby allowing the military to move, hunt, and attack with greater speed and freedom. But Crazy Horse knew that U.S. troops would not hesitate to kill unprotected women and children. A difficult decision was made, and Crazy Horse's forces surrendered to the United States in May 1877. Sitting Bull and his followers escaped U.S. repression by crossing the border into Canadian-claimed territory.[82]

Standing Rock

The Standing Rock Agency was created in the 1870s, before the end of the conflict with Crazy Horse and Sitting Bull. Sitting Bull was from the area and settled there for a time after the United States released him from prison. On the Standing Rock Agency and later reservation, the United States used federal marshals to enforce U.S. law. The United States also delivered treaty payments to Lakota people through various Indian agencies in such a way as to promote economic dependence and to undermine the authority of existing Lakota government leaders.[83]

By the end of the 1870s, conditions in the Lakota Nation had deteriorated significantly. In Standing Rock, immigrants from the United States squatted and took land at will. Agents of the federal government deposed local Lakota leaders and replaced them with their own henchmen. Forced schooling of children increased. In 1881 there was a tuberculosis outbreak. In 1882 the once-great Lakota Nation was broken up into five separate reservations, including the Standing Rock Sioux Reservation.[84]

The Lakotas were among the first to be subjected to the policies of forced assimilation via boarding schools and allotment. As boarding schools for the

Lakotas expanded in the 1880s, police officers were needed to round children up and take them away. The schools forbid the speaking of the Lakota language and the practicing of traditional Lakota religion. School punishments for violating these bans included hanging children by their thumbs. Later, in 1910, the United States outlawed the practice of the Sun Dance on Lakota reservations.[85]

Sitting Bull was lured back to the United States with the promise of an amnesty, but the United States lied to the great leader. Sitting Bull and 137 of his followers were arrested and imprisoned at Fort Randall upon entering lands occupied by the United States. Sitting Bull was released from prison in 1882 and returned to the Standing Rock Sioux Reservation. He was unhappy to find that the United States was now imposing leaders on the Lakotas; they had been elected by the Lakota people before. In 1885 Sitting Bull left the reservation to be part of William "Buffalo Bill" Cody's traveling Wild West show.[86]

The Lakotas were among the first to suffer the negative impacts of the General Allotment Act of 1887. While the treaty of 1868 required the agreement of at least three-quarters of the Lakota male population before any land could be sold, U.S. leaders quickly found they could not meet this condition. Sitting Bull opposed parting with any more land. The United States could find only twenty-two people willing to sign the agreement for sale of "surplus" lands of the Standing Rock Reservation. Nevertheless, the United States sold off more than half the reservation, leaving land only fit for submarginal grazing in possession of the Standing Rock Sioux.[87]

The new Ghost Dance religion, started by a Paiute shaman, Wovoka, was welcomed to Standing Rock by Sitting Bull and his followers. The Ghost Dance preached peace, as well as the return of the buffalo and the retreat of the United States. Fearing the spread of this new religious movement, the United States placed reservations, including the Standing Rock Reservation, under military command. Agents acting on behalf of the United States assassinated Sitting Bull in December 1890. In the violence that followed, 189 people were killed; only 39 of these were occupying troops. Some weeks later, the United States massacred more than three hundred followers of the Ghost Dance at Wounded Knee.[88]

By 1910 most Lakotas had been pushed onto allotments. The 1934 Indian Reorganization Act began to exacerbate divisions in Lakota societies. This act authorized Indian reservations to organize governing bodies. As the Lakotas were on six reservations, in 1937 they formed the pan-reservation Black Hills Sioux Nation Council to help coordinate litigation over the Black Hills. Those who continued to support traditional Lakota governing structures responded by forming the Black Hills Treaty and Claims Council, outside the IRA structure and governments.[89]

Congress authorized the Army Corps of Engineers to construct a series of dams along the Missouri River in 1844. Congress authorized construction of the Oahe Dam and the taking of fifty-six thousand acres of the best land of the Standing Rock Reservation in 1958. The dam reached its final height in 1959 and was dedicated in 1962, when it began generating power. The Standing Rock Sioux lost access to sacred sites, the best remaining timber lands, and other agricultural resources, causing significant economic, social, and physical dislocations.[90]

In pursuit of the emerging termination policy, Congress passed the Indian Claims Commission Act in 1946. This law established a special claims commission for all Indian grievances founded in duress, fraud, unconscionable consideration, and mistakes of fact, essentially addressing the treaty-making process as under contract law. In addition, the act authorized the commission to consider claims based not in legal theories but upon principles of fair and honorable dealings. The act provided for an investigative division, and the commission could rewrite treaties as they should have occurred. In 1950 attorneys for the Lakotas entered a claim for the Black Hills based on unconscionable consideration and consideration under the fair-and-honorable dealings provisions of the claims act. [91]

Termination policy backfired. Indians organized national groups to fight the policy: the National Congress of American Indians in 1958 and the more militant National Indian Youth Council in 1961. The NIYC joined Indians who reasserted their fishing rights, in violation of state laws and regulations, in civil disobedience. The Lakotas successfully organized to defeat laws designed to extend the criminal jurisdiction of South Dakota over the Sioux reservations.[92]

In 1964 the Sioux were still in the tight grip of crushing poverty. Forty percent of Sioux lived on less than a thousand dollars a year, and infant mortality was 30 percent above the national average. The Lakotas also suffered a high suicide rate. They had no natural resources left to develop, their land was too remote for industry, and less than one-fifth of them graduated high school. The expansion of the social spending programs of the New Frontier and the Great Society helped some.[93]

The late 1960s and early 1970s saw the rise of more militant Indian activism and the creation of the American Indian Movement. AIM made sovereignty the new Ghost Dance for the Lakotas (and others), and the young urban militants of AIM formed alliances with the older traditionalists. The two groups worked together in their struggles against those who ran IRA governments and popularized the idea of Sioux national sovereignty. AIM, Indian militants, and their allies argued in 1974 that the 1868 treaty was still legally intact. The militants and traditionalists moved Lakota popular opinion to the idea that the Black Hills and the remainder of the 1868 treaty lands were never lost. More and more people wanted the hills back rather than monetary compensation.[94]

On June 13, 1979, a claims court ruled that the taking of the Black Hills had been a Fifth Amendment taking of property and that compensation was appropriate. The judgment entered was for more than $17.5 million, plus interest, for a total of roughly $105 million. The United States appealed the Court of Claims award to the Supreme Court. On July 1, 1980, the Supreme Court, in an opinion written by Justice Blackmun, found that the history of unfair dealings on the part of the U.S. government was clear and affirmed the decision of the Court of Claims in finding that the taking of the Black Hills violated the Fifth Amendment protection of property. Judge Willian Rehnquist wrote a dissent, claiming that what happened with the Black Hills was generous and fair on the part of the U.S. government, without citation to authority.[95]

AIM denounced the attorneys for the Lakotas as parasites who would take an unconscionable share of the monetary damages. A new attorney for the Pine Ridge Reservation began launching lawsuits with innovative theories to get the Black Hills back. All were unsuccessful. The Lakotas approached the United Nations with no results. In 1985 U.S. senator Bill Bradley of New Jersey introduced a bill to return the Black Hills to the Sioux, but the reaction of South Dakota and its senator made passage impossible. Despite crushing poverty that continues to this day, the legally recognized governments of the Lakotas have refused to accept payment for the lands seized illegally by the United States. As of the publication of this book, the Black Hills award continues to collect interest.[96] The Standing Rock Sioux government takes the position that all lands recognized by the 1868 treaty are Lakota territory.

The Dakota Access Pipeline

The Dakota Access Pipeline (DAPL) is a 1,200-mile-long pipeline that crosses under Lake Oahe, a federally regulated water crossing, about half a mile north of the Standing Rock Sioux Reservation. The pipeline, completed in the spring of 2017, originates in North Dakota, crosses South Dakota and Iowa, and ends in Patoka, Illinois. Ninety-nine percent of the pipeline was constructed on private lands, which required no regulatory approval by the federal government. The pipeline does cross federally regulated waterways in hundreds of places, requiring approval by the Army Corps of Engineers. For the approval process, the Army Corps of Engineers treated each crossing as a separate project and conducted an environmental assessment for each. The National Environmental Policy Act requires a hard look at the impacts of a proposed project for an environmental assessment. If there is a finding of no significant impact (FONSI), an environmental impact statement, with its significantly more stringent requirements for consultation and public commenting, is not required. The Lake Oahe crossing was found to have no significant impact on the environment of the sacred waters that the Standing Rock Sioux Reservation requires for hunting, fishing, and religious ceremonies.[97]

Representatives of Energy Transfer Partners met with the governing council of the Standing Rock Sioux on September 30, 2014, to discuss the project and to express concern for the continuing interests of the Standing Rock Sioux in areas potentially impacted by the pipeline. Energy Transfer Partners, an energy company from Texas, owns the Dakota Access Pipeline project. During the meeting, Standing Rock chairman David Archiambault informed the company that the Standing Rock Sioux took the position that they retained rights throughout the boundaries of the 1868 Fort Laramie Treaty and opposed the construction of any pipeline impacting that territory. Tribal historic preservation officer Waste Win Young thanked Energy Transfer Partners for taking the time to speak with them about the issue and complained that the council had been having a difficult time contacting the Army Corps of Engineers regarding the project. He informed Energy Transfer Partners that the proposed Lake Oahe crossing would be under culturally sensitive resources and that the Historic Preservation Office could make more information available regarding culturally sensitive sites along the proposed route of the pipeline.[98]

The next month, Dakota Access Pipeline staff contacted the Army Corps of Engineers for an easement application. The easement application was submitted in June 2015. The Army Corps of Engineers granted the easement on July 25, 2016. The original path of the pipeline would have crossed the Missouri River ten miles upstream from the city of Bismarck, North Dakota, but this crossing was rerouted because of fears that potential spills or leaks could threaten municipal water sources.[99]

Two days after the approval of the easement by the Army Corps of Engineers, the Standing Rock Sioux filed suit, claiming violations of the National Historic Preservation Act, the National Environmental Policy Act, and other statutes. The Dakota Access Pipeline joined the suit on August 5, 2016, as an interested party. The Cheyenne River Sioux joined the case on the side of their kin on August 10,

2016. Initially the lawsuit sought injunctive relief and a temporary restraining order, claiming violations of the National Historic Preservation Act consultation process.[100]

Massive protests followed, with Indian Rights activists working together with environmental groups, including Earth Justice. Those opposed to the pipeline declared themselves to be "water protectors." As many as four thousand water protectors had participated in protests by late August. Private security forces working for DAPL reacted violently, siccing attack dogs on the water protectors. State security forces instituted roadblocks and checkpoints to deter water protectors. North Dakota governor Jack Dalrymple authorized a restricted state of emergency. State security forces also attacked the water protectors and arrested some of those covering the protests and broadcasting events to the world.[101]

The protests of the water protectors made a significant impact on leaders back in Washington. The Barack Obama administration waited until the Standing Rock and Cheyenne River Sioux lost their motion for a temporary restraining order on September 9, 2016, clearly in hopes that the courts would put the project on hold. When that did not happen, the Departments of Justice and the Interior, and the Army Corps of Engineers, put the Lake Oahe permit crossing on hold. On November 14, 2016, the assistant secretary of the army for civil work stated that additional discussions with the Standing Rock Sioux were necessary before the project could continue. After further discussions, on December 4, the U.S. government declared that the easement could not be approved on the current record and that the robust consultation and considerations of an environmental impact statement were necessary before an easement could be approved.[102]

The United States electoral college selected a new president on December 19, 2016, and that candidate, Donald Trump, had declared his support for the Dakota Access Pipeline. Trump took office on January 20, 2017. On January 24, he ordered the Army Corps of Engineers to approve the Lake Oahe easement with all due speed under the law. The army completed its review on February 8 and issued a new easement. The Standing Rock Sioux sought a preliminary injunction and temporary protective order the next day on the grounds that the pipeline would substantially burden their religion and violate the Religious Freedom Restoration Act, but this injunction was denied on March 7.[103]

> The Religious Freedom Restoration Act
> Does Not Protect Lake Oahe

The District Court for the District of Columbia provided, on March 7, 2017, what the Ninth Circuit Court of Appeals could not deliver in 2007: a coherent, if inadequate, opinion regarding why the pollution and desecration of a sacred site is not a substantial burden to the practice of religion. While the opinion of the district court was not definitive—it merely ruled on the likelihood of ultimate success—this court put forth a coherent argument based on the legislative history of the Religious Freedom Restoration Act without addressing the difficulties surrounding the differences of opinion between Justices Antonin Scalia and Sandra Day O'Connor as to what the *Lyng* decision ultimately means.

The Standing Rock Sioux took the position that Lake Oahe was sacred, its waters were necessary for religious ceremonies, and the Dakota Access Pipeline endangered the sacred character in two ways. First, the pipeline could leak and pollute the waters, rendering them useless for religious ceremonies. Second, many Standing Rock Sioux believed that a prophecy about a great black snake that would encircle and devour the people told of the coming of the pipeline. The mere presence of the pipeline, the black snake, under Lake Oahe desecrated the lake and endangered all. Thus the presence of the pipeline under the water substantially burdened religion.[104]

The court delivered an opinion with the interpretation that Congress intended the Religious Freedom Restoration Act to merely restore the compelling interest test from before the days of *Employment Division v. Smith*, including previous exceptions and precedents, including *Lyng*. To support this interpretation of legislative intent, the court quoted the Senate committee report on RFRA: "[P]re-*Smith* case law makes it clear that strict scrutiny does not apply to government actions involving only management of internal Government affairs or the use of the Government's own property or resources." Thus the court determined that the total desecration of a sacred site is, legally speaking, not a burden on religion. To further support this interpretation, the court listed a string of precedents, beginning with the *Navajo Nation* case of 2007 (discussed at length in chapter 2): "Just as the Ninth Circuit and other courts must follow *Lyng* until the Supreme Court instructs otherwise, this Court must do the same."[105]

While it may have been the intent of the United States Senate to keep alive the precedents before *Smith*, the specific language of the statute and the meaning of *Lyng*, as disputed by Justices O'Connor and Scalia, do not support this reasoning. RFRA was to apply in "all" cases, an expansion of the previous existing compelling interest test. In addition, Scalia argued, in *Smith*, that the compelling interest test had been abandoned, not by *Smith* but by *Lyng*. Thus, if RFRA is to restore the test before *Smith*, and if *Smith* is just following *Lyng* as Scalia wrote, then RFRA must restore the test that existed before *Lyng*. Alternatively, if O'Connor's interpretation—that

Lyng was a narrow exception to the compelling interest test—is correct, then RFRA would again end the value of *Lyng* as a relevant precedent, because the compelling interest test is now to be applied in all cases and the list of exceptions carved out by precedent has been significantly narrowed, by the plain language of the law.

Though the attempt to obtain a preliminary injunction failed, the litigation continued and the Standing Rock Sioux had some success in the summer of 2017. The Standing Rock Sioux retained significant rights to draw water from the Missouri River and Lake Oahe. In addition, the Standing Rock Sioux retained significant hunting and fishing rights in the area. The Standing Rock Sioux and their allies argued that none of the environmental assessments sufficiently considered the impact of the pipeline on the water, hunting, and fishing rights of the Standing Rock Sioux. The court found that the environmental assessments in this case largely complied with the law but that the assessments of both July 25, 2016, and February 3, 2017, failed to adequately consider the impacts of an oil leak or spill on the water, hunting, and fishing rights of the Standing Rock Sioux. While the presumption is that when an environmental assessment is inadequate, the approval should be vacated, if remediation of the assessment is possible without overturning the approval, that should be contemplated by the court. As neither party had, before June 14, briefed in detail the possible remedy for a faulty environmental assessment that largely complied with the law, the court ordered the parties to brief their arguments as to what should happen, as the environmental assessment was remanded for further action by the Army Corps of Engineers. While the court allowed the oil to continue to flow as the Army Corps of Engineers remedied the inadequate environmental assessment, in December 2017 the court required finalization and implementation of the oil-spill response plans for Lake Oahe, completion of a compliance audit by a third party selected in consultation with the plaintiff Indian nations, and public reporting of information regarding pipeline operations. The court took these steps as part of its oversight responsibilities during remediation of the deficiencies in the original assessment. As of publication, the Dakota Access Pipeline is fully functional, and crude oil is flowing beneath Lake Oahe. The assessment has been sent back to the Army Corps of Engineers for further consideration of the impacts of an oil spill on the treaty rights of the Standing Rock Sioux, and the district court is monitoring the situation.[106]

Again, the courts are consistently unwilling to protect indigenous sacred sites and religious resources when faced with government action that will desecrate them, but unlike many of the other cases examined here, the Standing Rock Sioux effectively allied themselves with environmental organizations and brought considerable publicity to their cause, effectively educating many that they were seeking to protect sacred waters, as water protectors. The effectiveness of the protests of the water protectors pushed the Obama administration to engage in the full consultation process required by environmental impact statements, but this case also demonstrates again the fragility of administrative decisions as avenues for protecting rights. The new administration simply reversed the decision and canceled further consultation. This lack of consultation was condemned by Victoria Tauli-Corpuz, United Nations special rapporteur on the rights of indigenous peoples, for not complying with the requirements of the United Nations Declaration on the Rights of Indigenous Peoples.[107]

Other commentators have pointed out that the lack of substantive consultation, combined with the costs of delays caused by ongoing protests and lawsuits, cost Energy Transfer Partners, Wells Fargo, and other investors considerable money. Banks have been targeted for their support of the Dakota Access Pipeline, and several have pulled their support for project. Wells Fargo remains invested but is the subject of growing boycotts. Some legal commentators have suggested that engaging in significant consultation with Indian nations before undertaking projects that may impact cultural, religious, economic, and treaty interests makes the most financial sense. Of course, this works only with a well-informed public that is willing to do what it takes to support indigenous interests.[108]

6 IMPROVING PROTECTION OF INDIAN SACRED SITES AND RECONCEIVING INDIAN SOVEREIGNTY

There are several recommendations for how to approach the wide range of discretion that courts have created for administrators in managing Indian sacred sites on public lands. It should be clear by now that the federal government can do whatever it likes with Indian cultural sites on public lands and that there are currently neither constitutional nor statutory protections for Indian religions. This chapter examines a wide range of proposals designed to address many difficulties facing Indian nations, including the protection of cultural and sacred sites.

Within the existing framework of Indian law and sovereign relations, there are strategies for promoting the protection of Indian sacred sites. Joshua A. Edwards has argued that the Ninth Circuit Court of Appeals clearly misinterpreted the new standard of "substantial burden" and that the Religious Freedom Restoration Act should have provided protection to the Hopis and other peoples concerned about the expansive desecration of the San Francisco Peaks. The D.C. federal district court followed this precedent with regard to the impact of the Dakota Access Pipeline on the sacred water of Lake Oahe. Absent a higher court revisiting the Ninth Circuit's tortured interpretation of RFRA, this position will not have practical impact. Kristen A. Carpenter has suggested that lawyers should craft arguments based in property rights, as the First Amendment and RFRA offer no protection to sacred sites. Carpenter has provided a series of clever arguments based in third-party property rights of easements, whereby indigenous religious practitioners may be able to claim enforcement of existing easements or monetary damages for the destruction of such easements.[1]

While the idea of using the law of easements to protect sacred sites is ingenious, it would likely run up against what Mike Myers has called the "just cuz" doctrine of Indian law. The "just cuz" doctrine is simply a more colloquial version of the damning assessment of the practices of the Supreme Court identified by David E. Wilkins: to deny Indian rights, the Supreme Court twists logic and reason while engaging in fear-mongering hypotheticals about Indians hunting whales to extinction, human sacrifice, or Indians ruling large parts of the Americas. These methods ensure that claimants lose otherwise excellent cases "just cuz" they are Indians.[2] One could argue that the tortured interpretation of "substantial burden" on religion created by the Ninth Circuit Court of Appeals, which Edwards takes issue with, is another instance of the "just cuz" doctrine in action.

In the face of the "just cuz" doctrine of a hostile Supreme Court, other Indian law commentators have urged pursuing political lobbying alternatives to constant losses in litigation. Louis Fischer makes this recommendation, noting that Indians have had more success in lobbying both Congress and the executive branch. Lobbying would be necessary in any effort to correct what Edwards sees as the failure of the courts to properly identify the intent of Congress with RFRA. Indian groups can lobby with regard to specific land issues, as Congress has full power over the final disposition of federal lands. The case of Oak Flat is a clear demonstration of Congress's ultimate power and how that power can be misused. The San Carlos Apaches may yet find success with their protest and lobbying efforts, but the Hopis and others appear to have largely failed in lobbying efforts regarding the San Francisco Peaks. (Recent efforts have provided a measure of success: the City of Flagstaff has agreed to another level of filtration of the reclaimed sewage effluent before it is piped to the snowmaking machines at the Peaks).[3]

Beyond lobbying to protect individual sacred sites, there are legislative proposals to generally expand protection of Indian sacred sites. One method would be for Congress to clarify the meaning of "substantial burden" and explicitly include management of Indian sacred sites. Alex Tallchief Skibine has called for an amendment to the American Indian Religious Freedom Act to offer more explicit protections. His three-part proposed law calls for a more precise definition of "sacred sites" modeled on a synthesis of Executive Order 13,007's definition of "traditional cultural properties" and other relevant approaches. (He remained unspecific.) Second, he argues for expanding the threshold for burdening religions beyond the scope of coercion or denial of a benefit to include such burdens as those suffered by the desecration or destruction of sacred sites. Finally Skibine called for the same type of intermediate scrutiny that has been used for free speech in public places rather than the strict scrutiny test. Under this proposed intermediate scrutiny test, when religion is burdened, the government would have to come up with "an important or substantial interest . . . unrelated to the suppression of religion, and the burden posed on religious freedom could be no greater than those essential to protect that governmental interest."[4] Presumably, under such a test, complete desecration of the Hopis' most sacred site would be a greater burden than the burden on the government of having only a profitable low-key ski resort available in the middle of a desert.

INDIAN SOVEREIGNTY

A more innovative solution to the problem lies in the possibility of formulating a new understanding of indigenous sovereignty. The legal history of Indian sovereignty has seen many changes. Initially, European nations, when they were not invading indigenous lands, made treaties with Indian nations, including military and political alliances, as fully sovereign partners. In North America, once the English immigrant presence was more secure, European-styled nations began to claim sovereignty over indigenous nations they had never met, let alone conquered in battle. Making some sense of this anomalous state of affairs, the Marshall Trilogy declared Indian nations to not be fully foreign sovereigns but instead to be domestic dependent nations that did not have the full sovereign right to sell their lands to anyone they pleased. The Doctrine of Discovery divested Indian nations of this power, so when Thomas Jefferson purchased the lands of hundreds of Indian nations from France with the Louisiana Purchase, he merely purchased the French claims to the exclusive right to obtain land from Indian nations, which retained their rights to occupy the land. In the final part of his famed trilogy, Marshall made it quite clear that Indian nations retained full internal sovereignty beyond the power of the states to interfere.

While Marshall's legal framework went unenforced and ethnic cleansing of the east was largely completed, the legal framework of the Marshall Trilogy remained in place for decades for the Indian nations forcibly removed to the west. The Supreme Court had long recognized exclusive Indian sovereignty over internal affairs, but the high court changed this position in redefining plenary power in the late nineteenth and early twentieth century. As late as 1883, in *Ex Parte Crow Dog*, 109 U.S. 556, the Supreme Court recognized Indian societies as separate and as having their own criminal justice systems. But liberal outrage over indigenous justice not being in line with Europe's vindictive notions of justice pushed Congress to pass the Major Crimes Act, taking felony criminal jurisdiction away from Indian societies and unilaterally extending federal criminal jurisdiction over reserved lands. While not yet mentioning plenary power, in 1886, with *U.S. v. Kagama*, 118 U.S. 375, the Supreme Court upheld the Major Crimes Act as being a proper exercise of congressional power over Indian affairs. The same year that the Supreme Court eliminated all constitutional limits on the exercise of congressional powers over Indian peoples, the court also decided that corporations had the same legal standing as persons and thus afforded constitutional protections to corporations from the excesses of Congress.[5] These protections for corporations have never been extended to Indian governments and societies.

It was not until 1886 that the Supreme Court recognized that the plenary power of Congress over Indian affairs was not "full" in the sense of "at the exclusion of the states" but was "full" in the sense of unchecked by the power of the Constitution, the Bill of Rights, or international law. What followed was a systematic attempt to eliminate Indian cultures, languages, and religions from the face of the Earth. This policy ended with the Indian Reorganization Act of 1934, and the theory that Indian nations retained sovereign powers not explicitly removed by Congress emerged in this legal era. Plenary power remained a specter stalking Indian nations, and the framework Marshall created, with Indian nations having full internal sovereignty, deteriorated with further congressional and judicial power grabs.

The Nixon administration reversed some congressional assaults on Indian sovereignty and denounced the renewed efforts to eliminate Indian nations. Government-to-government relations slowly took over the Indian policy of the federal government. By 1980 many new laws provided avenues for the protection of Indian national and cultural interests. The consultation process of the Indian Religious Freedom Act was one important component of this new, but imperfect, respect for indigenous rights.

For a time in the middle to late twentieth century, there was hope that assaults on indigenous sovereignty in the United States might come to an end and that Indian sovereignty would stabilize. Charles F. Wilkinson identifies the latest changes in Indian policy as starting not with the bold new direction established by President Nixon but instead with a change in direction by the United States Supreme Court. Wilkinson marks the change in direction with the 1959 Supreme Court decision in *Williams v. Lee*. This case arose from a dispute over unpaid bills between a trading post operating on the Navajo Reservation and a Navajo man, Paul Williams, living on the reservation. The non-Indian creditor sought payment through a court order from a county court in Arizona rather than from the Navajo court system. The Supreme Court determined that the Navajo courts had exclusive jurisdiction over the matter. This case began a string of Supreme Court decisions that protected indigenous water rights, Indian control of Indian education, and off-reservation fish and game rights, as well as reaffirmed the protection of indigenous national assets from state taxation.[6]

The Nixon administration continued the move to greater respect for indigenous sovereignty, and this culminated in the 1975 Indian Self-Determination Act and its 1994 amendments. The process enabled by the Self-Determination Act provided for Indian governments to take over and manage Bureau of Indian Affairs programs at their own pace. What emerged from this law was a process of BIA downsizing as Indian governments gained confidence and experience and took on additional management and government responsibilities.[7]

While the elected branches of the U.S. government had done much to reverse course, so too did the once-benign Supreme Court. While the high court had played its part in undermining constitutional protections for Indian nations and Indian peoples, it had been more like a benign tumor that slowly ate away at Indian sovereignty and rights while leaving the rest of the body of indigenous sovereignty intact. But starting in 1978, the United States Supreme Court became a malignant tumor on the political scene of U.S. Indian law and began an aggressive attack on the sovereignty and rights of indigenous peoples.

What emerged from the competing policies of the United States Supreme Court and the elected bodies of the U.S. government was a fundamental contradiction between the concept of Indian sovereignty and the contemporary Supreme Court interpretation of plenary power. Indigenous sovereignty predates the U.S. Constitution. The United States recognized Indian sovereignty in the Indian Commerce Clause of the Constitution and gave Congress the exclusive power to define and manage Indian affairs. For scholars like David E. Wilkins and K. Tsianina Lomawaima, the initial meaning of "plenary power" in the Marshall Trilogy was that the United States Congress, not the other branches of government or the states, had the exclusive and preemptive power to govern Indian affairs, not that Congress had absolute power over Indian peoples. The United States Supreme Court later redefined this term.[8]

The expansive interpretation of "plenary power" has no basis in the Constitution and nullified the constitutionally recognized concept of indigenous sovereignty found in the Indian Commerce Clause. While *Kagama* effectively established unlimited congressional power over Indian affairs, the Supreme Court first used the term "plenary power" in *Lone Wolf v. Hitchcock*, 187 U.S. 553 (1903). In this case, the taking of Indian lands was challenged as explicitly violating treaty terms. The Supreme Court alluded to early opinions by John Marshall describing the relationship between Indian nations and the United States as that of a ward to its guardian. From this premise, the Supreme Court disregarded the Supremacy Clause of the Constitution, where all treaties are said to be the supreme law of the land (and therefore on par in power with the requirements of the Constitution itself), and claimed that the power of Congress over the affairs of Indian peoples was without limit, and always had been. For Wilkins and Lomawaima, this was a deliberate twisting of the meaning of the phrase "plenary power," from an exclusive power of Congress to govern Indian relations to one of absolute and unchecked power.

For Wilkins the contemporary rulings of the Supreme Court on Indian issues have nothing to do with logic, sound reasoning, or legal ideals. Wilkins identifies the new direction of the court as ignoring the trust responsibility to Indian peoples and ignoring collective Indian rights. Wilkins found that Supreme Court justices, "individually and collectively, have engaged in the manufacturing, redefining, and burying of 'principles,' 'doctrines,' and legal 'tests' to excuse and legitimize constitutional, treaty, and civil rights violations" of Indian individuals and nations. Wilkins notes where the Supreme Court, to obtain its desired outcomes, has used such tactics as taking selected phrases out of context and creating unreasonable and exaggerated hypotheticals designed to generate fear of Indian sovereignty. As a remedy, Wilkins calls for Congress to disavow the legitimacy of the newer expansive definition of "plenary power."[9]

PLACING INDIAN SOVEREIGNTY IN CONTEXT

Another theoretically grounded approach to indigenous sovereignty is Thomas Biolsi's "Imagined Geographies," where he identifies four modular components of sovereignty that complicate the traditional territorial-based theories. Biolsi contemplates four types of political space where indigenous sovereignty existed inside the United States. The first was the traditional territorial space of Indian nations. The second was indigenous co-management, with state and federal agencies and governments, of resources such as fish, wildlife, water, religious sites, and cultural properties. The third sovereign space was that of individual portable rights that existed beyond reservation boundaries, including such things as possession of eagle feathers for religious and ceremonial purposes, and religious use and possession of peyote. The final indigenous space identified is that where Indian peoples act as citizens of the United States while retaining Indian cultural identity. This final space is where Indian peoples fight and struggle to be included in the community of the United States. One example of struggle in this space that Biolsi presents is the ongoing conflict over the use of insulting and derogatory mascots by national sports franchises. Biolsi identifies one of the greatest threats to the exercise of indigenous sovereignty in these spaces as the refusal to recognize indigenous peoples as political communities with the right of self-determination and an insistence on a "colorblind" society with no "special cases" and where every individual is treated the same, regardless of circumstances.[10]

Frank Pommersheim updates the ongoing examinations of Indian sovereignty with his 2009 book, *Broken Landscapes: Indians, Indian Tribes, and the Constitution*. He analyzes the alarming trajectory of Indian law, placing it in a changing international context and examining several options for making corrections. As to the constitutional basis of Indian law, Pommersheim identifies three basic schools of thought, tied to different historical eras. First was the era of Indian relations based in the Marshall Trilogy of cases. Second was the era of congressional plenary power that emerged in the late nineteenth century. Third was the Felix Cohen era of retained sovereignty that emerged with the Indian Reorganization Act. Pommersheim identifies the current era as one of Supreme Court plenary power that emerged with *Oliphant v. Suquamish*, 435 U.S. 191 (1978). Pommersheim concludes that with this case, the United States Supreme Court began down a path of making common law decisions that more and more reduced the sovereignty of Indian nations. The final theoretical era, Pommersheim hopes, would be some form of treaty-based federation for the future.[11]

While tracing a history of doctrinal confusion in federal Indian policy that exacerbated the Supreme Court's creation of what he identifies as the court's newly created common law plenary power, Pommersheim expands the understanding of the changing disposition of the Supreme Court by placing the court's decisions in a context of developments in international law. With increased activity of indigenous nongovernmental organizations in international affairs, international legal standards have changed considerably from the days when Marshall stripped Indian nations of full national sovereignty by invoking the Eurocentric Doctrine of Discovery (perhaps an early variant of the "just cuz" doctrine). In 2007 the United Nations General Assembly adopted the Declaration on the Rights of Indigenous Peoples. This emerging international consensus protects the self-determination of indigenous peoples in the areas of cultural integrity, land and natural resources, social welfare and development, self-government, and freedom from discrimination. Pommersheim also notes that while indigenous people won a victory over the government of Nicaragua in the Inter-American Court of Human Rights with regard to land occupation rights, the United States simply denied the legitimacy of that court's jurisdiction when faced with a similar challenge to removing an indigenous family from continuously occupied lands.[12]

While the United States has ignored developments in indigenous international law in respecting the rights of indigenous peoples, Pommersheim compares recent developments in three other settler–common law nations and finds that these nations have adjusted their laws to somewhat conform to emerging standards that recognize the humanity of indigenous peoples. In 1982 Canada amended its constitution to respect the continuing rights and treaties of indigenous peoples. The Supreme Court of Canada later placed indigenous oral history and tradition on the same level as other historical documents in determining land title. New Zealand entered into a single treaty with nearly all indigenous peoples of the land in the 1840 Treaty of Waitangi. To deal with later violations and difficulties, New Zealand authorized the Waitangi Tribunal to hear indigenous complaints. While the findings of the tribunal are not binding, they are official recommendations that the courts and parliament are to give attention to. In 1997 Australia changed its understanding of indigenous land title by recognizing it for the first time with *Mabo v. Queensland*. This case referenced the Marshall Trilogy and adopted many of the positions on retained indigenous rights. There the high court stated that contemporary common law must keep abreast of current international law. Pommersheim noted that the United States Supreme Court has, by contrast, repeatedly been unable or afraid to confront the reality of the past.[13]

MOVING FORWARD TOGETHER

In 2004 Raymond Cross, a professor at the University of Montana School of Law, called for a second American founding to address ongoing problems with indigenous development and sovereignty. Cross notes that the initial founding principles of American Indian law created a separation of societies that was in part based on fear. While Cross acknowledges significant differences in Indian and non-Indian communities that often cause difficulties in communications, total understanding is not necessary for living together; only mutual respect is needed.[14] In identifying the need for a second American founding, Cross explains the failures of government policy in finding solutions to issues of social participation and development.

Cross condemns both the policies of the 1960s and the later neoliberal approach as doomed to failure. He characterizes the 1960s Great Society programs as trying to recast Indians as ethnic minorities. In the past, voluntary minorities traveled to the United States, and by shedding much of their ethnic identity, these former outsiders were integrated into the larger community. The programs of the 1960s, in Cross's assessment, attempted to re-create this process with involuntary minorities, including Indian peoples. Indians, by and large, had little interest in shedding their cultural heritage. Cross acknowledges that there has been a great deal of progress made in regaining indigenous self-determination, but he characterized the Supreme Court's trajectory as refusing to allow Indians to participate in a greater American community *as Indians*. Cross identifies this approach of the United States Supreme Court as foisting a neoliberal form of agentalism on Indians, mirroring the neoliberal approach to African American poverty in the political realm. This approach refused to acknowledge the actual circumstances of individuals and peoples while leaving them to act as agents on their own.[15]

An example of this neoliberal approach to Indians is the case of *U.S. v. Navajo Nation*, 537 U.S. 488 (2003). In this case, the Navajo Nation negotiated a lease for coal development on reservations lands. The Interior Department conducted its own study of the situation and determined that a fair market rate for the lease would be 20 percent. As part of its trust responsibility, the Interior Department must sign off on any such leases. Navajo officials negotiated a rate with Peabody Coal for 12.5 percent, and the secretary of the interior both approved the lease and, at the request of Peabody Coal, never informed Navajo officials that the department's analysis placed a fair market rate at 20 percent. The difference in rates cost the Navajo Nation some $600 million, and the Navajo Nation sued the federal government for failure to live up to its trust responsibility. The Supreme Court found that the Navajo Nation was responsible for negotiating the lease and that there was no basis for finding that the secretary of the interior's approval duty included an enforceable action for money damages in court. Cross finds this approach to treating Indian nations as agents to appear merely vindictive, in the absence of any sustained programmatic assistance to provide the knowledge, skills, and training needed for them to act as effective agents.[16]

While not rejecting the notion of Indian nations and individuals as agents, Cross condemns the neoliberal approach while calling for the development of Indian peoples and nations as agents able to control their own affairs. In doing so, Cross looks to Amartya Sen's notion of development as freedom. Sen's approach to development is not to focus solely on economic indicators as a measure of development but to instead measure development in terms of expanding substantive freedom by eliminating poverty and tyranny. For Sen, economic growth is not an end in itself but a means to the end of enhancing the lives of people. For Sen, people must be at the center of any development program. People must be actively involved in their own destiny. Thus freedom is both a means and an end in development. Sen also noted that freedom is inherently diverse. For Cross, this freedom requires a new covenant between Indian and non-Indian peoples based upon mutual respect and a commitment to deep diversity. Deep diversity, here, is an acceptance of a plurality of ways of being with localized political institutions and practices. For Cross, the development of freedom requires expanding the capabilities of Indian peoples to act as agents by providing education that allows people to express their opinions meaningfully, exercise economic freedom, and participate in a larger community with respect and equality.[17]

Cross calls for Indian people to take the lead in promoting this new relationship with non-Indian peoples. Cross notes limited successes in the area of public education in Montana. Montana is the only state with a constitutional provision recognizing protecting Indian heritage as an important part of the state's educational duty. Cross also describes a great deal of fear of meaningful Indian participation in the larger political community in the United States. In 1992 the State of Montana sought to redistrict in a way as to disenfranchise Indian voters. Ultimately Montana was placed under the federal supervision provisions of the 1965 Voting Rights Act. Cross calls for improvements in communication and education to overcome the remaining fear in non-Indian communities as a necessary step in negotiating new arrangements based in deep diversity.[18]

Other studies similarly conclude that Indian development works better when Indian nations have sovereign control over resources to fit development needs to the specific local conditions. James Huffman and Robert Miller, as part of a series of studies on property rights and economic development in indigenous lands in Canada and the United States, conclude that a diversity of property arrangements controlled by sovereign Indian nations with state-like powers would best provide for indigenous economic development. Manley A. Begay Jr., Stephen Cornell, Miriam Jorgenson, and Joseph P. Kalt find that Indian development projects have been most successful when driven by Indian interests and needs in ways that account for local Indian culture.[19]

These authors argue that local indigenous institutions must work well with local Indian cultures and note that Indian nations that largely adopted Bureau of Indian Affairs–proposed Indian Reorganization Act constitutions without significant amendment have not done terribly well with these alien systems. The authors also note that institutions do not necessarily have to strictly follow traditional patterns and that if they are developed by the cultures themselves, they have a much greater chance of success. In support of this position, the authors present the example of the reservation government of the Confederated Salish and Kootenai Tribes. This reservation in northwestern Montana forced together three different Indian peoples with no shared history or culture: the Salish, Pend d'Orelle, and Kootenai. Together these groups crafted a parliamentary government with a legislatively chosen council chair. With a self-created government designed to meet the collective needs of its different traditions, the Confederated Salish and Kootenai Reservation was the first Indian nation to take over every government program available for self-management by Indian nations in 2003.[20]

Christine K. Gray reiterates a most troubling problem regarding indigenous sovereignty. Borrowing from Philip J. Deloria, Gray states that the right of Indian nations to exist, and thereby exercise their collective rights to self-determination and sovereignty, should be obvious. But in the American system, this right to exist is not obvious. Instead Indian peoples must fight and struggle for every bit of sovereignty. This difficulty is in part due to the lack of public understanding of the issues.[21]

THE PRESENT SUPREME COURT'S DISINCLINATION TO RECOGNIZE INDIAN SOVEREIGNTY

To address the recent historical animosity of the United States Supreme Court toward indigenous sovereignty and rights, Alex Tallchief Skibine suggests that Congress might enter into a compact of incorporation with each Indian nation. This measure would be similar to the compact of incorporation with Puerto Rico that recognized the home rule of that territory—although the recent bankruptcy and termination of local government of that territory indicate dangerous weaknesses in this approach. Skibine's plan calls for the compact to be approved by members of the various nations; the compact could be altered only by mutual consent of the compacting parties.[22] As opposed to some proposed constitutional amendments designed to protect Indian sovereignty from a hostile Supreme Court, discussed below, individually negotiated compacts would leave the possibility of Indian nations securing rights to access sacred sites and encumbrances on federal lands, requiring the preservation of these places in the compacts themselves.

A legislative alternative proposed by Michael Eitner calls for uniform statutory guidelines for the consultation process, with a right of action by Indian interests if the government has no good reason to ignore indigenous concerns. This legislative proposal merely addresses instances where administrative agencies clearly do not give any substantive consideration of indigenous concerns, and it would provide for regularity and substance in consultation procedures on a government-to-government basis. The first part of the law would require agencies to treat Indian claims regarding the sacredness of sites as true. This would be a rebuttable presumption (presumably to address concerns created by fear-mongering courts that false claims of sacredness would then appear everywhere). If the government disagreed with the Indian claims of sacred places being impacted, this law would provide for the government to overcome Indian claims by presenting evidence that might convince a neutral third party. If the agency, in its action, did not sufficiently address Indian concerns, Indian interests would have a cause of action in which the burden would shift to the government to convince the court that the agency properly ignored Indian claims regarding the action. Further, the proposed law would call for de novo review by the courts to determine whether or not the agency provided adequate consideration of Indian concerns. This would be a departure from the current situation, where the courts merely examine decisions for illegal or arbitrary and capricious reasoning. Eitner argues that this is necessary to guarantee that administrative decisions are actually based on facts in the record.[23]

The main difficulty with the proposed uniform consultation statute is that determined administrators would be able to craft environmental impact statements to comply with review standards that would emerge from an anti-Indian Supreme Court, but this problem would be substantively avoided by the expansion of co-management agreements. Martin Nie calls for the expansion of co-management of resources to protect Indian cultural resources, including sacred sites. Nie notes that co-management agreements already exist for fish, game, and wildlife management with interested Indian nations in the Pacific Northwest and the Great Lakes. Alaskan Natives have a long-standing co-management agreement under the Marine Mammal Protection Act through the Alaska Eskimo Whaling Commission. The Confederated Salish and Kootenai Tribes co-manage the National Bison Range in western Montana with the Fish and Wildlife Service and National Park Service. As Nie as points out, co-management elevates the interests of Indian nations beyond those of mere stakeholders to those of active participants in management and planning decisions.[24] Expansion of co-management programs to include Indian sacred sites has a multitude of advantages, and these are addressed below in an assessment of a Bears Ears National Monument proposal from late 2015 by a consortium of Indian governments.

Several constitutional amendments have been proposed to address widespread concerns regarding the United States Supreme Court's recent history of dismantling Indian rights. These proposed amendments focus on sovereignty in a traditional territorial manner and largely overlook Indian cultural concerns regarding the protection of sacred sites on federal lands. While the proposed amendments provide for indigenous peoples to be citizens of both their Indian nation and the United States, they do not contemplate collective religious rights for indigenous peoples and would leave the protection of indigenous religious freedoms outside Indian territory, in the hands of a hostile United States Supreme Court.

The National Congress of American Indians proposed the Tribal Sovereignty and Economic Enhancement Act, which has three provisions, largely directed at the integrity of territoriality-based sovereignty.[25] This proposed law would directly abrogate recent Supreme Court decisions designed to undermine Indian sovereignty. There is some reason to believe this law would not require a constitutional amendment. The Supreme Court expanded its attack on the jurisdiction of Indian courts from *Oliphant* with *Duro v. Reina*. In *Duro*, the Supreme Court declared not only that Indian courts did not have jurisdiction over non-Indians but also that Indian courts did not have jurisdiction over nonmembers, even when offenses took place on reservation lands. In 1991 Congress responded by amending the Indian Civil Rights Act to recognize the inherent jurisdictional power of Indian nations over members of other Indian nations, and the Supreme Court upheld this amendment in the 2004 case *United States v. Lara*. But some have interpreted dicta in the opinion to indicate that the Supreme Court might not accept a similar recognition of inherent sovereignty when it comes to jurisdiction over non-Indians and that a hostile future Supreme Court might declare that the inherent sovereignty of Indian nations is less than that of European nations and thus it is impossible for Congress to recognize Indian jurisdiction over European American visitors.[26] The three points of the NCAI proposed legislation are: (1) restoration of full inherent sovereignty, except as expressly divested by treaty or congressional act; (2) return to the impenetrable barrier to state authority found in the Marshall Trilogy; (3) enhanced federal review of Indian court cases, especially on matters related to the 1968 Indian Civil Rights Act.[27] The last part was seen as a necessary trade-off to extending jurisdiction to non-Indians on reservations. While this was a proposal of the NCAI, Indian governments have only partially supported the proposal, preferring the first two provisions and not caring much for the third.[28]

Russell Lawrence Barsh and James Youngblood Henderson have proposed a constitutional amendment designed to more formally recognize the incorporation of Indian nations into the United States as a federation created by treaties with Indian nations. This proposed amendment would formally recognize a third sovereign entity in U.S. federalism: Indian nations. This proposed amendment would, for the purposes of the law and the U.S. Constitution, recognize Indian nations as states, with a few exceptions. Indian nations would retain all powers of state governments, and no powers could be removed by Congress, except with approval of a three-quarters vote of the national population. Indian nations would have the ability to set criteria for membership, regardless of the provisions of the Fourteenth Amendment, and would have a modified form of representation in Congress. The proposed amendment calls for an election of Senate and House Indian caucuses. The House caucus would select representatives from each Indian nation based on population, and each Indian nation would have one representative in the Senate caucus. Members would serve four-year terms, and the caucuses would elect two members each to serve in the House and Senate as full members of those bodies with voting privileges. States would have no power over Indian lands, except by compact agreed to by all parties, and Indian members residing in Indian territory would have no vote in state elections. This proposal also calls for $500 million dollars in development funds to be delivered to Indian governments, apportioned by population, with no strings attached.[29]

The proposed amendment would address several outstanding problems Indian peoples have with the current arrangements imposed upon them by the U.S. federal system, but there remain difficulties. First, the proposed amendment provides for its application to Indian nations only if their members consent by a two-thirds vote.[30] The proposal also makes no provisions for Indian peoples currently not recognized by the federal government.[31] With regard to collective Indian rights to sacred sites on public lands, such an arrangement would provide Indians with a greater voice in formulating federal policies, but the territorial nature of the expansion of sovereignty does not address the protection of rights and interests outside the territorial jurisdiction of Indian governments. While this proposed amendment would address many concerns, further measures would have to be taken to protect religious concerns off-reservation.

Frank Pommersheim has proposed a much simpler amendment, but this proposal is also limited to the erosion of sovereignty in the face of Supreme Court hostility. Pommersheim's proposed amendment states that the inherent sovereignty of Indian nations shall not be infringed, except by those powers expressly delegated to the United States by the Constitution. Pommersheim argues that this proposed amendment would not displace existing treaties and would stabilize sovereignty in the face of the assault by the United States Supreme Court.[32] This amendment would leave in place all retained off-reservation rights of Indian peoples and leave room for compacts and other future agreements to incorporate substantive protections for Indian sacred sites outside of Indian territory.

COLLABORATIVE MANAGEMENT

When I started researching this project, I began to consider the possibilities of unconventional approaches to Indian sovereignty that might provide extraterritorial control or influence over Indian sacred sites as a possible solution to the ongoing problem of sacred site desecration. Any sensible analysis will recognize that the core problem is the lack of recognized Indian political authority, or sovereignty, over sacred sites. Of course, the most theoretically simple, yet politically difficult, method for guaranteeing protection of Indian sacred places on public lands is to return sufficient public lands to Indian nations to provide Indian peoples with a viable land base to operate as fully sovereign nations and to leave the management of sacred sites up to sovereign Indian governments. An estimated 45 million acres of additional land would be necessary to provide Indian peoples with a sufficient land base to have sustainable nations. The U.S. government holds more than 650 million acres as public lands, many of which contain Indian sacred sites.[33] A return of Indian lands and recognition of full sovereignty of Indian nations over those lands would likely provide the form of protection for Indian sacred sites that practitioners of traditional Indian religions would find most acceptable. But while the international consensus is moving toward recognizing indigenous peoples as "peoples" under international law, and thus recognizing entitlement to self-determination, the government of the United States is not moving in that direction. One branch is hostile to respecting the fundamental human rights of Indian peoples, and the public is woefully uninformed about Indian issues. So while it would be nice to live in a society free of domination, submission, and alienation, in the short term, sacred sites are being destroyed and Indian rights are being trampled. This is where collaborative management comes in. In the fall of 2015, several Indian nations for put forth a proposal for the most ambitious collaborative management plan for Indian sacred sites.

The ongoing policy of government-to-government relations has led to an increase in Indian management of many federal programs serving Indian reservations. With the change in policy initiated by the Nixon administration, the federal government has been willing to share more and more management responsibilities with Indian governments. Beyond this, Indian governments, such as the Blackfeet Nation, have entered compacts with surrounding states regarding the management of social services and law enforcement jurisdiction. Co-management agreements have succeeded in maintaining limited resources of game, fish, and whales.[34] A similar model could be expanded to where Indian interests are not mere stakeholders but have a deciding interest. A consortium of Indian governments has put forward a proposal for joint federal and Indian management of sacred sites designed to promote Indian self-determination and education of the general public regarding Indian cultures and values.

BEARS EARS

In the southeastern corner of Utah is a remote, ecologically intact area bounded by the eastern shore of the Colorado River. It is a place of historical, cultural, and religious importance to the Hopi, Navajo, Ute Mountain Ute, Uintah and Ouray Ute, and Zuni nations. Bordered on the south by the Navajo Nation and on the east stretching from White Mesa to the Colorado River near Moab, this area of 1.9 million acres is mostly Bureau of Land Management lands. Natural Bridges National Monument is within the region. A coalition of the above-mentioned Indian nations calls the region Bears Ears. All coalition members have some history with Bears Ears, and until the nineteenth century, Bears Ears was part of the Navajo Nation. Bears Ears contains more than one hundred thousand cultural sites, including granaries and complex villages.[35]

The Utah congressional delegation has had concern for how exactly to manage the Bears Ears region for some time. Senator Robert Bennett launched the Public Lands Initiative (PLI) to address outstanding concerns regarding eastern Utah public lands management. When Bennett lost his election in 2010, representatives Rob Bishop and Jason Chaffetz took over the project. The nonprofit group Utah Diné Bikeyah (UDB) formed to press for management of Bears Ears in a manner that would protect cultural and religious sites. The representatives designed the Public Lands Initiative as a way to put together a legislative proposal with public input that largely worked through county governments. While the congresspeople held several meetings on the PLI, Indian leaders were never invited.[36]

Despite feeling shut out of the PLI, Utah Diné Bikeyah leaders and members made efforts to participate in the process through San Juan County, Utah, where about half the population was Navajo. By 2014, UDB had created a draft cooperative management plan and was presenting it to both Utah representatives and the San Juan County commissioners. The San Juan County Commission became increasingly hostile to UDB participation in the process. At first commissioners assured UDB that their proposal would be among those polled for public response, but the co-management proposal was not included in the poll. Despite this, a write-in campaign returned 64 percent of the votes in favor of the UDB proposal. County commissioners ultimately recommended a plan for aggressively developing energy resources in the area. In December 2014, the San Juan County Commission informed UDB by letter that the organization was no longer welcome to participate in the Public Lands Initiative process.[37]

Feeling ignored and shut out, UDB took is collaborative management proposal to the governments of local Indian nations for action. In 2015 the Hopi, Navajo, Uintah and Ouray Ute, the Ute Mountain Ute, and Zuni governments entered into a formal alliance and created the Bears Ears Inter-Tribal Coalition. The coalition crafted a detailed proposal for collaborative management of Bears Ears and on October 15, 2015, submitted it to President Barack Obama and the Utah representatives working on the Public Lands Initiative.[38]

The response to the proposal has been mixed. Former secretary of the interior Bruce Babbitt, taking time off from efforts to expand ski resorts on Indian sacred sites, called for President Obama to adopt the Bears Ears joint management proposal. Congressman Bishop publicly opposed the proposal and put forth an alternative plan that would forbid consideration of Indian concerns not approved by county commissioners or the State of Utah. Bishop went further and demonstrated his fundamental ignorance of Indian affairs by describing the Bears Ears coalition member nations as a "self-appointed coalition." The members of the coalition are the legally elected governments of the neighboring Indian nations. Navajo Nation Council delegate Davis Filfred, representing tribal members from Utah, found the statement offensive and pointed out that the Navajo Nation Council had unanimously passed the bill of support for the project and that the council was unified with the executive in support for Bears Ears National Monument.[39]

The Bears Ears Coalition proposal urged Obama to create a 1.9-million-acre national monument by executive order, with collaborative management between the coalition member nations and the various agencies that manage the different parts of Bears Ears. The proposal recommended creating a management commission made up of eight members, one from each Indian nation in the coalition and one from each responsible federal agency. The commission would be responsible for management and crafting policies that would be reviewed by the secretary of agriculture. From beginning to end of commission decisions, Indian officials would be directly involved. If the commission reached an impasse, they would first attempt mediation. If that failed, the secretary of agriculture would retain ultimate authority and would be required to issue a written opinion explaining the decision. While the commission would set policy and create management plans, the day-to-day operations would be overseen by a single manager answering to the commission.[40]

The coalition proposal also had several goals and operational directives to be set out in the executive order creating the national monument. First, it recommended Indian hiring preferences for staffing. Bears Ears National Monument would be closed to mining, have regulated and reasonable off-road motor vehicle travel, continue the State of Utah's hunting regulations and laws, and keep the monument area open to public use. The coalition suggested that the order contain a directive to the secretary of agriculture to enter into agreements with the State of Utah to make exchanges for state land located in the interior of the monument's proposed borders. The proposal called for maintaining existing grazing permits and current firewood-removal management plans. There was also a directive for the commission to create a management plan to protect Indian sacred sites, traditional cultural properties, and items, including plants, used for religious purposes, to the fullest extent under the law. On January 7, 2017, President Obama accepted parts of the Bears Ears proposal, reducing the protected area to 1.35 million acres. But Obama stripped the collaborative management provisions from the proposal, leaving representatives of the coalition nations only sitting on an advisory panel. Since then, opponents have been pushing to reverse the national monument designation, with Utah congressional representatives spearheading a legislative push to destroy this first experiment in extensive collaborative management between Indian governments and the United States. In August 2017 the new secretary of the interior, Ryan Zinke, recommended reducing the size of three national monuments, including Bears Ears, but made vague statements regarding potentially increasing Indian co-management of the site. In any event, a protracted legal battle over the proposed reduction in size of the national monuments is expected.[41]

In December of 2017, President Donald Trump reduced Bears Ears to 202,000 acres, splitting the original monument into two noncontiguous areas. The five member nations of the coalition immediately filed lawsuits challenging the unprecedented reduction. In response to the law suits filed by the coalition members, Republican Congressional Representative John Curtis introduced a bill that would ratify Trump's ordered reduction in size of the national monument and further undermine the representation of Indian national interests in the management of a reduced Bears Ears. While Obama ignored the call for collaborative management of Bears Ears, as proposed by the coalition nations, Obama's order retained an advisory council made up of representatives selected by the coalition nations. The Curtis bill proposes restructuring the advisory council to include local and federal representatives and provides for the President of the United States hand picking the Indian members of reformulated advisory council.[42]

The Antiquities Act of 1906 offers the president wide discretion in creating national monuments. The courts have never overturned a presidential designation as of this writing. The Antiquities Act authorizes the president to create national monuments with the smallest area necessary to protect the monument, but in 1996 President Bill Clinton designated 1.7 million acres in Utah as the Grand Staircase–Escalante National Monument. This expansive national monument survived challenges in federal court. Presidents have also been increasing the management directives included in such orders, and these directives have also withstood court challenges. The proposal of the coalition is the first to have a collaborative directive with Indian nations, and the coalition stated that the proposed management would be infused with indigenous values.[43]

Collaborative management of public lands in agreement with Indian governments has several advantages. First, this would be a continuation of the historic trend begun in the Nixon years of turning over greater amounts of federal operations to day-to-day management and implementation by Indian officials. While such arrangements would not provide Indian interests with a veto, Indians would have strong influence over the entire decision-making procedure. In addition, moral suasion would have an exponentially higher impact on non-Indian decision-makers, as they would have ongoing professional and personal contacts with Indian staff and commissioners. It is harder to destroy someone's sacred places when you have to see them again at work on Monday. Further, the Bears Ears proposal called for using the collaborative management project as a method for expanding non-Indian understanding of Indian values, cultures, and perspectives. In the short term, the national monument designation is the most promising legal option for substantive improvements in the protection of Indian sacred sites that may be carried out without constitutional amendments or social revolution.

There are also several weaknesses to the collaborative management arrangements. First, the secretary of agriculture would still have ultimate management authority. While the Bears Ears proposal would require the secretary to publish a written explanation for decisions, nothing prevents the secretary from ignoring Indian concerns and there would be no avenue for judicial review. In addition, Congress would retain ultimate authority for the disposition of public lands, regardless of the delegated authority within the Antiquities Act. Congress may pass laws dismantling the collaborative management arrangement, as is currently being pushed, or a member of Congress could slip a rider onto a must-pass appropriations bill and simply give the land to commercial interests. Another potential weakness is that some lawmakers or judges might characterize the minimal respect for indigenous cultural, religious, and sovereign interests as extending "special rights" to a "privileged minority"—or even as a breach of the Establishment Clause of the First Amendment. Non-Indian communities will continue to be highly susceptible to such political lies for the foreseeable future as their education systems have by and large failed to provide them with even the most basic facts about their own history and the legal foundations of their own political structures. This lack of knowledge has left much of the non-Indian population of the United States unable to make informed and meaningful choices on Indian issues.

LACK OF EDUCATION

Lack of respect and empathy are among the prime causes of decisions that destroy both Indian sacred sites and sovereignty. This lack of empathy and respect stems from a lack of information about U.S. history as it relates to the theoretical and practical origins of non-Indian America. Even today indigenous people in the United States regularly face overt racial hostility that has been long socially unacceptable for other groups. Indian girls are sexualized and harassed at younger ages and with greater frequency than their peers. This is in part because images of Indians from films and mascots have deep roots in the non-Indian culture and consciousness of the United States. Exacerbating matters, many members of the general public have little to no knowledge of actual Indian lives, history, or experiences. For these people, there is little understanding of retained indigenous rights, sovereignty, or treaty obligations. Many non-Indians are under the mistaken impression that all Indians receive money from casinos and/or handouts from the government. Even in academic fields, such as critical race theory, Indians are largely ignored. Much ignorance about Native Americans has been perpetuated by the inadequate treatment of Indians and Indian issues in schools. While some states with larger Indian populations, such as Montana, have made progress, there is still a widespread lack of accurate Indian history presented in public education.[44]

The lack of accurate information about Indians in education not only promotes a lack of respect and empathy for indigenous peoples in the United States; it also creates a reserve of ill-informed people for anti-Indian organizing across the country. Property owners and those with business interests impacted by efforts to protect sacred sites have tended to form the membership basis of groups opposed to Indian self-determination. Some of these groups find additional support from large corporate interests and white supremacist circles. Anti-Indian groups take advantage of misinformation about the legal and historical origins of Indian reservations. Even non-Indians living on private lands within the borders of reservations that have been checker-boarded by allotment do not understand the basics of Indian sovereignty.[45]

The consultation process has been shown to address some of this ignorance. In the case of the Snowbowl expansion, Forest Service zone archaeologist Heather Cooper Provencio was well acquainted with Indian concerns and history regarding the San Francisco Peaks. She made sure to explain the religious and cultural importance of the Peaks to Forest Supervisor Nora Rasure. While Rasure ultimately decided to desecrate the Hopi holy site, she did not do so gleefully as an expression of her right to do so. She reluctantly made a necessary conclusion given how the project proposal was framed by the Arizona Snowbowl Resort.

The Blackfeet Indians had the greatest success in explaining their position to forest managers through the consultation process. After initial discussions, the Forest Service decided it needed to separate the record of decision for Badger-Two Medicine to better investigate Blackfeet retained rights and religious interests. Even then, the initial inclination of agency planners was to designate the entire area as roadless, conforming the plan to the interests on non-Indian hikers and horseback riders, but continued consultation revealed that the Blackfeet wanted the area to maintain a small portion of existing roads to facilitate the exercise of treaty rights and access to sacred sites for the disabled and elderly.

While the Washoe did not obtain their maximum objectives with regard to Cave Rock, they may have obtained the most important victory. The consultation process for the climbing management plan for Cave Rock, run by Supervisor Juan Palma's subordinates, provided the Washoe the opportunity to educate the climbing public about the importance of Cave Rock to the Washoe. While climbers' reverence for the landscape is more amenable to Indian perspectives than that of Australian mining corporations, the consultation process turned some climbers against the idea of permitting continued climbing at Cave Rock. More importantly, this educational effort turned climbers against their own lobbying organization when it tried to portray the Washoe as privileged and selfish. While the Access Fund continued to press for climbers to have access, the complaints of informed climbers prevented the Access Fund from engaging in anti-Indian rhetoric and promoting ignorant and racist views of Indians.

The differences in outcomes for Bear's Lodge, Cave Rock, Badger-Two Medicine, and the San Francisco Peaks can largely be explained by the different economic situations. With the Peaks, the entire process was driven by the economic interests of the Snowbowl ski resort and its well-connected lawyer, former interior secretary Bruce Babbitt. Portions of the Forest Service viewed the consultation process as an unfortunate obstacle to promoting a project that planners decided was necessary. With the Peaks, economic interests predetermined the outcome. Cave Rock and Bear's Lodge both involved rock climbing, but at Cave Rock the routes were the most difficult in the country, providing a unique climbing experience. This situation did not lend itself to the growth of a professional tourist climbing business, as had developed at Bear's Lodge. With fewer climbers impacted and no businesses jeopardized, the Washoe were able to narrowly gain significant protections for a highly important cultural site. Similarly, at Badger-Two Medicine, the impact on recreational snowmobile use was minimal and such use was expected to be merely displaced to other areas, including areas of the Blackfeet Reservation opened up to accommodate recreational use.

In its brief opposing of the Bear's Lodge climbing management plan, the Mountain States Legal Foundation demonstrated the central tension that causes difficulties in expressing empathy and respect for indigenous peoples in land management policies. The foundation objected to the educational aspect of the management plan and the proposed goal of full voluntary compliance with abstaining from climbing in June.[46] Those offering climbing tours had a direct financial interest in preventing the education necessary for cross-cultural empathy, consideration, and respect. Had the Access Fund membership not already been educated as to Washoe concerns, that membership would have been more susceptible to the hate-based propaganda the Access Fund initially engaged in. Instead, informed members of the Access Fund called out the leadership for their unconscionable actions. Those with financial interests that may be jeopardized by offering empathy and respect to Indians look to prevent education and to exploit the ignorance of the public.

The collaborative management of Bears Ears would directly address problematic non-Indian ignorance of Indian cultures and concerns. While the coalition proposal calls for the inclusion of extensive educational opportunities, it also maintains existing federal regulatory limitations for management. Management decisions would still be subjected to the environmental impact statement process with its layers of consultation requirements and opportunities for public scoping, collaborative meetings, brainstorming, and comments on draft proposals. Assuming the Indian collaborative management leadership would take the opportunity to engage in cross-cultural communications, as happened with the Cave Rock consultations, important work in improving non-Indian education may be accomplished, increasing opportunities for meaningful expression of freedom by non-Indians, who will now have a greater understanding of the world they live in.

The lack of understanding of the history and conditions of American Indians in the United States is staggering. For Sen and Cross, development requires education that allows people to express their opinions meaningfully, exercise economic freedom, and participate in a larger community with respect and equality. Under these measures of development, the non-Indian population of the United States is largely ill-prepared to discuss the relations of non-Indians and indigenous peoples through U.S. history. As Paul Chaat Smith has stated:

> [N]o reasonably sentient person of whatever background could seriously dispute the overwhelming evidence that Indians are at the very center of everything that happened in the Western Hemisphere (which, technically speaking, is half the world) over the past five centuries, and so that history is at the heart of everyone who lives here. . . .
>
> Yet that can't possibly be true, because everything you learn teaches you that the Indian experience is a joke, a cartoon, a minor sideshow. The overwhelming message from schools, mass media, and conventional wisdom says Indians might be interesting, even profound, but never important.[47]

Indians and Indian law have so little in importance in non-Indian education that Supreme Court justices remain disturbingly ignorant of the foundational concepts. Steven Newcomb's encounter with Justice Scalia revealed not only the latter's staggering ignorance but also the inability of political and intellectual leaders to see the Indian origins of North America, even when the first chapter of one of their favorite books discusses the matter extensively. Much like Scalia, Justice Stephen Breyer could not remember the legal designation of Indian nations, but this time in open court. Even though he was one of the better justices on understanding the implications of Indian issues, Breyer had to ask, at oral arguments, during a recent case in which a corporation was challenging the ability of Indian nations to have civil jurisdiction over U.S. corporations doing business on reservations (after having signed an explicit agreement recognizing said jurisdiction), "Now, is there any—and—and what is the word in *Cherokee?* I forget. It's 'something dependent nation.' What kind of—it was—there are two words."[48]

Not only are those alleged to have the top legal minds commonly uninformed of the legal foundations of the nation they sit in judgment over, college professors are sometimes completely unaware of major events in the history of the Western Hemisphere. In the fall of 2015, professor of history Maury Wiseman of Sacramento State University stated that indigenous populations of the Americas did not face genocide. When Chiitaanibah Johnson, a nineteen-year-old woman of Navajo and Maidu ancestry, objected to the professor's denial, he ended class early and characterized Johnson's reaction as a disruption. A university investigation later determined that neither Johnson nor Wiseman had violated any university policies.[49] The professor took the view that because no one had deliberately targeted the entire indigenous population of the Americas for extermination, there was no genocide in the Americas. Wiseman appears to have misunderstood that the term "Indian" is akin to "European." No one would argue that the Nazis did not commit genocide because it was not their deliberate policy to eliminate all Europeans. Any educated person in the United States should be aware that the Plymouth Colony sought to exterminate the Pequot people, that the territorial governor of Colorado during the U.S. Civil War called for extermination of the Cheyennes, that the government of the new territory of Arizona called for extermination of the Apaches, and that Christopher Columbus instituted slave labor policies that led to the complete elimination of the Arawak Indians from the face of the Earth. One needs no specific knowledge of the Convention on the Prevention and Punishment of the Crime of Genocide to understand that all are examples of genocide. (Though all teachers of twentieth-century U.S. history should be aware of the legal definition of genocide.)

Indian peoples have taken the initiative in promoting development and freedom by providing greater understanding and education in the United States, but the time has come for non-Indians to take responsibility for their own education. Non-Indian peoples of the United States have created a plurinational society. Cross and Sun have argued that sufficient education for meaningfully expressing opinions, with dignity and respect, and participating in society as part of human freedom should be both measures and ends of development. A person's abilities increase her or his freedom. Of critical importance, federal administrators, lawmakers, judges, and educators have commonly lacked sufficient understanding of Indian peoples and their experiences with non-Indian peoples and thus have not been prepared to meaningfully engage indigenous leaders on issues of Indian sovereignty and sacred sites or to render informed opinions regarding these issues. Indians can only do so much with their limited resources to educate the non-Indian community. It is necessary for the long-term healing of society for non-Indians to take responsibility for their education regarding their own history. In the area of historical and political education, non-Indian intellectual and political leaders, and the public they educate and govern, remain in need of development to achieve the freedom to meaningfully interact with others.

CONCLUSIONS

The consultation process has been part of a growing respect for Indian cultural and religious concerns in the management of public lands by the federal government. Starting the formal reversal of U.S. policy regarding the continued survival of Indian religions and cultures, the Indian Religious Freedom Act of 1978 initiated the requirement for federal administrators to consult with Indian governments and religious leaders when making decisions that impacted Indian sacred sites. The potential for federal protection of sacred sites improved with the 1992 amendments to the National Historic Preservation Act. These created the category "traditional cultural properties," which are places of cultural or religious significance to indigenous peoples and are eligible for inclusion on the National Register of Historic Places. The amendments expanded congressional recognition of the United States as a multicultural society. The consultation process was further strengthened by Executive Orders 13,007 (1996), 13,084 (1998), and 13,175 (2000). Executive Order 13,007 called upon administrators to avoid adverse impacts on sites of religious or cultural significance to indigenous peoples. The later orders called upon federal agencies to regularize and formalize their government-to-government consultation procedures.

While Congress and the executive made small but significant steps toward honestly addressing the reality of the United States as a plurinational society, the Supreme Court acted to curtail and eliminate constitutional protections for religious freedom, which hurt indigenous religions the most. While the late twentieth century demonstrated a fairly consistent pattern of Supreme Court hostility to Indian national sovereignty, practitioners of Indian religions were the first to discover that the United States Supreme Court no longer respected constitutional protections for religious freedom. With the 1988 *Lyng* decision, the court announced that the Free Exercise clause of the First Amendment provided no protection for religious expression on public lands, even when government destruction of sacred sites would make the exercise of religious ceremonies impossible. The potential for the government to achieve its ends with less destructive means was not even considered, as the government had absolute dominion over lands as property owner. Going further in 1990 with the *Smith* case, the United States Supreme Court declared that all generally applicable laws were constitutional, even if they curtailed the exercise of religion. Though the *Smith* case originated in the practices of Indian religious traditions, the broad nature of the ruling negatively impacted the religious freedom of all those living in the United States.

Reflecting public outrage, Congress acted to restore legal protections for religious freedom and the Supreme Court again acted to limit religious freedom. The 1993 Religious Freedom Restoration Act sought to restore and expand previous protections for religious freedom, calling on the courts to review laws that burdened religious freedom to determine whether they fostered a compelling governmental interest in the least restrictive means possible. The next year Congress amended the Indian Religious Freedom Act to specifically nullify the holding in *Smith* by protecting Indian use and possession of peyote for religious purposes. In 1997, the Supreme Court found that RFRA could not apply to state actions with *City of Boerne v. Flores*, 521 U.S. 507. Following the lead of the Supreme Court in *Lyng*, the Ninth Circuit Court of Appeals ruled that RFRA did not apply to the management of public lands in the case of the Snowbowl expansion in Coconino National Forest.

Writing in the wake of the *Lyng* case, Marcia Yablon predicted that leaving discretionary authority with administrators, after the mandatory consultation process, would provide the best and most practical protections for Indian sacred sites. Yablon argued that administrative discretion, combined with the consultation process, would give federal administrative agencies the opportunity to find creative and flexible compromises among competing interests. Courts do not like to take the time to educate themselves on anything and are bound by a long string of racist precedents emanating from a hostile Supreme Court, as Robert Williams has noted.[1] With another decade of consultation after Yablon made her optimistic predictions, the strengths and weaknesses of the evolving consultation process can more fully be assessed.

The greatest strength of the consultation process in practice was its ability to open communications and bridge cultural gaps, bringing greater understanding of Indian rights and concerns to non-Indian communities. As discussed in the introduction and throughout the case studies, many Indian religions have specific places of deep significance (with the notable exception in this book being the Makah interest in whaling). While the notion of specific places (the USS *Arizona*; Gettysburg) retaining cultural or religious significance was not completely alien to non-Indians, the near total lack of accurate information about Indian culture in non-Indian communities left a great chasm to be bridged. The consultation process brought non-Indian administrators to understand Blackfeet treaty and religious interests in Badger-Two Medicine. At Cave Rock, the Washoes communicated their concerns to both administrators and the climbing community, turning significant portions of the climbing community against their own lobbying organization. The Quechans obtained greater protections for their sacred sites from Glamis mining operations and obtained new state requirements for remedial measures. Even with the San Francisco Peaks, where administrators decided to desecrate the mountain, the Hopis and others successfully communicated their concerns to the forest supervisor, making her decision to disregard Indian concerns much more difficult, psychically speaking.

The cross-cultural communications of the consultation process have also been successful in communicating concerns of non-Indians to Indian community leaders, leading to creative solutions. At Bear's Lodge, after Indian leaders took the feelings of climbers back to their communities, many Indians decided that a voluntary ban on climbing would be more meaningful to them, as it provided people the opportunity to show their respect for Indian concerns by choosing to abstain from climbing in June. Additionally, the Blackfeet, through the consultation process, decided to open up parts of their territory to snowmobile use to provide recreational opportunities after Badger-Two Medicine was closed to all snowmobile use.

When administrators did not have preconceived goals, Indians were able to at least partially vindicate their interests. While the Blackfeet obtained their maximal objectives within the confines of a travel management plan, the retained treaty rights for hunting, fishing, logging, and religious access to Badger-Two

Medicine facilitated this outcome. The consultation process provided the Blackfeet the opportunity to educate administrators about their ongoing interests in the formulation of a new travel management plan. Similarly, the Washoes obtained significant protections for Cave Rock with the permanent total ban on climbing when the purpose of the Forest Service was to protect the integrity of the site through a new management plan. By contrast, the Forest Service set as its goal improving the financial viability and safety of the Snowbowl ski resort in the San Francisco Peaks.

When administrative agencies have a determined plan but refuse to engage in consultation, the courts have shown that they will enforce the Indian right to consultation. The Quechan Nation was good enough to inform the Bureau of Land Management of the need for consultation with regard to the placement of the Imperial Valley Solar Project, but the BLM ignored this courtesy notice. Two years later the BLM approved the project without ever consulting on a government-to-government level with the Quechans. A preliminary injunction derailed the project, as to obtain matching federal funds, the project had a hard deadline for beginning. Had the BLM engaged in consultation as required, it likely could have pushed the project through. But if consultation had occurred, the BLM might have been able to tailor the solar complex to avoid or minimize damage to Quechan cultural and religious sites.

When the consultation process occurs, it does not necessarily educate the general public. While there was no consultation in the Imperial Valley Solar Project case, an ignorant public denounced the Quechans as being backward and opposed to environmental progress rather than understanding that the Quechans were acting to protect a vital legal right necessary for the continued protection of cultural and religious sites. Similarly, the Makahs engaged in extensive consultations with different administrative agencies of the federal government, but this did not prevent unscrupulous animal rights activists making common cause with anti-Indian groups in promoting racist hatred toward the Makahs. Unaware that the Makahs had a deeper respect for whales than non-Indians had, with the Makahs viewing whales as part of their own community, the public was susceptible to the vile lies of Sea Shepherd founder Paul Watson. The consultation process has been able to provide much-needed education to only small segments of the non-Indian population.

Federal administrators also had total discretion in their decisions. So long as the consultation process was engaged in, regardless of the outcome, the courts supported the administrative decision. In the case of the Snowbowl expansion, there was never any question that the decision burdened Hopi and other Indian religions, but the Ninth Circuit ultimately refused to weigh this burden against the government's interest in protecting the profits of a mediocre ski resort in a desert. Administrative decisions have not been limited by either the First Amendment protection of the free exercise of religion (now nonexistent) or the Religious Freedom Restoration Act. Similarly, no establishment concerns remain, as the courts have affirmed mandatory total bans on climbing and snowmobiling that were designed, in part, to protect the cultural and religious interests of Indians. While international law will not penetrate U.S. courts anytime soon, even a North American Free Trade Agreement arbitration tribunal recognized the protection of indigenous cultural and religious sites as a legitimate function of government. So long as administrators consult Indian interests, they may manage sacred and cultural sites with complete discretion, with no court review.

Behind the minimal protections of the consultation process, there remains the danger of the power of Congress as landowner of record for Indian sacred sites. While international law has called for consultation in all cases, the power of Congress to dispose of public lands has the ability to eliminate any protections the consultation process might provide Indian sacred sites. Nowhere has this been more starkly demonstrated than in the case of Apache Leap and Oak Flat. Slipping them into a must-pass appropriations bill, Congress simply traded these culturally significant places to an Anglo-Australian mining company. Even the minimal protections of consultation were circumvented by determined politicians. Of course, this action merely serves as a reminder that the plenary power of Congress over Indian affairs remains unchecked by any legal limitations.

Admittedly there have been significant improvements in relations between federal officials and Indian peoples, in part because of the improved use of the consultation process, but there are outstanding concerns. Most significant of these concerns is the ongoing hostility of the United States Supreme Court to the growing international consensus on indigenous rights. While the international community now recognizes the inherent right of indigenous peoples to some self-determination and calls for respect for indigenous religions and their relationships to the land, the Supreme Court has undermined Indian sovereignty and stripped religious freedom protections from the Constitution, placing indigenous peoples at a distinct disadvantage in protecting what are generally considered, outside of the Supreme Court, fundamental human rights. In December 2012, the Forest Service Office of Tribal Relations prepared a report for the secretary of agriculture that reviewed the policies and procedures regarding Indian sacred sites.² In preparing this review, the Forest Service communicated with indigenous leaders and accepted public comments.

Many Indian concerns demonstrated a lack of faith in both the Forest Service and the U.S. legal system in general. Generally Indians believed that the system was not designed to protect Indian interests and that the law was not capable of protecting Indian sacred places. There was also a great deal of skepticism regarding the Forest Service's ability to protect sacred sites. Many felt that economic concerns "held greater weight" than cultural or traditional values. More specifically, Indians felt that the definition of "sacred sites" in Executive Order 13,007 was too limited by being focused on religion and did not adequately represent the scope of what was sacred. Some were concerned that confidential information presented to the Forest Service about the location of sacred sites would not remain confidential. Some felt the Forest Service lacked sufficient law enforcement capacity to protect historical sites, sacred places, and other areas of concern from disturbance, vandalism, and destruction. Many brought up their ongoing unhappiness with the decision regarding the San Francisco Peaks and asked that the Forest Service reverse the decision regarding the Snowbowl expansion. Some complained that wilderness and roadless designations created obstacles for the elderly or disabled in accessing sacred sites.³

With regard to the consultation process, Indian interests identified problematic areas and offered suggestions for improvement. The Forest Service concurred with Indian complaints that personnel turnover impeded ongoing communication efforts, adding that Indian government turnover exacerbated this difficulty. Others noted that the system provided no regular avenue of communication for nonfederally recognized tribes, hurting their access to sacred sites as well as protection of those places. Indians also expressed concerns over sufficient consultation when it came to traditional cultural properties under the National Historic Preservation Act. Indians requested that the Forest Service coordinate efforts to protect sacred sites with other agencies. Indian interests freely recommended to the Forest Service the expansion of co-management arrangements. Some expressed a desire for a veto over Forest Service actions. Some wanted greater Indian decision-making authority in working with the Forest Service. Some proposed entering more mutually beneficial management agreements with the Forest Service. Others complained that the Forest Service needed better training in consultation procedures, Indian law, and cultural competency.⁴

The Forest Service, by and large, addressed these concerns and offered recommendations to the secretary of agriculture. The Forest Service admitted that it needed to improve its competency in consultation procedures, Indian law, and cultural sensitivity. The Forest Service also agreed that its resources were stretched thin in areas such as enforcement but said that it could do a better job with what resources it had. As to ongoing confidentiality concerns, the Forest Service hoped that provisions within the 2008 Farm Bill that exempt confidential information about Indian sacred sites from Freedom of Information Act requests would help alleviate these concerns. To improve consultation and ongoing communication difficulties, the Forest Service recommended expanding written agreements with Indian governments and formal annual meetings on a government-to-government basis. As to indigenous officials proposing greater co-management, the Forest Service noted that it was not authorized to divest itself of decision-making authority but that it could enter into more co-management arrangements on a case-by-case basis.[5]

The report concluded that administrators had broad discretion, backed by recent court decisions, to do whatever they wanted but that these decisions had significant consequences for the Forest Service and local administrators. Many forest administrators commented that they understood that they had broad discretion in protecting Indian sacred sites, but many Forest Service personnel feared repercussions from other local constituencies, Congress, or the presidential administration. The report concluded that even with the Forest Service's legal authority to act with broad discretion, vindication in court against Indian claims not only injures relations with Indian groups involved in the litigation but also undermines cooperation and relations with all Indian groups, as they believe the law does not protect Indian interests and that the Forest Service is either not concerned with or incapable of respecting Indian concerns.[6]

The consultation process required in the administration of Indian sacred sites on public lands has grown into a powerful tool for education. In the hands of conscientious administrators, the consultation process has provided avenues for cross-cultural communications and education. At Bear's Lodge, local Indian communities and climbers cobbled together a fragile compromise that severely curtailed climbing access (though this compromise remains endangered by commercial climbing guide companies that have a direct financial interest in undermining cooperation). The Washoes succeeded in educating climbers at Cave Rock, and some climbers turned against their own lobbying group as it flirted with demonizing the Washoes by playing on the general ignorance of the public. The consultation process has been instrumental in educating federal administrators. This happened with the Quechans in their struggles against new gold mining in their former lands, and again with the Blackfeet in protecting their religious and treaty interests in Badger-Two Medicine. Even in the most disastrous case for Indian interests, the San Francisco Peaks, the Hopis and other Indian interests communicated their concerns to the forest supervisor in such a way that the supervisor made the horrible decision with a full understanding how she was harming various Indian religious communities.

While the consultation process can educate some, there remains a staggering amount of ignorance that cannot be overcome by the consultation process alone. Much of the ignorant non-Indian press and politicians demonized the Quechans when they turned to the courts to enforce their right to consultation, derailing a solar project. The Makahs, even when working with sympathetic federal administrators, found themselves attacked by racist anti-whaling activists, who knowingly preyed upon the ignorance of the general public while making common cause with politicians seeking to destroy what little recognition of Indian sovereignty remained.

There are numerous possible solutions to the U.S. legal system's lack of recognition of Indian sovereignty and Indian interests in sacred sites on public lands. Collaborative management with a robust consultation process is perhaps the best solution for both short-term implementation and long-term stability. An active consultation process will educate non-Indian interests as to the concerns of Indian cultural and religious communities and provide avenues for creative compromises that can bring communities together. There will always remain economic interests and opportunistic politicians who prey upon the ignorance of non-Indians outside of the consultation process. By exploiting a lack of information, these interests promote the growth of anti-Indian hostility, as occurred with the Access Fund, the Mountain States Legal Foundation, and the Sea Shepherd Conservation Society. As the prominence of white supremacist attitudes in non-Indian society has ebbed and peaked over time, it is not hard to imagine a future in which the U.S. government sweeps away any pretense of cooperation with Indian peoples in a plurinational society and completely rejects the emerging norms of the international community on the rights of indigenous peoples.

The United States created a plurinational society. As Europeans invaded the Western Hemisphere, they failed in their efforts to wipe out indigenous languages, religions, cultures, and peoples. While the United States was a racial dictatorship for centuries, European Americans finally started to acknowledge, in part, that it is a crime against humanity to try to wipe other peoples from the face of the Earth. No one is suggesting that the descendants of the invaders return to their lands of origin. Unless the European American community intends to reject the norms of international law on the rights of indigenous peoples, the lands of the United States must be a plurinational society based in mutual respect and dignity. The sooner this fact of history is admitted, the sooner real healing and society-building can begin.

The failure of many university and high school history programs to provide a thorough assessment of the historic reality of an inadvertent plurinational society in the middle of North America fuels the ignorance that groups such as the Mountain States Legal Foundation and the Sea Shepherd Society exploit with their anti-Indian bigotry. Jurists, congresspeople, college professors, and myriad other Americans in all walks of life are commonly ill-informed about the difficult historical experiences of and challenges facing Indian peoples. So those who assume positions of responsibility in the Forest Service and other agencies of the federal government lack the means to participate meaningfully in concert with indigenous leaders seeking to protect cultural and sacred sites, as well as their national interests. The consultation process can reach only a fraction of these decision-makers.

History education needs to significantly improve non-Indian understanding of American society by including basic lessons about the history of the United States and the highly significant role Indian societies have played in the creation of this unintended plurinational society. Four basic ideas about Indian nations should be understood by any person who successfully completes a U.S. history course. First is the fact in 1492 there was (and in many cases remains) more cultural, political, and religious diversity among Indian nations than among the nations of Europe. Second is the fact that the indigenous peoples of the Americas were the victims of genocide. Third is the U.S. claim to title to Indian lands and how this claim relates to Indian sovereignty. Fourth are the facts that more than 560 Indian nations remain within the United States alone; that Indian religions, cultures, languages, and governments exist today; and that Indian people are the poorest of all citizens, even with a small number of nations making a windfall with casino revenues. Without knowing these simple truths, one does not know the history of the United States.

Students need to learn that the term "Indian" is similar in scope to "European." In 1492 the Americas and Europe were each home to hundreds of nations with different languages. In the Americas, the religions and political organization of Indian peoples ran the entire spectrum, from the European-like monarchy of the Aztecs, with their feudal-type economic system, to the participatory democracies of the Crows and Hopis, which lacked any coercive state structure. Economically, many Indian nations participated in collective ownership, and prestige was gained by sharing with others. In European terms, American communities ranged from extreme leftist anarcho-socialist communes all the way to absolutist feudal monarchies, while Europeans had different variants of absolutist monarchies. Nominally, nearly all Europeans were Catholics in 1492, while the Americas had hundreds, if not thousands, of different religions with different teachings. Each American community has its own history, culture, and outlook, just as European communities do. Indians just happen to have more diversity. Presenting the extreme differences in Aztec and Hopi culture, economics, and politics is a simple way of presenting this truth. More relevant to U.S. history, addressing some of the difficulties Tecumseh faced in trying to unite all Indian nations against U.S. expansion is another way to quickly address this issue.

Common misunderstandings regarding the genocide of indigenous Americans seem to stem from two common misconceptions. The first is addressed above. There has never been a single Indian nation, culture, ethnicity, group, or identity. Thus it is completely irrelevant that no one ever attempted to engage in a systematic extermination of Indians as a whole. Claiming that there was no genocide because no one deliberately targeted all Indians for extermination is like denying the genocide of the Roma by the Nazis because there was no systematic attempt to exterminate all Europeans. The second mistake comes from the straw man argument that the high mortality rate Indian nations suffered because of exposure to new diseases due to sustained contact with Europeans was a form of metaphorical genocide. The issue of disease is largely irrelevant to the crime of genocide. The arguments that indigenous peoples suffered genocide are twofold and use both the common and legal definitions of "genocide."

The common definition of "genocide" is the murder or the attempt to murder all members of a racial, religious, ethnic, national, or cultural group. This undeniably happened in the Americas numerous times, beginning with Christopher Columbus. By instituting a brutal slave labor regime on the Arawak Indians, Columbus set in motion policies that led to the extermination of the Arawak by 1555. While one can quibble over whether or not genocide is a crime of specific intent, the argument is that Columbus intended a brutal regime of slave labor and it killed everyone. While it is arguable that Columbus may have merely had the specific intent of enslaving and massacring people, other examples from American history do not have any ambiguity in intent. The Plymouth Colony tried to exterminate the Pequot people. In the 1860s the appointed governor of

Colorado, John Evans, called for extermination of the Cheyennes, and Colonel John Chivington sought to carry out this policy in such places as Sand Creek. The Arizona Territorial Legislature called for extermination of the Apache people in 1864.[7] These are but four examples of commonplace genocide within American history, but there is a much broader, more overlooked, systematic case of legal genocide that every person who goes to school in the United States should know about if they are to have even the most basic understanding of the history of the U.S. government.

Understanding that genocide occurred in the Americas requires an understanding of the legal definition of "genocide." The Convention on the Prevention and Punishment of the Crime of Genocide includes in the definition the transfer of children from one group to another with the intent to destroy a national, ethnic, or religious group.[8] From the 1880s to the 1930s, the United States engaged in an aggressive policy of assimilation, designed to eliminate all Indian communities as separate political, religious, lingual, cultural, and ethnic groups. To facilitate this policy, the United States forced European property ownership on Indian nations, outlawed the use of Indian languages, outlawed Indian religious practices, and transferred Indian children to Christian-run boarding schools, where children were forced to abandon all aspects of their culture, including languages and religions. Many argue that the forced removal of Indian children to boarding schools, combined with the intent to eliminate the various indigenous peoples of the United States as separate national, ethnic, and religious groups, is a pretty clear case of a crime against humanity. The widespread use of boarding schools designed to destroy Indian religious life is not merely one example of genocide; hundreds of different religious groups suffered under this policy. Thus the indigenous peoples of North America suffered hundreds of cases of genocide or more.

This twentieth-century genocide against religious minorities in the United States is perhaps the most glaring omission in U.S. history survey courses, but it is easily remedied. While history instructors should also lecture on the topics, the fifth episode of the PBS series *We Shall Remain*, "Wounded Knee," provides an excellent introduction to twentieth-century Indian issues, including moving accounts by survivors of boarding schools. This highly recommended documentary also ties later attempts to destroy Indian societies through urban relocation programs of the termination policy to the unrest of the 1970s. While perhaps not necessarily reaching the level of genocide, the Eisenhower policy of termination was another overlooked attempt to destroy Indian communities of the twentieth century.[9]

While some presentation of the nineteenth-century policy of ethnic cleansing, euphemistically called "Indian removal," is common in many survey courses, such a presentation is insufficient if it does not teach the central holdings of the Marshall Trilogy. The Marshall Trilogy serves as the theoretical basis for federal sovereignty over the land of the entire United States. This is the entire legal foundation of the nation. It is more basic and fundamental than the U.S. Constitution and theoretically predates the Constitution. As this foundation is based in the ethnocentric and racist Doctrine of Discovery, it is understandable why non-Indians might find the topic embarrassing. But if the present is to be understood, embarrassing truths must be confronted when they have to do with the foundations of government. The holdings of the Marshall Trilogy are not difficult to explain. First, discovering European powers, by virtue of being Christian and therefore "better" than indigenous peoples, obtained underlying title to indigenous lands by being the first Christians to stumble upon the people in question. Indigenous peoples retained their right of occupancy but were limited in selling the occupied land to the discovering Christian power. Second, as indigenous nations have had their national sovereignty limited by the Doctrine of Discovery, Indian nations are not foreign nations under international law but are domestic dependent nations, with the United States serving as their "guardian." Third, though domestic dependent nations, Indian nations remain sovereign in their internal affairs and the states have no power over Indian nations.[10] While Andrew Jackson's subsequent lawlessness in the face of the Marshall Trilogy would be considered an important episode in U.S. constitutional history, those events are relatively minor when it comes to understanding the foundations of the U.S. claim to sovereignty over any part of the Americas.

Indian peoples are still here, are changing, and are not going anywhere. The U.S. government recognizes more than 560 Indian nations, and Indian people as a whole remain the financially poorest people in the United States, with the lowest life expectancy. One way to emphasize that Indian cultures continue to survive and change, making the United States a multicultural society, is to note that the film *Star Wars: A New Hope*, a product of Anglo-American culture of worldwide impact and significance, was dubbed into the Navajo language in 2013.

When more non-Indians know the basics of U.S. history and the significant Indian place in that history, more non-Indians will understand how offensive it is to desecrate cultural or sacred sites for profit. When faced with a public outraged at the prospect of economically developing part of the Gettysburg Battlefield, the federal government moved to protect it with eminent domain.[11] Today, supposedly educated opinion leaders are unaware of the basics of the foundational principles of the United States, and the general non-Indian population knows little of the plurinational society it lives in. Greater understanding among non-Indians is necessary for the non-Indian populations of the United States to make meaningful decisions regarding how to live together with others in a plurinational society. Despite the best efforts of past non-Indian political leadership, Indians will remain part of their homelands and try to protect places of cultural and religious significance. While there are many good suggestions about how to better allocate power to protect Indian cultural and sacred sites, increasing respect for Indian sovereignty and protecting Indian self-determination, including self-determination in cultural and religious matters, will require concerted efforts by non-Indian communities to educate themselves about their own history and the world their ancestors created. When non-Indians have some basic understanding of reality, they can begin to act in meaningful ways, with some dignity, to move forward with others and improve their own freedom.

To sum up, the consultation process implemented by the 1978 Indian Religious Freedom Act has proved effective in offering indigenous peoples some means to educate non-Indians about their cultures and sacred sites and to garner protection for them. As has been shown, however, a more innovative and better solution to the problems posed by federal management of public lands encompassing Indian sacred sites lies in formulating a new understanding of Indian sovereignty. This solution would necessarily recognize Indian political authority over sacred sites. Such a change in the fundamental law of the United States undoubtedly presents a mammoth challenge to those wedded to hidebound understandings of constitutional provisions concerning "Indian Tribes" and hundreds of years of judicial interpretation thereof. Even so, the best solution would be to return sufficient public lands to Indian peoples to allow them to operate as fully sovereign nations and to leave the management of sacred sites up to sovereign Indian governments. Raymond Cross and other legal thinkers agree that Indian people should take the lead in promoting this new compact. Indian development will proceed more quickly when Indian nations have sovereign control over resources and can fit development needs to specific local conditions. Equally important, educators can improve prospects for the expression of indigenous sovereignty and stewardship of their own sacred sites by conveying accurate and complete information to non-Indians about the relationships of Indian and non-Indian peoples from 1492 to the present.

AFTERWORD

When the hardcover printing of this book was going to press in late 2017, the struggles of the Standing Rock Sioux Tribe and their allies to prevent the Dakota Access Pipeline from crossing under the sacred waters of Lake Oahe were at an odd place, in the middle of a contentious and ongoing litigation. The case was relevant to the research of this book in that it was one of the most recent applications of the Religious Freedom Restoration Act (RFRA), confirming that the act did not protect indigenous sacred sites in the United States, but indicating that the courts were still willing to consider the potential impact of federal actions on established treaty rights to water and resources. As that litigation continued, major changes in the makeup of the Supreme Court was shifting the balance of power on indigenous issues.

In 2017, the court found itself with a new justice knowledgeable about Indian law and determined to maintain the status quo on indigenous rights, even as he eagerly assisted in stripping rights from almost every other group.[1] Justice Neil Gorsuch's support for the status quo on indigenous sovereignty was fully on full display in his majority opinion in *McGirt v. Oklahoma* in 2020.[2] While the mainstream press wildly exaggerated the holding in that case (the Court merely applied existing principles of Indian law to it), Justice Gorsuch made it clear that he intended to follow existing precedent and protect indigenous sovereignty, even if a state had been ignoring the law for many decades. The balance of power shifted again just two years after the *McGirt* decision when newly appointed justice Amy Coney Barret authored an opinion that ignored the long history of precedent. As Justice Gorsuch noted of this majority opinion, "[T]his declaration comes as if by oracle, without any sense of the history recounted above and unattached to any colorable legal authority. Truly, a more ahistorical and mistaken statement of Indian law would be hard to fathom."[3]

The Lakotas' opposition to the Dakota Access Pipeline continued in this changing political climate and has encountered a similar morass of legal nonsense. Just before this book went to press, the district court ordered the United States Army Corps of Engineers (USACE) to correct the environmental assessment and address the concerns of the Standing Rock and Cheyenne River Sioux tribes. The pipeline construction continued as the USACE completed a new assessment in February 2019 and found, again, that the pipeline would have no significant impact on tribal treaty resources or access to clean water. At this point, litigation resumed. The pipeline was completed even as the courts found that the new environmental assessment had again failed to comply with the requirements of the National Environmental Policy Act.[4]

Finding that the Corps of Engineers failed to adequately address the scientific controversy surrounding the risks of a pipeline discharge, inadequately considered how a spill might impact treaty-protected resources, and did not account for the social justice implications of the DAPL project, the District of Columbia district court ordered the Corps of Engineers to engage in the much more extensive process of creating a full environmental impact statement. The court further ordered a halt to use of the pipeline while the more extensive evaluation was completed.[5] USACE appealed.

The appellate court agreed that the environmental assessment was inadequate and that there was no legal basis for issuing the easement, but it noted that it lacked the power to order the pipeline shut down as a remedy for this deficiency. USACE, as the decision-making entity, had the authority to order the pipeline to shut down, but, as it stood, the district court could not force it to do so.[6]

The draft environmental impact statement (DEIS) was issued in September 2023, while the pipeline the DEIS is supposed to have assessed for potential approval continued to pump oil under the sacred waters of Lake Oahe. USACE has refused to turn off the pipeline, even as the courts have repeatedly agreed that there remains significant scientific controversy as to the likelihood of a spill. The Standing Rock and Cheyenne River Sioux tribes have sought participation in producing the DEIS, but their concerns have been ignored at every turn. The Sioux governments find themselves in the strange position of objecting to the adequacy of an assessment of a pipeline that is currently operating with no legal approval. The Lakotas won the battle in court, demonstrating that the prior process violated the law, but the pipeline remains in operation, just 'cuz the executive branch, now led by a Democratic administration, doesn't care to follow the law when Indians are involved.

Still, there is hope: the Supreme Court recently rejected a call to ignore precedents and wipe away what remains of recognized indigenous sovereignty, largely maintaining the status quo.[7] The courts continue to recognize limited sovereignty for indigenous nations and the supremacy of the federal government in protecting that sovereignty. As long as they do not comply with the requirements of the United Nations Declaration on the Rights of Indigenous Peoples or of international law, the laws of the United States remain tools of limited utility for protecting indigenous sovereignty, rights, and freedoms.

NOTES

INTRODUCTION

1. Steven Newcomb, "A Conversation with a Justice of the U.S. Supreme Court," *Indian Country Today*, June 24, 2011, https://indiancountrymedianetwork.com/news/opinions/a-conversation-with-a-justice-of-the-us-supreme-court (accessed December 22, 2016).
2. *Johnson v. McIntosh*, 21 U.S. 543 (1823).
3. The case from the previous spring that Newcomb identified for Scalia was *City of Sherrill, New York v. Oneida Indian Nation of New York*, 544 U.S. 197 (2005); Newcomb, "A Conversation."
4. Steven Newcomb, "What Justice Scalia Said He Did Not Know about U.S. Indian Law," *Indian Country Today*, February 26, 2016, https://indiancountrymedianetwork.com/news/opinions/what-justice-scalia-said-he-didnt-know-about-us-indian-law (accessed December 22, 2016); Newcomb, "A Conversation."
5. In particular, Allison M. Dussias, "Friend, Foe Frenemy: The United States and American Indian Religious Freedom," *Denver University Law Review*, Vol. 90 (2012), is a broad examination of government briefs in some of the cases examined here.
6. *Cherokee Nation v. Georgia*, 30 U.S. 1 (1831); Valerie Richardson, "Obama Adopts U.N. Manifesto on Rights of Indigenous Peoples," *Washington Times*, December 16, 2010.
7. National Environmental Policy Act, 42 U.S. Code § 4321 *et seq*.
8. Philip Deloria, "Historiography," in *A Companion to American Indian History*, ed. Philip J. Deloria and Neal Salisbury (Malden, MA: Blackwell, 2004), 7–8.

CHAPTER 1

1. Philip Deloria, "Historiography," in *A Companion to American Indian History*, ed. Philip J. Deloria and Neal Salisbury (Malden, MA: Blackwell, 2004), 6.
2. Donald Fixico, "Federal and State Policies and American Indians," in Deloria and Salisbury, *A Companion*, 380–81.
3. Jill Norgren, "The Cherokee Nation Cases of the 1830s," *Journal of Supreme Court History*, Vol. 19, No. 1 (1994): 65, 71–72.
4. Fixico, "Federal and State Policies," 381–82.
5. *Johnson v. M'Intosh*, 21 U.S. 543 (1823); *Cherokee Nation v. Georgia*, 30 U.S. 8 (1831); *Worcester v. Georgia*, 31 U.S. 515 (1832).
6. Tim Alan Garrison, "Beyond *Worcester:* The Alabama Supreme Court and the Sovereignty of the Creek Nation," *Journal of the Early Republic*, Vol. 19, No. 3 (Autumn 1999): 423–50.
7. John H. Vinzant, *The Supreme Court's Role in American Indian Policy* (El Paso: LFB Scholarly Publishing, 2009), 48–50; Fixico, "Federal and State Policies," 383.
8. Fixico, "Federal and State Policies," 383–84.
9. Fixico, "Federal and State Policies," 384.
10. Vinzant, *Supreme Court's Role*, 53.
11. Fixico, "Federal and State Policies," 385.
12. James Riding In, "Scholars and Twentieth-Century Indians," in *New Directions in American Indian History*, ed. Colin G. Calloway (Norman: University of Oklahoma Press, 1988), 133–34. Frederick Hoxie presents an account of the role social scientists played in the effort to destroy indigenous culture in *A Final Promise: The Campaign to Assimilate the Indians, 1880–1920* (Lincoln: University of Nebraska Press, 2001). Hoxie argues that ethnocentric social scientists played a key role in shaping public and congressional opinion and thereby federal Indian policy.
13. Fixico, "Federal and State Policies," 385.
14. Fixico, "Federal and State Policies," 386–87.
15. William T. Hagan, "The New Indian History," in *Rethinking American Indian History*, ed. Donald L. Fixico (Albuquerque: University of New Mexico Press, 1997), 30.
16. Fixico, "Federal and State Policies," 388.
17. Paul Vandevelder, "What Do We Owe the Indians?" *American History*, Vol. 44, No. 2 (June 2009): 36.
18. Fixico, "Federal and State Policies," 389.
19. Fixico, "Federal and State Policies," 389.
20. *Lyng v. Northwest Indian Cemetery Protective Association*, 485 U.S. 439 (1989); *Employment Division v. Smith*, 494 U.S. 872 (1990).
21. Fixico, "Federal and State Policies," 391; Allison Dussias, "Friend, Foe, Frenemy: The United States and American Indian Religious Freedom," *Denver University Law Review*, Vol. 90 (2012): 357, 367–68; Marcia Yablon, "Property Rights and Sacred Sites: Federal Regulatory Responses to American Indian Religious Claims on Public Land," *Yale Law Journal*, Vol. 113, No. 7 (May 2004): 1646.

22. Vine Deloria Jr. and Clifford M. Lytle, *American Indians, American Justice* (Austin: University of Texas Press, 1983), 11.
23. *Center for Biological Diversity v. United States Forest Service*, 349 F.3d 1157, 1165 (9th Cir. 2003), as quoted in *Navajo Nation, et al. v. U.S. Forest Service, et al.*, Case Nos. CV 05-1824-PCT-PGR, CV 05-1914-PCT-EHC, CV 05-1949-PCT-NVW, CV 05-1966-PCT, United States District Court for the District of Arizona, the Honorable Paul G. Rosenblatt presiding, *Order of the Court*, January 11, 2006, 5.
24. Brian Edward Brown, *Religion, Law, and the Land: Native Americans and the Judicial Interpretation of Sacred Land* (Westport, CT: Greenwood Press, 1999), 66–67.
25. Brown, *Religion, Law*, 73–74, 87; *Wilson v. Block*, 708 F.2d 735, 747 (D.C. Cir. 1983). ("We find that the Forest Service complied with AIRFA in the present case. Before approving the Preferred Alternative, the Forest Service held many meetings with Indian religious practitioners and conducted public hearings on the Hopi and Navajo reservations at which practitioners testified. The views there expressed were discussed at length in the Final Environmental Statement and were given due consideration in the evaluation of the alternative development schemes proposed for the Snow Bowl. Development of the Snow Bowl under the Preferred Alternative will not deny the plaintiffs access to the Peaks, nor will it prevent them from collecting religious objects. The Forest Service has not burdened the plaintiffs' religious practices in any manner prohibited by AIRFA.")
26. Vine Deloria Jr., *For This Land: Writings on Religion in America* (New York: Routledge, 1999), 223; Brown, *Religion, Law*, 73, 136, 172.
27. Brown, *Religion, Law*, 119, 123–24, 150. David E. Wilkins, *American Indian Sovereignty and the U.S. Supreme Court* (Austin: University of Texas Press, 1997), 247, characterizing the Forest Service choice as most destructive.
28. *Lyng*, 485 U.S. 451; Brown, *Religion, Law*, 151.
29. *Lyng*, 485 U.S. 451–52.
30. *Lyng*, 486 U.S. 476–77.
31. *Lyng*, 486 U.S. 454; Wilkins, "Who's in Charge of U.S. Indian Policy? Congress and the Supreme Court at Loggerheads Over American Indian Religious Freedom," *Wicazo Sa Review*, Vol. 8, No. 1 (Spring 1992): 58.
32. *Smith*, 494 U.S. 872; Wilkins, "Who's in Charge?" 57.
33. Garrett Epps, *To an Unknown God: Religious Freedom on Trial* (New York: St. Martin's Press, 2001), 9–10.
34. Epps, *To an Unknown God*, 14–16.
35. Epps, *To an Unknown God*, 17–19.
36. Epps, *To an Unknown God*, 42–43, 46, 49.
37. Epps, *To an Unknown God*, 51–52, 94.
38. Epps, *To an Unknown God*, 59–60, 64.
39. Epps, *To an Unknown God*, 107–9.
40. Epps, *To an Unknown God*, 111.
41. Epps, *To an Unknown God*, 147, 149.

42. *Sherbert v. Verner*, 374 U.S. 398 (1963); Epps, *To an Unknown God*, 216.
43. *Smith*, 494 U.S. 883, 890.
44. *Smith*, 494 U.S. 894–95.
45. *Smith*, 494 U.S. 902.
46. *Smith*, 494 U.S. 908–9.
47. David W. Inlander, "Don't Let Laws Impede Religion Practices," *Chicago Sun Times*, March 7, 1992; Ethan Bronner, "Curbs on Religious Freedoms Rally Crusade," *Oregonian*, January 12, 1991; Samuel Rabinove, "The Supreme Court and Religious Freedom," *Christian Science Monitor*, June 25, 1990.
48. Rabinove, "Supreme Court and Religious Freedom"; Nat Hentoff, "Justice Scalia vs. the Free Exercise of Religion," *Washington Post*, May 19, 1990; Larry Witham, "Bill on Religion Gathers Support across Spectrum," *Washington Times*, March 13, 1993; Nat Hentoff, "Is Religious Freedom a Luxury?" *Washington Post*, September 15, 1990; Peter Steinfels, "Clinton Signs Boost for Religious Freedom; Liberals, Conservatives Back New Law," *Houston Chronicle*, November 17, 1993.
49. Religious Freedom Restoration Act of 1993, 42 U.S.C. § 2000bb; Allison Dussias, "Ghost Dance and Holy Ghost: The Echoes of Nineteenth-Century Christianization Policy in Twentieth-Century Native American Free Exercise Cases," *Stanford Law Review*, Vol. 49, No. 4 (April 1997): 844–45.
50. Epps, *To an Unknown God*, 235. It is worth noting that the statutory exception for American Indian use and possession of peyote has caused the Supreme Court to protect the religious rights of other groups to possess and use others banned substances. See *Gonzales v. O Centro Espirita Beneficente Uniao do Vegetal*, 546 U.S. 418 (2006).
51. Wilkins, "Who's in Charge?" 57–58; Brown, *Religion, Law*, 151; *Navajo Nation v. United States Forest Service*, 535 F.3d 1058 (9th Cir. 2008), 1085–87.
52. Lloyd Burton and David Ruppert, "Bear's Lodge or Devil's Tower: Inter-Cultural Relations, Legal Pluralism, and the Management of Sacred Sites on Public Lands," *Cornell Journal of Law and Public Policy*, Vol. 8, No. 2 (Winter 1999): 201.
53. Burton and Ruppert, "Bear's Lodge," 202–3; *Bear Lodge Multiple Use v. Babbitt*, 175 F.3d 814 (10th Cir. 1999), 816; Joel Brady, "'Land Is Itself a Sacred Being': Native American Sacred Site Protection on Federal Public Lands Amidst the Shadows of *Bear Lodge*," *American Indian Law Review*, Vol. 24, No. 1 (1999/2000): 165, on the outlawing of the Sun Dance; Raymond Cross and Elizabeth Brenneman, "Devils Tower at the Crossroads: The National Park Service and the Preservation of Native American Cultural Resources in the 21st Century," *Public Land and Resource Law Review*, Vol. 18 (1997): 16.
54. *Bear Lodge*, 175 F.3d 818; Eric Freedman, "Protecting Sacred Sites on Public Land, Religion and Alliances in the Mato Tipila-Devils Tower Litigation," *American Indian Quarterly*, Vol. 31, No. 1 (Winter 2007): 14; Burton and Ruppert, "Bear's Lodge," 210–11.
55. Cross and Brenneman, "Devils Tower," 24; Burton and Ruppert, "Bear's Lodge," 212–15.
56. Cross and Brenneman, "Devils Tower," 25; Burton and Ruppert, "Bear's Lodge," 215, 217.

57. Cross and Brenneman, "Bear's Lodge," 26; *Bear Lodge*, 175 F.3d 821.
58. Dussias, "Friend, Foe," 357–58.
59. *Bear Lodge*, 175 F.3d 820.
60. Cross and Brenneman, "Devils Tower," 34; Freedman, "Protecting Sacred Sites" 18; *Bear Lodge*, 175 F.3d 820.
61. Burton and Ruppert, "Bear's Lodge," 229; *Bear Lodge Multiple Use Association v. Babbitt*, 2 F. Supp. 2d 1448 (1998).
62. *Bear Lodge*, 2 F. Supp. 1454; Cross and Brenneman, "Devils Towers," 28–29; Cross and Brenneman are among the contemporary commentators.
63. *Bear Lodge*, 2 F. Supp. 1455, 1456.
64. *Bear Lodge*, 2 F. Supp. 1455.
65. Freedman, "Protecting Sacred Sites," 10; *Bear Lodge*, 175 F.3d 821–22.
66. Freedman, "Protecting Sacred Sites," 2.
67. *Natural Arch & Bridge Society v. Alston*, 209 F. Supp. 2d 1207 (Federal District Court of Utah, Central Division, 2002), 1210.
68. *Natural Arch*, 209 F. Supp. 2d, 1210–11.
69. *Natural Arch*, 209 F. Supp. 2d, 1211; *Badoni v. Higgins*, 638 F.2d 172 (10th Cir. 1980), 175.
70. *Badoni*, 638 F.2d 176, 177.
71. *Badoni*, 638 F.2d 179–80.
72. *Natural Arch*, 209 F. Supp. 2d 1212–14.
73. *Natural Arch*, 209 F. Supp. 2d 1213–15.
74. *Natural Arch*, 209 F. Supp. 2d 1213–15.
75. *Natural Arch*, 209 F. Supp. 2d 1214–15.
76. *Natural Arch*, 209 F. Supp. 2d 1222–26
77. *Natural Arch & Bridge Society v. Alston*, 98 Fed. Appx. 711 (10th Cir. 2004), cert. denied, 543 U.S. 1145 (2005).
78. Yablon, "Property Rights," 1646; Dussias, "Friend, Foe," 357, 367–68; United States Department of Agriculture, Office of Tribal Relations, and United States Forest Service, *Report to the Secretary of Agriculture: USDA Policy and Procedures Review and Recommendations: Indian Sacred Sites* (Washington, DC: U.S. Department of Agriculture, 2012), 20.
79. Lloyd Burton, *Worship and Wilderness: Culture, Religion, and Law in the Management of Public Lands and Resources* (Madison: University of Wisconsin Press, 2002), 160, 261–63, 292–95.
80. Joel W. Martin, *The Land Looks After Us: A History of Native American Religion* (New York: Oxford University Press, 2001), 92.
81. Brown, *Religion, Law*, 2.
82. Walter Echo-Hark, "Five Hundred Nations within One: The Search for Religious Justice," in *A Seat at the Table: Huston Smith in Conversation with Native Americans on Religious Freedom*, ed. Phil Cousineau (Berkeley: University of California Press, 2006), 30, on religion as a way of life; Martin, *Land Looks After Us*, x, on the study of religion as a study of all culture; Vine Deloria Jr., "The Spiritual Malaise in America:

The Confluence of Religion, Law, and Community," in Cousineau, *Seat at the Table*, 9, on religion centered on the larger community, including the dead; Deloria, "Spiritual Malaise," 14, on Indian responsibility to the land; Robert S. Michaelson, "Dirt in the Courtroom: Indian Land Claims and American Property Rights," in *American Sacred* Space, ed. David Chidester and Edward T. Linenthal (Bloomington: Indiana University Press, 1995), 49, "Does the land" quote; Charlotte Black Elk, "The Homelands of Religions: The Clash of Worldviews Over Prayer, Place, and Ceremony," in Cousineau, *Seat at the Table*, 62, on European conflict with Earth; Brown, *Religion, Law*, 2, final quote.

83. David Chidester and Edward T. Linenthal, *American Sacred Space* (Bloomington: Indiana University Press, 1995), 5, 9. One can debate whether or not those who called the USS *Arizona* or Gettysburg a "national shrine" and "sacred" meant what they said, but this debate is irrelevant to the arguments here. What is undeniable is that many of those who identified these places as national shrines and sacred were at least nominally practitioners of religions of European origins, such as various denominations of Christianity, and that these same people identified these places as extraordinary in some sense and worthy of special reverence and protection. Thus it was within the normal understandings of the practitioners of settler religions (regardless of whether or not these understandings were religious in origin) that certain places deserve different treatment than others and that not all common activities, including commercial activities, should necessarily be conducted at such places. As there is some notion of "sacred" that sets aside places from ordinary use or treatment that is not necessarily religious in origin, and this was the language used by those who sought to set aside these places, albeit for political, historical, and cultural reasons that were likely not directly religious. The word "sacred" was used to describe these likely secular notions of extraordinary places of significance that should not be treated like ordinary places.

84. Michaelson, "Dirt in the Courtroom," 79, on sacred ground of Gettysburg; *U.S. v. Gettysburg Electric Rail Co.*, 160 U.S. 668 (1896).

85. Yablon, "Property Rights," 1648–49.

86. Christine K. Gray, *The Tribal Moment in American Politics: The Struggle for Native American Sovereignty* (New York: Rowman & Littlefield, 2013), 198.

87. Erich Fromm, *Marx's Concept of Man* (New York: Continuum, 2000), 44, 65; see page 68 for more on the goals of social organization. It is worth noting that the form of freedom here, and its centrality to the human experience, differs in no significant ways from Amartya Sen's concept of freedom as a measure and end of economic development, discussed in chapter 6.

CHAPTER 2

1. See *Navajo Nation v. U.S. Forest Service*, 408 F. Supp. 2d 866 (D. Ariz. 2006), affirmed in part and reversed in part, 479 F.3d 1024 (9th Cir. 2007); affirmed en banc, 535 F.3d 1058 (9th Cir. 2008); certiorari denied, 556 U.S. 1281 (2009).

2. *Navajo Nation v. Forest Service*, Case Nos. CV 05-1824-PCT-PGR, CV 05-1914-PCT-EHC, CV 05-1949-PCT-NVW, CV 05-1966-PCT, trial transcript (hereinafter "Tr."), 1070, 1701.
3. Harry C. James, *Pages from Hopi History* (Tucson: University of Arizona Press, 1974), xii; Tr. 427, 531.
4. Armin W. Geertz, "Contemporary Problems in the Study of Native North American Religions with Special Reference to the Hopis," *American Indian Quarterly*, Vol. 20, No. 3 (1996): 46–47, 75–76, 408, 409; Maria Glowacka, Dorothy Washburn, and Justin Richland, "*Nuvatukya'ovi*, San Francisco Peaks: Balancing Western Economies with Native American Spiritualities," *Current Anthropology*, Vol. 50, No 4 (August 2009): 553; Jonathan Haas, "Power, Objects, and a Voice for Anthropology," *Current Anthropology*, Vol. 37, supplement (February 1996): S4; Tr. 427, 439, 531.
5. Tr. 430–33, 442–44, 575.
6. Tr. 444–45, 447, 448, 564, 585, 586, 595.
7. Scott Rushforth and Steadman Upham, *A Hopi Social History* (Austin: University of Texas Press, 1992), 16; Frederick Dockstader, *The Kachina and the White Man: Influences of White Culture on the Hopi Kachina Cult* (Albuquerque: University of New Mexico Press, 1985), 162–63, 172; James F. Brooks, *Mesa of Sorrows: A History of the Awat'ovi Massacre* (New York: W. W. Norton & Company, 2016).
8. Richard O. Clemmer, *Roads in the Sky: The Hopi Indians in a Century of Change* (Boulder, CO: Westview Press, 1995), 88.
9. Richard O. Clemmer, "'Then Will You Strike My Head from My Neck': Hopi Prophecy and the Discourse of Empowerment," *American Indian Quarterly*, Vol. 19, No. 1 (1995): 56; Clemmer, *Roads in the Sky*, 91.
10. James, *Pages,* 185; Armin W. Geertz, *The Invention of Prophecy: Continuity and Meaning in Hopi Indian Religion* (Berkeley: University of California Press, 1994), 133; Clemmer, *Roads in the Sky*, 108, 132.
11. Clemmer, *Roads in the Sky*, 108–9; Geertz, *Invention of Prophecy*, 128.
12. James, *Pages*, 189–91; Geertz, *Invention of Prophecy*, 133.
13. James, *Pages*, 203; Justin B. Richland, "The State of Hopi Exception: When Inheritance Is What You Have," *Law and Literature*, Vol. 20, No. 2 (2008): 266–67.
14. Geertz, *Invention of Prophecy*, 134; Clemmer, *Roads in the Sky*, 151–52.
15. Clemmer, *Roads in the Sky*, 152.
16. Richland, "Hopi Exception," 268; Clemmer, *Roads in the Sky*, 151–52.
17. James, *Pages*, 204–5; Clemmer, *Roads in the Sky*, 154–55, 160.
18. Clemmer, *Roads in the Sky*, 161, 164.
19. Geertz, *Invention of Prophecy*, 134.
20. Clemmer, "Strike My Head," 62.
21. Clemmer, *Roads in the Sky*, 190.
22. Richard O. Clemmer, "The Hopi Traditionalist Movement," *American Indian Culture and Research Journal*, Vol. 18, No. 3 (1994): 144; James, *Pages*, 205.
23. James, *Pages*, 205; Clemmer, "Hopi Traditionalist," 145.

24. Geertz, *Invention of Prophecy*, 149–50. See, for example, Peter M. Whiteley, *Rethinking Hopi Ethnography* (Washington, DC: Smithsonian Institution Press, 1998), which describes the book as a "notorious confabulation of fact and imagination."
25. Geertz, *Invention of Prophecy*, 151; Clemmer, "Hopi Traditionalist," 146–47; Clemmer, *Roads in the Sky*, 272.
26. Justin B. Richland, "Pragmatic Paradoxes and Ironies of Indigeneity at the 'Edge' of Hopi Sovereignty," *American Ethnologist*, Vol. 34, No. 3 (January 2008): 543–44.
27. Geertz, *Invention of Prophecy*, 143; Clemmer, *Roads in the Sky*, 238.
28. Tr. 510, 594; Dockstader, *Kachina*, 147–48.
29. Dockstader, *Kachina*, 147–48, 158–59; Richland, "Hopi Exception," 264–65.
30. Clemmer, "Hopi Traditionalist," 157.
31. Klee Benally, dir., *The Snowbowl Effect* (Flagstaff: Indigenous Action Media, 2005), DVD; *Navajo Nation v. Forest Service*, Case Nos. CV 05-1824-PCT-PGR, CV 05-1914-PCT-EHC, CV 05-1949-PCT-NVW, CV 05-1966-PCT, *Order* of January 11, 2006, 37; Brian Edward Brown, *Religion, Law, and the Land: Native Americans and the Judicial Interpretation of Sacred Land* (Westport, CT: Greenwood Press, 1999), 61–62, 66.
32. *Wilson v. Block*, 708 F.2d 735 (D.C. 1983), 738; Brown, *Religion, Law*, 62–63, 66.
33. Brown, *Religion, Law*, 63, 66.
34. *Wilson*, 708 F.3d 738–39.
35. Clemmer, *Roads in the Sky*, 195; Brown, *Religion, Law*, 63.
36. Clemmer, *Roads in the Sky*, 195; Brown, *Religion, Law*, 63, 67.
37. Tr. 1096.
38. Brown, *Religion, Law*, 64, 67, 87–88; *Wilson*, 708 F.2d 735, 747; Tr. 1024.
39. *Navajo Nation v. United States Forest Service*, 479 F.3d 1024 (9th Cir. 2007), 1030.
40. Tr. 1022, 1024, 1698.
41. Tr. 1024, 1041, 1056–57, 1126–27.
42. Tr. 1024–45.
43. Benally, *Snowbowl Effect*; *Navajo Nation v. Forest Service*, Case Nos. CV 05-1824-PCT-PGR, CV 05-1914-PCT-EHC, CV 05-1949-PCT-NVW, CV 05-1966-PCT, *Order*, 3; *Navajo Nation* 535 F.3d 1082; *Navajo Nation v. Forest Service*, Case Nos. CV 05-1824-PCT-PGR, CV 05-1914-PCT-EHC, CV 05-1949-PCT-NVW, CV 05-1966-PCT, *Order*, 3–4; Tr. 1043; *Navajo Nation*, 479 F.3d 1045.
44. Tr. 1041–42, 1070, 1171, 1701.
45. Tr. 1023, 1042–43, 1092.
46. Tr. 1051, 1108–9.
47. Document 74-5, filed August 21, 2005, Navajo Nation document attachment to *Motion for Summary Judgment, Navajo Nation v. Forest Service*, Case Nos. CV 05-1824-PCT-PGR, CV 05-1914-PCT-EHC, CV 05-1949-PCT-NVW, CV 05-1966-PCT, 21 (emphasis added).
48. Document 74-5, filed August 21, 2005, Navajo Nation document attachment to *Motion for Summary Judgment, Navajo Nation v. Forest Service*, Case Nos. CV 05-1824-PCT-PGR, CV 05-1914-PCT-EHC, CV 05-1949-PCT-NVW, CV 05-1966-PCT, 21.

49. Tr. 1172.
50. Benally, *Snowbowl*.
51. Tr. 1181–82.
52. Tr. 1183, 1185, 1190.
53. Tr. 1188–89, 1191.
54. Tr. 1192, 1194, 1196.
55. Tr. 1199, 1237, 1268, 1269.
56. Tr. 1136, 1164, 1636–41.
57. Tr. 1044–45, 1239; *Navajo Nation*, 479 F.3d 1024, 1045.
58. Tr., 1198, 1240.
59. Tr. 1194, 1242, 1243, 1264, 1664.
60. Tr. 1250, 1272, 1273, 1279.
61. Tr. 1250, 1268, 1273.
62. Tr. 1232–34, 1248–49.
63. Tr. 1233, 1281–83.
64. Tr. 1664, 1672.
65. Tr. 1199, 1669, 1670.
66. Tr. 1673, 1684, 1715.
67. Tr. 1683–84.
68. Tr. 1674–75.
69. United States Forest Service, *Arizona Snowbowl Facilities Improvements Final Environmental Impact Statement Record of Decision and Forest Plan Amendment 21* (Washington, DC: US Forest Service, 2005), 4.
70. Tr. 1675–76.
71. Tr. 1679–80, 1722.
72. Tr. 1678–79.
73. U.S. Forest Service, *Record of Decision*, 26.
74. Tr. 1146.
75. Benally, *Snowbowl*; "Sierra Club and Tribes Act to Protect the Peaks from More Development," *Navajo-Hopi Observer*, June 29, 2005; S. J. Wilson, "Tribes, Activists Gather in Celebration of the Peaks," *Navajo-Hopi Observer*, March 27, 2007.
76. Editorial, "Tribal Sovereignty Over Peaks a Stretch," *Arizona Daily Sun*, February 22, 2002; Randy Wilson and Roy Callaway, "An Apology on Language, a Commitment on Coverage," *Arizona Daily Sun*, March 3, 2002, on real racism.
77. Seth Muller, "Coalition Formed to Oppose Snowbowl Report," *Arizona Daily Sun*, February 10, 2004.
78. Benally, *Snowbowl*.
79. See *Navajo Nation v. U.S. Forest Service*, 408 F. Supp. 2d 866 (D. Ariz. 2006), affirmed in part and reversed in part, 479 F.3d 1024 (9th Cir. 2007), affirmed en banc, 535 F.3d 1058 (9th Cir. 2008), certiorari denied, 556 U.S. 1281 (2009).
80. *Navajo Nation v. Forest Service*, Case Nos. CV 05-1824-PCT-PGR, CV 05-1914-PCT-EHC, CV 05-1949-PCT-NVW, CV 05-1966-PCT, *Civil Docket*, Item No. 1, Item No. 23. Summary judgment is judgment by the court without presentation of evidence.

Summary judgment is appropriate where no factual matters are in dispute and when an issue can be determined as a matter of law, as opposed to a matter of contested fact. A bench trial is a trial without a jury. In administrative appeals, a bench trial without a jury is standard procedure. *Navajo Nation v. Forest Service*, Case Nos. CV 05-1824-PCT-PGR, CV 05-1914-PCT-EHC, CV 05-1949-PCT-NVW, CV 05-1966-PCT, *Order* of the District Court, 23; Tim Wiederaenders, "Native Americans Have Valid Stance on Snowmaking for Snowbowl," *Navajo-Hopi Observer*, November 16, 2005.

81. "Lynelle K. Hartway—Lawyer Profile," Martindale.com, www.martindale.com/Lynelle-K-Hartway/42106-lawyer.htm; Shanker Law Firm, "Howard M. Shanker," www.shankerlaw.net/index.php?option=com_content&task=view&id=197&Itemid=77 (accessed July 1, 2010); Cindy Cole, "Kirkpatrick Wins Dem Nod," *Arizona Daily Sun*, September 2, 2008; Tr. 2.
82. Tr. 127, 128, 138, 494, 510, 594.
83. Tr. 139, 146.
84. Tr. 145, 147, 156–59.
85. Tr. 555–59.
86. Tr. 127–26.
87. Tr. 414–18.
88. Johnny Cruz, "U of A, Hopi Tribe Mourn Passing of Sekaquaptewa," *Navajo-Hopi Observer*, December 27, 2007; Tr. 573–74.
89. Tr. 450–52.
90. Tr. 136.
91. Tr. 134–35.
92. Tr. 601–2.
93. Tr. 530.
94. Tr. 530–31.
95. Steve Talbot, "Spiritual Genocide: The Denial of American Indian Religious Freedom, from Conquest to 1934," *Wicazo Sa Review*, Vol. 21, No. 2 (Autumn 2006): 7.
96. *Navajo Nation v. Forest Service*, Case Nos. CV 05-1824-PCT-PGR, CV 05-1914-PCT-EHC, CV 05-1949-PCT-NVW, CV 05-1966-PCT, *Order*, 19, 41–42, 56; Tr. 421–23, 463–85, 489; *Navajo Nation v. Forest Service*, 408 F. Supp. 2d 866 (2006), 895.
97. Cindy Cole, "Judge OKs Snowmaking on Peaks," *Arizona Daily Sun*, January 11, 2006, quoting Nora Rasure; Cindy Cole, "Snowmaking Opponents Now Targeting City Council," *Arizona Daily Sun*, January 12, 2006, quoting Jeneda Benally and Miguel Vasquez.
98. *Navajo Nation*, 479 F.3d 1024, 1032–34, 1044–45.
99. Howard Fischer, "Snowbowl Fight Rages On," *Arizona Daily Sun*, March 12, 2007.
100. Randy Wilson, "Snowbowl Coverage a Moving Target," *Arizona Daily Sun*, April 7, 2007; Fischer, "Snowbowl Fight."
101. Cindy Cole, "Court Sides with Snowbowl," *Arizona Daily Sun*, August 8, 2008, quoting Bucky Preston; "Responses to News on Snowbowl," *Arizona Daily Sun*, June 8, 2009, quoting Robert Greene.

102. Berkeley Law, "Faculty Profiles, William A. Fletcher," University of California, www.law.berkeley.edu/php-programs/faculty/facultyProfile.php?facID=39 (accessed July 1, 2010).
103. *Navajo Nation*, 479 F.3d 1040–3.
104. *Navajo Nation*, 479 F.3d 1044.
105. *Wisconsin v. Yoder*, 406 U.S. 205 (1972), 215, quoted in *Navajo Nation*, 479 F.3d 1043; *Navajo Nation*, 479 F.3d 1044.
106. *Navajo Nation*, 479 F.3d 1044–45.
107. *Navajo Nation*, 479 F.3d 1045.
108. *Lynch v. Donnelly*, 465 U.S. 668 (1984), 673, quoted in *Navajo Nation*, 479 F.3d 1045; *Navajo Nation*, 479 F.3d 1045–46.
109. *Navajo Nation*, 535 F.3d 1048, 1058, 1067.
110. *Navajo Nation*, 535 F.3d 1058, 1067.
111. *Navajo Nation*, 535 F.3d 1058, 1063.
112. *Navajo Nation*, 535 F.3d 1062–63.
113. *Navajo Nation*, 535 F.3d 1063.
114. *Navajo Nation*, 535 F.3d 1086, 1090.
115. *Navajo Nation*, 535 F.3d 1070–73.
116. *Northwest Indian Cemetery Protective Association v. Lyng*, 485 U.S. 439 (1989), 451, quoted in *Employment Division v. Smith*, 494 U.S. 872 (1990), 883.
117. *Smith*, 494 U.S. 900.
118. *Navajo Nation v. Forest Service*, 129 S. Ct. 2763, 174 L. Ed. 2D 270, 2009 U.S. LEXIS 4206. Allies of the Hopis, using the same law firm as the Navajo Nation, filed a challenge to the proposed expansion based upon environmental and health grounds on September 21, 2009. Save the Peaks Coalition, "New Lawsuit Filed against Forest Service," September 21, 2009, www.indigenousaction.org/save-the-peaks-new-lawsuit-filed-against-forest-service/ (accessed July 1, 2010).
119. Burton noted that this was the impact of *Lyng*, and writing Indians out of the Religious Freedom Restoration Act has the same impact. Lloyd Burton, *Worship and Wilderness: Culture, Religion, and Law in the Management of Public Lands and Resources* (Madison: University of Wisconsin Press, 2002), 292.
120. United States Department of Agriculture, Office of Tribal Relations and U.S. Forest Service, *Report to the Secretary of Agriculture: USDA Policy and Procedures Review and Recommendations: Indian Sacred Sites* (Washington, DC: USDA, 2012), 15, 30.

CHAPTER 3

1. James F. Downs, *The Two Worlds of the Washo: An Indian Tribe of California and Nevada* (New York: Holt, Rinehart & Winston, 1966), 8, 36.
2. Downs, *Two Worlds*, 34; Edgar E. Siskin, *Washoe Shamans and Peyotists: Religious Conflict in an American Indian Tribe* (Salt Lake City: University of Utah Press, 1983), 3, 12.
3. Downs, *Two Worlds*, 45, 49, 51; Siskin, *Washoe Shamans*, 9.

4. Downs, *Two Worlds*, 54; Stephen Powers, Don. D. Fowler, and Catherine S. Fowler, eds., "Stephen Power's 'The Life and Culture of the Washo and Paiutes,'" *Ethnohistory*, Vol. 17, No. 3/4 (Summer–Autumn 1970): 121, on Washoe warfare and troop accuracy with the bow.
5. Siskin, *Washoe Shamans*, 22, 27, on the power and its sources; Downs, *Two Worlds*, 56, 60.
6. Siskin, *Washoe Shamans*, 123, 143.
7. Mathew S. Makley and Michael J. Makley, *Cave Rock, Climbers, Courts, and a Washoe Indian Sacred Place* (Reno: University of Nevada Press, 2010), 2, 10, 27, 28.
8. Downs, *Two Worlds*, 60.
9. James F. Downs, "Washo Religion," *Anthropological Records*, Vol. 16, No. 9 (1961): 366; Makley and Makley, *Cave Rock*, 27.
10. Downs, *Two Worlds*, 60.
11. Downs, "Washo Religion," 366, 370.
12. Makley and Makley, *Cave Rock*, 97; Downs, "Washo Religion," 367.
13. Downs, *Two Worlds*, 73; Barrik Van Winkle, "Cannibals in the Mountains, Washoe Teratology and the Donner Party," *New Perspectives on Native North America* (Lincoln: University of Nebraska Press, 2006), 398, 400, 406.
14. Downs, *Two Worlds*, 75–77, 79.
15. Downs, *Two Worlds*, 76.
16. Downs, *Two Worlds*, 76.
17. Downs, *Two Worlds*, 77, 79.
18. Downs, *Two Worlds*, 79.
19. Downs, *Two Worlds*, 83, 90.
20. Downs, *Two Worlds*, 95–96.
21. Makley and Makley, *Cave Rock*, 13; Downs, *Two Worlds*, 88, 95–96.
22. Downs, *Two Worlds*, 96, 102.
23. Siskin, *Washoe Shamans*, 102; Downs, *Two Worlds*, 102.
24. Downs, *Two Worlds*, 104; Siskin, *Washoe Shamans*, 116, 143.
25. Siskin, *Washoe Shamans*, 113, 122, 123.
26. Siskin, *Washoe Shamans*, 116, 127, 158, 160.
27. *Downs, Two Worlds*, 107; United States Forest Service, *Cave Rock Management Direction Final Environmental Impact Statement* (Washington, DC: U.S. Forest Service, 2002), 2–55.
28. Makley and Makley, *Cave Rock*, 28–32.
29. Makley and Makley, *Cave Rock*, 32–33.
30. Makley and Makley, *Cave Rock*, 33–34.
31. Makley and Makley, *Cave Rock*, 34–35.
32. Makley and Makley, *Cave Rock*, 35–36.
33. Makley and Makley, *Cave Rock*, 36–37.
34. Makley and Makley, *Cave Rock*, 37–38.
35. U.S. Forest Service, *Cave Rock Management Direction*, 3–10. Makley and Makley, *Cave Rock*, 25, 30, 38.

36. U.S. Forest Service, *Cave Rock Management Direction*, 3–2, 3–5, 3–9, 3–12.
37. U.S. Forest Service, *Cave Rock Management Direction*, 3–12.
38. Makley and Makley, *Cave Rock*, 18–19.
39. Makley and Makley, *Cave Rock*, 20–21.
40. U.S. Forest Service, *Cave Rock Management Direction*, 3–9, 3–12.
41. U.S. Forest Service, *Cave Rock Management Direction*, 3–28.
42. U.S. Forest Service, *Cave Rock Management Direction*, 3–30, 3–31; Makley and Makley, *Cave Rock*, 41.
43. Makley and Makley, *Cave Rock*, 41.
44. Makley and Makley, *Cave Rock*, 42–43.
45. Makley and Makley, *Cave Rock*, 43–44.
46. Makley and Makley, *Cave Rock*, 44–45.
47. Makley and Makley, *Cave Rock*, 45.
48. Makley and Makley, *Cave Rock*, 47.
49. Makley and Makley, *Cave Rock*, 47–48.
50. Makley and Makley, *Cave Rock*, 46; U.S. Forest Service, *Cave Rock Management Direction*, 1–4.
51. Makley and Makley, *Cave Rock*, 46.
52. Makley and Makley, *Cave Rock*, 46–47.
53. Makley and Makley, *Cave Rock*, 58.
54. Makley and Makley, *Cave Rock*, 58, 61–62.
55. Lynn Armitage, "The Washoe: The First People of Lake Tahoe," *Indian Country Today*, August 5, 2012, http://indiancountrytodaymedianetwork.com/2012/08/05/washoe-first-people-lake-tahoe-125703 (accessed September 27, 2015); Makley and Makley, *Cave Rock*, 58.
56. Makley and Makley, *Cave Rock*, 60.
57. U.S. Forest Service, *Cave Rock Management Direction*, 3–9, 3–12, 3–25.
58. U.S. Forest Service, *Cave Rock Management Direction*, 4–1; Makley and Makley, *Cave Rock*, 59, 60, 63.
59. Makley and Makley, *Cave Rock*, 63.
60. Makley and Makley, *Cave Rock*, 63–64.
61. Makley and Makley, *Cave Rock*, 64.
62. Makley and Makley, *Cave Rock*, 64–65.
63. Makley and Makley, *Cave Rock*, 65.
64. Makley and Makley, *Cave Rock*, 65–66.
65. Makley and Makley, *Cave Rock*, 66.
66. Makley and Makley, *Cave Rock*, 66.
67. U.S. Forest Service, *Cave Rock Management Direction*, 3–42; Makley and Makley, *Cave Rock*, 67–68.
68. Makley and Makley, *Cave Rock*, 69–70.
69. Makley and Makley, *Cave Rock*, 71. U.S. Forest Service, *Cave Rock Management Direction*, 2–5, 2–7, 2–10.
70. U.S. Forest Service, *Cave Rock Management Direction*, 4–3.

71. U.S. Forest Service, *Cave Rock Management Direction*, 4–15 to 4–18.
72. U.S. Forest Service, *Cave Rock Management Direction*, 4–17 to 4–20.
73. Makley and Makley, *Cave Rock*, 78, 80.
74. Makley and Makley, *Cave Rock*, 80, 81.
75. U.S. Forest Service, *Cave Rock Management Direction*, 2–2 to 2–4.
76. U.S. Forest Service, *Cave Rock Management Direction*, 2–9.
77. U.S. Forest Service, *Cave Rock Management Direction*, 2–16.
78. Makley and Makley, *Cave Rock*, 86–88.
79. *Access Fund v. USDA*, 499 F.3d 1036 (9th Cir. 2007), 1042, 1046.
80. *Access Fund*, 499 F.3d 1043.
81. *Access Fund*, 499 F.3d 1043–44.
82. *Access Fund*, 499 F.3d 1045–46.
83. *Access Fund*, 499 F.3d 1046.
84. *Van Orden v. Perry*, 545 U.S. 677 (2005); *Access Fund*, 499 F.3d 1047, 1048.
85. Makley and Makley, *Cave Rock*, 97–100.

CHAPTER 4

1. Jay Hansford C. Vest, "Traditional Blackfeet Religion and the Sacred Badger-Two Medicine Wildlands, *Journal of Land and Religion*, Vol. 6, No. 2 (1998): 461–62.
2. Vest, "Traditional Blackfeet," 462, 464, 469; John C. Jackson, *The Piikani Blackfeet: A Culture Under Siege* (Missoula, MT: Mountain Press, 2000), 4.
3. Vest, "Traditional Blackfeet," 466.
4. Vest, "Traditional Blackfeet," 468–69.
5. Vest, "Traditional Blackfeet," 470, 479.
6. Vest, "Traditional Blackfeet," 471–72.
7. Vest, "Traditional Blackfeet," 474
8. Vest, "Traditional Blackfeet," 478.
9. Jackson, *Piikani Blackfeet*, x; Clark Wissler and Alice Beck Kehoe, *Amskapi Pikuni: The Blackfeet People* (Albany: SUNY Press, 2012), xiii.
10. Wissler and Kehoe, *Amskapi Pikuni*, 38, 72.
11. Wissler and Kehoe, *Amskapi Pikuni*, 2–3, 3–5, 24; Jackson, *Piikani Blackfeet*, 10.
12. Wissler and Kehoe, *Amskapi Pikuni*, 5, 6, 25.
13. Wissler and Kehoe, *Amskapi Pikuni*, 8, 9.
14. Wissler and Kehoe, *Amskapi Pikuni*, 17–18, 28; Jackson, *Piikani Blackfeet*, 15.
15. Wissler and Kehoe, *Amskapi Pikuni*, 22, 30–31.
16. Wissler and Kehoe, *Amskapi Pikuni*, 33, 36, 37.
17. Wissler and Kehoe, *Amskapi Pikuni*, 40, 41, 86.
18. Wissler and Kehoe, *Amskapi Pikuni*, 41.
19. Wissler and Kehoe, *Amskapi Pikuni*, 42, 96.
20. Wissler and Kehoe, *Amskapi Pikuni*, 42.
21. Wissler and Kehoe, *Amskapi Pikuni*, 46, 81, 98.
22. Wissler and Kehoe, *Amskapi Pikuni*, 46–49, 103.
23. Wissler and Kehoe, *Amskapi Pikuni*, 47, 49, 87, 106, 107.

24. Wissler and Kehoe, *Amskapi Pikuni*, 109, 121–22.
25. Wissler and Kehoe, *Amskapi Pikuni*, 124; Mark David Spence, "Crown of the Continent, Backbone of the World: The American Wilderness Ideal and Blackfeet Exclusion from Glacier National Park," *Environmental History*, Vol. 1, No. 3 (July 1996): 34; Robert H. Keller and Michael F. Turek, *American Indians and National Parks* (Tucson: University of Arizona Press, 1998), 46.
26. Spence, "Crown of the Continent," 35; Keller and Turek, *American Indians and National Parks*, 49–50.
27. Spence, "Crown of the Continent," 35.
28. Wissler and Kehoe, *Amskapi Pikuni*, 126.
29. Spence, "Crown of the Continent," 35; Wissler and Kehoe, *Amskapi Pikuni*, 124; Keller and Turek, *American Indians and National Parks*, 52.
30. Wissler and Kehoe, *Amskapi Pikuni*, 153, 154.
31. Paul C. Rosier, *Rebirth of the Blackfeet Nation, 1912–1954* (Lincoln: University of Nebraska Press, 2001), 16–19.
32. Rosier, *Rebirth*, 18, 21.
33. Rosier, *Rebirth*, 3, 21, 31–45.
34. Rosier, *Rebirth*, 31–45.
35. Keller and Turek, *American Indians and National Parks*, 53–55; Little Chief quote, 55.
36. Keller and Turek, *American Indians and National Parks*, 56–57, 59.
37. Rosier, *Rebirth*, 59, 63.
38. Keller and Turek, *American Indians and National Parks*, 60–61.
39. Rosier, *Rebirth*, 69, 70, 73, 74, 89, 107.
40. Wissler and Kehoe, *Amskapi Pikuni*, 160; Rosier, *Rebirth*, 82.
41. Rosier, *Rebirth*, 84, 91, 92.
42. Rosier, *Rebirth*, 93.
43. Rosier, *Rebirth*, 96–97.
44. Rosier, *Rebirth*, 85–86.
45. Rosier, *Rebirth*, 92, 128; Wissler and Kehoe, *Amskapi Pikuni*, 161, quote from Joe Brown.
46. Rosier, *Rebirth*, 117–27, 143, 144; Wissler and Kehoe, *Amskapi Pikuni*, 161, 163.
47. Rosier, *Rebirth*, 151–52, 169, 207.
48. Rosier, *Rebirth*, 222, 246.
49. Wissler and Kehoe, *Amskapi Pikuni*, 167–68; Rosier, *Rebirth*, 250.
50. Rosier, *Rebirth*, 252–53, 258–59.
51. Rosier, *Rebirth*, 170, 250, 274–75.
52. Rosier, *Rebirth*, 262.
53. Keller and Turek, *American Indians and National Parks*, 62–63; Wissler and Kehoe, *Amskapi Pikuni*, 177.
54. Wissler and Kehoe, *Amskapi Pikuni*, 179–80; James J. Lopach, Margery Hunter Brown, and Richmond L. Clow, *Tribal Government Today: Politics on Montana Indian Reservations* (Niwot: University of Colorado Press, 1998), 36.

55. Keller and Turek, *American Indians and National Parks*, 60–61.
56. Wissler and Kehoe, *Amskapi Pikuni*, 173, 180.
57. Lopach, Brown, and Clow, *Tribal Government Today*, 38–39.
58. Timothy J. Preso, letter to Sally Jewell, secretary of the U.S. Department of the Interior, and Tom Vilsack, secretary of the U.S. Department of Agriculture, Earth Justice, October 28, 2014, http://earthjustice.org/sites/default/files/files/B2M%20lease%20 cancellation%20letter%20—%20final.pdf (accessed December 17, 2015). Had there been a finding of significant impact, a full environmental impact statement would have been required by the National Environmental Policy Act. Terri Lee Nelson, "Legal Protection for Native American Sacred Landscapes Involving Forest Service Lands" (master's thesis, University of Montana, 1991); Preso to Jewell and Vilsack.
59. *Solenex, LLC, v. Sally Jewell, Secretary of Interior,* Case No. 13-993-RJL, U.S. District Court for the District of Columbia, *Memorandum of Points and Authorities in Support of Motion to Intervene as Defendants,* September 26, 2013, 3, 4; Preso, 3.
60. *Solenex, Memorandum,* 5; Preso, 4, 5.
61. *Solenex, Memorandum,* 5; Preso, 6; *Solenex v. Jewell,* Case No. 13-993-RJL, U.S. District Court for the District of Columbia, July, 27, 2015; Terri Hansen, "Sacred Blackfoot Land Saved! BLM Cancels Oil and Gas Leases in Badger-Two Medicine Region," *Indian Country Today,* March 18, 2016, http://indiancountrytodaymedianetwork.com/2016/03/18/sacred-blackfoot-land-saved-blm-cancels-oil-and-gas-lease-badger-two-medicine-region (accessed April 14, 2016).
62. Wissler and Kehoe, *Amskapi Pikuni,* 175.
63. Wissler and Kehoe, *Amskapi Pikuni,* 175.
64. United States Forest Service, *Final Environmental Impact Statement Rocky Mountain Ranger District Travel Management Plan* (Washington, DC: U.S. Forest Service, 2007), 156.
65. U.S. Forest Service, *Final Environmental Impact Statement,* xiv, 3–5, 156.
66. U.S. Forest Service, *Final Environmental Impact Statement,* 5; United States Forest Service, *Rocky Mountain Ranger District Travel Management Plan Record of Decision for Badger-Two Medicine* (Washington, DC: U.S. Forest Service, 2009), 7–9.
67. U.S. Forest Service, *Final Environmental Impact Statement,* xiii, 6, 7, 12.
68. U.S. Forest Service, *Record of Decision,* 23; U.S. Forest Service, *Final Environmental Impact Statement,* xiv.
69. U.S. Forest Service, *Final Environmental Impact Statement,* xii–xiii.
70. U.S. Forest Service, *Record of Decision,* 22.
71. U.S. Forest Service, *Final Environmental Impact Statement,* xiv.
72. U.S. Forest Service, *Record of Decision,* 9.
73. U.S. Forest Service, *Record of Decision,* 4, 16.
74. U.S. Forest Service, *Record of Decision,* 4–5, 14.
75. U.S. Forest Service, *Record of Decision,* 4–5, 9, 12, 16.
76. *Appeal Reviewing Officer's Review and Recommendation—Badger-Two Medicine Travel Management ROD—Lewis & Clark NF—Appeal* Nos. 09-01-00-0022, 0023, 0025, 0027, 0029, 0030, 0031, 0033, 0036, 0037, 0039, 0040, 0041, 0042, and 0043, June 13, 2009, 6,

45–51; Jane L. Cottrell, *Final Administrative Determination, Department of Agriculture, Appeal* Nos. 09-01-00-0022, 0023, 0025, 0027, 0029, 0030, 0031, 0033, 0036, 0037, 0039, 0040, 0041, 0042, and 0043, June 18, 2009; *Fortune v. Thompson*, 2011 U.S. Dist. LEXIS 5343.
77. *Fortune*, 6–10.
78. Order of the Ninth Circuit Court of Appeals, *Fortune v. Thompson*, Case No. 11-35242, October 28, 2011.

CHAPTER 5

1. Robert J. Miller, "Exercising Cultural Self-Determination: The Makah Indian Tribe Goes Whaling," *American Indian Law Review*, Vol. 25, No. 2 (2000/2001): 183, 185–87.
2. Miller, "Exercising Cultural Self-Determination," 174, 189, 190, 196, 198, 199.
3. Miller, "Exercising Cultural Self-Determination," 202–4.
4. Christina Roberts, "Treaty Rights Ignored: Neocolonialism and the Makah Whale Hunt," *Kenyon Review*, Vol. 3, No. 1 (2010): 82; Miller, "Exercising Cultural Self-Determination," 226.
5. Zachary Tomlinson, "Abrogation or Regulation? How *Anderson v. Evans* Discards the Makah's Treaty Whaling Rights in the Name of Conservation Necessity," *Washington Law Review*, Vol. 78 (2003): 1116; Miller, "Exercising Cultural Self-Determination," 254, 255.
6. Tomlinson, "Abrogation or Regulation?" 248.
7. Tomlinson, "Abrogation or Regulation?" 258.
8. Rob van Ginkel, "The Makah Whale Hunt and Leviathan's Death: Reinventing Tradition and Disputing Authenticity in the Age of Modernity," *Etnofoor*, Vol. 17, Nos. 1–2 (2004): 65, 66, 69; Miller, "Exercising Cultural Self-Determination," 239, 262–63.
9. Mark Lee, "You Talkin' to Me? Racism Sells: The Anti-Whaling Movement and Japan," *Northwest Asian Weekly*, March 26, 2011, http://nwasianweekly.com/2011/03/you-talkin-to-me-racism-sells-the-anti-whaling-movement-and-japan (accessed February 6, 2018); Van Ginkel, "Makah Whale Hunt," 76, 80, "Save a whale"; Miller, "Exercising Cultural Self-Determination," 262, 265–66.
10. Trey Parker, dir., *South Park*, season 13, episode 11, "Whale Whores" (Comedy Central, October 28, 2009); Lee, "You Talkin' to Me?"; Paul Lee Watson, "Makah Whaling: Whales Must Be Protected in U.S. Waters," Sea Shepherd Conservation Society, March 11, 2015, www.seashepherd.org/commentary-and-editorials/2015/03/11/makah-whaling-whales-must-be-protected-in-us-waters-692 (accessed April 14, 2016); Van Ginkel, "Makah Whale Hunt," 68, Watson quote.
11. Van Ginkel, "Makah Whale Hunt," 67; Frank Hopper, "Whale Wars Groups vs. Makah: Who Decides if Traditions Are Authentic?" *Indian Country Today*, June 23, 2015, http://indiancountrytodaymedianetwork.com/2015/06/23/whale-wars-group-vs-makah-who-decides-if-traditions-are-authentic-160741 (accessed December 12, 2015).
12. Hopper, "Whale Wars Groups vs. Makah."

13. Tomlinson, "Abrogation or Regulation?" 1103.
14. *Anderson v. Evans*, 314 F.3d 1006 (9th Cir. 2002); Tomlinson, "Abrogation or Regulation?" 1113, 1127.
15. Tomlinson, "Abrogation or Regulation?" 1113, 1119, 1125.
16. Tomlinson, "Abrogation or Regulation?" 1116; Roberts, "Treaty Rights Ignored," 83; United States Department of Commerce, National Oceanic and Atmospheric Administration, National Marine Fisheries Service, West Coast Region, *Draft Environmental Impact Statement on the Makah Tribe Request to Hunt Gray Whales* (Washington, DC: U.S. Department of Commerce, 2015), ES-1.
17. U.S. Department of Commerce, *Draft EIS*, ES-1 to ES-3.
18. Jack D. Forbes, *Warriors of the Colorado: The Yumas of the Quechan Nation and Their Neighbors* (Norman: University of Oklahoma Press, 1965), 63; United States Bureau of Land Management, *Environmental Assessment, CA-760-EA2000-34, For the Indian Pass Withdrawal, CACA-39853* (Washington, DC: U.S. Bureau of Land Management, 2000), 12.
19. Forbes, *Warriors of the Colorado*, 64, 65, 68.
20. Forbes, *Warriors of the Colorado*, 68–69.
21. Robert L. Bee, *Crosscurrents along the Colorado: The Impact of Government Policy on the Quechan Indians* (Tucson: University of Arizona Press, 1981), 9; Forbes, *Warriors of the Colorado*, 67, 69, 70.
22. Forbes, *Warriors of the Colorado*, 80, 81; Bee, *Crosscurrents along the Colorado*, 28.
23. Bee, *Crosscurrents along the Colorado*, 20, 37, 40, 50.
24. Bee, *Crosscurrents along the Colorado*, 92–93, 96–97.
25. Bee, *Crosscurrents along the Colorado*, 152.
26. U.S. Bureau of Land Management, *Environmental Assessment*, 2, 3, 8, 12, 13.
27. U.S. Bureau of Land Management, *Environmental Assessment*, 1; Non-Party Initial Submission of the Quechan Indian Nation, *Glamis Gold v. United States of America*, International Center for Settlement of Investment Disputes, North American Free Trade Agreement Arbitral Tribunal, August 19, 2005, 5.
28. Non-Party Supplemental Submission of the Quechan Indian Nation, *Glamis Gold v. United States of America*, International Center for Settlement of Investment Disputes, North American Free Trade Agreement Arbitral Tribunal, October, 16, 2006, 13.
29. U.S. Bureau of Land Management, *Environmental Assessment*, 1; Non-Party Initial Submission, *Glamis*, 2, 3.
30. Non-Party Initial Submission, *Glamis*, 3–5.
31. *Glamis Gold v. United States of America*, 48 ILM 1038 (2009), 1042; Application for Leave to File a Non-Party Submission of the Quechan Indian Nation, *Glamis Gold v. United States of America*, International Center for Settlement of Investment Disputes, North American Free Trade Agreement Arbitral Tribunal, August 19, 2005, 1; Indian Law Resource Center, "NAFTA Tribunal Recognizes Sacred Place of Quechan Tribe—Denies Glamis Gold's Claim in Full," Indian Law Resource Center, June 9, 2009, http://indianlaw.org/Quechan_Glamis_NAFTA_Tribunal (accessed April 14, 2016).
32. *Glamis v. USA*, 48 ILM 1066–67.

33. *Quechan Indian Tribe v. United States Department of the Interior*, 755 F. Supp. 2d 1104 (S.D. Cal. 2010), 1107, 1119, 1120.
34. *Quechan*, 755 F. Supp. 2d 1119.
35. *Quechan*, 755 F. Supp. 2d 1107, 1118, 1119.
36. *Quechan*, 755 F. Supp. 2d 1107, 1120.
37. *Quechan*, 755 F. Supp. 2d 1106.
38. *Quechan*, 755 F. Supp. 2d 1112, 1119, 1121.
39. Ryan D. Dreveskracht, "Alternative Energy in American Indian Country: Catering to Both Sides of the Coin," *Energy Law Journal*, Vol. 33, No. 2 (2012): 431, 434.
40. Richard J. Perry, *Apache Reservation, Indigenous Peoples and the American State* (Austin: University of Texas Press, 1993), 77–78.
41. Perry, *Apache Reservation*, 77, 176; Lydia Millet, "Selling Off Apache Holy Land," *New York Times*, May 29, 2015.
42. Perry, *Apache Reservation*, 47, 51, 70.
43. Perry, *Apache Reservation*, 47, 70, 89.
44. Perry, *Apache Reservation*, 55.
45. Perry, *Apache Reservation*, 63–64, 84.
46. Perry, *Apache Reservation*, 84, 87.
47. Perry, *Apache Reservation*, 89, 97.
48. Perry, *Apache Reservation*, 97.
49. Perry, *Apache Reservation*, 99.
50. Perry, *Apache Reservation*, 99.
51. Perry, *Apache Reservation*, 102.
52. Perry, *Apache Reservation*, 99.
53. Perry, *Apache Reservation*, 106.
54. Lacy Johnson, "At U.S. Capitol, Arizona Apache Protest Planned Copper Mine," Reuters New Service, July 21, 2015; Perry, *Apache Reservation*, 118, 129, 134.
55. Gale Courey Toensing, "Grijalva's Save Oak Flat Bill Boosted by Historic Preservation Listing," *Indian Country Today*, July, 20, 2015, http://indiancountrytodaymedianetwork.com/2015/07/20/grijalvas-save-oak-flat-bill-boosted-historic-preservation-listing-161136 (accessed April 14, 2016).
56. Perry, *Apache Reservation*, 134, 136, 147.
57. Perry, *Apache Reservation*, 191.
58. Perry, *Apache Reservation*, 155, 158.
59. Perry, *Apache Reservation*, 174, 176, 177.
60. Perry, *Apache Reservation*, 193, 194.
61. Christina Rose, "From Neil Young to a Flash Mob: Apache Stronghold Blazes through Country," *Indian Country Today*, July 22, 2015, http://indiancountrytodaymedianetwork.com/2015/07/22/neil-young-flash-mob-apache-stronghold-blazes-through-country-161156 (accessed April 14, 2016); Millet, "Selling Off Apache Holy Land"; Joseph Huff-Hannon, "Meet the Apache Activists Opening for Neil Young," *Rolling Stone*, July 21, 2015, www.rollingstone.com/politics/news/meet-the-apache-activists-opening-for-neil-young-20150721 (accessed April 14, 2016).

62. Huff-Hannon, "Meet the Apache Activists"; Millet, "Selling Off Apache Holy Land."
63. Gale Courey Toensing, "57 Affiliated Tribes of Northwest Indians Urge Senate to Nix Sacred Land Giveaway," *Indian Country Today*, December 12, 2014, http://indiancountrytodaymedianetwork.com/2015/07/20/grijalvas-save-oak-flat-bill-boosted-historic-preservation-listing-161136 (accessed April 14, 2016); Millet, "Selling Off Apache Holy Land"; Huff-Hoffman, "Meet the Apache Activists."
64. Lee Allen, "We Want to Talk: Resolution Copper Breaks Silence Over Land Swap," *Indian Country Today*, June 17, 2015, http://indiancountrytodaymedianetwork.com/2015/06/17/we-want-talk-resolution-copper-breaks-silence-over-land-swap-160750 (accessed April 14, 2016).
65. Huff-Hoffman, "Meet the Apache Activists"; PR Newswire, "Senators Bernie Sanders and Tammy Baldwin Introduce the Save Oak Flat Act in the Senate," PR Newswire, November 5, 2015, www.prnewswire.com/news-releases/senators-bernie-sanders-and-tammy-baldwin-introduce-the-save-oak-flat-act-in-the-senate-300173851.html (accessed December 17, 2015).
66. "National Register of Historic Places; Notification of Pending Nominations and Related Actions," 80 Fed. Reg. 110, 32945 (June 9, 2015); Gale Courey Toensing, "Yavapai-Apache Chairman: 'Oak Flat Holy Sites Are Central to Apache Spiritual Beliefs,'" *Indian Country Today*, February 4, 2015, http://indiancountrytodaymedianetwork.com/2015/02/04/yavapai-apache-chairman-oak-flat-holy-sites-are-central-apache-spiritual-beliefs-159016 (accessed July 8, 2016); Michael Bastach, "Lawmakers Accuse Feds of 'Stealth Land Grab' to Stop an Arizona Mining Project," *Daily Caller*, February 4, 2016, http://dailycaller.com/2016/02/04/lawmakers-accuse-feds-of-stealth-land-grab-to-stop-an-arizona-mining-project/ (accessed July 4, 2016); Jessica Swarner, "Did Obama Just Block the Sale of Sacred Apache Land to a Foreign Mining Company? Well . . ." *Indian Country Today*, March 17, 2016, http://indiancountrytodaymedianetwork.com/2016/03/17/oak-flat-historic-designation-win-mine-opponents-fight-may-continue-163775 (accessed July 8, 2016); United States Forest Service, *Apache Leap Special Management Area Environmental Assessment and Finding of No Significant Impact* (Washington, DC: U.S. Forest Service, 2017), 7–8.
67. Peter d'Errico, "Oak Flat Deal Violates Apache Rights, Mining Best Practices," *Indian Country Today*, March 3, 2016, http://indiancountrytodaymedianetwork.com/2016/03/30/oak-flat-deal-violates-apache-rights-mining-best-practices (accessed July 9, 2016).
68. Joseph M. Marshall III, *The Lakota Way* (New York: Penguin Compass, 2001), 207.
69. Marshall, *Lakota Way*, 207, 208; Joseph M. Marshall III, *The Journey of Crazy Horse: A Lakota History* (New York: Penguin, 2004), 19.
70. Marshall, *Lakota Way*, 211; Edward A. Milligan, *Dakota Twilight: The Standing Rock Sioux, 1874–1890* (Hicksville, NY: Exposition Press, 1976), 7, 18.
71. Marshall, *Crazy Horse*, 113, 114; Milligan, *Dakota Twilight*, 11. Marshall, *Lakota Way*, 209.
72. Marshall, *Crazy Horse*, 28, 31–35.

73. Marshall, *Crazy Horse*, 107, 109.
74. Marshall, *Crazy Horse*, 107, 109.
75. Milligan, *Dakota Twilight*, 8; Marshall, *Crazy Horse*, xv, xvi, xxi, 127.
76. Marshall, *Crazy Horse*, 126, 178, 186, 189; Edward Lazarus, *Black Hills: White Justice* (New York: HarperCollins, 1991), 38–39.
77. Lazarus, *Black Hills*, 48–51, 54–64.
78. Lazarus, *Black Hills*, 64–69.
79. Lazarus, *Black Hills*, 78–80; Marshall, *Crazy Horse*, 198, 201–3, 212.
80. Marshall, *Crazy Horse*, 271, 272, 273. Lazarus, *Black Hills*, 86–89.
81. Lazarus, *Black Hills*, 86–90.
82. Marshall, *Crazy Horse*, 175, 273, 276–77; Marshall, *Lakota Way*, 217; Milligan, *Dakota Twilight*, 76.
83. Milligan, *Dakota Twilight*, 20, 22, 30, 35, 48.
84. Milligan, *Dakota Twilight*, 92–96, 98, 104, 107.
85. Milligan, *Dakota Twilight*, 104; Marshall, *Lakota Way*, 220, 221.
86. Milligan, *Dakota Twilight*, 101, 103, 106, 110.
87. Milligan, *Dakota Twilight*, 119, 122.
88. Milligan, *Dakota Twilight*, 126–31, 133, 135; Lazarus, *Black Hills*, 115.
89. Lazarus, *Black Hills*, 125, 138–41, 161, 164.
90. Plaintiff Standing Rock Sioux Tribe's Memorandum in Support of Its Motion for Partial Summary Judgment, *Standing Rock Sioux Tribe v. U.S. Army Corps of Engineers*, Case No. 1:16-cv-1534-JEB, United States District Court for the District of Columbia, February 14, 2017, 4.
91. Lazarus, *Black Hills*, 183–86, 191–92.
92. Lazarus, *Black Hills*, 251–56.
93. Lazarus, *Black Hills*, 257–60.
94. Lazarus, *Black Hills*, 311, 325, 327.
95. Lazarus, *Black Hills*, 378–80, 400, 401.
96. Lazarus, *Black Hills*, 403–9, 412–13, 419, 420.
97. *Standing Rock Sioux Tribe v. U.S. Army Corps of Engineers*, 205 F. Supp. 3d 4 (United States District Court, D.C. 2016), 7; *Standing Rock Sioux Tribe v. U.S. Army Corps of Engineers*, 239 F. Supp. 3d 77 (United States District Court, D.C. 2017), 80.
98. Standing Rock Sioux Tribal Council, transcript of DAPL meeting, September 30, 2014.
99. *Standing Rock*, 239 F. Supp. 3d 81; Plaintiff Standing Rock Sioux Tribe's Memorandum in Support of Its Motion for Partial Summary Judgment, *Standing Rock Sioux Tribe v. U.S. Army Corps of Engineers*, Case No. 1:16-cv-1534-JEB, United States District Court for the District of Columbia, February 14, 2017, 8.
100. *Standing Rock*, 239 F. Supp. 3d 81.
101. Amnesty International "Police Must Protect the Right to Peacefully Protest Pipeline Construction in North Dakota," Amnesty International USA, August 23, 2016, www.amnestyusa.org/press-releases/police-must-protect-the-right-to-peacefully-protest-pipeline-construction-in-north-dakota (accessed February 5, 2018); Amnesty

International, "Amnesty International USA Calls on Authorities to Protect Peaceful Protest at Dakota Access Oil Pipeline Site," Amnesty International USA, August 30, 2016, www.amnestyusa.org/press-releases/amnesty-international-usa-calls-on-authorities-to-protect-peaceful-protest-at-dakota-access-oil-pipeline-site (accessed February 5, 2018); Tarah Demant, "'We have become a disposable people': Why Amnesty Went to Cannon Ball, North Dakota," Amnesty International USA, September 1, 2016, https://blog.amnestyusa.org/uncategorized/we-have-become-a-disposable-people-why-amnesty-went-to-cannon-ball-north-dakota (accessed February 5, 2018); Amnesty International, "Amnesty International USA to Monitor North Dakota Pipeline Protests," Amnesty International USA, October 28, 2016, www.amnestyusa.org/press-releases/amnesty-international-usa-to-monitor-to-north-dakota-pipeline-protests (accessed February 5, 2018); Josh Fox, "The Arrest of Journalists and Those Covering the Dakota Pipeline Is a Threat to Democracy—and the Planet," *The Nation*, October 14, 2016.
102. *Standing Rock*, 239 F. Supp. 3d 81–2.
103. *Standing Rock*, 239 F. Supp. 3d 82–3.
104. *Standing Rock*, 239 F. Supp. 3d 89–90.
105. S. Rep. No. 103-111 at 8–9 (1993) as quoted by 239 F. Supp. 3d 93; 239 F. Supp. 3d. 94.
106. *Memorandum Opinion* of June 14, 2017, *Standing Rock Sioux v. U.S. Army Corps of Engineers*, Case No. 16-cv-15344-JEB, United States District Court for the District of Columbia, 2017 WL 2573994, pp. 66–67 of the original publication by the court; *Memorandum Opinion* of December 4, 2017, *Standing Rock Sioux v. U.S. Army Corps of Engineers*, Case No. 16-cv-15344-JEB, United States District Court for the District of Columbia, 3, 8.
107. Native News Online Staff, "UN Special Rapporteur: Sacred Sites Not 'Dots on a Map' and Feds Failed Consultation Process Marred By 'Lack of Good Faith,'" *Native News Online*, March 4, 2017, http://nativenewsonline.net/currents/un-special-rapporteur-sacred-sites-not-dots-map-feds-failed-consultation-process-marred-lack-good-faith/ (accessed September 24, 2017).
108. Andrew Westney, "Dakota Access Saga Highlights Value of Tribal Consultation," *Law 360*, June 7, 2017.

CHAPTER 6

1. Joshua A. Edwards, "Yellow Snow on Sacred Sites: A Failed Application of the Religious Freedom Restoration Act," *American Indian Law Review*, Vol. 34, No. 1 (2009–10): 151, 168–69; Kristen A. Carpenter, "A Property Rights Approach to Sacred Sites Cases: Asserting a Place for Indians as Nonowners," *UCLA Law Review*, Vol. 32 (2004–5): 1061, 1063–64, 1094–99.
2. Justice Scalia commented on human sacrifice during oral arguments for *Employment Division v. Smith*, 494 U.S. 872 (1990), on November 6, 1989, 52:44; Mike Myers, "The Supreme Court's 'Just Cuz' Doctrine for Cheating Natives," *Indian Country Today*, January 18, 2016, http://indiancountrytodaymedianetwork.com/2016/01/18/supreme-courts-just-cuz-doctrine-cheating-natives (accessed April 14, 2016).

3. Louis Fisher, "Indian Religious Freedom: To Litigate or Legislate?" *American Indian Law Review,* Vol. 26, No. 1 (2001–2002):1, 39; Anne Minard, "San Francisco Peaks Settlement between Hopi and Flagstaff Comes Under Fire," *Indian Country Media Network,* March 10, 2016, https://indiancountrymedianetwork.com/news/environment/san-francisco-peaks-settlement-between-hopi-and-flagstaff-comes-under-fire/ (accessed February 23, 2017).
4. Alex Tallchief Skibine, "Towards a Balanced Approach for the Protection of Native American Sacred Sites," *Michigan Journal of Race and Law,* Vol. 17 (2011–2012): 269, 288, 291, 299–300.
5. David E. Wilkins and K. Tsianina Lomawaima, *Uneven Ground: American Indian Sovereignty and Federal Law* (Norman: University of Oklahoma Press, 2001), 108, 109, 112.
6. *Williams v. Lee,* 358 U.S. 217 (1959). Charles F. Wilkinson, *American Indians, Time, and the Law: Native Sovereignty in a Modern Constitutional Democracy* (New Haven, CT: Yale University Press, 1987), 7, 121.
7. Todd M. Johnson and James Hamilton, "Self-Government for Indian Tribes: From Paternalism to Empowerment," *Connecticut Law Review,* Vol. 27 (1994–95): 1251, 1278.
8. Wilkins and Lomawaima, *Uneven Ground,* 5, 9, 99, 107.
9. David E. Wilkins, *American Indian Sovereignty and the United States Supreme Court: The Masking of Justice* (Austin: University of Texas Press, 1997), 3–4, 99, 111, 256, 257, 297, 300–1, 309.
10. Thomas Biolsi, "Imagined Geographies: Sovereignty, Indigenous Space, and American Indian Struggle," *American Ethnologist,* Vol. 32, No. 2 (May 2005): 239, 248, 250, 255.
11. Frank Pommersheim, *Broken Landscapes: Indians, Indian Tribes, and the Constitution* (New York: Oxford University Press, 2009), 5, 256.
12. Pommersheim, *Broken Landscapes,* 256, 274, 277, 284, 297.
13. Pommersheim, *Broken Landscapes,* 285, 288, 290, 293.
14. Raymond Cross, "Reconsidering the Original Founding of Indian and Non-Indian America: Why a Second American Founding Based on Principles of Deep Diversity Is Needed," *Public Land and Resource Law Review,* Vol. 25 (2004): 61, 63–64.
15. Cross, "Reconsidering," 69, 75, 80, 81–83.
16. Cross, "Reconsidering," 81–83.
17. Cross, "Reconsidering," 65, 84, referring to Amartya Sen, *Development as Freedom* (New York: Alfred A. Knopf, 1999), 3, 14, 53, 298.
18. Cross, "Reconsidering," 86–88, 91, 92.
19. James Huffman and Robert Miller, "Indian Property Rights and American Federalism," In *Self-Determination: The Other Path for Native Americans,* ed. Terry L. Anderson, Bruce L. Benson, and Thomas E. Flanagan (Stanford, CA: Stanford University Press, 2006), 293; Manley A. Begay Jr., Stephen Cornell, Miriam Jorgenson, and Joseph P. Kalt, "Development, Governance, Culture: What Are They and What Do They Have to Do with Rebuilding Native Nations?" In *Rebuilding Native Nations: Strategies for Governance and Development,* ed. Miriam Jorgensen (Tucson: University of Arizona Press, 2007), 22.

20. Begay et al., "Development, Governance, Culture," 48, 52.
21. Christine K. Gray, *The Tribal Moment in American Politics: The Struggle for Native American Sovereignty* (New York: Roman & Littlefield, 2013), 24, 198.
22. Pommersheim, *Broken Landscapes*, 302.
23. Michael Eitner, "Meaningful Consultation with Tribal Governments: A Uniform Standard to Guarantee that Federal Agencies Properly Consider Their Concerns," *University of Colorado Law Review*, Vol. 86 (2014): 867, 896, 897.
24. Martin Nie, "The Use of Co-Management and Protected Land-Use Designations to Protect Cultural Resources and Reserved Treaty Rights on Federal Lands," *Natural Resources Journal*, Vol. 48 (2008): 585, 595, 603, 606, 609.
25. Pommersheim, *Broken Landscapes*, 300.
26. Pommersheim, *Broken Landscapes*, 300.
27. Pommersheim, *Broken Landscapes*, 300.
28. Pommersheim, *Broken Landscapes*, 300, 301; *Duro v. Reina*, 495 U.S. 676 (1991); *United States v. Lara*, 541 U.S. 193 (2004).
29. Pommersheim, *Broken Landscapes*, 304–5.
30. Pommersheim, *Broken Landscapes*, 305.
31. Pommersheim, *Broken Landscapes*, 305, 306.
32. Pommersheim, *Broken Landscapes*, 307.
33. H. D. Rosenthal, *Their Day in Court: A History of the Indian Claims Commission* (New York: Garland Publishing, 1990), 253–54.
34. Nie, "Co-Management and Protected Land-Use Designations," 603, 606.
35. The Bears Ears Inter-Tribal Coalition, *Proposal to President Barack Obama for the Creation of Bears Ears National Monument* (Utah: Bears Ears Inter-Tribal Coalition, October 15, 2015), 4–6, 8–9.
36. Bears Ears Coalition, *Proposal*, 15.
37. Bears Ears Coalition, *Proposal*, 15, 16; Bears Ears Inter-Tribal Coalition, *Exhibit One, a Timeline: The Relationship of the Public Lands Initiative with the Tribes and Their Members* (Utah: Bears Ears Inter-Tribal Coalition, October 15, 2015).
38. Bears Ears Coalition, *Proposal*, 18, 19.
39. Bruce Babbitt, "It's Time for Obama to Make Bear Ears in Utah a National Monument," *Los Angeles Times*, January 21, 2016; Anne Minard, "Bears Ears Coalition Splits from 'Disrespectful' Congressional Reps," *Indian Country Today*, January 22, 2016, http://indiancountrytodaymedianetwork.com/2016/01/22/bears-ears-coalition-splits-disrespectful-congressional-reps-163127 (accessed April 14, 2016).
40. Bears Ears Coalition, *Proposal*, 20–2, 29, 31.
41. Hiring preferences for Indians is not racial discrimination but a political preference akin to preferring city residents for city jobs, according to the United States Supreme Court; *Morton v. Mancari*, 417 U.S. 535 (1974); Bears Ears Coalition, *Proposal*, 29, 31, 35–37; Ryan Benally, "Rescind Bears Ears National Monument Designation," *Indian Country Media Network*, May 16, 2017, https://indiancountrymedianetwork.com/news/opinions/rescind-bears-ears-national-monument-designation/ (accessed October 1, 2017); Rob Capriccioso, "Zinke Says Tribes Are 'Happy' to Have Bears Ears

Modifications; Tribes Disagree," *Indian Country Media Network*, June 13, 2017, https://indiancountrymedianetwork.com/news/native-news/zinke-says-tribes-happy-bears-ears-modifications-tribes-disagree (accessed October 1, 2017); Juliet Eilperin and Daryl Fears, "Interior Secretary Recommends Trump Alter at Least Three National Monuments, Including Bears Ears," *Washington Post*, August 24, 2017; Kim Baca, "Battle Lines Form as Trump Sets Sights on Bears Ears," *Indian Country Media Network*, January 30, 2017, https://indiancountrymedianetwork.com/news/native-news/bears-ears-battle-trump-sets-sights (accessed February 23, 2017).

42. Aubry Weiber, "Tribes Fight to Keep Bears Ears Lawsuit in D.C." *Salt Lake Tribune*, February 2, 2018; Carleton Bowekaty and Shaun Chapoose, "Utah Bill Tramples on Tribal Sovereignty at Bears Ears," *The Hill*, January 3, 2018.

43. *Utah Association of Counties v. Bush*, 316 F. Supp. 2d 1172 (2004), *appeal dismissed*, 455 F.3d 1094 (10th Cir. 2006); *Tulare County v. Bush*, 306 F.3d 1138 (D.C. Cir. 2002), 1142, *cert. denied*, 540 U.S. 813; Bears Ears Coalition, *Proposal*, 23, 33.

44. Dwanna L. Robertson, "Invisibility in the Color-Blind Era, Examining Legitimized Racism against Indigenous Peoples," *American Indian Quarterly*, Vol. 39, No. 2 (Spring 2015): 30, 113, 114, 120, 131, 132, 140–43; Raymond Cross, "American Indian Education: The Terror of History and the Nation's Debt to the Indian Peoples," *UALR Law Review*, Vol. 21 (1999): 941.

45. Zoltan Grossman, "Treaty Rights and Responding to Anti-Indian Activity," in *Sovereignty, Colonialism and the Indigenous Nations: A Reader*, ed. Robert Odawi Porter (Durham, NC: Carolina Academic Press, 2005), 304, 307, 320.

46. Lloyd Burton and David Ruppert, "Bear's Lodge or Devil's Tower: Intercultural Relations, Legal Pluralism, and the Management of Sacred Sites on Public Lands," *Cornell Journal of Law and Public Policy*, Vol. 8, No. 2 (Winter 1999): 201–47.

47. Paul Chaat Smith, *Everything You Know about Indians Is Wrong* (Minneapolis: University of Minnesota Press, 2009), 71.

48. Justice Stephen Breyer, *Dollar General v. Mississippi Band of Choctaw Indians*, United States Supreme Court Case No. 13-1496, *Transcript of Oral Arguments*, December 7, 2015, 40.

49. Vincent Schilling, "History Professor Denies Native Genocide: Native Student Disagreed, Then Says Professor Expelled Her from Course," *Indian Country Today*, September 6, 2015, http://indiancountrytodaymedianetwork.com/2015/09/06/history-professor-denies-native-genocide-native-student-disagrees-gets-expelled-course (accessed April 14, 2016); Vincent Schilling, "Native Genocide Issue at Sac State, 'No University Policies Violated,' Says President," *Indian Country Today*, October 13, 2015, http://indiancountrytodaymedianetwork.com/2015/10/13/native-genocide-issue-sac-state-no-university-policies-violated-says-president-162070 (accessed April 14, 2016).

CONCLUSIONS

1. Marcia Yablon, "Property Rights and Sacred Sites: Federal Regulatory Responses to American Indian Religious Claims on Public Land," *Yale Law Journal*, Vol. 113, No. 7 (May 2004): 1658–59; Robert A. Williams Jr., *Like a Loaded Weapon: The Rehnquist*

Court, Indian Rights, and the Legal History of Racism in America (Minneapolis: University of Minnesota Press, 2005).

2. United States Department of Agriculture, Office of Tribal Relations, and United States Forest Service, *Report to the Secretary of Agriculture: USDA Policy and Procedures Review and Recommendations: Indian Sacred Sites* (Washington, DC: USDA, 2012).

3. USDA, *Report*, 15, 18, 19, 21, 22, 27, 30.

4. USDA, *Report*, 19, 20, 23.

5. USDA, *Report*, 16, 20, 24.

6. USDA, *Report*, 28, 30.

7. James W. Loewen, *Lies My Teacher Told Me: Everything Your American History Textbook Got Wrong* (New York: New Press, 1995), 55; Robert W. Venables, *American Indian History: Five Centuries of Conflict and Coexistence*, Vol. 2 (Santa Fe, NM: Clear Light Publishers, 2004), 200; Richard J. Perry, *Apache Reservation, Indigenous Peoples and the American State* (Austin: University of Texas Press, 1993), 102.

8. United Nations General Assembly, Convention on the Prevention and Prohibition of the Crime of Genocide, December 9, 1948.

9. Stanley Nelson, dir., *We Shall Remain*, episode 5, "Wounded Knee" (Brighton, MA: PBS Distribution, 2009).

10. *Johnson v. McIntosh*, 21 U.S. 543 (1823); *Cherokee Nation v. Georgia*, 30 U.S. 1 (1831); *Worcester v. Georgia*, 31 U.S. 515 (1832).

11. *U.S. v. Gettysburg Electric Rail Co.*, 160 U.S. 668 (1896).

AFTERWORD

1. *Dobbs v. Jackson Women's Health Organization*, 597 U.S. 215 (2022).

2. 140 S. Ct. 2452, 207 L. Ed. 2d 985 (2020).

3. *Oklahoma v. Castro-Huerta*, 597 U.S. ___ , 2022 WL 2334307, first paragraph of section II.A. of Justice Gorsuch's dissent.

4. *Standing Rock Sioux Tribe v. U.S. Army Corps of Engineers*, 440 F. Supp. 3d 1, 11 (D.D.C. 2020).

5. *Standing Rock Sioux Tribe v. U.S. Army Corps of Engineers*, 471 F. Supp. 3d 71, 87 (D.D.C. 2020).

6. *Standing Rock Sioux Tribe v. U.S. Army Corps of Engineers*, 985 F.3d 1032, 1054 (D.C.C. 2021).

7. *Haaland v. Brackeen*, Docket No. 21-376, June 15, 2023.

BIBLIOGRAPHY

PRIMARY SOURCES

Cases and Statutes

Access Fund v. USDA, 499 F.3d 1036 (9th Cir. 2007).
Anderson v. Evans, 314 F.3d 1006 (9th Cir. 2002).
Badoni v. Higgins, 638 F.2d 172 (10th Cir. 1980).
Bear Lodge Multiple Use v. Babbitt, 175 F.3d 814 (10th Cir. 1999).
Bear Lodge Multiple Use v. Babbitt, 2 F. Supp. 2d 1448 (Dist. Ct. D. Wyoming 1998).
Cherokee Nation v. Georgia, 30 U.S. 1 (1831).
Dollar General v. Mississippi Band of Choctaw Indians, United States Supreme Court Case No. 13-1\496, *Transcript of Oral Arguments*, December 7, 2015.
Duro v. Reina, 495 U.S. 676 (1991).
Employment Division v. Smith, 494 U.S. 872 (1990).
Fortune v. Thomson, 2011 U.S. Dist. LEXIS 5343.
Gonzales v. O Centro Espirita Beneficente Uniao do Vegetal, 546 U.S. 418 (2006).
Glamis Gold v. United States of America, 48 ILM 1038 (2009).
Johnson v. McIntosh, 21 U.S. 543 (1823).
Lyng v. Northwest Indian Cemetery Protective Association, 485 U.S. 439 (1989).
Morton v. Mancari, 417 U.S. 535 (1974).
Natural Arch & Bridge Society v. Alston, 209 F. Supp. 2d 1207 (Federal District Court of Utah, Central Division, 2002).
Natural Arch & Bridge Society v. Alston, 98 Fed. Appx. 711 (9th Cir. 2004).

Navajo Nation v. Forest Service, Case Nos. CV 05-1824-PCT-PGR, CV 05-1914-PCT-EHC, CV 05-1949-PCT-NVW, CV 05-1966-PCT, United States District Court for the District of Arizona.

Navajo Nation v. Forest Service, 479 F.3d 1024 (9th Cir. 2007).

Navajo Nation v. Forest Service, 535 F.3d 1058 (9th Cir. 2008).

Navajo Nation v. Forest Service, 129 S. Ct. 2763, 174 L. Ed. 2D 270, 2009 U.S. LEXIS 4206.

Quechan Indian Tribe v. United States Department of the Interior, 755 F. Supp. 2d 1104 (S.D. Cal. 2010).

Religious Freedom Restoration Act, 42 U.S.C. § 2000bb (1993).

Sherbert v. Verner, 374 U.S. 398 (1963).

Solenex v. Jewell, Case No. 13-993-RJL, United States District Court for the District of Columbia, July, 27, 2015.

Solenex, LLC, v. Sally Jewell, Secretary of Interior, Case No. 13-993-RJL, U.S. District Court for the District of Columbia, *Memorandum of Points and Authorities in Support of Motion to Intervene as Defendants*. September 26, 2013.

Standing Rock Sioux Tribe v. U.S. Army Corps of Engineers, Case No. 1:16-cv-1534-JEB, United States District Court for the District of Columbia, *Plaintiff Standing Rock Sioux Tribe's Memorandum in Support of Its Motion for Partial Summary Judgment*, February 14, 2017.

Standing Rock Sioux Tribe v. U.S. Army Corps of Engineers, 205 F. Supp. 3d 4 (United States District Court, D.C. 2016).

Standing Rock Sioux Tribe v. U.S. Army Corps of Engineers, 239 F. Supp. 3d 77 (United States District Court, D.C. 2017).

Standing Rock Sioux v. U.S. Army Corps of Engineers, Case No. 16-cv-15344-JEB, United States District Court for the District of Columbia, 2017 WL 2573994, June 14, 2017.

Tulware Country v. Bush, 308 F.3d 1138 (D.C. Cir. 2002).

United States v. Gettysburg Electric Rail Co., 160 U.S. 668 (1896).

United States v. Lara, 541 U.S. 193 (2004).

Utah Association of Counties v. Bush, 455 F.3d 1094 (10th Cir. 2006).

Van Orden v. Perry, 545 U.S. 677 (2005).

Wilson v. Block, 708 F.2d 735 (D.C. 1983).

Worcester v. Georgia, 31 U.S. 515 (1832).

Other Primary Sources

Allen, Lee. "We Want to Talk: Resolution Copper Breaks Silence Over Land Swap." *Indian Country Today,* June 17, 2015. http://indiancountrytodaymedianetwork.com/2015/06/17/we-want-talk-resolution-copper-breaks-silence-over-land-swap-160750 (accessed April 14, 2016).

Amnesty International USA. "Amnesty International USA Calls on Authorities to Protect Peaceful Protest at Dakota Access Oil Pipeline Site," August 30, 2016. www.amnestyusa.org/press-releases/amnesty-international-usa-calls-on-authorities-to-protect-peaceful-protest-at-dakota-access-oil-pipeline-site (accessed February 5, 2018).

———. "Amnesty International USA to Monitor North Dakota Pipeline Protests," October 28, 2016. www.amnestyusa.org/press-releases/amnesty-international-usa-to-monitor-to-north-dakota-pipeline-protests (accessed February 5, 2018).
Appeal Reviewing Officer's Review and Recommendation—Badger-Two Medicine Travel Management ROD—Lewis & Clark NF—Appeal Nos. 09-01-00-0022, 0023, 0025, 0027, 0029, 0030, 0031, 0033, 0036, 0037, 0039, 0040, 0041, 0042, and 0043, June 13, 2009.
Application for Leave to File a Non-Party Submission of the Quechan Indian Nation, *Glamis Gold v. United States of America*, International Center for Settlement of Investment Disputes, North American Free Trade Agreement Arbitral Tribunal, August 19, 2005.
Armitage, Lynn. "The Washoe: The First People of Lake Tahoe." *Indian Country Today*, August 5, 2012. http://indiancountrytodaymedianetwork.com/2012/08/05/washoe-first-people-lake-tahoe-125703 (accessed September 27, 2015).
Baca, Kim. "Battle Lines Form as Trump Sets Sights on Bears Ears," *Indian Country Media Network*, January 30, 2017. https://indiancountrymedianetwork.com/news/native-news/bears-ears-battle-trump-sets-sights (accessed February 23, 2017).
Bears Ears Inter-Tribal Coalition. *Exhibit One, A Timeline: The Relationship of the Public Lands Initiative with the Tribes and Their Members*. Utah: Bears Ears Inter-Tribal Coalition, October 15, 2015.
———. Bears Ears Inter-Tribal Coalition. *Proposal to President Barack Obama for the Creation of Bears Ears National Monument*. Utah: Bears Ears Inter-Tribal Coalition, October 15, 2015.
Capriccioso, Rob. "Zinke Says Tribes Are 'Happy' to Have Bears Ears Modifications; Tribes Disagree." *Indian Country Media Network*, June 13, 2017. https://indiancountrymedianetwork.com/news/native-news/zinke-says-tribes-happy-bears-ears-modifications-tribes-disagree/ (accessed October 1, 2017).
Cottrell, Jane L. *Final Administrative Determination, Department of Agriculture, Appeal* Nos. 09-01-00-0022, 0023, 0025, 0027, 0029, 0030, 0031, 0033, 0036, 0037, 0039, 0040, 0041, 0042, and 0043, June 18, 2009.
Demant, Tarah. "'We have become a disposable people': Why Amnesty Went to Cannon Ball, North Dakota." Amnesty International USA, September 1, 2016. https://blog.amnestyusa.org/uncategorized/we-have-become-a-disposable-people-why-amnesty-went-to-cannon-ball-north-dakota (accessed February 5, 2018).
Fox, Josh. "The Arrest of Journalists and Those Covering the Dakota Pipeline Is a Threat to Democracy—and the Planet." *The Nation*, October 14, 2016.
Hansen, Terri. "Sacred Blackfoot Land Saved! BLM Cancels Oil and Gas Lease in Badger-Two Medicine Region." *Indian Country Today*, March 18, 2016. http://indiancountrytodaymedianetwork.com/2016/03/18/sacred-blackfoot-land-saved-blm-cancels-oil-and-gas-lease-badger-two-medicine-region (accessed April 14, 2016).
Hopper, Frank. "Whale Wars Groups vs. Makah: Who Decides if Traditions Are Authentic?" *Indian Country Today*, June 23, 2015. http://indiancountrytodaymedianetwork.com/2015/06/23/whale-wars-group-vs-makah-who-decides-if-traditions-are-authentic-160741 (accessed December 12, 2015).

Huff-Hannon, Joseph. "Meet the Apache Activists Opening for Neil Young." *Rolling Stone*, July 21, 2015. www.rollingstone.com/politics/news/meet-the-apache-activists-opening-for-neil-young-20150721 (accessed April 14, 2016).

Indian Law Resource Center. "NAFTA Tribunal Recognizes Sacred Place of Quechan Tribe—Denies Glamis Gold's Claim in Full." Indian Law Resource Center, June 9, 2009. http://indianlaw.org/Quechan_Glamis_NAFTA_Tribunal (accessed April 14, 2016).

Minard, Anne. "Bears Ears Coalition Splits from 'Disrespectful' Congressional Reps." *Indian Country Today*, January 22, 1016. http://indiancountrytodaymedianetwork.com/2016/01/22/bears-ears-coalition-splits-disrespectful-congressional-reps-163127 (accessed April 14, 2016).

———. "San Francisco Peaks Settlement between Hopi and Flagstaff Comes Under Fire." *Indian Country Media Network*, March 10, 2016. https://indiancountrymedianetwork.com/news/environment/san-francisco-peaks-settlement-between-hopi-and-flagstaff-comes-under-fire (accessed February 23, 2017).

Native News Online Staff. "UN Special Rapporteur: Sacred Sites Not 'Dots on a Map' and Feds Failed Consultation Process Marred by 'Lack of Good Faith.'" *Native News Online*, March 4, 2017. http://nativenewsonline.net/currents/un-special-rapporteur-sacred-sites-not-dots-map-feds-failed-consultation-process-marred-lack-good-faith (accessed September 24, 2017).

Ninth Circuit Court of Appeals, Order of the Court, *Fortune v. Thompson,* Case No. 11-35242, October 28, 2011.

Newcomb, Steven. "A Conversation with a Justice of the U.S. Supreme Court." *Indian Country Today*, June 24, 2011. https://indiancountrymedianetwork.com/news/opinions/a-conversation-with-a-justice-of-the-us-supreme-court (accessed December 22, 2016).

———. "What Justice Scalia Said He Did Not Know about U.S. Indian Law." *Indian Country Today*, February 26, 2016. https://indiancountrymedianetwork.com/news/opinions/what-justice-scalia-said-he-didnt-know-about-us-indian-law/ (accessed December 22, 2016).

Parker, Trey, dir. *South Park*. Season 13, episode 11, "Whale Whores." Aired October 28, 2009, on Comedy Central.

Preso, Timothy J. Letter to Sally Jewell, secretary of the U.S. Department of the Interior, and Tom Vilsack, secretary of the U.S. Department of Agriculture. Earth Justice, October 28, 2014. http://earthjustice.org/sites/default/files/files/B2M%20lease%20cancellation%20letter%20—%20final.pdf (accessed December 17, 2015).

PR Newswire. "Senators Bernie Sanders and Tammy Baldwin Introduce the Save Oak Flat Act in the Senate." PR Newswire, November 5, 2015. www.prnewswire.com/news-releases/senators-bernie-sanders-and-tammy-baldwin-introduce-the-save-oak-flat-act-in-the-senate-300173851.html (accessed December 17, 2015).

Quechan Indian Nation. Non-Party Initial Submission, *Glamis Gold v. United States of America*, International Center for Settlement of Investment Disputes, North American Free Trade Agreement Arbitral Tribunal, August 19, 2005.

———. Non-Party Supplemental Submission, *Glamis Gold v. United States of America*, International Center for Settlement of Investment Disputes, North American Free Trade Agreement Arbitral Tribunal, October, 16, 2006.

Rose, Christina. "From Neil Young to a Flash Mob: Apache Stronghold Blazes through Country." *Indian Country Today*, July 22, 2015. http://indiancountrytodaymedianetwork.com/2015/07/22/neil-young-flash-mob-apache-stronghold-blazes-through-country-161156 (accessed April 14, 2016).

Save the Peaks Coalition. "New Lawsuit Filed against Forest Service." Save the Peaks Coalition, September 21, 2009. www.indigenousaction.org/save-the-peaks-new-lawsuit-filed-against-forest-service (accessed July 1, 2010).

Schilling, Vincent. "History Professor Denies Native Genocide: Native Student Disagreed, Then Says Professor Expelled Her from Course." *Indian Country Today*, September 6, 2015. http://indiancountrytodaymedianetwork.com/2015/09/06/history-professor-denies-native-genocide-native-student-disagrees-gets-expelled-course (accessed April 14, 2016).

———. "Native Genocide Issue at Sac State, 'No University Policies Violated,' Says President." *Indian Country Today*, October 13, 2015. http://indiancountrytodaymedianetwork.com/2015/10/13/native-genocide-issue-sac-state-no-university-policies-violated-says-president-162070 (accessed April 14, 2016).

Standing Rock Sioux Tribal Council. Transcript of DAPL meeting, September 30, 2014.

Toensing, Gale Courey. "57 Affiliated Tribes of Northwest Indians Urge Senate to Nix Sacred Land Giveaway." *Indian Country Today*, December 12, 2014. http://indiancountrytodaymedianetwork.com/2014/12/12/57-affiliated-tribes-northwest-indians-urge-senate-nix-sacred-land-giveaway-158266 (accessed April 14, 2016).

———. "Grijalva's Save Oak Flat Bill Boosted by Historic Preservation Listing." *Indian Country Today*, July, 20, 2015. http://indiancountrytodaymedianetwork.com/2015/07/20/grijalvas-save-oak-flat-bill-boosted-historic-preservation-listing-161136 (accessed April 14, 2016).

United Nations General Assembly. Convention on the Prevention and Prohibition of the Crime of Genocide, December 9, 1948.

United States Bureau of Land Management. *Environmental Assessment, CA-760-EA2000-34, For the Indian Pass Withdrawal, CACA-39853*. Washington, DC: U.S. Bureau of Land Management, 2000.

United States Department of Agriculture, Office of Tribal Relations, and United States Forest Service. *Report to the Secretary of Agriculture: USDA Policy and Procedures Review and Recommendations: Indian Sacred Sites*. Washington, DC: U.S. Department of Agriculture, 2012.

United States Department of Commerce, National Oceanic and Atmospheric Administration, National Marine Fisheries Service, West Coast Region. *Draft Environmental Impact Statement on the Makah Tribe Request to Hunt Gray Whales*. Washington, DC: U.S. Department of Commerce, 2015.

United States Forest Service. *Apache Leap Special Management Area Environmental Assessment and Finding of No Significant Impact*. Washington, DC: U.S. Forest Service, 2017.

———. *Arizona Snowbowl Facilities Improvements Final Environmental Impact Statement Record of Decision and Forest Plan Amendment 21*. Washington, DC: U.S. Forest Service, 2005.

———. *Cave Rock Management Direction Final Environmental Impact Statement*. Washington, DC: U.S. Forest Service, 2002.

———. *Final Environmental Impact Statement Rocky Mountain Ranger District Travel Management Plan*. Washington, DC: U.S. Forest Service, 2007.

———. *Rocky Mountain Ranger District Travel Management Plan Record of Decision for Badger-Two Medicine*. Washington, DC: U.S. Forest Service, 2009.

Watson, Paul. "Makah Whaling—Whales Must Be Protected in U.S. Waters." Sea Shepherd Conservation Society, March 11, 2015. www.seashepherd.org/commentary-and-editorials/2015/03/11/makah-whaling-whales-must-be-protected-in-us-waters-692 (accessed April 14, 2016).

SECONDARY SOURCES

Banks, Kimball M. "Indians, Reclamation, and Historic Preservation." *Plains Anthropologist*, Vol. 44, No. 170 (1999): 5–12.

Banner, Stuart. *How the Indians Lost Their Land: Law and Power on the Frontier*. Cambridge, MA: Belknap Press of Harvard University, 2005.

Baton, Marietta W. "Consultation on Grand Staircase–Escalante National Monument from Planning to Implementation." *American Indian Quarterly*, Vol. 25 No. 1 (Winter 2001): 28–34.

Bee, Robert L. *Crosscurrents along the Colorado: The Impact of Government Policy on the Quechan Indians*. Tucson: University of Arizona Press, 1981.

Benally, Klee, dir. *The Snowbowl Effect*. DVD. Flagstaff: Indigenous Action Media, 2005.

Benally, Ryan. "Rescind Bears Ears National Monument Designation." *Indian Country Media Network*, May 16, 2017. https://indiancountrymedianetwork.com/news/opinions/rescind-bears-ears-national-monument-designation (accessed October 1, 2017).

Biolsi, Thomas. "Imagined Geographies: Sovereignty, Indigenous Space, and American Indian Struggle." *American Ethnologist*, Vol. 32, No. 2 (May 2005): 239–59.

Brady, Joel. "'Land Is Itself a Sacred Being': Native American Sacred Site Protection on Federal Public Lands Amidst the Shadows of *Bear Lodge*." *American Indian Law Review*, Vol. 24, No. 1 (1999–2000): 153–68.

Brooks, James F. *Mesa of Sorrows: A History of the Awat'ovi Massacre*. New York: W. W. Norton, 2016.

Brown, Brian Edward. *Religion, Law, and the Land: Native Americans and the Judicial Interpretations of Sacred Lands*. Westport, CT: Greenwood Press, 1999.

Burton, Lloyd. *Worship and Wilderness: Culture, Religion, and Law in the Management of Public Lands and Resources*. Madison: University of Wisconsin Press, 2002.

Burton, Lloyd, and David Ruppert. "Bear's Lodge or Devil's Tower: Intercultural Relations, Legal Pluralism, and the Management of Sacred Sites on Public Lands." *Cornell Journal of Law and Public Policy*, Vol. 8, No. 2 (Winter 1999): 201–47.

Campbell, Gregory R., and Thomas A. Foor. "Entering Sacred Landscapes: Cultural Expectations versus Legal Realities in the Northwestern Plains." *Great Plains Quarterly*, Vol. 24, No. 3 (June 2004): 163–83.

Carpenter, Kristen A. "A Property Rights Approach to Sacred Sites Cases: Asserting a Place for Indians as Nonowners." *UCLA Law Review*, Vol. 32 (2004–2005): 1061.

Carroll, Mark M. *Homesteads Ungovernable: Families, Sex, Race, and the Law in Frontier Texas, 1823–1860*. Austin: University of Texas Press, 2001.

Charles, James N. "Involvement of Native Americans in Cultural Resources Programs." *Plains Anthropologist*, Vol. 44, No. 170 (1999): 25–34.

Clemmer, Richard O. "The Hopi Traditionalist Movement." *American Indian Culture and Research Journal*, Vol. 18, No. 3 (1994): 125–66.

———. *Roads in the Sky: The Hopi Indians in a Century of Change*. Boulder, CO: Westview Press, 1995.

———. "'Then Will You Strike My Head from My Neck': Hopi Prophecy and the Discourse of Empowerment." *American Indian Quarterly*, Vol. 19, No. 1 (1995): 31–73.

Cousineau, Phil, ed. *A Seat at the Table: Huston Smith in Conversation with Native Americans on Religious Freedom*. Berkeley: University of California Press, 2006.

Cross, Raymond. "American Indian Education: The Terror of History and the Nation's Debt to the Indian Peoples." *UALR Law Review*, Vol. 21 (1999): 941–77.

———. "Reconsidering the Original Founding of Indian and Non-Indian America: Why a Second American Founding Based on Principles of Deep Diversity Is Needed." *Public Land and Resource Law Review*, Vol. 25 (2004): 61.

Cross, Raymond, and Elizabeth Brenneman. "Devils Tower at the Crossroads: The National Park Service and the Preservation of Native American Cultural Resources in the 21st Century." *Public Land and Resource Law Review*, Vol. 18 (1997): 5–45.

David, Ethan. "An Administrative Trail of Tears," *American Journal of Legal History*, Vol. 50, No. 1 (2008): 49–100.

Deloria, Philip. "Historiography." In *A Companion to American Indian History*, edited by Philip J. Deloria and Neal Salisbury, pp. 6–24. Malden, MA: Blackwell, 2004.

Deloria Jr., Vine. *For This Land: Writings on Religion in America*. New York: Routledge, 1999.

Deloria Jr., Vine, and Clifford M. Lytle. *American Indians, American Justice*. Austin: University of Texas Press, 1983.

Dockstader, Frederick. *The Kachina and the White Man: Influences of White Culture on the Hopi Kachina Cult*. Albuquerque: University of New Mexico Press, 1985.

Downs, James F. *The Two Worlds of the Washo: An Indian Tribe of California and Nevada*. New York: Holt, Rinehart and Winston, 1966.

———. "Washo Religion." *Anthropological Records*, Vol. 16, No. 9 (1961): 365–85.

Dreveskracht, Ryan D. "Alternative Energy in American Indian Country: Catering to Both Sides of the Coin." *Energy Law Journal*, Vol. 33, No. 2 (2012): 431–48.

Dussias, Allison M. "Friend, Foe, Frenemy: The United States and American Indian Religious Freedom." *Denver University Law Review*, Vol. 90 (2012): 347–432.

———. "Ghost Dance and Holy Ghost: The Echoes of Nineteenth-Century Christianization Policy in Twentieth-Century Native American Free Exercise Cases." *Stanford Law Review*, Vol. 49, No. 4 (April 1997): 773–852.

Edwards, Joshua A. "Yellow Snow on Sacred Sites: A Failed Application of the Religious Freedom Restoration Act." *American Indian Law Review*, Vol. 34, No. 1 (2009–2010): 151–70.

Eitner, Michael. "Meaningful Consultation with Tribal Governments: A Uniform Standard to Guarantee That Federal Agencies Properly Consider Their Concerns." *University of Colorado Law Review*, Vol. 86 (2014): 867–900.

Epps, Garrett. *Peyote v. the State: Religious Freedom on Trial*. Norman: University of Oklahoma Press, 2009.

———. *To an Unknown God: Religious Freedom on Trial*. New York: St. Martin's Press, 2001.

Fisher, Louis. "Indian Religious Freedom: To Litigate or Legislate?" *American Indian Law Review*, Vol. 26, No. 1 (2001–2002): 1–39.

Fixico, Donald. "Federal and State Policies and American Indians." In *A Companion to American Indian History*, edited by Philip J. Deloria and Neal Salisbury, pp. 379–96. Malden, MA: Blackwell, 2004.

Forbes, Jack D. *Warriors of the Colorado: The Yumas of the Quechan Nation and Their Neighbors*. Norman: University of Oklahoma Press, 1965.

Forbes-Boyte, Kari. "*Fools Crow versus Gullett*: A Critical Analysis of the American Indian Religious Freedom Act." *Antipode*, Vol. 31, No. 3 (July 1999): 304–23.

Freedman, Eric. "Protecting Sacred Sites on Public Land: Religion and Alliances in the Mato Tipila-Devils Tower Litigation." *American Indian Quarterly*, Vol. 31, No. 1 (Winter 2007): 1–22.

Fromm, Erich. *Marx's Concept of Man*. New York: Continuum, 2000.

Garrison, Tim Alan. "Beyond *Worcester*: The Alabama Supreme Court and the Sovereignty of the Creek Nation." *Journal of the Early Republic*, Vol. 19, No. 3 (Autumn 1999): 423–50.

Geertz, Armin W. "Contemporary Problems in the Study of Native North American Religions with Special Reference to the Hopis." *American Indian Quarterly*, Vol. 20, No 3 (1996): 393–414.

———. *The Invention of Prophecy: Continuity and Meaning in Hopi Indian Religion*. Berkeley: University of California Press, 1994.

Ginkel, Rob van. "The Makah Whale Hunt and Leviathan's Death: Reinventing Tradition and Disputing Authenticity in the Age of Modernity." *Etnofoor*, Vol. 17, No. 1/2 (2004): 58–89.

Glowacka, Maria, Dorothy Washburn, and Justin Richland. "*Nuvatukya'ovi*, San Francisco Peaks: Balancing Western Economies with Native American Spiritualities." *Current Anthropology*, Vol. 50, No. 4 (August 2009): 547–62.

Gray, Christine K. *The Tribal Moment in American Politics: The Struggle for Native American Sovereignty*. New York: Roman & Littlefield, 2013.

Grossman, George S. "Indians and the Law." In *New Directions in American Indian History*, edited by Colin G. Calloway, pp. 97–126. Norman: University of Oklahoma Press, 1988.

Grossman, Zoltan. "Treaty Rights and Responding to Anti-Indian Activity." In *Sovereignty, Colonialism and the Future of Indigenous Nations, a Reader*, edited by Robert Odawi Porter, pp. 304–20. Durham, NC: Carolina Academic Press, 2005.

Haas, Johnathan. "Power, Objects, and a Voice for Anthropology." *Current Anthropology*, Vol. 37, supplement (February 1996): S1–22.
Haes, Brenda L. "Devils Tower, Wyoming: An Examination of a Clash in Cultures." *Annals of Wyoming: Wyoming History Journal*, Vol. 75, No. 3 (July 2003): 2–7.
Hagan, William T. "The New Indian History." In *Rethinking American Indian History*, edited by Donald L. Fixico, pp. 29–42. Albuquerque: University of New Mexico Press, 1997.
Harjo, Suzan Shown. "American Indian Religious Freedom Act after Twenty-Five Years: An Introduction." *Wicazo Sa Review*, Vol. 19, No. 2 (Fall 2004): 129–36.
Harring, Sidney L. "Indian Law, Sovereignty, and State Law: Native People and the Law." In *A Companion to American Indian History*, edited by Philip J. Deloria and Neal Salisbury, pp. 441–459. Malden, MA: Blackwell, 2004.
Huffman, James, and Robert Miller. "Indian Property Rights and American Federalism." In *Self-Determination: The Other Path for Native Americans*, edited by Terry L. Anderson, Bruce L. Benson, and Thomas E. Flanagan, pp. 273–96. Stanford, CA: Stanford University Press, 2006.
Irwin, Lee. "Freedom, Law, and Prophecy: A Brief History of Native American Religious Resistance." *American Indian Quarterly*, Vol. 21, No. 1 (Winter 1997): 35–55.
Jackson, John C. *The Piikani Blackfeet: A Culture Under Siege*. Missoula, MT: Mountain Press, 2000.
James, Harry C. *Pages from Hopi History*. Tucson: University of Arizona Press, 1974.
Johnson, Todd M., and James Hamilton. "Self-Government for Indian Tribes: From Paternalism to Empowerment." *Connecticut Law Review*, Vol. 27 (1994–1995): 1251–79.
Jorgensen, Miriam, ed. *Rebuilding Native Nations: Strategies for Governance and Development*. Tucson: University of Arizona Press, 2007.
Keller Robert H., and Michael F. Turek. *American Indians and National Parks*. Tucson: University of Arizona Press, 1998.
Lazarus, Edward. *Black Hills: White Justice*. New York: Harper Collins, 1991.
Lee, Mark. "You Talkin' to Me? Racism Sells: The Anti-Whaling Movement and Japan." *Northwest Asian Weekly*, March 26, 2011. http://nwasianweekly.com/2011/03/you-talkin-to-me-racism-sells-the-anti-whaling-movement-and-japan (accessed February 5, 2018).
Long, Carolyn N. *Religious Freedom and Indian Rights: The Case of Oregon v. Smith*. Topeka: University Press of Kansas, 2000.
Lopach, James J., Margery Hunter Brown, and Richmond L. Clow. *Tribal Government Today: Politics on Montana Indian Reservations*. Niwot: University of Colorado Press, 1998.
Loewen, James W. *Lies My Teacher Told Me: Everything Your American History Textbook Got Wrong*. New York: New Press, 1995.
Macklem, Patrick. "Distributing Sovereignty: Indian Nations and Equality of Peoples." *Stanford Law Review*, Vol. 45 (1993): 1311–67.
Makley, Mathew S., and Michael J. Makley. *Cave Rock: Climbers, Courts, and a Washoe Indian Sacred Place*. Reno: University of Nevada Press, 2010.

Maroukis, Thomas C. *The Peyote Road: Religious Freedom and the Native American Church*. Norman: University of Oklahoma Press, 2010.

Martin, Joel W. *The Land Looks After Us: A History of Native American Religion*. New York: Oxford University Press, 2001.

Marshall, Joseph M. *The Journey of Crazy Horse: A Lakota History*. New York: Penguin, 2004.

———. *The Lakota Way*. New York: Penguin Compass, 2001.

McCoy, Ron. "Repatriation of Cultural Objects." *American Indian Art Magazine*, Vol. 40, No. 2 (Spring 2015): 86–87.

Michaelson, Robert S. "Dirt in the Courtroom: Indian Land Claims and American Property Rights." In *American Sacred Space*, edited by David Chidester and Edward T. Linenthal, pp. 43–96. Bloomington: Indiana University Press, 1995.

Miller, Robert J. "Exercising Cultural Self-Determination: The Makah Indian Tribe Goes Whaling." *American Indian Law Review*, Vol. 25, No. 2 (2000/2001): 165–273.

Millet, Lydia. "Selling Off Apache Holy Land." *New York Times*, May 29, 2015.

Milligan, Edward A. *Dakota Twilight: The Standing Rock Sioux, 1874–1890*. Hicksville, NY: Exposition Press, 1976.

Myers, Mike. "The Supreme Court's 'Just Cuz' Doctrine for Cheating Natives." *Indian Country Today*, January 18, 2016. http://indiancountrytodaymedianetwork.com/2016/01/18/supreme-courts-just-cuz-doctrine-cheating-natives (accessed April 14, 2016).

Nelson, Terri. "Legal Protection for Native American Sacred Landscapes Involving Forest Service Lands." Master's thesis, University of Montana, 1991.

Nelson, Stanley, dir. *We Shall Remain*. Episode 5, "Wounded Knee." DVD. Brighton, MA: PBS Distribution, 2009.

Nie, Martin. "The Use of Co-Management and Protected Land-Use Designations to Protect Cultural Resources and Reserved Treaty Rights on Federal Lands." *Natural Resources Journal*, Vol. 48 (2008): 585–647.

Norgren, Jill. "The Cherokee Nation Cases of the 1830s." *Journal of Supreme Court History* (1994): 65–82.

Perry, Richard J. *Apache Reservation, Indigenous Peoples and the American State*. Austin: University of Texas Press, 1993.

Pommersheim, Frank. *Broken Landscapes: Indians, Indian Tribes, and the Constitution*. New York: Oxford University Press, 2009.

Powers, Stephen, Don. D. Fowler, and Catherine S. Fowler, eds. "Stephen Powers' 'The Life and Culture of the Washo and Paiutes.'" *Ethnohistory* Vol. 17, No. 3/4 (Summer–Autumn 1970): 117–49.

Richland, Justin B. "Pragmatic Paradoxes and Ironies of Indigeneity at the 'Edge' of Hopi Sovereignty." *American Ethnologist*, Vol. 34, No. 3 (January 2008): 540–57.

———. "The State of Hopi Exception: When Inheritance Is What You Have." *Law and Literature*, Vol. 20, No. 2 (2008): 261–78.

Riding In, James. "Scholars and Twentieth-Century Indians: Reassessing the Recent Past." In *New Directions in American Indian History*, edited by Colin G. Calloway, pp. 127–50. Norman: University of Oklahoma Press, 1988.

Roberts, Christina. "Treaty Rights Ignored: Neocolonialism and the Makah Whale Hunt." *Kenyon Review*, Vol. 3, No. 1 (2010): 78–90.

Robertson, Dwanna L. "Invisibility in the Color-Blind Era: Examining Legitimized Racism against Indigenous Peoples." *American Indian Quarterly*, Vol. 39, No. 2 (Spring 2015): 113–53.

Robinson, Lindsay G. *Conquest by Law: How the Discovery of America Dispossessed Indigenous Peoples of Their Lands.* Oxford: Oxford University Press, 2005.

Rosenthal, H. D. *Their Day in Court: A History of the Indian Claims Commission.* New York: Garland Publishing, 1990.

Rosier, Paul C. *Rebirth of the Blackfeet Nation, 1912–1954.* Lincoln: University of Nebraska Press, 2001.

Rushforth, Scott, and Steadman Upham. *A Hopi Social History.* Austin: University of Texas Press, 1992.

Sen, Amartya. *Development as Freedom.* New York: Alfred A. Knopf, 1999.

Shreve, Bradley Glenn. "Of Gods and Broken Rainbows." *New Mexico Historical Review*, Vol. 82, No. 3 (Summer 2007): 369–90.

Siskin, Edgar E. *Washoe Shamans and Peyotists: Religious Conflict in an American Indian Tribe.* Salt Lake City: University of Utah Press, 1983.

Skibine, Alex Tallchief. "Towards a Balanced Approach for the Protection of Native American Sacred Sites." *Michigan Journal of Race and Law*, Vol. 17 (2011–2012): 269–302.

Smith, Paul Chaat. *Everything You Know about Indians Is Wrong.* Minneapolis: University of Minnesota Press, 2009.

Smith, Paul Chaat, and Robert Allen Warrior. *Like a Hurricane: The Indian Movement from Alcatraz to Wounded Knee.* New York: New Press, 1997.

Spence, Mark David. "Crown of the Continent, Backbone of the World: The American Wilderness Ideal and Blackfeet Exclusion from Glacier National Park." *Environmental History*, Vol. 1, No. 3 (July 1996): 29–49.

Talbot, Steve. "Desecration and American Indian Religious Freedom." *Journal of Ethnic Studies*, Vol. 12, No. 4 (1985): 1–18.

———. "Spiritual Genocide: The Denial of American Indian Religious Freedom, from Conquest to 1934." *Wicazo Sa Review*, Vol. 21, No. 2 (Autumn, 2006): 7–39.

Tomlinson, Zachary. "Abrogation or Regulation? How *Anderson v. Evans* Discards the Makah's Treaty Whaling Rights in the Name of Conservation Necessity." *Washington Law Review*, Vol. 78 (2003): 1101–32.

Vandevelder, Paul. "What Do We Owe the Indians?" *American History*, Vol. 44, No. 2 (June 2009): 30–39.

Venables, Robert W. *American Indian History: Five Centuries of Conflict and Coexistence*, Vol. 2. Santa Fe, NM: Clear Light, 2004.

Vest, Jay Hansford C. "Traditional Blackfeet Religion and the Sacred Badger-Two Medicine Wildlands." *Journal of Land and Religion*, Vol. 6, No. 2 (1998): 455–89.

Vinzant, John H. *The Supreme Court's Role in American Indian Policy.* El Paso: LFB Scholarly Publishing, 2009.

Wenger, Tesa. *We Have a Religion: The 1920s Pueblo Indian Dance Controversy and American Religious Freedom*. Chapel Hill: University of North Carolina Press, 2009.

Westney, Andrew. "Dakota Access Saga Highlights Value of Tribal Consultation." *Law 360*, June 7, 2017.

Wilkins, David E. *American Indian Politics and the American Political System*. 2nd ed. New York: Rowman & Littlefield, 2007.

———. *American Indian Sovereignty and the United States Supreme Court: The Masking of Justice*. Austin: University of Texas Press, 1997.

———. "Who's in Charge of U.S. Indian Policy? Congress and the Supreme Court at Loggerheads over American Indian Religious Freedom." *Wicazo Sa Review*, Vol. 8, No. 1 (Spring 1992): 40–60.

Wilkins, David E., and K. Tsianina Lomawaima. *Uneven Ground: American Indian Sovereignty and Federal Law*. Norman: University of Oklahoma Press, 2001.

Wilkinson, Charles F. *American Indians, Time, and the Law: Native Sovereignty in a Modern Constitutional Democracy*. New Haven, CT: Yale University Press, 1987.

Williams Jr., Robert A. *Like a Loaded Weapon: The Rehnquist Court, Indian Rights, and the Legal History of Racism in America*. Minneapolis: University of Minnesota Press, 2005.

Winkle, Barrik Van. "Cannibals in the Mountains, Washoe Teratology and the Donner Party." In *New Perspectives on Native North America*, edited by Sergei A. Kan and Pauline Turner Strong, pp. 395–413. Lincoln: University of Nebraska Press, 2006.

Wissler, Clark, and Alice Beck Kehoe. *Amskapi Pikuni: The Blackfeet People*. Albany: State University of New York Press, 2012.

Yablon, Marcia. "Property Rights and Sacred Sites: Federal Regulatory Responses to American Indian Religious Claims on Public Land." *Yale Law Journal*, Vol. 113, No. 7 (May 2004): 1623–62.

INDEX

Abbie, Ruth, 107
Access Fund, 108, 110–13, 158, 194
Access Fund v. USDA (2007), 135
Advisory Council on Historic
 Preservation, 109
agentalism, 181
Alabama Supreme Court, 13
Alaska Eskimo Whaling Commission, 184
Alaskan Natives, 184
Alcatraz Island, 17
allotment, 11, 14–16, 26, 51–52, 95, 122–23,
 125–26, 146, 164–65, 193
American Indian Movement, 17, 166
American Indian Religious Freedom Act,
 7, 18–24, 30, 37–38, 40, 45, 59, 60, 76,
 83, 159, 174, 176, 198–99, 210
American Jewish Congress, 9
American Recovery and Reinvestment
 Act, 149
Anaimtapoi, 145
Anderson v. Evans (2002), 227, 228
Annunciation Chapel, 34

Antiquities Act, 32, 191, 192
Apache Leap, 138, 139, 155, 157, 158, 159, 202
Apache-Sitgreaves National Forest, 63
Apache Stronghold, 157
Arawak Indians, 196, 207
Archiambault, David, 168
Arikawa Indians, 160
Arizona Daily Sun, 69
Arizona Snowbowl Resort, 22, 48–51, 53,
 55, 57–67, 69, 71–73, 75, 77, 79, 81–83, 85,
 87, 88, 193–94, 199, 201, 203
Arizona Territorial Legislature, 155, 208
Arlington National Cemetery, 34
Army Corps of Engineers, 137, 139, 166,
 168, 169, 171
Assiniboines, 119
Aubrey, Mae, 128
Avikwaame, 145, 147
Awatavi, 51

Babbitt, Bruce, 49, 61, 189, 194
Backbone of the World, 117–18, 122

253

Badger-Two Medicine, 2, 8, 31, 115–19, 121–23, 125, 127, 129, 130–36, 193–94, 200, 205
Badoni v. Higgins (1980), 36–38
Baker Massacre, 120
Baldwin, Tammy, 158
Barsh, Russell Lawrence, 186
Battle of Greasy Grass, 121, 163
Battle of the Little Bighorn. *See* Battle of Greasy Grass
Baucus, Max, 131
Bavavi, 73
Bea, Carlos, 84, 85, 86, 87
Bear Lodge Multiple Use v. Babbitt (1998), 215
Bear Lodge Multiple Use v. Babbitt (1999), 214
Bears Ears, 41, 188, 189, 190–91, 194
Bears Ears Inter-Tribal Coalition, 189–91, 194
Bears Ears National Monument, 2, 184, 189, 190
Bear's Lodge, 2, 31–33, 36, 41, 89–90, 103, 106, 108, 111–12, 114, 194, 200, 204
Beleliwe, 97
Benally, Jeneda, 77
Bennett, Robert, 188
Bethesda Baptist Church, 34
Biolsi, Thomas, 178–79
Bishop, Rob, 188–89
Blackfeet Agency, 125
Blackfeet Indian Welfare Association, 128
Blackfeet Nation, 16, 115, 117–31, 133–36, 188
Blackfeet National Bank, 131
Blackfeet Reservation, 117, 121–26, 135, 194
Blackfeet Tribal Business Council p.16, 124, 126, 127, 133
Blackfeet Tribal Council, 120
Blackfire, 77
Black-footed People, 118, 120–21
Blackfoot Nation (Canada), 118, 131
Black Hills, 160, 162–67
Black Hills Sioux Nation Council, 165

Black Hills Treaty and Claims Council, 166
Black Mesa Ranger District, 63
Blackmun, Harry, 67
Blind Old Man, 144, 145
boarding schools, 15, 25, 97, 122, 140, 146, 156, 164, 208
Bobcat, 17
Book of Hopi, The (Waters), 56
Borowsky, Eric, 79–80
Bradley, Bill, 167
Brennan, William J., Jr., 24, 28, 81
Breyer, Stephen, 195
Broken Landscapes: Indians, Indian Tribes, and the Constitution (Pommersheim), 179
Brown, Brian Edward, 42
Brown, Joseph, 126–27
Buffalo Bill's Wild West, 165
Bureau of Indian Affairs, 16, 17, 25, 52–56, 58, 97, 122, 123, 124–29, 131, 146, 156, 177, 182
Burns, Larry Alan, 150
Burton, Lloyd, 41, 43

California State Legislature, 148
Capital Trail Vehicle Riders Association, 135
Captain Jim, 95
Carpenter, Kristen A., 173, 232, 243
Carson City, Nev., 97, 99
Carson Colony, 98
Carson Indian School p.97
Cave Rock, 8, 31, 36, 38, 40, 89–92, 97–114, 135–36, 158, 193–95, 200, 201, 204
Center for Biological Diversity, 69, 71
Century of Dishonor: A Sketch of the United States Government's Dealings with Some Indian Tribes, A (Jackson), 14
Chaffetz, Jason, 188
Cherokee Nation, 12–13
Cherokee Nation v. Georgia (1831), 6, 12–13, 196

Cheyenne Indians, 32, 162–63, 196, 208
Cheyenne River Sioux Indians, 168–69
Chihuahua, state of (Mexico), 154
Chinese laborers, 94
Chiricahua Apache Indians, 154
Chivington, John, 208
Citizenship Act, 15, 53
City of Boerne v. Flores (1997), 199
Clan of Greasewood, 73
Clinton, William J. (Bill), 19, 24, 34, 71, 81, 104, 191
Cochise, 154–55
Coconino National Forest (Ariz.), 7, 58–59, 64, 199
Codell, Elouise Pepion, 131
Cody, William (Buffalo Bill), 165
Cohen, Felix, 128–29, 179
COINTELPRO, 18
Cold Maker, 117
collaborative management, 178, 184, 187–92, 194, 195, 203–5
Collier, John, 16, 53–54, 126–27
Columbus, Christopher, 196, 207
Commentaries on the Constitution of the United States (Story), 4
Comstock Lode, 93
Confederated Salish and Kootenai Tribes, 183–84
Confederate States of America, 154
Connaughton, Kent P., 10
Conquering Bear, 161
"Constitutional Originalism" (Scalia), 4
Convention on the Prevention and Punishment of the Crime of Genocide, 196, 208
Coolidge Dam, 156
Coronado National Forest, 64
Cottrell, Jane L., 135
Council at Horse Creek, 161
Council of Seven Fires, 160
court of claims, 167
Crazy Horse, 161–64
Creation Man, 92

Creation Mother, 92
Cree Indian Nation, 121
Cross, Raymond, 45–46, 180–82, 195–96, 201
Crow Indians, 32, 117, 160, 207
Custer, George Armstrong, 120, 163
Custer Died for Your Sins, 17
Cypress Hill Conference, 120

Daily Caller, 158
Dakota Access Pipeline, 79, 137, 139, 167–73
Dalrymple, Jack, 169
Damalali, 92
Daniels, Robert, 52
Dark Skies Coalition, 65
Davis, Gray, 148
Dawes Act. *See* General Allotment Act (Dawes Act)
Declaration on the Rights of Indigenous Peoples, 6, 159, 179
De'ek Wadapush, 99
Defense Authorization Act, 157, 159
Deloria, Philip J., 183
Deloria, Vine, Jr., 17, 87
Devils Tower. *See* Bear's Lodge
DeWaal, Earl, 39, 40
DNA Legal Services, 71
Doctrine of Discovery (or Doctrine of Christian Discovery), 3–4, 13, 175, 179, 209
Dollar General v. Mississippi Band of Choctaw Indians (2015), 235
Donner Party, 93
Douglas County Council on Alcohol and Drug Abuse Prevention and Treatment, 26
Downes, William F., 34–36, 38, 112
Duro v. Reina (1991), 185

Earth Justice, 169
Ebenezer Baptist Church, 34
Edwards, Joshua A., 173, 173

Eisenhower, Dwight, 6, 157, 208
Eitner, Michael, 183, 184
Employment Division v. Smith (1990), 19, 25, 27–30, 41, 78, 85, 170, 199
Energy Transfer Partners, 168, 172
Establishment Clause, U.S. Constitution, 20, 30–31, 34–35, 38–40, 44, 83, 103, 109, 111–12, 114, 135, 192, 202
European Americans, 3, 16, 41, 93, 185, 205, 206
Evans, John, 208
Executive Order 13,007, 19, 34, 102, 174, 198, 203
Executive Order 13,084, 20, 198
Executive Order 13,175, 20, 198
Ex Parte Crow Dog (1883), 175

Farm Bill of 2008, 40, 204
Feather Woman, 116
Filfred, Davis, 189
Fischer, Louis, 174
Flagstaff Activist Network, 69, 71, 77
Flagstaff Chamber of Commerce, 79
Flagstaff City Council, 77
Flagstaff Indian Days, 77
Flake, Jeff, 157
Flathead Indian Nation, 123
Fletcher, William A., 78–83, 85, 87
Forest Service. *See* U.S. Forest Service
Forest Service Office of Tribal Relations, 202
Fort Laramie Treaty, 120, 162, 168
Fort Kearny, 162
Fort Randall, 165
Fortune v. Thomson (2011), 227
Fourteenth Amendment, U.S. Constitution, 186
Franciscan missionaries, 57
Freedom of Information Act, 40, 204
Free Exercise Clause, U.S. Constitution, 19, 20, 23, 24, 25, 27, 36, 37, 85, 199, 202
Fromm, Erich, 45–46

gaans, 152
Garrison, Tim Alan, 14
General Allotment Act (Dawes Act), 14, 95, 165
genocide, 196, 206–8
Georgetown University, 71
Georgia, 12–13
Geronimo, 156
Gettysburg Battlefield, 43, 80, 209
Ghost Dance, 165–66
Glacier County School Board, 126
Glacier National Park, 123, 125, 127, 129–30
Glacier-Two Medicine Alliance, 135
Glamis Gold v. United States of America (2009), 228
Glamis Imperial, 147
Glen Canyon Dam, 37–38
gold mining, 147, 156, 205
Gonzales v. O Centro Espirita Beneficente Uniao do Vegetal (2006), 214
Grand Staircase–Escalante National Monument, 191
Gratten, John, 161
Gray, Christine K., 183
gray whales, 140–41, 143–44
Great Lakota Nation, 160, 164
Great Mystery, 116
Great Northern Hotel, 125
Great Sioux Reservation, 162
Great Society, 166, 181
Great Spirit, 56, 107, 116
Greene, Robert, 80
Greenpeace, 142
Grijalva, Raul, 158
Gumalanga, 95
Gustafson, Maribeth, 109–11, 114

Haddon, Sam E., 135–36
Handbook of Federal Indian Law (Cohen), 128
Harney, William. *See* Woman Killer (William Harney)
Harris, Robert, 103, 109

Hartway, Lynelle K., 71
Havasupais, 58, 81
Henderson, James Youngblood, 186
Henderson, Thelton E., 78
Highway 50, 99
Honanie, Antone, 73, 74
Hoover, J. Edgar, 18
Hopi Cultural Preservation Office, 65, 73
Hopi Cultural Resource Advisory Task Force, 63, 65
Hopi Dictionary/Hopiikwa Lavaytutuveni: A Hopi-English Dictionary of the Third Mesa Dialect (Sekaquaptewa), 74
Hopi Health Department, 73
Hopi Nation/Hopi Tribal Council, 8, 52, 53, 54, 55, 56, 57, 58, 59, 71, 73
Hotevilla, 74
House Made of Dawn (Momaday), 17
Hualapai Tribe, 58, 71, 72, 81, 84
Huffman, James, 46, 182
Hundred in the Hands, 162
Hunkpapa Indians, 160
Hunt, Helen, 14

Imperial County, Calif., 147
Imperial Valley Solar Project, 150, 201
Indian Child Welfare Act, 18, 21
Indian Civil Rights Act, 185
Indian Claims Commission, 16–17, 55–56, 100, 147
Indian Claims Commission Act, 166
Indian Commerce Clause, 177–78
Indian New Deal. *See* Indian Reorganization Act
Indian Office, 14
Indian Pass, 145, 147, 148
Indian Reorganization Act, 11, 15, 16, 22, 53–54, 95, 126–28, 146, 156, 165–66, 176, 179, 182, 198–99, 210
Indian Religious Freedom Act. *See* American Indian Religious Freedom Act

Indian Self-Determination and Education Act, 18, 177
Indians of All Tribes, 17
Indians of California, 90, 92
Indian Welfare League, 53
Indigenous Law Institute, 3
Inter-American Court of Human Rights, 180
International Council on Mining and Metals, 147
International Dark Sky City, 65
International Whaling Commission, 140
Iroquois League, 12
Itsapichpaupe, 117

Jackson, Andrew, 12, 209
Jefferson, Thomas, 175
Jenkins, Bruce S., 39, 40
Jewell, Sally, 131
Jiji Kin, 161–64
Johnson, Ben, 142
Johnson, Chiitaanibah, 196
Johnson, Thomas, 3
Johnson, Wayne, 141
Johnson v. M'Intosh (1823), 3–4, 6, 13
"just cuz" doctrine, 174, 179

Karok Nation, 23, 24
kawanami, 145
Kennedy, Anthony, 35
Kianaa Indians, 118
Kikmongwi, 53, 54, 55
Kilma, Don, 109
Kiowa Indians, 31–32
Kipp, Woodrow L., 130
Klamath Indians, 25–26
Klamath National Forest, 26
Kootenai Indians, 183–84
Kumastamxo, 145
Kuwanwisiwma, Leigh, 72–74, 76
Kwikumat, 144–45
kwoxots, 145
Kykotsmovi, 73

LaFarge, Oliver, 53–54
Lake Oahe, 2, 137, 139, 160, 167–71, 173
Lake Powell, 37–39
Lake Tahoe Basin Management Unit, 103, 109–10
Lake Tahoe Summit, 104
Lakota Nation, 120, 160, 164
Lancaster, Ben, 95
leave-no-trace movement, 100, 103, 107
Lee v. Weisman (1992), 35
Lemon v. Kurztman (1971), 35, 39, 111–12, 135
Leon, Richard, 131
Lewis and Clark expedition, 161
Lewis and Clark Forest Reserve, 123
Lewis and Clark National Forest, 115, 132–33
Lilienfield, Terry, 105, 110
Lincoln, Abraham, 154
Little Chief, 125
Little Dog, 122
Little Thunder, 161–62
Lomawaima, K. Tsianina, 117, 178
Lone Bear, 95
Lone Wolf v. Hitchcock (1903), 178
Louisiana Purchase, 3, 175
Lyng v. Northwest Indian Cemetery Protective Association (1989), 19, 22–24, 27–30, 41, 78, 85–86, 170–71, 199

Maasaw, 50, 56, 74
Mabo v. Queensland (1997), 180
Maher, John, 105–6
Maidu Indians, 196
Major Crimes Act, 176
Makah Culture and Research Center, 142
Makah Nation, 2, 9, 137, 139, 141–43
Makah Tribal Council, 142
Makah Whaling Commission, 141
Marine Mammal Protection Act, 138, 143, 184
Marshall, John, 3, 6, 12–13, 178
Marshall Trilogy, 175–77, 179–80, 185, 209
Marx, Karl, 45–46

Marxokuvek, 145
McCain, John, 157
McKeown, M. Margaret, 111, 112
McKibben, Howard, 110
McNichols, Jean, 105
Medicine Elk, 117
Medicine Grizzly, 117
Medicine Wolf, 117
Meeks Bay Resort and Marina, 104
Miller, Robert, 46, 182
Mimbres Apaches, 156
Minault, Paul, 108
Mineral Strip, 122
Mining Association of Canada, 147
Missouri River, 139, 161, 166, 168, 171
Modoc Point, Ore., 25
Momaday, N. Scott, 17
Montanans for Multiple Use, 135
Montana State Constitution, 130
Montana Trail Vehicle Riders Association, 135
Montana Wilderness Society, 135
Mormon Lake, 63
Morning Star, 116–17
Morton v. Mancari (1974), 234
Moses Street, 97
Mountain States Legal Foundation, 34, 41, 131, 194, 205–6
Muddy River Indians, 118
mushege, 93
Myer, Dillon, 128–29
Myers, Mike, 174

Na'api, 116–18
naahks, 116, 117
Naddewasioux, 160
Napoleonic Wars, 161
National Bison Range, 184
National Cathedral, 111
National Conference of Catholic Bishops, 29
National Congress for American Indians, 129, 148, 166, 185

National Council of Churches, 29
National Environmental Justice Advisory Council, 71
National Environmental Policy Act, 6–7, 18, 59, 131, 168
National Forest Service, 89
National Historic Preservation Act, 19, 61, 131, 168–69, 198, 203
National Indian Youth Council, 166
National Marine Fisheries Service, 143
National Native American Honor Roll Society, 77
National Oceanic and Atmospheric Administration, 143
National Park Service; Park Service, 20, 31–40, 43, 89, 117, 123–25, 130, 159, 184
National Register of Historic Places, 19, 99, 103–5, 111, 158, 198
National Tribal Employment Rights Organization, 130
Native American Bank Corporation, 131
Native American Church, 25–27, 29, 95–96
Native American Community Development Corporation, 31
Native American Graves Protection and Repatriation Act, 19, 21
Natural Arch and Bridge Society, 39
Natural Arch & Bridge Society v. Alston (2002), 215
Natural Bridges National Monument, 188
Navajo Medicinemen's Association, 59
Navajo Mountain, 37
Navajo Nation, 16, 22, 34, 38, 58, 71–72, 181, 188–89
Navajo Nation v. Forest Service (2007), 48, 49, 70–83, 170
Navajo Nation v. Forest Service (2008), 48–49, 78, 80–88
Neah Bay Treaty, 138
Nevada Indian Agency, 97
Nevada State Historic Preservation Office, 109
Newcomb, Steven, 3–4, 195

New Frontier, 166
Nez, Nora, 72
Nez Perce, 118
Nie, Martin, 184
Ninth Circuit Court of Appeals, 29–30, 49, 71, 78, 80–81, 83–84, 86, 111, 136, 143, 169, 173–74, 199
Nixon, Richard, 6–7, 17–18, 56, 132, 147, 157, 176–77, 187, 191
Noche-do-Klinne, 155
North American Free Trade Agreement, 138, 202
North American Free Trade Agreement Arbitral Tribunal, 138, 147–48, 151–52, 160, 202
Northern Cheyenne, 163
Northern Paiute, 98
Northland Recreation Company, 58
Norton, Gale, 148
Nuvamsa, Ben, 79
Nuvatukyaovi, 48, 57, 70, 75, 80

Oahe Dam, 166
Oak Flat, 41, 138–39, 152–53, 155, 157–59, 174, 202
Obama, Barack, 6, 40, 169, 172, 189–91
O'Connor, Sandra Day, 23, 28, 35, 39, 78, 85–86, 170
Office of Emergency Preparedness, 81
Office of Tribal Relations, U.S. Forest Service, 202
Ojibwe Indians, 160
Old Oraibi, 73
Old Man. *See* Na'api
Old Person, Chief, 129
Old Woman, 116
Oliphant v. Suquamish, 179
Oregon Supreme Court, 27
Osman, Dan, 100–103, 110, 113
Ozette Village, 139

Pahaana, 50, 55
Paiutes, 25, 37, 90, 92, 94

Palma, Juan, 103–5, 107–9, 113–14, 193
Parker, Theron, 141
Parker, Trey, 142
Patoka, Ill., 167
Peabody Coal, 80, 181
Pearl Harbor, 43
Pend d'Orelle, 183
People for the American Way, 29
Pequot, 196, 207
Peterson, R. Max, 59
Pewetsoli, 92
Peyote Cult. *See* Native American Church
Piankeshaw Indians, 3
Piikani Indians, 118
Pike, Nizhoni, 158
Pima Indians, 156
Pine Ridge Reservation, 167
pipa taxa (good for the people), 145
plenary power, Congress, 45, 47, 176–79, 202
Plymouth Colony, 196, 207
Poia, 116–17
Pommersheim, Frank, 179–80, 186–87
Powder River, 162
Prescott, Ariz., 48, 71, 77
Preston, Bill Bucky, 65, 70, 72–75, 79–80
Proclamation 1043, 37
Progressive Leadership Alliance of Nevada, 109
prophecy, 50, 55, 57, 170
Provencio, Heather Cooper, 63–68, 193
Public Lands Initiative, 188–89
Public Law 280, 17
Pueblo Revolt (1680), 51

Quechan Historical Preservation Office, 149
Quechan Indian Nation, 137–38, 144–52, 200–201, 204–5
Quechan Indian Tribe v. United States Department of the Interior (2010), 229
Quechan League, 145

Quechan Tribal Council, 146
Quiver, Elaine, 33

Rain Boss, 97
Rainbow Bridge National Monument, 31, 34, 38
Rapid City, South Dakota, 126
Rasure, Nora, 49, 63–64, 66–69, 77, 88, 193
Rawlinson, Johnnie B., 78
Red Cloud, 162–63
Red Coyote. *See* Smith, Al
Red Power, 17
Rehnquist, William, 167
Religious Freedom Restoration Act, 19, 29, 49, 70, 77–78, 81, 85–86, 88, 139, 169–70, 173, 199, 202
Reno Evening Gazette, 97
Resolution Copper, 157–59
Rio Tinto, 157
Rocky Mountain Ranger District, 132–34
Rosenblatt, Paul G., 71, 76–77
Rupert, Henry "Moses," 96–99, 104–5, 110
Running Man geoglyph, 147

Sagetown, 95
Salazar, Ken, 150
Salish, 183–84
San Carlos Reservation Apache Indians, 137–38, 153, 155–58, 174
Sand Creek Massacre, 162
Sanders, Bernie, p.158
San Francisco Aquarium, 93
San Francisco Mountain Forest Reserve, 58
San Francisco Peaks, 7–8, 22, 38, 48, 50–51, 57–63, 65–70, 72, 74–77, 79, 81–84, 88–89, 173–74, 193–94, 200–201, 203, 205
Save the Peaks Coalition, 69–70, 77
Scalia, Antonin, 3–4, 7, 9, 27–30, 78, 85–86, 170, 195
Sea Shepherd Conservation Society, 201, 205–6

Second Wounded Knee, 17
Sekaquaptewa, Emory, 73–75
Sen, Amartya, 181–82, 195
Sett Pine, 117
Seven Years' War, 11
Shanker, Howard M., 71–72, 80
Shell River Trail, 161
Sherbert v. Verner (1963), 27–28, 85
Shoshones, 160
Siberian Natives, 141
Siksika Indians, 18
Silverman, Aaron, 107
Sitting Bull, 160, 162–65
Sixteenth Street Baptist Church, 111
Skibine, Alex Tallchief, 174–75, 183
Sky Father, 36
Smith, Al, 25–37
Smith, Paul Chaat, 195
Snake Clan, 37
Snowbowl. *See* Arizona Snowbowl Resort
Solenex, 131
Solenex v. Jewell (2015), 226
Sonora, State of, Mexico, 154
Southern District of California, U.S. District Court for the, 150
Spirit Mountain, 145, 147
Standing Rock, 160, 164–65, 169
Standing Rock Agency, 164
Standing Rock Sioux Indians, 9, 79, 139, 160, 165–72
Standing Rock Sioux Reservation, 137, 139, 160, 164–68
Standing Rock Sioux Tribe v. U.S. Army Corps of Engineers (2016), 231
Standing Rock Sioux Tribe v. U.S. Army Corps of Engineers (2017), 232
Star Boy, 116
Star Wars: A New Hope, 209
State-Tribal Cooperative Act, 130
Story, Joseph, 4
Southern Baptist Convention, 29
sovereignty, 4–11, 13–14, 16–19, 21, 44–46, 54, 56–57, 71–72, 127–28, 142, 144, 153–54, 166–67, 173, 175–80, 183, 185–87, 192–93, 197, 199, 202, 205–6, 209–10
Sun Dance, 32, 116–17, 160, 165
Supremacy Clause, U.S. Constitution, 178
Supreme Court of Canada, 180

Tax Relief and Health Care Act of 2006, 131
Tecumseh, 207
Tenth Circuit Court of Appeals, 34–37, 39–40, 112
Tessera Solar, LLC, 149
termination, 6, 11, 16–18, 21, 25–26, 37, 58, 95, 129, 166, 183, 208
Tewa Indians, 51
Texas State Capitol, 112
Thieves' Road, 163
Third Mesa, 73–74
Three State Order, 132–34
Thunderdreamer, 162
Tolowa Nation, 23
Tonto National Forest, 139, 153, 155, 157
Touro Synagogue, 111
traditional cultural property, 63, 70, 104–5, 109–10, 114, 158–59
traditionalist movement, Hopi, 17, 55–57
Traditional Values Coalition, 29
Trail of Broken Treaties, 17
Treaty of Waitangi, 180
Tribal Sovereignty and Economic Enhancement Act, 185
Trump, Donald, 41, 169, 190–91

Uintah and Ouray Ute Indians, 188–89
United Nations Declaration on the Rights of Indigenous Peoples, 46, 149, 151, 160, 172
United Nations General Assembly, 6, 56, 179
United States v. Gettysburg Electric Rail Co. (1896), 216, 236
United States v. Lara (2004), 185
University of Montana School of Law, 180

U.S. Coast Guard, 141
U.S. Department of the Interior, 14, 80, 127, 131, 181
U.S. Department of War, 14
U.S. District Court of Wyoming, 34
U.S. Forest Service, 8–9, 20, 22–24, 30, 36, 48–49, 58–66, 68–73, 76–83, 86, 88–90, 97, 99, 101–17, 130, 132–38, 152, 159, 193, 194, 201–6
USS *Arizona*, 43, 200
U.S. v. Kagama (1886), 176
U.S. v. Navajo Nation (2003), 181
Utah Association of Counties v. Bush (2004), 235
Utah Diné Bikeyah, 188
Ute Mountain Ute, 188–89
utihi'I, 50

Van Orden v. Perry (2005), 112
Vasquez, Miguel, 77
Virginia City, 99
Voting Rights Act, 157, 182

Waitangi Tribunal, 180
waju seeds, 90
Wakantanka, 160
waktoglakapi, 162
Waldrip, Gene, 60–66, 68–70
Wallace, Brian, 102, 104, 106–8
Wallace, J. Clifford, 112
Wampanoag Nation, 11
Washington, D.C., 17
Washoe Indians, 8, 16, 36, 89–96
Water Beings, 92–93, 97
water protectors, 169, 172
Waters, Frank, 56
Watson, Paul, 142, 144, 201
Welewkushkush, 97–98
We Shall Remain (Nelson, dir.), 208
Western Apaches, 9, 137, 152–59

Western Hemisphere, 195–96, 205
Western Regional Office, U.S. Forest Service, 103
Whale Wars, 142
White Mesa, 188
White Mountain Apache Nation, 58, 71
Wilderness Act, 132
Wilderness Society, 135
Wilkins, David E., 174, 177–78, 213–14, 233, 248
Wilkinson, Charles F., 176, 233, 248
Williams, Paul, 177
Williams, Robert, 200, 236, 248
Williams v. Lee (1959), 176, 233
Wilson, Dick, 80
Wilson v. Block (1983), 22, 80, 213, 218, 238
Wind Maker, 117
Wisconsin v. Yoder (1972), 23, 221
Wiseman, Maury, 196
Woman Killer (William Harney), 161–62
Wood, John, 120
Worcester v. Georgia (1832), 13, 212, 236, 238
Worship and Religion: Culture, Religion, and Law in the Management of Public Lands and Resources (Burton), 41
Wounded Knee, 17, 165, 208
Wovoka, 165

Yablon, Marcia, 199–200
Yavapai-Apache Nation, 58, 65, 71, 158–59
Yellow Woman, 162
York, Franklin, 95
Yosemite National Park, 102
Young, Neil, 158
Young, Waste Win, 168
Yurok Nation, 23–24

Zinke, Ryan, 190
Zuni Nation, 188

www.ingramcontent.com/pod-product-compliance
Lightning Source LLC
Chambersburg PA
CBHW020944230426
43666CB00005B/160